D0041832

ESCAPING THE RESOURCE CURSE

INITIATIVE FOR POLICY DIALOGUE AT COLUMBIA

INITIATIVE FOR POLICY
DIALOGUE AT COLUMBIA

JOSEPH E. STIGLITZ AND SHARI SPIEGEL,
SERIES CO-EDITORS

Ann Florini, editor,
The Right to Know: Transparency for an Open World, 2007

Macartan Humphreys, Jeffrey D. Sachs, and Joseph E. Stiglitz, editors,
Escaping the Resource Curse, 2007

ESCAPING THE RESOURCE CURSE

EDITED BY MACARTAN HUMPHREYS,
JEFFREY D. SACHS, AND JOSEPH E. STIGLITZ

Foreword by George Soros

Columbia University Press

NEW YORK

Columbia University Press
Publishers Since 1893
New York   Chichester   West Sussex

Copyright © 2007 Columbia University Press

Library of Congress Cataloging-in-Publication Data

Escaping the resource curse / edited by Macartan Humphreys,
Jeffrey D. Sachs, and Joseph E. Stiglitz ;
foreword by George Soros.
p. cm.
Includes bibliographical references and index.

ISBN-13: 978-0-231-14196-3 (clothbound : alk. paper)
ISBN-13: 978-0-231-51210-7 (electronic)

1. Petroleum industry and trade—Government policy—
Developing countries.   2. Petroleum industry and trade—
Developing countries—Planning.   3. Economic development
projects—Developing countries—Evaluation.   I. Humphreys,
Macartan.   II. Sachs, Jeffrey D.   III. Stiglitz, Joseph E.
HD9578.D44R47   2007
333.8'232091724—dc22
2006036062

Columbia University Press books are printed
on permanent and durable acid-free paper.
This book was printed on paper with
recycled content.

Printed in the United States of America
c   10   9   8   7   6   5   4   3   2   1

References to Internet Web sites (URLs) were accurate at the
time of writing. Neither the author nor Columbia
University Press is responsible for URLs that may have
expired or changed since the manuscript was prepared.

INITIATIVE FOR POLICY DIALOGUE AT COLUMBIA

JOSEPH E. STIGLITZ AND SHARI SPIEGEL, SERIES CO-EDITORS

The Initiative for Policy Dialogue (IPD) at Columbia University brings together academics, policy makers, and practitioners from developed and developing countries to address the most pressing issues in economic policy today. IPD is an important part of Columbia's broad program on development and globalization. The Initiative for Policy Dialogue at Columbia: Challenges in Development and Globalization presents the latest academic thinking on a wide range of development topics and lays out alternative policy options and trade-offs. Written in a language accessible to policy makers and students alike, this series is unique in that it both shapes the academic research agenda and furthers the economic policy debate, facilitating a more democratic discussion of development policies.

The discovery of oil or other natural resources often brings about dreams of wealth and prosperity for developing countries. In all too many cases, though, these discoveries have instead been associated with devastating political conflict and lasting economic setbacks. The fact that countries that are well endowed with resources often do so badly is referred to as the *resource curse*. The purpose of this book is to help understand the reasons for the resource curse. By examining the lessons from both the successes and failures and by comparing the wide range of experiences of natural resource exporting countries, this volume thus provides a number of principles by which to counter the effects of the resource curse. It explains what can be done to lift the resource curse, to enable those dreams of prosperity to be realized, and to ensure that the benefits of that wealth are fairly shared. It provides a practical framework for policy makers, policy analysts, and activists who are concerned with the management of extractive industries in developing countries. In presenting their policy recommendations, the contributors to this volume show that it is possible to manage resource revenues in a way that promotes sustainable economic growth and poverty alleviation.

For more information about IPD and its upcoming books, visit www.policydialogue.org.

REVENUE WATCH INSTITUTE

The Revenue Watch Institute (RWI) works with civil society, media and policy makers in resource-dependent countries to counter the effects of the so-called resource curse and enhance public participation in these countries' economic governance. RWI has helped create local coalitions advocating revenue and expenditure transparency, and has created public finance monitoring centers in several countries. It has created a body of research and reference tools to assist citizens in monitoring natural resource revenues and public expenditures, and facilitates a wide range of training for local actors to enhance their skills. RWI also helps policy makers improve their capacity to transparently and efficiently manage their country's public finances and provides journalists with the reference tools and training necessary to cover extractive industries and public finances effectively. *Escaping the Resource Curse* is the third volume in the Revenue Watch Institute's publications series. The series provides practical guides for various groups, such as policy makers, journalists, and civil society groups trying to counter the resource curse.

For more information about these publications and RWI's activities, visit www.revenuewatch.org.

CONTENTS

FOREWORD

George Soros

"Resource curse" is the term used to describe the failure of resource-rich countries to benefit from their natural wealth. Perversely, many countries rich in natural resources are poorer and more miserable than countries that are less well endowed. This is clearly visible in Africa. The Congo, Angola, and Sudan have been torn by civil strife, and Nigeria suffers from endemic corruption, while resource-poor countries such as Burkina Faso and Ghana are equally poor but more peaceful and democratic.

Lifting the resource curse could change the fate of the countries concerned and make a significant contribution to achieving the United Nations' Millennium Development Goals. It should be easier to recapture existing but misappropriated mineral wealth than to create wealth where it does not exist. Thus the resource curse offers a fertile field for benevolent intervention, and much progress has already been made.

As this book explains, the resource curse is a complex phenomenon. Three different processes come into play. The first is the currency appreciation due to resource revenues and its negative effect on the competitive position of other industries. This is called the "Dutch Disease." The second is the fluctuation in commodity prices and its disruptive effects. And the third is the effect on political conditions. The first two are purely economic and have been studied extensively. It is the third factor that needs to be better understood, especially as its impact is far greater than that of the other two. The explanation has to connect economic theory with political theory.

I should like to use this occasion to summarize my own views on the subject. For purposes of analysis, I distinguish between four sets of players: international oil companies, national oil companies, and the governments and the people of the countries concerned. I am using oil for the sake of simplicity. A similar analysis can be applied to other commodities, although it will differ in many particulars. I couch my analysis in terms of three kinds of asymmetry: asymmetric information, asymmetric agency, and asymmetric bargaining power. Of the three, asymmetric agency problems are by far the most important. I shall make it the focal point of my analysis, giving the other two asymmetries a supporting role.

Agency problems arise when the agent does not faithfully serve the interests of the principal. The first step in an analysis is therefore to identify the principal. This is where political theory comes in. The ownership of natural resources is an attribute of sovereignty. According to modern political theory, sovereignty belongs to the people. That was not always the case. Before the French Revolution, sovereignty belonged to the king, but in the French Revolution the people deposed the king and they assumed his sovereignty. In other parts of the world, such as Saudi Arabia, the symbolic transfer of power never occurred. Nevertheless, for the purposes of studying the agency problem, we identify the people as the principal.

Foreign oil and mining companies need to obtain concessions to exploit natural resources. They can obtain them only from the rulers of the countries, but the rulers are not the principals. They are agents of the people. The rulers get their rewards from the companies, not from the people whose interests they are supposed to safeguard. They have much greater incentives to remain in power than the rulers of resource-poor countries and they have greater financial means at their disposal. That is why resource-rich countries are less democratic and often fall into the hands of repressive rulers. The countries concerned are also prone to civil strife.

This is the key agency problem and the primary source of the revenue curse. It is asymmetric in the sense that it affects only the principals on one side, namely the people of the countries concerned, not the other side, the owners of the oil and mining companies. The managers of these companies faithfully represent the companies' interests and that involves doing whatever they can to obtain concessions on the most favorable terms possible. This has, in the past, included bribing and exerting other pressures on the rulers.

The resource curse has a murky history. International mining and oil companies could often enlist the support of their governments. They used to routinely pay off the rulers and colluded with them in not disclosing payments. They also used to exert themselves in keeping the right people in power, or on occasion support armed insurrections in the expectation of obtaining concessions. More recently, U.S.-based companies have come under the constraints of the Foreign Corrupt Practices Act and other OECD-based companies under its anti-bribery codes. Publicly traded companies are also subject to pressure by public opinion, and some managements, exemplified by British Petroleum, have developed their own ethical standards. But history has not come to an end. Constraints imposed on international oil and mining companies do not apply to Russia, China, or India. And there are many international operators who are not similarly constrained. The no-holds-barred hunt for natural resources continues unabated.

Historically, international oil and mining companies benefited from asymmetric information and asymmetric bargaining power. That is how they managed to capture most of the natural resources in the less developed world. But conditions have changed. After World War II, rising nationalism and democratic aspirations made resource-rich countries more assertive. In 1951, Mohammed Mossadeq nationalized the Anglo-Iranian Oil Company. He was overthrown by a CIA-led coup, but some 20 years later a wave of nationalizations swept through the major oil-producing countries, leading to the first oil crisis. Since then, bargaining power has shifted in favor of the oil-producing countries. Nondemocratic governments could count on acceptance and support from the governments of oil-consuming countries. This has been an important element in the lack of democratic development in the Middle East. The current tightness in oil supplies has reinforced this unfavorable trend.

The creation of national oil companies has largely cured the asymmetry in information and the formation of OPEC has shifted the bargaining power in favor of oil-producing countries. Since then international oil companies have been largely confined to newly emerging oil-producing countries where they still enjoy informational and bargaining power advantages.

National oil companies give rise to a different set of agency problems, however. Depending on their stage of development, they can offer an effective antidote vis-à-vis the international oil companies with regard to all three asymmetries. They are liable, however, to aggravate the agency problem at the governmental level and run into agency problems of their own. National oil companies can serve as a power base for nondemocratic governments as well as a source of internal corruption. Resource revenues provide a nondemocratic government both with the financial means and the incentive to maintain itself in power. Elections can be rigged using the resources of national oil companies because the companies are not accountable to the public. When the rulers are in possession of revenues that do not pass through the national budget, or the budgets are not transparent, there is an agency problem and democracy is endangered. Russia is the best example but the problem arises whenever governments depend on rents from resource revenues rather than from taxes.

While the establishment of national oil and mining companies may have largely eliminated the asymmetry of information between international companies and the governments of the resource-rich countries, a different kind of asymmetric information persists. The citizens of resource-rich countries have very little information about the extractive industry-related activities in which their government engages. Unless the people understand better how much money is flowing and where, the asymmetry will persist. The obvious remedy is greater transparency and accountability. This is an area where a broad-based international transparency campaign is beginning to make inroads.

The resource curse is a major scourge, but it can be cured. It has now been recognized that transparency and accountability are the remedies. A powerful movement has emerged to advocate it. It started with the Publish What You Pay campaign launched in early 2003 by Global Witness and other nongovernmental organizations. This was taken up almost immediately by the British government and became the Extractive Industries Transparency Initiative. My foundations have sponsored revenue watch initiatives in several countries. The Revenue Watch Institute, which is being established with the help of the Hewlett Foundation and others, will seek to institutionalize these initiatives and to broaden public understanding of the resource curse phenomenon and its cures.

Escaping the Resource Curse is the first volume in the Initiative for Policy Dialogue (IPD) series at Columbia University Press, but it is also the third in the Revenue Watch publication series. The first, *Follow the Money,* provides practical information to civil society groups in resource-rich countries on how to become effective monitors of government earnings and expenditures. The second, *Covering Oil,* was also produced together with IPD and offers journalists practical information about the petroleum industry to give them the background information needed to write in-depth analytical and investigative reports on the effects of extractive industries in their countries. *Escaping the Resource Curse* fulfils an important role not addressed by these other publications. Directed toward policy makers and those interested in influencing policy, it provides practical and independent advice from leading experts to policy makers in resource-rich countries about how to maximize long-term benefits from their natural wealth and avoid the pitfalls of the resource curse.

I am happy to endorse the book and the movement to hold governments accountable by contributing this Foreword.

ACKNOWLEDGMENTS

The initial idea for this book came in discussions with Karin Lissakers, George Soros, and Svetlana Tsalik of the Open Society Institute (OSI). Their work and experience was invaluable for identifying key gaps in our understanding of how to respond to the problems that arise from natural resource wealth. William Masters of Purdue and Paul Collier of Oxford University played a central role in these early discussions and were instrumental in giving shape to the structure of this project. We thank them for their wisdom and insight.

We also benefited from timely inputs from practitioners and experts in the oil and gas industry. Drafts of the chapters in this volume were presented at a conference at Columbia University in July 2005 and benefited greatly from the comments and suggestions provided by participants who generously gave of their time and expertise. These include Luis dos Prazeres, Executive Director of the National Petroleum Agency of Sao Tome and Principe; Jeffrey Davis, Deputy Director of the Fiscal Affairs Department of the International Monetary Fund; Ian Gary of Catholic Relief Services; Xixi Chen, Matleena Kniivila, David O'Connor, and Yimeng Zhang of the United Nations Division for Sustainable Development, Economic and Social Affairs; Kevin Conrad of the Rainforest Carbon Coalition; Keith Myers of Chatham House; Hurst Groves and David Nissen from the Columbia Center for Energy, Marine Transportation and Public Policy; and Keith Slack of Oxfam America. We thank especially Tom Heller of Stanford University who provided critical comments throughout these stages of writing.

Throughout the process, we benefited from wonderful support and guidance from Julie McCarthy, Morgan Mandeville, and Ari Korpivaara from OSI. We gratefully acknowledge financial support from OSI that made the writing of this volume possible. Shari Spiegel, Sylvia Wu, and Siddhartha Gupta from the Initiative for Policy Dialogue and Ben Cahill at Columbia University Earth Institute provided excellent support throughout this process. We would like to thank Myles Thompson and Marina Petrova at Columbia University Press for their support, guidance, and patience as well as two anonymous referees who provided thoughtful comments and criticisms on the structure of the volume and the individual chapters. The final manuscript benefited from the scrutiny of a number of readers who read through and provided written comments on the entire manuscript. For this we thank especially Laura Paler and Sylvia Wu. Special thanks to Karin Lissakers and Svetlana Tsalik, whose overall vision and perceptive comments on individual chapters have been simply invaluable.

Macartan Humphreys, Jeffrey D. Sachs, and Joseph E. Stiglitz
New York, September 2006

ESCAPING THE RESOURCE CURSE

———

CHAPTER 1

Introduction

What Is the Problem with Natural Resource Wealth?

Macartan Humphreys, Jeffrey D. Sachs, and Joseph E. Stiglitz

There is a curious phenomenon that social scientists call the "resource curse" (Auty 1993). Countries with large endowments of natural resources, such as oil and gas, often perform *worse* in terms of economic development and good governance than do countries with fewer resources. Paradoxically, despite the prospects of wealth and opportunity that accompany the discovery and extraction of oil and other natural resources, such endowments all too often impede rather than further balanced and sustainable development.

On the one hand, the *lack* of natural resources has not proven to be a fatal barrier to economic success. The star performers of the developing world—the Asian Tigers (Hong Kong, Korea, Singapore, and Taiwan)—all achieved booming export industries based on manufactured goods and rapid economic growth *without* large natural resource reserves. On the other hand, many natural resource–rich countries have struggled to generate self-sustaining economic takeoff and growth and have even succumbed to deep economic crises (Sachs and Warner 1995). In country after country, natural resources have helped to raise living standards while failing to produce self-sustaining growth. Controlling for structural attributes, resource-rich countries grew less rapidly than resource-poor countries during the last quarter of the twentieth century. Alongside these growth failures are strong associations between resource wealth and the likelihood of weak democratic development (Ross 2001), corruption (Sala-i-Martin and Subramanian 2003), and civil war (Humphreys 2005).

This generally bleak picture among resource-rich countries nonetheless masks a great degree of variation. Some natural resource–rich countries have performed far better than others in resource wealth management and long-term economic development. Some 30 years ago, Indonesia and Nigeria had comparable per capita incomes and heavy dependencies on oil sales. Yet today, Indonesia's per capita income is four times that of Nigeria (Ross 2003). A similar discrepancy can be found among countries rich in diamonds and other nonrenewable minerals akin to oil and gas. For instance, in comparing the diamond-rich countries of Sierra Leone and Botswana, one sees that Botswana's economy has grown at an average rate of 7 percent over the past 20 years while Sierra Leone has plunged into civil strife, its gross domestic product (GDP) per capita actually dropping 37 percent between 1971 and 1989 (World Bank Country Briefs).

The United Nation's Human Development Index illustrates the high degree of variation in well-being across resource-rich countries (Human Development Report 2005). This measure summarizes information on income, health, and education across countries worldwide. Looking at this measure, we find that Norway, a major oil producer, ranks at the very top of the index. Other relatively high-ranking oil-producing countries include Brunei, Argentina, Qatar, United Arab Emirates, Kuwait, and Mexico. Yet, many oil-producing countries fall at the other extreme. Among the lowest ranked countries in the world are Equatorial Guinea, Gabon, The Republic of Congo, Yemen, Nigeria, and Angola. Chad comes in close to the bottom at 173 out of 177.

Variation in the effects of resource wealth on well-being can be found not only across countries but also *within* them. Even when resource-rich countries have done fairly well, they have often been plagued by rising inequality—they become rich countries with poor people. Approximately half the population of Venezuela—the Latin American economy with the most natural resources—lives in poverty; historically, the fruits of the country's bounty accrued to a minority of the country's elite (Weisbrot et al. 2006). This reality presents yet another paradox. At least in theory, natural resources can be taxed without creating disincentives for investment. Unlike in the case of mobile assets—such as capital, where high taxes can induce capital to exit a country—oil is a nonmovable commodity. Since tax proceeds from the sale of oil can be used to create a more egalitarian society, one could expect less, not more, inequality in resource-rich countries. In reality, however, this is rarely the case.

The perverse effects of natural resources on economic and political outcomes in developing states give rise to a wide array of difficult policy questions for governments of developing countries and for the international community. For instance, should Mexico privatize its state-run oil companies? Should the World Bank help finance the development of oil in Chad; if so, under what conditions? Should the international community have "allowed" Bolivia and Ecuador to mortgage future oil revenues to support deficit spending during the recessions they faced in the past decade? Should Azerbaijan use its oil revenues to finance a reduction in taxes or should it put the money into a stabilization fund? Should Nigeria offer preferential exploration rights to China rather than requiring open competitive bidding in all blocks? Should Sudan use the proceeds from oil sales to support oil-producing regions or spread the wealth more evenly across different regions?

The chapters in this volume lay out a broad framework for thinking about these issues, a framework that seeks simultaneously to help countries avert the natural resource curse and address the myriad of serious questions on how a resource endowment should be managed. While an extensive literature on the resource curse exists, few books attempt to tackle this issue by drawing on both theory and practice, as well as on both economics and politics. In undertaking this task, we have asked leading economists, political scientists, and legal practitioners active in research and policy making on natural resource management to write down the key lessons they have learned on best practice for managing these resources. For concreteness, we asked them to focus especially on oil and gas, which makes for cleaner and more focused analyses throughout. While some features of oil and gas economics are specific to these industries, much of the logic and many of the proposals presented here can be applied also to other forms of natural resources. The result of their studies is a rich collection of analyses into the causes and patterns of the perverse effects of oil and gas and the identification of a series of steps that can be taken to break the patterns of the past.

But before we start exploring the solutions let us begin our study with an examination of the origins of the resource curse—why does oil and gas wealth often do more harm than good? The basic paradox calls for an explanation, one that will allow countries to do something to undo the resource curse. Fortunately, over the past decade, research by economists and political scientists has done much to enhance our understanding of the issues.

WHERE DOES THE RESOURCE CURSE COME FROM?

To understand the natural resource paradox we need first a sense of what makes natural resource wealth different from other types of wealth. Two key differences stand out. The first is that unlike other sources of wealth, natural resource wealth does not need to be produced. It simply needs to be extracted (even if there is often nothing simple about the extraction process). Since it is not a result of a production process, the generation of natural resource wealth can occur quite independently of other economic processes that take place in a country; it is, in a number of ways, "enclaved."[1] For example, it can take place without major linkages to other industrial sectors and it can take place without the participation of large segments of the domestic labor force. Natural resource extraction can thus also take place quite independently of other political processes; a government can often access natural resource wealth regardless of whether it commands the cooperation of its citizens or effectively controls institutions of state. The second major feature stems from the fact that many natural resources—oil and gas in particular—are nonrenewable. From an economic aspect, they are thus less like a source of income and more like an asset.

These two features—the detachment of the oil sector from domestic political and economic processes and the nonrenewable nature of natural resources—give rise to a large array of political and economic processes that produce adverse effects on an economy. One of the greatest risks concerns the emergence of what political scientists call "rent-seeking behavior." Especially in the case of natural resources, a gap—commonly referred to as an economic *rent*—exists between the value of that resource and the costs of extracting it. In such cases, individuals, be they private sector actors or politicians, have incentives to use political mechanisms to capture these rents. Rampant opportunities for rent-seeking by corporations and collusion with government officials thereby compound the adverse economic and political consequences of natural resource wealth.

UNEQUAL EXPERTISE

The first problems arise even before monies from natural resource wealth make it into the country. Governments face considerable challenges in their dealings with international corporations, which have great interest and expertise in the sector and extraordinary resources on which to draw. Since oil and gas exploration is both capital and (increasingly) technologically intensive, extracting oil and gas typically requires cooperation between country governments and experienced international private sector actors. In many cases, this can produce the unusual situation in which the buyer—the international oil company—actually knows more about the value of the good being sold than the seller—the government of the resource-rich country. Companies can, in such instances, be in very strong bargaining positions relative to governments. The challenge for host countries is to find ways to contract with the international corporations in a manner that also gives them a fair deal. If, of course, there are large numbers of corporations that have the requisite knowledge, competition should be able to eliminate the rents associated with expertise, thereby allowing the resource-rich country to receive a larger fraction of the resource's market value. But countries cannot always rely on the existence of such competition.

"DUTCH DISEASE"

Once a contract has been negotiated and the money begins to flow in, new problems arise. In the 1970s, the Netherlands discovered one of these problems. Following the discovery of natural gas in the North Sea, the Dutch found that their manufacturing sector suddenly started performing more poorly than anticipated.[2] Resource-rich countries that similarly experience a decline in preexisting domestic sectors of the economy are now said to have caught the "Dutch disease" (Ebrahim-Zadeh 2003). The pattern of the "disease" is straightforward. A sudden rise in the value of natural resource exports produces an appreciation in the real exchange rate. This, in turn, makes exporting non–natural resource commodities more difficult and competing with imports across a wide range of commodities almost impossible (called the "spending effect"). Foreign exchange earned from the natural resource meanwhile may be used to purchase internationally traded goods, at the expense of domestic manufacturers of the goods. Simultaneously, domestic resources such as labor and materials are shifted to the natural resource sector (called the "resource pull effect"). Consequently, the price of these resources rises on the domestic market, thereby increasing the costs to producers in other sectors. All in all, extraction of natural resources sets in motion a dynamic that gives primacy to two domestic sectors—the natural resource sector and the nontradables sector, such as the construction industry—at the expense of more traditional export sectors. In the Dutch case, this was manufacturing; in developing countries, this tends to be agriculture. Such dynamics appear to occur widely, whether in the context of Australian gold booms in the nineteenth century, Colombian coffee in the 1970s, or the looting of Latin America's gold and silver by sixteenth-century Spanish and Portuguese imperialists.

Globally, these shifts can have adverse effects on the economy through several channels. Any shift can be costly for an economy, as workers need to be retrained and find new jobs, and capital needs to be readjusted. Beyond this, the particular shifts induced by the Dutch disease may have other adverse consequences. If the manufacturing sector is a long-term source of growth—for example, through the generation of new technologies or improved human capacity—then the decline of this sector will have adverse growth consequences (Sachs and Warner 2001). Another channel is through income distribution—if returns to export sectors such as agriculture or manufacturing are more equitably distributed than returns to the natural resource sector, then this sectoral shift can lead to a rise in inequality. In any case, the Dutch disease spells trouble down the road—when activities in the natural resource sector eventually slow down, other sectors may find it very difficult to recover.

VOLATILITY

The Dutch disease problem arises because of the *quantity* of oil money coming in; other problems arise because of the *timing* of the earnings. Earnings from oil and gas production, if viewed as a source of income, are highly volatile. The volatility of income comes from three sources: the variation over time in rates of extraction, the variability in the timing of payments by corporations to states, and fluctuations in the value of the natural resource produced. As an example of the first two sources of variability consider figure 1.1, which shows one projection for Chad's earnings from the sale of oil over the period 2004–2034. We see a sharp rise, followed by a rapid decline, a second rise, and a second decline. This pattern emerges from two distinct sources. The first is the variation over time in the rate of extraction. A typical pattern is to have a front-loading of extraction rates since production volumes tend to reach a peak within the first few years of production and then gradually descend until production stops. In practice, risks exist in Chad—as in Nigeria and elsewhere—that this volatility will be compounded further by interruptions that result from political instability in the country and in producing regions. The second major source of volatility derives from the nature of the agreement between the producing companies and the government. In the Chad case, the oil consortium was exempted from taxes on earning for the first years of production. Since taxes constitute a major source of government earnings, the eventual introduction of taxes should provide a major boost to Chad's earnings.

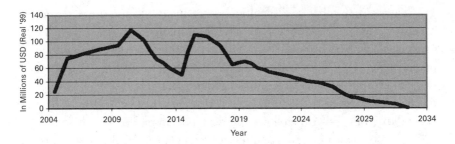

Figure 1.1   Revenues to Chad, Base Case 917 MM BBLs, US$15.25/BBL.

Source: Based on estimates presented in the World Bank Inspection Panel (2000).

The third major source of volatility—not even accounted for in Figure 1.2—arises from the highly volatile nature of oil and gas prices. The figure presented by the World Bank is based on prices of $15.25 a barrel, a number that now appears hopelessly out of date. Figure 1.2 shows the price of oil over the past 20 years. Note that while there is a very clear upward trend over these years, the variation around this trend is very great with week on week changes of plus or minus 5 to 10 percent relatively common.

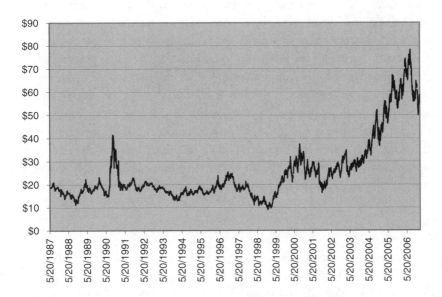

Figure 1.2   All Countries Spot Price FOB Weighted by Estimated Export Volume (Dollars per Barrel).

There are a number of difficulties with a highly volatile income source. Most obvious is the fact that longer term planning is rendered difficult by great uncertainty over future financing, especially as a result of fluctuations in the value of the commodity. Even when the volatility is not associated with uncertainty, with capital market imperfections, volatility in receipts often translates into volatility in expenditure. The result can be high levels of expenditure in good years followed by deep cuts in bad years. These in turn lead to "boom–bust cycles." All too often, the benefits in the good years are transitory whereas the problems generated during the bad years endure.

The magnitude of these fluctuations can be increased by international lending. When times are good (prices and output are high), the country borrows from abroad, exacerbating the boom. But when prices fall, lenders demand repayment, forcing expenditure reductions which increase the magnitude of the downturn. On some occasions, most famously in the oil price booms of the 1970s, several oil states mortgaged their futures by borrowing against booming oil revenues, only to end up in debt crisis when oil prices fell in the early 1980s. Mexico, Nigeria, and Venezuela typified the oil-debt boom and bust. This is not quite as irrational as it seems. Most poor countries are rationed in international borrowing, and may be unable to borrow to secure financing for infrastructure needed for growth. Oil can serve as collateral, or at least as an informal guarantee (since the oil earnings are easy to identify and direct toward debt servicing). Thus, an oil boom, either through higher prices or quantities, can unleash not only a higher cash flow but also increased access to international loans. If the infrastructure investments are indeed high economic priorities, it might make sense to borrow against future oil earnings in this way. However, that "if" has been a big one, since much international borrowing has been wasted or stolen, and international capital inflows have been subject to panic and sharp reversals, often throwing the borrowing countries into a deep debt crisis. This is true for non-oil as well as oil states, but the very nature of natural resource endowments makes resource-rich countries even more susceptible to this dynamic.

LIVING OFF YOUR CAPITAL

A new set of problems arises once governments start spending their earnings. Because oil and gas resources are nonrenewable, any consumption of revenues from sales should be viewed as a consumption of capital rather than a consumption of income. If all revenues are consumed in each period, then the value of the country's total capital declines. Ignoring extraction costs, an optimal strategy involves converting most of the natural resource stock into financial assets, investing the assets in a diversified portfolio and treating the interest on the financial assets as income. With extraction costs, Hotelling's analysis (see chapter 6) provides a framework for determining the optimum time to undertake resource extraction. In principle, the portfolio composition problem can be fully separated from the expenditure decision. It may be optimal to convert oil below the ground into gold, apartment buildings, dollars, or some other assets above the ground. Indeed doing so—for example, by selling oil rights on futures markets—could entirely remove the income volatility associated with natural resources. Similarly, complete privatization of oil rights (with up-front payments) might—in perfectly functioning markets—serve a similar role. It turns out, however, that the implicit price governments pay for this conversion of a risky natural resource asset into a financial asset is extremely high, so that in general governments would be ill-advised to do so.[3]

In practice, the income and expenditure sides get linked. International advisers often emphasize that the country is not *wealthier* as a result of resource extraction; it has just changed the composition of its asset base. But this argument has only limited resonance. In practice, along with access to capital stock and rising income comes pressure to spend sooner rather than later. This pressure comes from many sources. As discussed in chapters 8 and 10, politicians with an uncertain hold on power have an incentive to spend sooner rather than to leave opportunities on the table for future political opponents. And their incentives are greater if spending can help ensure that they will remain in power longer. Other pressures may arise from populations demanding rapid and visible improvements in welfare or from constituents demanding favors in return for political support. Particularly compelling arguments can be made for the use of the resources (or even borrowing against future resources) when the economy is operating below full capacity and a small amount of pump priming will have large effects on national income. International Monetary Fund (IMF) rules of budgetary stringency make little sense in this context.

The far more difficult cases arise when a government has a worthwhile project that entails drawing on significant domestic resources. It can be tempting to use oil revenues to cover the costs of domestic resource mobilization. But unless paired with other policies, this approach would likely give rise to currency appreciation, reducing jobs elsewhere in the economy. The net benefits might be negative. Nevertheless, if a government can use resource wealth to cover foreign exchange needs while mobilizing domestic tax revenue to finance the domestic component, such investments can still enable growth *without* exchange rate appreciation. Indeed, as discussed in chapter 7, in many cases, high levels of investment in the short run may be optimal, but the pressure to spend even beyond the optimum may still be very great.

INSUFFICIENT INVESTMENTS IN EDUCATION

Along with overconsumption comes underinvestment. Studies show that education as a form of investment especially suffers in resource-rich countries (Gylfason 2001). When states start relying on natural resource wealth, they seem to forget the need for a diversified and skilled workforce that can support other economic sectors once resource wealth has dried up. As a result, the share of national income spent on education declines, along with secondary school enrollment and the expected years of schooling for girls. While the costs of such declines might not be felt in the short term, as capital-intense activities take up a larger share of national production, their effects are likely to become more significant in the longer run as soon as economies start trying to diversify.

It is possible to understand this bias in terms of the nature of the sources of wealth. When a country's wealth depends on investments in manufacturing or other productive activities, human capital investment is an essential part of wealth creation. When a country's wealth arises from an endowment of natural resources, however, investment in a skilled workforce is not necessary for the realization of current income. Without a focus on wealth creation, or sustainability, insufficient attention will be paid to investments in human capital (or other productive investments.)

*   *   *

Beyond these economic and financial concerns, a series of political dynamics associated with oil and gas dependence can exacerbate adverse economic effects. As mentioned earlier, oil-dependent economies, for example, are considerably more likely to have limited political freedoms, to be governed by nondemocratic regimes, to have higher levels of corruption, and to suffer from civil wars within their boundaries. Evidence suggests that natural resource dependency causes these outcomes through a variety of mechanisms, as described in the following sections.

SPOLIATION

Higher levels of corruption present the most obvious political risk that can arise from large holdings of natural resources. The short run availability of large financial assets increases the opportunity for the theft of such assets by political leaders. Those who control these assets can use that wealth to maintain themselves in power, either through legal means (e.g., spending in political campaigns) or coercive ones (e.g., funding militias). By some accounts, corruption is a hallmark of the oil business itself.[4] But oil and gas dependence can also affect corruption indirectly. As discussed later, the presence of oil and gas wealth can produce weak state structures that make corrupt practices considerably easier for government officials. These risks are also likely to be exacerbated if the growth of the oil and gas sector is associated with a concentration of bureaucratic power, which increases the difficulty of securing transparency and other constraints on those in power. Not surprisingly, statistical studies that seek to account for variation in levels of corruption across different countries find that natural resource dependence is a strong predictor (Leite and Weidmann 1999).

Corruption related to natural resources takes many forms. International mining and oil companies that seek to maximize profits find that they can lower the costs of obtaining resources more easily by obtaining the resources at below market value—by bribing government officials—than by figuring out how to extract the resources more efficiently. In other cases, the natural resource is sold to domestic firms at below full value, with government officials either getting a kickback or an ownership share. In practice, the risks of corruption in resource-rich environments are very large and the costs of such corruption to the national economy are enormous. By some accounts, for example, Nigeria's president Abacha was responsible for the theft of as much as US$3 billion (Ayittey 2006).

WEAK, UNACCOUNTABLE STATES

Although one might expect that the added resources available to states from oil and gas revenues might make them stronger, there are a number of reasons why, paradoxically, it can make them weaker (Karl 1997). States that are able to generate revenue from the sale of oil and gas are less reliant on citizens, which can result in weak linkages between governments and citizens. When citizens are untaxed they sometimes have less information about state activities and, in turn, may demand less of states. Even if they disapprove of state action, they lack the means to withdraw their financial support from states. As a result, states have less need to engage with civilians. Moreover, in relying on external income sources rather than on domestic revenue, states have less of a need to develop a bureaucratic apparatus to raise revenue (Fearon and Laitin 2003). The need to collect taxes is widely thought to have contributed to the emergence of strong state and even democratic institutions in many Western countries (Ross 2004). The *lack* of reliance on tax revenue in favor of reliance on external sources of revenue is thus thought to hinder the development of effective states in many resource-rich developing countries (Moore 1998).

Further, since a resource-rich country's revenue is largely independent of the strength and success of the overall economy, the government of the resource-rich country has less of a need to engage in activities that support the economy. Without a broad support base in the economy, a government can instead invest its earnings in an oppressive capacity. Doing so does not, however, produce strong states. The structures that result are often not resilient and indeed, the capacity of repression can be turned against the incumbent. Even if such a strategy is successful at protecting leaders, it will not necessarily produce the capacity needed to engage productively with the national economy. In chapter 10, Terry Lynn Karl discusses these dynamics and suggests ways in which states may attempt to respond to the erosion of capacity.

THREATS TO DEMOCRACY

The adverse political effects associated with high levels of corruption and weak states ultimately have consequences for the political system itself. Countries rich in natural resources—in particular, in oil and gas—are less likely to have democratic political systems. Specifically, nondemocratic oil states are less likely to become democratic than states that do not export oil. This relationship has been found in cross-national studies that relate the discovery of oil in a given period to democratic changes over the coming decades (Tsui 2005). In effect, access to oil wealth can allow leaders to successfully repress or co-opt their oppositions, and thus avoid having to relinquish power through electoral competition.

These adverse political effects of oil are not just a problem for developing countries; such patterns have even been seen within the United States. One recent study examined the relationship between oil and coal production within each of the American states over the period 1929 to 2002 and related this to gubernatorial turnover. The study found that a 1 percent increase in state dependence on these resources is associated with a rise of approximately half a percent in the governor's margin of victory in these states (Goldberg et al. 2005). Overall, at least three features of oil dependent states help to explain the relationship between natural resource dependence and the lack of democratization (Ross 2001). First, governments do not feel the same pressures to exchange political power for the rights to tax, since they can raise their revenues from other sources. Second, they can invest in coercive capacity that can be used to quell threats to their political power. Finally, citizens in these states are less likely to undergo the transformative effects of industrializing countries that have been associated with demands for democratization elsewhere.

GRIEVANCES IN PRODUCING REGIONS

The production of natural resources is liable to give rise to various types of political frustrations within a country and especially in producing regions. The extraction process itself may result in forced out-migration, new in-migration, and, with attendant population pressures, environmental pollution or degradation. Even if such changes to local conditions are minimal, resource-rich regions may feel that they have a particular claim on resource wealth and may be aggrieved if they see the wealth leaving their region and benefiting others. Such complaints have been raised in oil regions including Cabinda in Angola, Doba in Chad, and even in the small island of Principe in Sao Tome and Principe. The effect of grievances of this form and ways to try to manage them are discussed in chapter 9.

MILITARY CHALLENGES TO GOVERNMENTS

Oil exporters spend much more on their militaries even in the absence of civil war—between 2 and 10 times more. In the most difficult cases, the resource curse results not only in militarization but also in civil war. Civil wars are, statistically speaking, more likely to occur in oil-rich states (Humphreys 2005). Indeed, some oil-rich states such as Angola, Colombia, or Sudan have had civil wars within their borders for decades on end. There are a number of reasons for this. If oil and gas wealth accrues to political leaders simply by virtue of the fact that they maintain nominal control of a state, this increases the incentives of nonstate actors to attempt to capture the state in order to benefit from the resource wealth, often through the use of violence (Collier and Hoeffler 2000; Fearon and Laitin 2003). This can lead to secessionist bids in some countries—sometimes aided by the grievances that arise in producing regions—or to attempts to topple the central government outright, as, for example, in the Republic of Congo (Englebert and Ron 2004). These incentives are all the stronger if the resource-rich state has weak capacity and lacks legitimacy. Because of the major international interest in these resources, outside actors—states, as well as corporations—may have an interest then in supporting threats to a central government in anticipation of special relations with the new regime. Foreign powers have often meddled shamelessly in the politics of oil-producing countries to try to maintain a hold on oil resources and revenue flows. The CIA-backed coup in Iran in 1953 is the most famous example (Gasiorowski 1987).

POLITICAL AND ECONOMIC INTERACTIONS

There are strong interactions between the economic problems discussed in the first part of this section and the political problems discussed in the second. Even in democracies, when governments privatize natural resources they often receive less than their full market value. Firms in extractive industries care first and foremost about minimizing what they have to pay for access to the resources. They therefore seek to ensure that the deals are structured in a way that benefits them over the government. Often, this is achieved through political action such as campaign contributions and other forms of public–private alliances. Moreover, while selling access to natural rents is seen as a relatively easy way to reduce budget deficits, the possibilities for shortsighted deals and complicity in rent-seeking abound. Various administrations in the United States have, at times, practically given away natural resources to raise additional budgetary funds. Ronald Reagan, for example, designed a "fire sale" of oil leases, rapid auctions that resulted in a significant depression in the prices government received. Corporations in the extractive industries also have an incentive to limit transparency, to make it more difficult for citizens to see how much their government is getting in exchange for sale of the country's resources. In most cases, such corporations have an incentive to limit government regulations that would restrict environmental damage or that would force corporations to pay for the cost of the damage they inflict.[5]

WHAT TO DO?

The chapters in this book address the challenges posed by the many adverse effects of oil and gas wealth. They assume throughout that both countries and companies can and should do something to more effectively and fairly develop oil resources. We assume in particular that governments are willing to take sometimes bold and difficult steps to try to succeed where most states have failed. If states are unable or unwilling to take such steps, then the best solution may well be to leave the oil and gas in the ground. The fact is that oil in the ground is a nonwasting asset.[6] Although leaving oil in the ground means that interest is forgone, the ground just might be the safest place for the asset, especially if there exists the risk that governments may use revenue for their purposes rather than for the good of society, as has happened so often already. In such cases, the people may benefit *some,* but clearly not as much as if the money were spent in ways that were directly intended to enhance their well-being. A judgment call is required, and not solely by the government of the host country, which often lacks the political will necessary to postpone extraction of natural resource reserves. In addition to governments and international corporations, civil society and the international community play an important role in influencing the extraction of natural resources. If the orientation of a government is such that there are likely to be few benefits to the people, then domestic groups and the international community should provide no help for extraction. Plausibly, the prospects of the money being used better later are greater than the prospects today, and so patience may be what is required.

Assuming, however, that a government is willing to take some of the difficult measures, what can be done? The chapters in Part I address a set of basic questions regarding how governments should interact with oil corporations. The first question that a country faces is: should the government get involved at all, or can the problem of extraction be left entirely in the hands of the private sector? Joseph Stiglitz considers this question in chapter 2. He argues that privatization is not the panacea that some advocates suggest;[7] rather, privatization can lead to a considerable loss of value for a state without necessarily resolving either the micro problems of good management or the macroeconomic problems that plague oil- and gas-rich countries. Stiglitz also discusses the design of the auction and contractual relationships between the government and the private sector, should the government decide to use private companies for resource extraction. These optimal auctions/contractual relationships are markedly different from those commonly employed, largely because of the political economy factors discussed earlier.

Some level of engagement with the private sector is, however, generally unavoidable and can be highly productive. Chapters 3 and 4 engage the problem of ensuring that a resource-rich country gets the best possible deal from its negotiations with international oil corporations. In chapter 3, David Johnston provides key information for evaluating the fiscal terms of oil contracts. He demonstrates the weaknesses with the most common methods used for evaluating the returns to a country of an oil contract and identifies the elements of a contract that should be a key focus of analysis for assessing whether a country has struck a good deal. In chapter 4, Jenik Radon argues that the benefits that accrue to government can depend greatly on one often overlooked feature—the skills of the negotiators. In fact, oil contract negotiation is more complex than many governments believe. While Radon emphasizes the likely returns to investing in the hiring of an experienced negotiation team, he also identifies a key set of areas that should be followed closely by all parties to oil and gas negotiations. In most cases, competitive bidding is likely to be the best way to offer drilling rights; not only does it generally fetch the highest bidding price, but it also can protect the country from corrupt dealings. In chapter 5, Peter Cramton describes the lessons that can be learned from auction theory for the case of oil and gas. Certain auction designs can help countries gain knowledge about the extent and nature of the information companies have about their blocks while also encouraging competition. Such transparency and competition results in greater revenues and prevents collusion among companies. The merits of different auction designs are discussed and one new auction design—the clock-proxy auction—is described in detail.

As we have seen, however, once oil and gas monies start coming into a country, new problems arise. The chapters in Part II address the macroeconomic and political economy issues associated with managing intertemporal expenditures of this form. In chapter 6, Geoffrey Heal describes the economic logic underlying the economically optimal way to divorce the pattern of earnings from expenditure patterns. Optimal expenditure paths typically require much higher levels of expenditure smoothing than would occur if expenditure tracked revenues closely. In his analysis, Heal further emphasizes the problems associated with treating revenues as income without taking into account the depletion of natural resource stocks, and offers a better method for factoring natural resource extraction into national accounting. A country's optimal expenditure path depends on how well it can balance the adverse macroeconomic consequences of large inflows of foreign exchange earnings with the need to invest in other sectors in order to achieve higher growth rates in the long run. This difficult trade-off is taken up by Jeffrey Sachs in chapter 7. Sachs shows the conditions under which natural resources are likely to have adverse effects on other sectors of an economy. These effects can be avoided, however, and indeed reversed, with appropriate investment strategies. The optimal investment strategy might involve much higher levels of front-loaded expenditure than many analysts suggest. A problem arises, however, in that—for any given optimal expenditure path, whether or not it is front loaded—there will generally exist political pressures to spend too much too soon. The reasons for these pressures are discussed in chapter 8 by Macartan Humphreys and Martin Sandbu. Some solutions to this problem can be found in the deployment of Natural Resource Funds, but only if these funds actually alter the incentives facing political actors. Incentives can be influenced in at least three key ways: by broadening the set of actors who play a role in expenditure decisions; by giving these actors a way to make commitments to particular expenditure paths; and by making it costly for them to deviate later from earlier decisions.

The chapters in Part III then turn to examine the political economy and legal issues associated with good revenue management. In chapter 9, Michael Ross examines the options available to states to manage the thorny distributive questions associated with resource wealth. The chapter looks at how mineral wealth can affect vertical and horizontal inequality, and what governments can do about it. Ross explores the advantages and disadvantages of the decentralization of mineral revenues and offers a series of guidelines for states that seek to better manage the distributional problems caused by mineral booms. Direct distribution of revenues to the citizens of a producing country, although attractive, raises a series of problems of its own. Similarly, the decentralization to local government authorities of responsibilities for raising revenues is highly problematic, while the decentralization of expenditure—once smoothing is undertaken by a more centralized structure—offers a number of benefits. Chapter 10 by Terry Lynn Karl turns to the problem of state–society linkages. Karl asks: If natural resource dependence has historically resulted in weaker links between states and their societies, can anything be done to stop this, going forward? She examines a number of the options that have been proposed and focuses especially on one key prerequisite for strong state–society linkages: public information regarding the state's finances and its operations in the oil and gas sectors. This, she argues, is a prerequisite for all other attempts to escape the resource curse. The final chapter by Joseph Bell and Teresa Maurea Faria examines the legal options that exist to help overcome the problems that have been identified. Their chapter—supported by appendices that provide abridged versions of innovative oil and gas revenue management laws—provides a set of very practical next steps for governments aiming to implement the recommendations of previous chapters.

Collectively, these chapters take us full cycle from the initial difficulties inherent in negotiating a deal with international corporations to the hard economic and political decisions that need to be made on when and how to spend natural resource earnings. Plaguing all well-meaning prescriptions, however, is the problem that the resource curse is such that many individuals in governments and in the private sector fare quite well in the short run when resources are misused. Even if such behavior does not benefit them in the long run, changing this behavior unilaterally may be too costly in the absence of reform by other actors. The challenge is to find ways to alter the incentives facing these actors to make it in their interest to do a better job. A theme running throughout the chapters in this volume is that this can be done only if greater light is shed on the industry so that publics are provided with much better information with which to evaluate the choices of their political leaders. Absent changes to the structure of oil and gas politics that can ensure much greater access to information about how deals are made, who gets what, and how resources are managed by incumbents, the lost opportunities that we see on a daily basis in oil- and gas-rich countries are set to continue for a long time to come.

NOTES

1. Natural resource extraction is therefore sometimes referred to by social scientists as "enclaved" (Hirschman 1958; Seers 1964).

2. See "The Dutch Disease" (1977).

3. Bonus (upfront) payments can be viewed as a loan from the corporation to the government; but the interest rate on this loan is the cost to capital of the corporation, which is typically much, much higher than the rate at which government can borrow.

4. In one testimony before French magistrates, the former Africa manager of Elf Aquitaine argued that "All international oil companies have used kickbacks since the first oil shock of the 1970s to guarantee the companies' access to oil." ("Oil Firm ELF" 2001).

5. They even have an incentive to restrict the use of accounting frameworks (like green GDP) that would call attention to the costs of resource depletion and environmental degradation. During the Clinton Administration, there was an attempt to develop and implement green GDP accounting, but congressional pressure, especially from coal mining states, led to a cutoff of funding. There is a vicious circle: extractive

industries have an incentive to maintain political systems or administrations which allow them to have greater voice.

6. According to Hotelling (1931), in perfectly functioning markets, on average, prices of natural resources will increase—in an amount just sufficient to offset the loss of interest. In such perfectly functioning markets, it would pay for those with high extraction costs to leave their resources in the ground; global efficiency would, for instance, focus current extraction on the low cost producers (probably in the Middle East).

7. For a recent study that argues in favor of privatization of the oil sector, see Weinthal and Luong (2006).

REFERENCES

Auty, R. 1993. *Sustaining Development in Mineral Economies: The Resource Curse Thesis.* London: Routledge.

Ayittey, G. B. N. 2006. "Nigeria's Struggle with Corruption." Testimony before the Committee on International Relations' Subcommittee on Africa, Global Human Rights and International Operations House Sub-Committee on Africa, U.S. House of Representatives, May 18, Washington, DC.

Collier, P. and A. Hoeffler. 2000. "Greed and Grievance in Civil Wars." Working Paper, World Bank. WPS 2000-18.

"The Dutch Disease." 1977. *The Economist*, November 26: 82–83.

Ebrahim-zadeh, C. 2003. "Back to Basics: Dutch Disease. Too Much Wealth Managed Unwisely." *Finance and Development* 40(1): 50–51.

Englebert, P. and J. Ron. 2004. "Primary Commodities and War: Congo-Brazzaville's Ambivalent Resource Curse." *Comparative Politics* 37(1): 61–81.

Fearon, J. D. and D. Laitin. 2003. "Ethnicity, Insurgency, and Civil War." *American Political Science Review* 97(1): 75–91.

Gasiorowski, M. 1987. "The 1953 Coup d'Etat in Iran." *International Journal of Middle East Studies* 19(3): 261–86.

Goldberg, E., E. Wibbels, and E. Mvukiyehe. 2005. "Lessons from Strange Cases: Democracy, Development, and the Resource Curse in the U.S. States, 1929–2002." Paper presented at the 2005 meeting of the American Political Science Association.

Gylfason, T. 2001. "Natural Resources, Education, and Economic Development." *European Economic Review* 45(4–6): 847–59.

Hirschman, A. O. 1958. *The Strategy of Economic Development.* New Haven: Yale University Press.

Hotelling, H. 1931. "The Economics of Exhaustible Resources." *Journal of Political Economy* 39(2): 137–75.

Human Development Report. 2005. http://hdr.undp.org/reports/global/2005/ (accessed July 15, 2006).

Humphreys, M. 2005. "Natural Resources, Conflict and Conflict Resolution." *Journal of Conflict Resolution* 49: 508–37.

Karl, T. L. 1997. *The Paradox of Plenty: Oil Booms and Petro-States*. Berkeley: University of California Press.

Leite, C. and J. Weidmann. 1999. "Does Mother Nature Corrupt?" Working Paper, IMF.

Moore, M. 1998. "Death without Taxes: Democracy, State Capacity, and Aid Dependence in the Fourth World." In *The Democratic Developmental State*, M. Robinson and G. White, eds. Oxford: Oxford University Press, pp. 84–124.

"Oil Firm ELF Accused of Bribing African Officials." 2001. Inter-Press Service, November 22.

Ross, M. 2001. "Does Oil Hinder Democracy?" *World Politics* 53(3): 326–61.

Ross, M. 2003. "Nigeria's Oil Sector and the Poor." Prepared for the UK Department for International Development.

Ross, M. 2004. "Does Taxation Lead to Representation?" *British Journal of Political Science* 34: 229–49.

Sachs, J. and A. M. Warner. 1995. "Natural Resource Abundance and Economic Growth." NBER Working Paper No. 5398.

Sachs, J. and A. M. Warner. 2001. "The Curse of Natural Resources." *European Economic Review* 45(4–6): 827–38.

Sala-i-Martin, X. and A. Subramanian. 2003. "Addressing the Natural Resource Curse: An Illustration from Nigeria." NBER Working Paper No. 9804.

Seers, D. 1964. "The Mechanism of an Open Petroleum Economy." *Social and Economic Studies* 13: 233–42.

Tsui, K. 2005. "More Oil, Less Democracy? Theory and Evidence from Crude Oil Discoveries." http://are.berkeley.edu/courses/envres_seminar/KTsuijobmarketpaper.pdf

Weinthal, E. and P. Luong. 2006. "Combating the Resource Curse: An Alternative Solution to Managing Mineral Wealth." *Perspectives on Politics* 4(1): 35–53.

Weisbrot, M., L. Sandoval, and D. Rosnick. 2006. *Poverty Rates in Venezuela: Getting the Numbers Right*. Center for Economic and Policy Research.

World Bank Country Briefs. http://web.worldbank.org (accessed June 15, 2006).

PART I

DEALING WITH OIL CORPORATIONS

CHAPTER 2

What Is the Role of the State?

Joseph E. Stiglitz

ABSTRACT

In their dealings with the global extractive industries, national governments frequently fail to get full value for their resources. The key problem is that private-sector parties have interests to maximize their revenues and to minimize those accruing to the country. Full privatizations of rights to oil and gas wealth have been marked by some of the worst abuses, with governments getting the worst deal. For countries with high-quality public management, and where there are not particularly difficult extraction problems, national oil companies should often play a central role in managing resources. Others face the difficult choice of trying either to improve public sector management or to rely on an imperfect and possibly corrupt public sector to define relationships with a private sector whose goal runs counter to that of the public interest—minimizing payments to the public. Even in these cases there are a number of important guidelines that governments can follow to ensure they get better value for their assets: Institutions should always be strengthened *before* engaging in privatization; patience should be practiced—it is sometimes better to keep oil wealth in the ground than to sell it badly; provisions should be identified for contract renegotiation ex ante; contracts should be minimally complex and evaluated on the basis of the incentives they generate and their performance under different scenarios; finally, the timing of payments should be a function of the ability of the state to bear risk. Whatever the approach, the aim of government decisions should be to ensure transparency, ownership, and fairness.

INTRODUCTION

In the first chapter of this volume, we identified one of the central problems underpinning the resource curse: Too often countries do not get the full value of their resources. Consider a government genuinely interested in using its good luck of an abundant resource endowment for the benefit of its people. But first it must somehow extract the resources from below the ground and sell them. To do that, it will have to rely on public employees and/or private contractors. It can hire the private contractors to undertake specific tasks, or it can sell them the natural resource in return either for a fixed amount or a royalty on whatever is sold. Many of the parties upon whom it must rely, however, have another objective: maximizing their own income or well-being, which in turn means minimizing the amount paid to the government. This is a natural and inevitable conflict of interest. Both in the public and private sectors, there are many who would also like to use the country's wealth for their own private purposes. Thus, a key challenge any government faces is to work out how to engage with these other actors, whose objectives inevitably differ radically from its own.

In this chapter, I focus on one issue that is particularly relevant to answering the question: How should governments work with the private sector to maximize the total (expected present discounted value of) revenue it receives from its natural endowment?

The traditional saying *caveat emptor*—let the buyer beware!—puts buyers on notice of the natural risks they face in buying goods in the marketplace. This chapter adds a new maxim: Let the owner beware! Be skeptical of those offering to manage your resources or to buy them from you. Their objective is not to increase your well-being, but theirs. And too often, the conditions that are required to be satisfied so that you can "trust the market" are not satisfied.[1] There is another maxim: "A fool and his money are soon parted." This is an even stronger warning to the publics in resource-rich countries: *It is all too easy for politicians to connive with those in the private sector to take from you what is yours.* This maxim may be less catchy but no less important: When it comes to natural resources, even a reasonably informed citizenry and their money can soon be parted.

THE PROBLEM OF CHEATING

The prospects of cheating are very real and great, and can arise at every stage of the transaction. The government may get less for the lease than

it should—there may even be attempts to restrict competition in bidding. Whatever the contract that has been signed, corporations are tempted
to cheat—to pay less than they are supposed to—because the amount of
money that can sometimes be made by doing so is so large. The occasions to cheat arise not just in developing countries. In the 1980s I worked
on a case involving cheating by the major oil companies in Alaska. This
oil-rich state had a mineral lease requiring the oil companies to pay it
12.5 percent of the gross receipts, less the cost of transporting the oil
out from the far-flung site at Prudhoe Bay on the Arctic Circle.[2] By
overestimating their costs by just a few pennies per gallon (and multi-
plying those pennies by hundreds of millions of gallons) the oil companies would increase their profits enormously. They could not resist the
temptation.

They also found other ways to cheat, such as selling their oil to
their own subsidiaries, recording a lower than fair market value (see
chapter 4); or using other subsidiaries to ship their oil out and then reporting a fictionally high shipping cost. Each piece of the cheating
puzzle was hard to detect, and government prosecutors had to analyze
thousands of transactions—at a cost of tens of millions of dollars. In
the end, there was no doubt that cheating had occurred—and on a
massive scale. There followed a series of settlements involving a who's
who of global oil companies—including what are now BP, ExxonMobil, and ConocoPhillips—for an amount in excess of 6 billion
dollars.[3]

Alabama successfully brought an even more outrageous case: *State of
Alabama v. Exxon Mobil Corp.*[4] At suit was whether or not Exxon could
deduct production costs from royalty payments as well as deduct gas
used to fuel the wells. The contract very clearly stated that they could
not. Moreover, internal Exxon memos presented at trial suggested that
they were aware of this and that they had conducted a cost-benefit analysis of the likelihood of getting caught. The court found for Alabama,
awarding $11.8 billion in punitive damages and $63.6 million in unpaid
royalties.[5]

While such possibilities exist in the United States, many more possibilities for cheating exist in countries where institutions are weaker.

In this chapter, I provide some guidelines for governments attempting
to navigate in this difficult environment; I describe the various ways that
countries can be, and have been, deprived of the true value of their resources; and I show what can be done to reduce the risk of being cheated.

If there is a single message of this chapter, it is this: There is no easy way out of this problem. Privatization—the process of turning over natural resource assets to the control of the private sector—is *not* the answer, or at least it is not necessarily the answer. But while there is no simple solution, some governments have done better than others in obtaining for their citizens a large fraction of the value of their resources. This chapter describes some of the things governments can do to increase that fraction, including strengthening institutional structures *before* engaging in privatization, holding corporations to higher standards, and carefully evaluating contract terms.

PRIVATIZATION AND PROBLEMS OF AGENCY

The central problem facing resource-rich countries may be easily stated: Various individuals wish to divert as much of that endowment as possible for their own private benefit. Modern economic theory has analyzed the generic problem of inducing agents (here government officials) to act in the interests of those they are supposed to serve (the principals, here citizens more generally). Agency problems arise whenever information is imperfect, and hence there is a need to emphasize *transparency,* or improving the openness and availability of information in the attempt to control corruption.[6]

Information is not the only way by which agency problems might be mitigated. Constraints can be imposed on actions that can be undertaken. Constraints on decision-making processes might affect the magnitude of the distortions that arise—for instance, requiring multiple approvals might increase the number of people who have to be bribed to get resources at below-market prices. The more people involved, the greater the probability that at least one is incorruptible (at least at going prices), thereby decreasing significantly the risks of corruption.[7] With the cost-benefit calculus for corruption changed, there might be less corruption.[8]

Every interaction opens up scope for an agency problem (and corruption is only one form that agency problems take). There are agency problems within firms, within the government, and in the transfer of assets from government control to the private sector. The entire set of rules governing the extraction of natural resources affects the magnitude of the agency problem—and the benefits that accrue to society from that country's natural resources.[9]

THE GENERAL PROBLEM OF DIVERSION

A look at experiences around the world shows a rich catalogue of ways by which resources get diverted and in which, in accomplishing the diversion, economic efficiency is impaired. In many developing countries, government-run oil companies have been marked by high levels of corruption; even when there is no overt corruption, those running the oil companies often pay themselves and their workers above-market wages—resulting in less money left over for the rest of the country. In countries with high levels of unemployment, the government-run oil companies become bloated with employees, a sort of welfare program directed disproportionately at the well connected.

Much of the public discourse has focused on government corruption— the attempt by government officials to divert as much as possible for their own use. This has led many (including the international financial institutions) to encourage privatization—turning over, in one way or the other, the development of natural resources to the private sector. Two decades ago, at the beginning of the wave of privatization, it was hoped that privatization would solve these problems. The private enterprises would have an incentive to be efficient. Especially if the resources were put up for auction, the winner would be the firm best able to extract resources; economic efficiency would be assured, at the same time that government revenue was maximized. But what has happened in the last two decades has made it abundantly clear that privatization does not eliminate scope for corruption, or more generally, eliminate agency problems. There are agency problems within private firms, just as there are in government enterprises. This is especially the case in those countries without good corporate governance (which means almost all developing countries). Those controlling the corporation (the company's officers) typically have the opportunity to divert the company's resources to their own benefit—and they not infrequently take advantage of that opportunity. Indeed, because public scrutiny of corporations, even public corporations, is typically less than public scrutiny of government enterprises, the scope for diversion is all the greater.[10]

We are concerned here, however, with the impact of these agency problems on the revenue obtained by the government. Privatizations typically entail not only a one-time payment from the private sector to the government but also an ongoing stream of payments, in the form of taxes. Leasing tracts of land entails further streams of payments, in the form of royalties. In many cases, government is a (minority) shareholder in the corporation given the right to extract the oil or natural resources. Each of these arrangements entails different potentials for "diversion" and different agency problems, and there is potential for diversion at each stage of the transaction, for example, both at the time the contract is signed and at the time it is implemented. When, for instance, private corporations in which the government is a minority shareholder are entrusted to develop a mine or oil field, there is a standard set of corporate governance problems: the abuse of minority shareholders by the controlling shareholder, or of shareholders by the "manager." Often, for instance, the company hires a foreign firm to "manage" the oil well. The question then is: What is the appropriate compensation? Even if the manager is directly compensated appropriately, he may pay a related third party more than fair market value for services—diverting value away from the government.

Even when the only ongoing relationship involves taxes or royalties, there are problems, as the company may attempt to cheat, hoping that if the amounts per barrel are small enough, they will go undetected. But pennies a barrel times hundreds of millions of barrels adds up. In the beginning of this chapter, we described two episodes of such cheating in the United States.

ADAM SMITH, THE INVISIBLE HAND, AND DIVERSION

It should have come as no surprise that privatization failed to solve the problem of resource diversion: profit-maximizing private enterprises naturally seek to minimize what they give to the government for their rights to control the use of the asset.[11] Modern capitalism is, by and large, based on a simple calculus: Each individual is concerned with how much he can get for himself. Under highly restrictive (never satisfied) conditions, Adam Smith was right that the pursuit of self-interest leads, as if by an invisible hand, to economic efficiency; but more generally, it may not. Adam Smith and his followers assumed perfect information; or at least that there were no agency problems (see Arnott et al. 1994; Greenwald and Stiglitz 1986). In many cases, the pursuit of self-interest (greed, by any other name) by American CEOs, investment banks, and accounting firms has not led to efficient investment, though some individuals have themselves been amply rewarded. And, so far at least, few have wound up paying any criminal penalties (for an extended discussion, see Stiglitz 2003).

It is standard doctrine, at least among American economists and in much of the business community, that firms should maximize the stock market value.[12] Almost every business school teaches that this is what managers are supposed to do. If they do not, they will be punished, either by being dismissed by their shareholders or by being taken over.[13] These doctrines have strong implications: If a firm can get control of oil at one-tenth of the market price by paying a $10 million bribe to a government official, a firm maximizing shareholder value should do so, so long as the expected penalties (the probability of being caught for violating the Foreign Corrupt Practices Act multiplied by the expected size of the fine if one is caught) are not too great.[14] If a mining company can somehow get out of a country without having to pay the full costs of cleanup, it should do so; if it is necessary to bribe some government official, or to make a campaign contribution, then that is just a necessary business expense.[15]

While some Western firms would shy away from the crassness of the behavior just described, the market economy rewards it. If a country auctions off its natural resources, the firm willing to pay the highest price is not necessarily the firm that is most efficient in extracting the resources. Rather, it might be the one most efficient in having the government pick up the cleanup costs, for example, minimizing the bribes required.

And few Western firms would shy away from active involvement in politics, in making campaign contributions ("investments" from which they expect, and typically do get, returns).

PRIVATIZATION AND THE SCOPE FOR DIVERSION

Privatization actually increases the scope (opportunities and incentives) for corruption, by increasing the potential for connivance between government officials and others for diverting resources away from the public good. The returns to corruption are higher and there is now a much wider range of hard-to-detect mechanisms for diversion. Prior to privatization, government officials can divert only a fraction of the flow of revenues; with privatization, government officials today can divert a fraction of the total value of the resource—the present discounted value of the future flow of revenues. The greater payoff for corruption provides greater incentives for corruption—and the record shows that individuals do respond to incentives. As we shall explain below, privatization often affords enormous opportunities for apparently legal (though typically nontransparent) ways of driving down the price paid for the resource.

The problems detailed in the paragraphs that follow are, for the most part, jointly problems of the private and public sectors—the agency problems in the two reinforce each other. The private sector exploits the public sector agency problem, the fact that the interests of the government official do not coincide completely with those he or she is supposed to serve. Even if the corporation, as a matter of official policy, does not seek to exploit the public sector, standard compensation schemes in the private sector provide incentives for their "agents" to do so.

EFFICIENCY

While the discussion in this chapter centers on the problem of maximizing the revenue accruing to the government, and focuses in particular on the problem of diversion, it should be clear that this is not a zero-sum game. It is not *just* a matter of diversion. In the process, resources often are not used well; resources may be extracted too quickly, without due attention to environmental consequences. Taking the wealth generated out of the country to protect it from recapture may have large macroeconomic consequences.

By most accounts, Norway's state oil company was both efficient and incorruptible; probably few countries have been able to realize for its citizens a larger fraction of the potential value of a country's resources. In the case of Norway, institutional change may make little difference in either direction; elsewhere, however, such opportunities for resource diversion may be quickly seized upon.

Norway's story is important (see chapter 4) because it destroys the shibboleth that efficiency and welfare maximization can be obtained only through privatization. Nor is Norway alone. Malaysia also makes claim to being the global champion and argues that its state-run oil company is able to garner for Malaysia a larger fraction of the value of that country's oil resources than it could have otherwise achieved.[16] The very process of privatization introduces a major opportunity for resource diversion, and those arguing for privatization must show that the losses from maintaining the resources within the public sector are greater than the combined losses associated with the transfer and the losses from agency problems after privatization.[17]

MECHANISMS FOR DIVERSION IN PRIVATIZATION

There are basically four (sometimes interrelated) mechanisms for "corrupt" privatizations, besides the obvious ones—just giving the resource to one's cronies, or, as in the United States, having a first-come system in which those already in the field are in a better position to grab the resources. First, reduce competition; second (particularly relevant in economies in transition when capital markets were not well developed), channel funds to favorites; third, provide favorites with inside information about the value of what is being sold; and fourth, enforce terms asymmetrically.

LIMITING COMPETITION

When competition for the resources is limited—and especially when it is known that it is limited—then the prices that prevail will be lower. There are three ways of limiting competition. The first is suddenly to put up for lease a large number of tracts—increase the supply so that the bidding on each tract is limited. This is what President Reagan did in the early 1980s. It was like a fire sale—as if the government *had* to get rid of its holdings *immediately*. But in fact, there was no reason for it; it was not as if the oil was going to disappear, or as if the United States needed to raise cash quickly. On a very large fraction of tracts, there was only one bidder (and, of course, the oil companies knew this). In a study I conducted with Jeff Leitzinger (1984) we quantified the impact on the price the government received. The government got a fraction of what it would have earned had the tracts been put up in a more orderly process, and the extra profits went into the coffers of the oil companies.[18]

There are several things the government can do to *increase* competition and to mitigate the magnitude of the asymmetries of information and their consequences. One approach is to require all companies to disclose their geological information concerning the tract and provide all bidders with information from that pre-bidding exploration that is publicly funded, which should be undertaken more extensively.[19] Checkerboard leasing (such as undertaken by Alberta, Canada) may allow more relevant information to become available before bidding, again resulting in government receiving more for its tracts.

Another way is to design the auction in ways that reduce the consequences of information asymmetries and thus increase the magnitude of competition. For instance, royalty bidding (in which bidding is over the percentage of the value of production to be given to the government) may produce significantly greater competition than bonus bidding. First, under royalty bidding, information asymmetries about the quantity of oil matter less (more important are information asymmetries about the magnitude of the costs of extraction). Second, bonus bidding favors large companies that can afford to make large up-front payments. Up-front bonuses constitute, in effect, a loan from the oil company to the government—the government gets money up front, which the oil company recovers later through sales of oil. While the current government benefits from money that otherwise would accrue to successor governments, the interest rate implicit in the loan is typically higher, sometimes much higher, than that at which the government can borrow abroad.[20] Third, bonus bidding favors larger, more diversified firms that are better able to bear risk, since, under bonus bidding, the risk (concerning the price of oil, the amount of oil, and the costs of extraction) is imposed on the bidder.[21]

Royalty bidding has one major disadvantage: a larger royalty rate reduces the incentive for companies to invest ex post, and may result in premature shutdown of wells as extraction costs rise; in contrast, the signature bonus is a sunk cost and does not distort subsequent investments.[22] The problem of premature shutdown has especially become a source of concern; but contractual arrangements, entailing reducing royalty rates at later stages of production, have been devised that have mitigated, if not eliminated, the problem.[23] Of course, if there were little uncertainty over the value of the resource, and capital markets were perfect (so there would be no discrepancy between the government and corporate borrowing rates), then this advantage of bonus bidding would predominate over the disadvantages noted earlier (see chapter 5). But realistically, there appears to be a strong presumption in favor of royalty bidding.[24]

The processes for limiting competition through the design and scale of the auction and the disclosure of information, which we have described in the case of the United States and other developed countries, are far more subtle than those often employed in developing and transition economies. When corrupt officials wish to limit competition, they may simply design qualifying conditions that allow only preferred bidders to compete.[25]

Not surprisingly, large multinationals have opposed reforms that would increase competition and lead to higher overall payment, and they have by and large prevailed.[26] The bonus bidding system still prevails, and there is limited pre-bidding disclosure of information.[27]

CHANNELING FUNDS

In the economies in transition in the former Soviet Union, another approach was often used in corrupt privatizations. The government did not allow foreign bidders, and at the early stages of transition, few domestic bidders had large resources of their own. The ostensible solution for firms then was to borrow from a bank. But in some countries, the government still controlled the banks—and so it could determine who got the money to bid and how much money they got. One pocket of the government was giving money to another pocket through an intermediary. There was no net transfer of cash to the government; the situation was only slightly different from what would have happened if the government had bought the mine or oil field from itself. That slight difference had enormous consequences, however. By going through the private intermediary, the government's equity position was converted into a creditor position. If the government had received fair market value, it would simply have entailed a transfer of risk. Yet, the government did not receive fair market value. Moreover, because it was easy for the buyer to default, there was not even any transfer of risk. It was simply a transfer of the upside potential to the private party.

I illustrated the point in the context of countries in which there are state banks, but matters differ little if the government controls the licensing of private banks. The granting of a license, with lax regulation, is granting the right to print money—or in this case, to determine who is able to bid for the government's resources. (Even with some regulation, government can affect who wins in that it can determine at whose bank deposits are put, and therefore who has the potential for making loans.)[28]

There is a clear implication. If privatization is to occur in countries in which there are limited numbers of private parties capable of bidding for the resources in a bonus bid, then: (1) bidding should be converted to royalty bidding—augmenting the argument for royalty bidding given in the previous section—and/or (2) foreign bidders must be allowed. Alternatively, the privatization should be postponed until there are enough viable bidders within the country to give rise to a competitive auction.

ASYMMETRIC INFORMATION

We have already noted the adverse consequences of asymmetries in information. It is not just that those who have inside information know what to bid. The effect is more subtle: When some have an informational advantage, the others, knowing that they are informationally disadvantaged, bid less than they otherwise would. They suffer from a version of the "winner's curse"—the fear that they will win only if they bid too much, in particular, only if they bid more than the "informed" bidder (see chapter 5).[29] As a result, companies shave their bids down; the insider, knowing this, can, on average, obtain the asset at a lower price—meaning the government receives less.

Such problems of asymmetric information are likely to arise in many oil-producing developing countries. They are obviously particularly likely to arise if those involved in management of the enterprise when it was run by the state are involved in one of the bidding consortiums.

Such problems are easily illustrated by a case that arose in the United States in the privatization of the U.S. Enrichment Corporation (USEC), the government enterprise responsible for making enriched uranium, required by atomic power plants and in manufacture of atomic and hydrogen bombs.[30] In this case, the government official who headed USEC led the consortium that won the bid. Clearly it had an information advantage.[31] Making matters worse, at the last minute, the U.S. government changed the terms of the bidding, putting into the deal more of its stock of uranium. The net effect was that, when the value of cash and uranium was netted out of the deal, as well as the commissions taken by the Wall Street firm that managed the privatization, the government got little for its business—almost surely a fraction of the present discounted value of what it would have received had it remained in the government's hands.

ASYMMETRIC ENFORCEMENT

Asymmetric enforcement of contract terms presents further problems. Most leases, for instance, have requirements that the lessee develop the field within a certain period of time. The value of the lease depends on how strictly such a requirement is enforced. If, for instance, there is price variability, then bidding on a lease with a high extraction cost (without such a provision) can be viewed as an option. If the price turns out to be high, the firm develops the lease; otherwise it does not. Even if the firm intends eventually to develop the field, if extraction costs are high, it pays for it to wait. If most bidders are bidding assuming that the contract will be enforced, an insider who knows that it will not be can easily win the bid—paying far less than the true value (given the lax enforcement).[32]

EXPERIENCES WITH PRIVATE CONTROL
AND ECONOMIC EFFICIENCY

Many of the advocates of privatization in the 1980s and 1990s were not much worried about corruption. They were often not even worried about the government getting fair value for the resources. They were focused on efficiency.[33] They believed that once resources were turned over to the private sector, they would be efficiently utilized. Corrupt privatizations affected the distribution of income, but the advocates were little concerned with that.

But they were wrong in their conclusion that corrupt privatizations would lead to economic efficiency because they did not understand property rights as a social construct. Property rights can be secure only if they are viewed as legitimate. Illegitimately obtained property cannot be secure, and, from a societal perspective, corrupt privatizations generate illegitimately held property.

Those who steal property know that their rights to the property they control are not secure; and so too for those who knowingly buy stolen property. There is an important lesson in this: A successful market economy requires secure property rights; but, in a democracy, property rights can only be secure if they are viewed as legitimate. Property acquired through fraud or coercion has no real legitimacy. Discussions of the sanctity of property rights have to be accompanied by policies and actions that give widespread legitimacy to property holdings. Without that, the turmoil so prevalent in resource-rich countries will continue.[34]

Those who obtained the property in the illegitimate privatizations understood this. Their incentive then was to exploit for themselves as much of the property as they could and to move it to a safe locale—outside of the country. Doctrines of free capital market mobility thus aided and abetted the diversion of the resources. With money fleeing the country, no wonder that many of the resource-rich countries did not obtain the benefits that one would have expected.[35]

In the end, then, privatization did not always achieve even the modest objective of economic efficiency for four reasons:

1. Without long-run secure property rights (and, as I have argued, there *could not* be long-run secure property rights) there is an incentive to extract as much as one can as fast as one can—faster extraction than is efficient. (In the case of renewable resources, this may even entail pushing extraction beyond the level of sustainability.)

2. Without long-run secure property rights, incentives to make the complementary investments required for efficient extraction are attenuated.

3. Without long-run secure property rights, there will be reluctance on the part of lenders to provide capital to finance these complementary

investments—even if the putative owners had been willing to make those investments.

4. It pays for each market participant to take his money out of the country, even though social efficiency would have required leaving it in.[36]

PRIVATIZATION AND INSTITUTIONAL STRUCTURES

There were further problems with the timing and manner of privatization. The International Monetary Fund (IMF), in Russia and elsewhere, had urged as rapid a privatization as possible. They worried that so long as resources remained under the control of government, the resources would not be efficiently utilized, and that there was scope for corruption. Yet, corruption was only one of the reasons these governments got so little for their resources. Bidders knew that the governments were under pressure to privatize quickly, so they bid more conservatively, knowing that the government's reservation price (the minimum price that it would accept) was low.

But there were further consequences of the pressure to privatize quickly: Fast privatization meant (in many countries) that privatization occurred before the institutional infrastructure—a developed legal system, a tax administration that could collect the revenues due, a corporate governance structure that could mitigate agency problems *within* firms, or financial institutions that could provide money to finance needed investments to realize the full value of the resources—was in place.[37] This, in turn, had several implications.

1. It meant that laws ensuring good corporate governance were not in place, so wealth was shifted from the corporation to those who controlled the corporation.

2. Many of the advocates of rapid privatization said that a rule of law would develop as those with control of resources would demand it. There was, however, no historical or theoretical basis for the claim. Quite the contrary: As Karla Hoff and I (2005) have shown, those who controlled the assets preferred to maintain a system that gave them more leeway to strip assets.

3. In the absence of the financial infrastructure, firms could not get access to the capital they required to improve the efficiency of resource extraction. Again, the balance was shifted toward stripping assets rather than building wealth, and all the other problems noted so far were thereby reinforced.

4. Privatizations occurred before the development of effective tax institutions, so one had the anomalous situation of the government turning over massive amounts of the country's most valuable resources to private entrepreneurs and yet having insufficient funds to finance basic social safety net and education programs.

Given all of these problems, it was perhaps no surprise that privatization failed to yield the benefits promised—a few people became very rich, but the country as a whole saw little benefit.

THE LESSONS OF RUSSIA

Russia provides a dramatic case in which the government has received but a pittance for the country's most important asset—its inheritance of natural resources. With the end of communism and the decay of an effective state, Russia, once a world superpower, became increasingly natural resource dependent—with, by some estimates, some 70 percent of its gross domestic product (GDP) related directly to natural resources.[38]

In 1996, Yeltsin needed help getting reelected and a small group of "oligarchs" had the organizational and financial capacity to help him—in exchange for control of the nation's vast natural resources.[39] Yeltsin allowed them to take control of these resource assets *legally*, at prices that were but a fraction of the fair market value, and *using the very rules of the game that they had helped to make.* The critical events occurred in 1995–1996, in a sale that Crystal Freeland called the "Sale of the Century" (Freeland 2000). There were auctions. But the auctions were rigged. As a result, the oligarchs got that country's vast natural resources for a pittance—some senior government officials believe the amount "stolen" exceeds a trillion dollars.[40] If Russia was not under such pressure to privatize, it could have rejected the bids. In the rush to privatization, those controlling the bidding process "disqualified" many of the bidders, ensuring that the competition was limited. No safeguards were set up to ensure that the country was receiving full value for its money: The IMF put conditions on speed, not on how well the privatizations were conducted.[41]

The privatization in Russia set in motion a vicious circle. Even without corruption, as we have noted, rapid privatization means that governments receive less than fair market value for the companies they sell off. With corruption, the prices were still lower. Either way, the legitimacy of the transfer of public resources to the private sector was questioned. And investors, those who had acquired the assets in the "illegitimate" privatizations, felt, quite rightly, that their property rights were not secure—a new government under popular pressure might reverse the privatization, or demand more money. Without a sense of security, new owners limited their investments and then took as much of their profits out of the country as they could—leading to further disillusionment with the privatization process, making property rights still less secure. Though Russia had been told repeatedly by its Western advisers from the IMF, the U.S. Treasury and elsewhere, that privatization would lead to growth and investment, the outcome was disappointing: Output fell by 40 percent. And there were massive capital outflows; one of the oligarchs, Roman Abramovich, famously purchased the Chelsea football team and numerous country estates in the United Kingdom (see, e.g., Garrahan and Ostrovsky 2005). Ordinary Russians, naturally, found it hard to see how this helped Russia's growth.

Russia has struggled to find a compromise so that the oligarchs who obtained the nation's assets on the cheap might pay a certain amount, perhaps over time, in return gaining legitimacy for their ownership and security for their property rights. Though such a compromise could be of benefit not only to the oligarchs but also to the country—helping to stimulate investment—it has so far eluded Russia.

While Russia's privatization has highlighted the problem, conflicts over the fairness of natural resource privatizations and contracts are endemic around the world. In the case of Russia, it was Russians stealing money from their own country; in most other cases, those extracting the resources are foreigners, which only heightens the tensions. Governments have been toppled because of this problem—as in Bolivia—and the sense of outrage has given support to populists, like Chavez in Venezuela. The ordinary citizens see rich Venezuelans and foreign companies benefiting from their wealth, but none of the wealth seems to trickle down to them. Chavez's ability to renegotiate old contracts, to get better terms for his country, simply reinforced the belief that, in the past, they had been cheated.

RESPONDING TO THESE RISKS

Agency problems are endemic. They cannot simply be wished away. And there are no magic solutions. The hope that privatization would solve agency problems (including problems of corruption) was a dream only of those who did not understand the underlying economics.

But while agency problems cannot be eliminated, I have argued some contractual and institutional arrangements make them worse than others. As I noted, the reason that net profit contracts are not used—even though they might *seem* efficient—is that they exacerbate agency problems.

In the paragraphs that follow, I describe some of the steps (beyond those already discussed) that governments can take to mitigate these risks.

STRENGTHEN INSTITUTIONS BEFORE ENGAGING IN PRIVATIZATION

I explained earlier that it is no accident that privatization has been beset with so many problems. Privatization has often occurred before good institutions that can conduct, for instance, fair, competitive, and efficient auctions, are in place. And privatizations have also occurred before institutions that can collect taxes and enforce contracts are in place. This suggests that these governmental institutions need to be strengthened before engaging in privatization. Yes, there may be some losses of public revenues in the interim, but these losses (essentially of a short-run cash flow) pale in comparison to the losses that have occurred in the privatization process (which are related to the value of the *stock*, not just the cash flow).

But this raises a problem: If the government has developed these strong institutions, perhaps it is better for it to go one step further, and develop the institutions for oil extraction itself, i.e., develop efficient and honest state-owned enterprises for oil extraction, as Norway and Malaysia did (and as Chile did in the case of copper.) There is one marked advantage of this strategy: It avoids the agency problem of privatization itself, in the process of which the government may lose a substantial fraction of the value of the asset.

BE PATIENT: OIL DOESN'T DISAPPEAR

In the case of fields that have not been developed, there is a strong argument for waiting: the assets will not disappear. Indeed, if the price of oil rises over time, the value of the assets beneath the ground grows over time. Especially in cases where costs of extraction are currently high, and might be lowered over time with the progress of technology, the return to waiting may be higher than on any other investment the government might make.

Hotelling's analysis (1931) offers a framework for determining the optimum time to take resources out of the ground (see also chapter 6). In principle, the portfolio composition problem (whether to hold one's wealth as oil beneath the ground or as some asset above the ground) can be fully separated from the expenditure decision. But in practice, the two get linked. As mentioned in the Introduction to this volume, as the country sees its income rise (as a result of extraction) there will be pressure to spend the money. International advisers will emphasize that the country is not wealthier; it has just changed the composition of its asset base—but this argument may have only limited resonance with the electorate. This suggests delaying extraction of resources below the ground until the country can reinvest the resources well above the ground.

A further problem arises when it is known that the government—when it gets hold of the money from the extraction of the resources—will use it for its own purposes and not more broadly for the people. For instance, the government might buy arms to perpetuate its power. The people might benefit to *some* extent, but clearly not as much as they could or should. The prospects of the money being used better later may be greater than the prospects today, even after some time discount factor is taken into account. Again, patience is what is required. Institutional arrangements can be designed to help ensure the proceeds *do* help the people, but they are hard to enforce ex post and it is difficult to know what to do in the presence of a variety of forms of reneging on the terms.[42]

IDENTIFY PROVISIONS FOR RENEGOTIATION EX ANTE

We should recognize that when large deposits of oil or minerals are found, or when the price of the oil or mineral rises markedly in an unexpected way, there are likely to be incentives to renegotiate contracts, especially if the original contract is not subtle enough in identifying the different circumstances in which such renegotiation might be desirable. Inevitably, with fixed costs already invested, these renegotiations can put governments in a bind. If the private company doesn't accede to the demands, it loses the contract. By the same token, oil companies may claim that the quality of oil is worse than they anticipated, or costs are greater than they anticipated, and demand better terms, threatening to leave. Again, the country government is in a bind. If the company leaves, there will be a costly delay in bringing the oil on line, and any new company brought in may demand terms not much different from those being demanded by the oil company. Often governments simply accede to the demands.

Every contract is subject to dispute, and this is no less true of oil contracts. In some cases, the company may have made investment commitments as part of terms of the lease (or sale). But when the commitments are made in terms of dollars invested, there might be non–arm's length accounting, with the company overvaluing the investments. On the other hand, there are a myriad of ways short of losing the contract in which the government can harass the contractor, many of which might not have been precluded by the contract. Since the discovery of a large find is likely to change the economic circumstances of the parties, producing both political and economic interest in a renegotiation, the parameters under which a renegotiation can occur should be identified ex ante so that agreements can be reached with less hostility than otherwise.

In the end, too often the country loses twice—first from the unfair contract or privatization, and second from political turmoil and adverse international attention from the investment community when an attempt is made to set things right.

AVOID COMPLEX CONTRACTS

A risk associated with complex contracts is that the true market value of the contract may be better understood by the oil companies than by the government (see chapter 4). For instance, if oil prices are highly volatile, and there is no due diligence clause for development, getting an oil lease is simply getting an option on the price of oil, and the price of the lease should reflect that option. A contract with a compulsory development clause would presumably lower the value of the lease—the contractor is forced to develop the lease at some time other than he would have chosen—but one needs to compare the extra development benefits with the loss of revenues. Contracts can be written that are sufficiently complicated so that it may be hard to tell whether there was a material breach; or provisions can be included that lead to breaches by both sides, making a determination of the fair resolution even more difficult.

There is a tension between the concerns just raised and those raised in the preceding section. Simple contracts, with few contingency clauses, are more likely to encounter circumstances in which there will be pressure to renegotiate.

Of use would be the development of a set of standard contracts, not written by the oil companies but by the oil producers, reflecting their experiences and attempting, in the best way they can, to guard against the various ways in which they have been cheated.

EVALUATE CONTRACTS ON THE BASIS OF THE INCENTIVES THEY GENERATE AND THEIR PERFORMANCE UNDER DIFFERENT SCENARIOS

Over the years, there have been a series of fads in extracting oil and other natural resources. There have been, for instance, various forms of contracting for the services provided. The general theory of contracting provides a lens through which these arrangements can be assessed—whatever the names attached to the arrangement—and calls attention to the fact that, so long as information is imperfect and contracts incomplete (i.e., always) issues of agency arise. Once the contract is specified, we can analyze payments in each of a different set of contingencies, and identify incentives and actions to which they lead. In short, we can, in principle, ascertain the fraction of the potential value of the resource that accrues to the government for a range of different price, quantity, or quality scenarios (see chapter 3).

MAKE THE TIMING OF PAYMENTS A FUNCTION OF THE ABILITY OF THE STATE TO BEAR RISK

Different contractual terms provide money to the government at different times—and with different risk. As we noted, most bonus bidding puts money up front and imposes risk on the oil companies. For oil companies dealing with the United States, this is foolish and expensive: The United States can borrow far more cheaply than even the best of the oil companies, and it can diversify its risks far better. The implicit risk and time discount factors disadvantage government. This pattern may be reversed when it comes to a large oil company dealing with a small oil-producing country.

ENSURE AGAINST OIL RISK

Long-term oil markets, extending decades into the future, effectively do not exist. As a result, countries may wish to maintain their *real reserves* as a form of asset protection—long-term risk management. This argument seems to have carried some weight in Bangladesh's decisions concerning the speed with which to develop a field.

CONCLUSION

Modern welfare economics has provided us with tools with which we can assess alternative strategies for developing a country's natural resources—the impact on "social welfare" (chapter 6). This is an approach which integrates the impact of natural resource extraction on the environment, on different groups within the country, as well as on subsequent generations. It incorporates macro- and microeconomics. It entails trade-offs, for example trade-offs between the magnitude of the agency problems, the risks of resource diversion, and exposure to risk. But for many applications, its comprehensiveness is matched by its cumbersomeness.

There are two simplified alternatives. One is to focus on how much the public has benefited from the sale, measured, for instance, by the present discounted value of revenues to the government.[43] The second is to measure the present discounted value of the change in the country's GDP—*green* GDP, of course, not GDP as conventionally measured (for more on the importance of correct measures of GDP, see chapter 6).[44] Both of these are, of course, inadequate: The first because it puts no weight either on what happens outside the public sector or on what the government itself does with the money; and the second because it puts no weight on concerns about distribution (median incomes might go down even as total income goes up). But each is useful in highlighting the various abuses that can occur.

This chapter should have made clear that inevitably, in the contractual arrangements between a country and those who have the knowledge and skill to take the oil out, there arise a large number of agency problems. In addition, the form of the contractual arrangements may make some of the problems worse, while it mitigates others.

At this juncture, the research community has not provided a full compendium of provisions—with costs and benefits, successes and failures—in alternative situations. We noted, however, that among the most successful approaches are those of Norway and Malaysia, countries that decided to own and run their own oil companies, learning the requisite skills in the diverse areas of management and control from a range of oil companies.[45]

Full privatizations—bonus bid, long-term leases to private companies with no government stake—have been marked by some of the worst abuses, with governments getting the worst deal (e.g., payments as a value of the oil).

For countries with high-quality public management, and where there are not particularly difficult extraction problems (such as those associated with deep water extraction), the route taken by Malaysia seems desirable. For others, the answer is less clear. They face the difficult choice of trying either to improve public sector management or to rely on an imperfect and possibly corrupt public sector to define relationships with a private sector whose goal runs counter to that of the public interest—minimizing payments to the public. Where possible, the path set forth by Malaysia is desirable—while initially relying on the private sector, a key objective should be the transfer of technology, skills, and understanding of organizational structures to enable the creation of an honest and efficient public sector extractive industry.

Whatever the approach, the following principles should guide the government:

Transparency: Open and transparent agreements, openly arrived at. Any oil firm not willing to disclose all terms of the contract, volumes extracted and prices sold, should be barred from operating within the country. Business secrecy is too often simply a cover for bad behavior. By the same token, when there are adjustments to the terms of the contract, they should be made in an open and transparent manner.

Ownership: The developing country should remain the ultimate owner of the natural resource. This means that residual rents and residual control rights should reside with the country. Of course, it may be in the interests of both parties to specify as clearly and extensively as possible what happens in various contingencies, but no contract can be fully complete.

Fairness: Natural resource rents belong to the country; foreign oil companies should get only a fair rate of return, adjusted for the risks they face. This means that the contracts should provide that increases in the price of oil or gas should go disproportionately to the developing country.

Earlier I described the principles that should guide the auction process, for instance, a strong presumption for royalty bidding, with the results of pre-bidding exploration publicly disclosed. When there is only one (or a few) bidder(s) on a tract, there should be real concern that the country will not receive fair value for its resources. In some cases, it may be desirable to have bidding for particular services, rather than leasing the tract. The reforms described in this chapter will not be welcome by all: There are many who benefit from current arrangements. They will raise worries that development will be impeded or growth slowed. These are issues of political economy, discussed, for example, in chapters 8, 9, and 10. Suffice it to say here, reforms in political processes—including those relating to campaign contributions—might in the end be necessary to achieve some of the simple institutional reforms advocated here. But the argument that a strategy of privatizing the assets somehow avoids the need for such political reforms is inconsistent both with theory and experience.

For many of the developing countries, the central problem is not so much the lack of adequate foreign assistance but the failure of the international community to pay adequately and fully for the resources that they have taken from the country, and to provide money in ways which go toward the development and well-being of the people in the country. Much of the responsibility for ensuring that countries are fully paid and that resources are well used lies, of course, with developing country governments. But I have shown, in this chapter, that there are incentives on the part of multinationals that go in quite the opposite direction, and that, in the past, their actions have sometimes undermined democracies and contributed to pervasive corruption, one of the defining characteristics of those countries with the resource curse.

It is possible that countries with more resources could actually face better prospects for growth. But if this is to happen, at the very least, developing countries must get full value for their resources, and the money that is received for the resources must be directed at benefiting the country as a whole rather than particular groups only. The resource curse is not inevitable, and there is much that can be done—by developing country governments, multinational companies, and the international community—to ensure that all the people in those countries lucky enough to have an abundance of resources will in fact enjoy the fruits of that bounty.

ACKNOWLEDGMENTS

The research described in this chapter was supported in part by the Ford, MacArthur, and Mott Foundations. I have also benefited from participation in the IPD journalist training programs on the resource curse in Kazakhstan, Nigeria, and Azerbaijan, sponsored by the Open

Society Institute. Discussions in Malaysia and Venezuela on the problems addressed in this chapter, including talks with the leaders of those countries, were also extremely informative.

NOTES

1. The general set of conditions under which it is efficient for government to turn over a complex activity (like national defense or oil extraction) to the private sector is highly restrictive. See Sappington and Stiglitz (1988).

2. In addition, the oil companies were required to pay 10 to 15 percent of the value of oil produced in Alaska to the state as severance taxes.

3. See Fineberg (2003). In what came to be known as the "Amerada Hess case" for the first company on the list of 15 defendants, BP alone settled for $185 million in royalties (in 1991) and $1.4 billion in back taxes (in 1994), though the federal government provided substantial tax relief to BP that cut its settlement cost in half. For more on the BP case, see Corzine (1994). I served as an expert witness in the suit. For more background on the Amerada Hess case and its resolution, see Thomas (1995). Alaska was only the first of a long line of suits by states and the federal government alleging that the oil companies had cheated on hundreds of millions of dollars of payments. The government has already prevailed on a number of these cases. During the Clinton Administration, new regulations were issued to try to limit the scope for such cheating.

4. The decision in the case, *State of Alabama v. Exxon Mobil Corp.* (no. cv-99-2368), can be found at http://www.verdictsearch.com/news/docs/national-nwltr_120303/1.jsp.

5. An original ruling, requiring Exxon to pay $3.4 billion in punitive damages and $88 million in compensatory damages, was thrown out after the Alabama state high court determined jurors should not have been allowed to see a letter by an Exxon-Mobil lawyer discussing legal interpretations of the royalty agreement (see Davis 2003).

6. The problem of agency in the context of corporations was discussed in Stiglitz (1985) and Jensen and Meckling (1976). For a brief discussion of some of the subsequent literature, see Stiglitz (2000). The role of the failings in corporate governance in the lack of success in Russia's privatization is discussed in Hoff and Stiglitz (2005).

7. A particularly useful device is constantly to rotate government officials, making it virtually impossible to bribe every official who might be involved in the transaction.

8. Another way of controlling agency costs is to limit the scope for conflicts of interest. When officials from the oil industry help formulate a nation's energy policy there is an obvious conflict of interest: an energy policy that is good for the energy industry is not, in general, an energy policy which is good for the nation. Regulations on "revolving doors" are intended to circumscribe the extent of these conflicts of interest.

9. This is true whether done by a government company or a private company; if by a private company, whether it is given control over the assets or just given respon-

sibility for extraction with, say, a five-year contract. If the assets are turned over to a private firm, how the "sale" is conducted also matters.

10. On the other hand, the "owners" may have a stronger incentive not to allow the diversion. But if ownership is diverse, there is a public good problem in oversight (see Stiglitz 1985). The difference between incentives for oversight in the public and private sector may differ relatively little.

11. The objectives of the optimal contract are several. They include (a) paying the agent as little as possible for extracting the oil and (b) ensuring that the agent extracts the oil in the most efficient way so that the total present discounted value of the oil that is extracted is maximized and at as little cost as possible. Governments with tight budget constraints and limited ability to access capital markets may also worry about risk and time profiles of payments. If appropriate budgetary frameworks are not in place, even advanced industrial countries may worry about these variables.

12. I call these "doctrines" because, except under highly restrictive conditions, stockholder value maximization does *not* lead to (constrained) Pareto efficiency, and may not even be in the interests of shareholders (see, e.g., Stiglitz 1972; Grossman and Stiglitz 1976, 1977; Stiglitz 1982).

13. There are important limitations in the takeover mechanism (see, e.g., Stiglitz 1972; or Grossman and Hart 1980). Takeovers are subject to the free-rider problems. Moreover, there are many ways by which managers reduce the likelihood of takeovers, some of which are, in effect, value destructing (Edlin and Stiglitz 1995).

14. When there are criminal penalties, some monetization of the cost of those penalties needs to be included in the analysis.

15. The media have uncovered numerous instances of such bribery, with relatively few convictions. Among those receiving considerable attention in recent years is that of ExxonMobil in Kazakhstan (see, e.g., Catan and Chaffin 2003) and Freeport Mining in Indonesia (see Waldman 1998). In the latter case, the company openly admitted paying government (defense department) officials for services rendered (providing security protection for the mine), saying there was no alternative to relying on Indonesian military for security. Indonesian government officials also asserted that payments by companies to soldiers or police officers violated their laws (Perlez and Bonner 2005).

16. Malaysia has since corporatized its oil industry (with the government still remaining a majority shareholder). The change may have released Malaysia from some of the constraints imposed on a government enterprise. While the freedom may result in greater efficiency, it also may simply provide more opportunities for diverting resources to private use (including through paying corporate officials high salaries).

17. Agency problems are not the only reasons that privatizations sometimes fail—or at least fail to perform as expected. There are also problems of commitment. On the one hand, once the investments have been made, governments may attempt to renegotiate for better terms, threatening to take over the assets. To protect themselves, investors may extract resources more rapidly than is optimal. On the other hand, at some point, the oil or mining company may threaten to shut down operations unless better terms are negotiated. The problem for the government is that it may not know whether such threats are credible because it does not know the true operating costs of

the firm. For instance, if the costs really are too high, then it pays for the government to renegotiate to improve the incentives of the company. If it does not pay, however, the government could find some other firm to operate the well under the original terms. This last option, however, might not be feasible if *other* oil companies also do not know the extraction costs. Then, assuming there are fixed costs to entering into the contract, they might infer that costs are prohibitive from the very fact that the other company left. Making matters worse, in simple bargaining problems with imperfect information, it may even pay the oil company to shut down operations (effectively go on strike) to improve the terms of its contract, even when production would be profitable for the company. Such asymmetries of information mean that, even when ex ante markets were highly competitive, ex post, the existing operator has some market power. It is often hard to design renegotiation-proof contracts. Requiring companies to post large bonds may make it less likely for firms to engage in such behavior. But there may be a large cost to such a requirement because of what is sometimes called the double moral hazard problem; the oil or mining company may worry that, even if it behaves impeccably, some future government may impose conditions that make operations so unattractive that it will want to withdraw, thereby "unfairly" forfeiting the bond.

18. I served as an expert witness in a suit by the State of Texas to try to stop Reagan's fire sale. Even though we showed that the losses to the government—and the gains to the oil companies—were enormous, the court ruled that this was within the discretionary powers of the Administration (see Leitzinger and Stiglitz 1984).

19. Clearly, oil companies will resist this initiative, saying that if they are forced to disclose the information, they will reduce their bid. In equilibrium, one would expect, however, the increase in the amounts bid in the follow-on auction to more than offset the losses in the amount bid in the original auction. There may, however, be problems in enforcement.

20. This is especially the case for advanced industrial countries, like the United States; the corporate borrowing rate, which would typically be used in preparing bids, is considerably higher than the T bill rate at which the U.S. government can borrow, or the rate at which, say, the state of Alaska can borrow.

21. Note that beyond the effects on competition, by imposing the risk on the company, bonus bidding also lowers prices as private sector participants demand compensation for bearing this risk (a risk premium is taken out of the price).

22. There is a second disadvantage: With no bonus payment, a firm may bid aggressively on the royalty, viewing the contract as an option. If it discovers that the cost of extraction is low, it develops the field; otherwise, it abandons it. It has little to lose. In one sense, the government too has little to lose: The oil is not a wasting asset; it will still be there. With a performance commitment, the tract may be put up for rebidding. If the government is concerned with getting cash flow quickly, it can mitigate this problem by increasing the (fixed) up-front bonus that has to be paid, discouraging firms from simply viewing the bid as a low cost option.

23. That is, a contract can provide that when the production from the field falls below a critical level, the royalty rate is reduced. The problem arises even in the standard bonus bidding contracts, which typically include a fixed (limited) royalty rate.

24. There is another nondistorting contract—royalty on net profit. The problem is that it is difficult to observe "true" net profits, and with net profit contracts, the agency problems noted earlier become overwhelming.

25. There is a certain subtlety even here. Even in well functioning auctions, there may be a process of qualification to ensure that bidders can actually pay what they bid. This process of qualification can easily be abused, however.

26. As a result of the fire sales during the Reagan Administration, there were only one or two bidders on many of the tracts. Indeed, the General Accounting Office released a study in 1986 reporting that the fire sales had "significantly decreased competition and government bid revenues" for oil leases, estimating that the government had foregone $7 billion in revenue it would have received had the auction been better designed. The oil industry responded by claiming that the fast and expansive sell-off of leases would accelerate the pace of oil production, so that "gains from early receipts of bonuses, rents, royalties and taxes will be more than sufficient to offset" the lost bid revenues (Shabecoff 1985).

27. In the case of minerals, the problems are more extreme, as evidenced by the Clinton Administration's failed attempt to revise the leasing laws.

28. See Freeland (2000) for a discussion of the privatizations of resources in Russia, which entailed many of the problems discussed in this and the previous section. Many of the privatizations in Czech Republic were intermediated through loans from state-owned banks—banks were not privatized in the early stages of the transition.

29. The winners curse phenomenon was first noted by Capen, Clapp, and Campbell (1971) and the mathematics was analyzed by Wilson (1977).

30. There were strong national security arguments for privatization (see chapter 6 of Stiglitz 2002). I am concerned here, however, with the narrower issue of obtaining fair market value.

31. The other major bidder was the contractor that had run the facilities for USEC.

32. Even worse are situations of asymmetric enforcement. If some firm knows the government is less likely to enforce certain terms of the contract, it can bid more. The special relationship with the government is converted into an advantage in bidding, even if the government does not overtly intervene in the auction process.

33. For a more general discussion of these issues, see Hoff and Stiglitz (2005).

34. See Stiglitz (2006) and Hoff and Stiglitz (2005) for a more extensive discussion of these issues.

35. There are, in effect, significant externalities; with so many pulling capital out of the country, output and returns are lower. Even those who did not need to move their capital abroad to protect it might, under these circumstances, find it more attractive to invest their money in the booming economy of the United States rather than the depressed economy of Russia. This can be formally modeled as a prisoner's dilemma Nash equilibrium: Pareto efficiency requires that all keep their money in the country; but it is in the interest of each to pull his money out. In other formulations, there is a coordination failure problem. There are multiple equilibria; one entails everyone pulling their money out, the other entails everyone leaving their

money in. The latter Pareto dominates the former. Changing the rules of the game—making it illegal to take your money out—essentially forces the economy into the good equilibrium.

36. There is a fifth set of problems related to the details of the contract. If the contract has a royalty provision which cannot be reset, then extraction stops when the net receipt by the oil company—net of the royalty payment—is zero; there is still a positive economic return to extracting oil.

37. See Stiglitz (2002) and Freeland (2000) for a more extensive discussion of Russian privatizations.

38. There are difficult problems in ascertaining the value, partly because of incentives (both for tax reasons and for reasons noted earlier) to report a lower value for the resources extracted than the true market value.

39. Actually, they were sufficiently astute that they provided little of their own money; mostly, they discovered how to use the government's own resources to get Yeltsin reelected.

40. I participated in a seminar with senior government officials in Moscow in March 1994, in which the central issue was about how to draw a line on the past. The officials shared a perception that between a trillion and a trillion and a half of assets had been stolen and, unless a significant fraction of that was somehow recovered, it would be difficult to move forward. The defenders of the theft point out that the assets would not have been worth so much, but for the efforts of the oligarchs to restructure them.

41. As always, matters are more complicated. The Russian government was also desperately in need of money. The government, however, was effectively forced to borrow from the private banks (much of the money in which came from deposits by government corporations). If the Central Bank had been allowed to lend the government money, or if the West had lent them more money in the short term, then the government would not have had to turn to the private banks in what looked like little more than a charade intended to mask the turning over of vast amounts of public resources to private hands.

42. The case of Chad (where a trust account was set up, but the government reneged on the agreement not long after oil revenues started to be generated) is telling. This is an argument for why it may be a mistake for multilateral institutions to help countries governed by corrupt dictators. Even though the country is desperately poor it would nonetheless likely be better off waiting.

43. Obviously, since different strategies of development entail different risks, and the proceeds are stochastic, a more refined analysis would take into account (with appropriate shadow prices) this variability. What matters is not just what actually happened, but also what might have happened.

44. One should really focus on green net national product—not the adjusted output produced within the country but the income (increment of wealth) of the citizens of the country. When countries sell their assets to foreigners at below fair market value, their national wealth is diminished. In many cases where this happened, governments spent the proceeds on consumption, and the country experienced a mini-boom. In other words, it appeared that privatization led to an increase

in GDP. This highlights how different measures can give different perspectives on the benefits of a so-called reform.

45. Chile's government seems similarly to run its copper mines efficiently, and to receive a large return—larger than it receives (on a comparable basis) from the privatized mines.

REFERENCES

Arnott, R., B. Greenwald, and J. Stiglitz. 1994. "Information and Economic Efficiency." *Information Economics and Policy* 6(1): 77–88.

Capen, E., R. Clapp, and W. Campbell. 1971. "Competitive Bidding in High-Risk Situations." *Journal of Petroleum Technology* 23: 641–53.

Catan, T. and J. Chaffin. 2003. "Bribery Has Long Been Used to Land International Contracts; New Laws Will Make That Tougher." *Financial Times* May 8: 19.

Corzine, R. 1994. "BP to Pay Dollars 1.4bn Tax to Alaska." *Financial Times* November 19: 3.

Davis, M. 2003. "ExxonMobil to Appeal Huge Award; Punitive Damages Total 11.8 Billion." *The Houston Chronicle* November 15: 1.

Edlin, A. and J. Stiglitz. 1995. "Discouraging Rivals: Managerial Rent-Seeking and Economic Inefficiencies." *American Economic Review* 85(5): 1301–12.

Fineberg, R. 2003. "Securing the Take: Petroleum Litigation in Alaska." In *Caspian Oil Windfalls: Who Will Benefit?*, ed. S. Talik, pp. 53–69. New York: OSI.

Freeland, C. 2000. *Sale of the Century: Russia's Wild Ride from Communism to Capitalism.* New York: Crown Business.

Garrahan, M. and A. Ostrovsky. 2005. "Chelsea Draws as Roman Scores with Oil." *Financial Times* September 30: 30.

Greenwald, B. and J. Stiglitz. 1986. "Externalities in Economies with Imperfect Information and Incomplete Markets." *Quarterly Journal of Economics* 101(2): 229–64.

Grossman, S. and O. Hart. 1980. "Takeover Bids, the Free Rider Problem and the Theory of the Corporation." *Bell Journal of Economics* 11(1): 42–64.

Grossman, S. and J. Stiglitz. 1976. "Information and Competitive Price Systems." *American Economic Review* 66(2): 246–53.

Grossman, S. and J. Stiglitz. 1977. "On Value Maximization and Alternative Objectives of the Firm." *Journal of Finance* 32(2): 389–402.

Hoff, K. and J. Stiglitz. 2005. "The Creation of the Rule of Law and the Legitimacy of Property Rights: The Political and Economic Consequences of a Corrupt Privatization." National Bureau of Economic Research, Working Paper 11772.

Hotelling, H. 1931. "The Economics of Exhaustible Resources." *Journal of Political Economy* 39(2): 137–75.

Jensen, M. and W. Meckling. 1976. "Theory of the Firm: Managerial Behavior, Agency Costs and Ownership Structure." *Journal of Financial Economics* 3: 305–60.

Leitzinger, J. and J. Stiglitz. 1984. "Information Externalities in Oil and Gas Leasing." *Contemporary Economic Policy* 0(5): 44–57.

Perlez, J. and R. Bonner. 2005. "Below a Mountain of Wealth, a River of Waste." *The New York Times* December 27: 1.

Sappington, D. and J. Stiglitz. 1988. "Privatization, Information and Incentives." NBER Working Paper No. W2196, June.

Shabecoff, P. 1985. "U.S. Government Lost $7 Billion on Offshore Leases, Study Finds." *New York Times* July 29: B5.

Stiglitz, J. 1972. "Optimality of Stock Market Allocation." *Quarterly Journal of Economics* 86(1): 25–60.

Stiglitz, J. 1982. "The Inefficiency of the Stock Market Equilibrium." *Review of Economic Studies* 49(2): 241–61.

Stiglitz, J. 1985. "Credit Markets and the Control of Capital." *Journal of Money, Credit, and Banking* 17(2): 133–52.

Stiglitz, J. 2000. "The Contributions of the Economics of Information to Twentieth Century Economics." *Quarterly Journal of Economics* 115(4): 1441–78.

Stiglitz, J. 2002. *Globalization and Its Discontents.* New York: W. W. Norton.

Stiglitz, J. 2003. The *Roaring Nineties.* Washington, DC: W. W. Norton.

Stiglitz, J. 2006. *Making Globalization Work.* New York: W. W. Norton.

Thomas, R. 1995. "State Settles Oil Fight $100 Million Ends 18-Year-Old Battle." *Anchorage Daily News* April 7: A1.

Waldman, P. 1998. "Hand in Glove: How Suharto's Circle and a Mining Firm Did So Well Together." *Wall Street Journal* September 29: 1.

Wilson, R., 1977. "A Bidding Model of Perfect Competition." *Review of Economic Studies* 44(3): 511–18.

CHAPTER 3

How to Evaluate the Fiscal Terms of Oil Contracts

David Johnston

ABSTRACT

This chapter addresses the dual issues of how country governments, national oil companies, and international oil companies work together to negotiate oil contracts; and what types of contractual relations are likely to lead to better outcomes than witnessed in the past. In particular, this chapter provides guidelines for evaluating the fiscal terms of oil contracts. While different families of oil contracts exist, I show that, contrary to popular belief, the *type* of system matters less than other design elements in determining the overall nature of the contract. In other words, governments can achieve their fiscal objectives with whichever fiscal system they choose as long as the system is designed properly. This chapter first discusses the different types of fiscal terms in oil contracts and then identifies the few substantial differences among them. I next consider the different ways to study the design of a deal in order to evaluate its merits. I assess the strengths and weaknesses of the commonly used Government Take statistic and discuss how it can be supplemented by the Effective Royalty Rate (ERR) measure, which better captures crucial issues of timing. Finally, I consider five additional features of importance to governments and companies during the oil contracting process: the degree of government participation (which can benefit governments but cost companies); the "savings index" (which accounts for the incentives facing companies to keep costs down); the responsiveness of the deal to changing economic conditions; provisions for minimizing risk; and provisions that allow companies to "book barrels."

INTRODUCTION

Oil is the world's number one strategic commodity. It is vitally important to developed and developing nations that rely on imported oil and gas, as well as to exporting nations, many of them among the poorest countries in the world—the Middle East aside. For countries with petroleum resources, the contribution from the petroleum sector to the nation's budget is often dramatically greater than the contribution to the country's gross national product (GNP). For example, if the petroleum sector were to represent 10 percent of GNP it would likely represent from 30 to 40 percent of the nation's budget. Not only is petroleum very profitable relative to most other industries, but the effective tax rate for the petroleum industry is also especially high.

Numerous dynamics influence today's industry. Oil demand continues to grow, and at a faster rate than anticipated. Consumption grew from 79 million barrels of oil per day (BOPD) in 2002 to 84.5 million in 2004, leaping by 2 to 3 million BOPD each year for a period in which expectations had been on the order of 1 to 1.5 million BOPD growth per year. Much of the new demand comes from the Asian giants India and China. Supply of oil and gas, however, is a function of exploration and production. There is now every indication that exploration and the resultant discoveries have peaked—although it remains uncertain when *production* will peak, since production lags behind exploration, sometimes by as much as 30 years. Gas is becoming increasingly important, even if, because of the higher transportation and management costs, gas discoveries in many regions of the world are still often characterized as being "worse than a dry hole."[1]

As these features change, the relationships among the main players in the industry change as well. On one side stand the country governments and national oil companies (NOCs) that control the bulk of the available oil and gas reserves, and on the other side stand the international oil companies (IOCs) that meet the majority of the financial, technical, organizational, and marketing needs of exporting and importing countries. On the side of the producing countries, numerous economic and political complexities associated with managing oil and gas exist. These issues are important not only to domestic affairs in any given country but also to the relationship between national actors and private oil companies. Many of the problems associated with oil and gas exploration and production, particularly in low-income countries, can be associated with corruption.

But in some cases the problems stem from misunderstandings and poor communication in the course of negotiating and implementing an oil contract. In these cases, the government, the NOC, and the IOC can fall suspect to accusations of theft of a nation's oil wealth. Moreover, as discussed in chapter 10, the publics in these countries often no longer sit idly by. The results are usually not healthy for a country's economic and political development.

While relationships among major actors may be fraught with political difficulties, they are also important from a practical point of view. There is great competition among countries for the limited resources of the IOCs. The ability of countries to attract IOC investment depends on their prospectivity and stability, as well as on their marketing skills. When they succeed in attracting investment, they want the best terms they can get. Oil companies, meanwhile, want to explore in regions where there is a reasonable chance of finding oil and gas. They want to deal with stable governments, and prefer contract terms that will provide a potential return-on-investment that is commensurate with the associated risks. They are also interested in (or rather obsessive about) "booking barrels"— adding reserves as assets to their balance sheets. Overall, the contract is the best indicator of how well the different goals of country governments and IOCs have been met. There is, however, no single clause or number contained in a contract that can tell you whether the country or the company (or neither or both) got a good deal. Rather, evaluating the contract requires examining a series of conditions, which is the subject of this chapter.

How do governments, NOCs, and IOCs work together in the process of negotiating an oil contract, and what types of contractual relationships are likely to lead to better outcomes for country governments? This question is often examined by focusing on the broad differences between the *families* of systems that exist (Johnston 2001, 2003). Indeed, there are myriad ways to structure business relationships in the petroleum sector. Yet, the first observation elaborated here is that, for all practical purposes, only two main families of petroleum fiscal regimes exist: "concessionary" systems and "contractual based" systems. Although differences exist between them, as will be discussed, they are not great from either a mechanical or a financial point of view. Instead, working out the merits of a particular agreement requires a deeper understanding of how the different systems operate and, in particular, of the core fiscal elements. These issues are discussed in the next section ("Fiscal System").

In the section on "Beneath the Surface: Evaluating Key Elements of an Oil Contract," I provide a framework for analyzing the properties of different agreements, identifying what is at stake with different provisions in an oil contract, regardless of which family an agreement comes from. I examine two measures, beginning with the most commonly cited—Government Take. Government Take is the government's share of economic profits from almost all income sources, including bonuses, royalties, profit oil, taxes, and government working interest. While an important statistic and widely used, it is nonetheless flawed because it does not take into account factors such as the timeframe for payouts to government and the level of government participation. In response to the issue of the time frame, I discuss and show how to calculate a companion statistic known as the Effective Royalty Rate (ERR), which measures the degree to which a contract "front-end loaded" payments to governments. Finally, I consider five additional features important to governments and companies: the degree of government participation, which comes at some benefit to governments but at a cost to companies; the "savings index," which gives a sense of the incentives facing companies to keep costs down; responsiveness of the deal to changing economic conditions; provisions for minimizing risk; and provisions that allow companies to "book barrels." I conclude with some observations on the options available to governments deciding how to allocate acreage.

FISCAL SYSTEM

In the universe of oil contracts, two main families of fiscal system exist. The first family includes "concessionary" systems, so called because the government grants the company the right to take control of the entire process—from exploration to marketing—within a fixed area for a specific amount of time. Since production and sale of the oil are then subject to royalties, taxes, and other concessions, contracts in this family are commonly known as Royalty/Tax Systems (R/T systems). "Contractual-based" systems comprise the second family. Agreements in the family belong to two predominant groups: production-sharing contracts (PSCs) and service agreements (SAs) (Johnston 1994).

In short, the distinguishing characteristic of each family of contract is where, when, and if ownership of the hydrocarbons transfers to the international oil company. While numerous variations and twists are found in both concessionary and contract-based systems,[2] from a mechanical and financial point of view *there are practically no differences between the various*

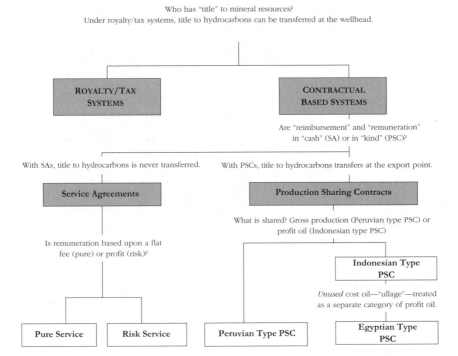

Figure 3.1   Classification of Petroleum Fiscal Regimes.

systems. As shown in the following sections, where the components of each system are discussed in detail, the key calculations in both families follow the same hierarchy. Any oil agreement takes into account, in the following order: (1) the generation of production and revenue; (2) the royalty or royalty equivalent elements for the government; (3) the cost recovery, tax deductions, or reimbursement for the corporation; and (4) the way profits are divided (such as profit-oil sharing and/or taxes). While some interesting exceptions to this general rule exist, they are most likely to be found only among the SAs of this world. The taxonomy of petroleum fiscal systems is outlined in figure 3.1. In fact, preferences for one system over another and certain elements or conventions generally tend to be regional.[3] Some of the geographic influences can be seen in table 3.1.

The belief that systems are somehow fundamentally different from a financial aspect has led to a number of common misconceptions. For instance, one common claim in discussions of the oil industry is that R/T systems and PSC systems each allocate different amounts of risk to either

Table 3.1   Regions of the World and the Most Prominent Types of Agreement

Region	Type of Agreement
Latin America and Middle East	Service agreements
Africa and the Former Soviet Union	Royalty/Tax systems with ROR features, in which the government collects a share of a company's cash flow in excess of the specified ROR
Africa	PSCs with cost recovery limits (limits to the amount of deductions that can be taken for cost recovery purposes) based on net production
Former British Colonies	Competition for blocks based not on a bonus payment but rather on "work program bidding," meaning the competitiveness of a plan for profit maximization of a particular block
Former Soviet Union	PSA terminology (vs. PSC)
West Africa	PSCs with "cost stop" terminology (rather than the "cost recovery limit" terminology used in Africa)
Middle East	PSCs with taxes paid "in lieu" ("for and on behalf of the contractor") out of the NOC's share of profit oil.

NOC, national oil company; PSA, production sharing agreement; PSC, production sharing contract; ROR, rate-of-return.

the NOC or the IOC. In actuality, neither R/T systems nor PSCs are *inherently* more likely to allocate greater risk either to the NOC or the IOC. Similarly, it is not the case that PSCs allow the IOCs to get their costs back faster, or even that they allow IOCs to get them back at all. Nor is it necessarily true that PSCs are more or less stable than R/T systems. There are differences, however. I discuss these below, but first I consider each of the different systems in more detail.

ROYALTY TAX SYSTEMS (R/T)

Before the late 1960s, R/T Systems—or "concessionary systems"—were, for all practical purposes, the only arrangements available. R/T systems are characterized by a number of features:

- Oil companies are contracted for the right to explore for hydrocarbons.
- If a discovery is deemed commercially viable, the international oil company has the right to develop and produce the hydrocarbons.

- When hydrocarbons are produced, the international oil company will take title to its share at the wellhead (this "entitlement" equals gross production less royalty). If the royalty is 10 percent the international oil company can 'lift' (take physical and legal possession of its entitlement of crude oil) 90 percent of production. If the royalty is paid in cash from another source of funds, then the IOC can 'lift' 100 percent of production.
- Exploration and production equipment is owned by the IOC.
- The IOCs pay taxes on profits from the sale of the oil.

Sample calculation. The example in figure 3.2 demonstrates the arithmetic performed to calculate Contractor and Government Take, and entitlement. Even though this analysis is "full cycle" the hierarchy of arithmetic that would be expected in any given accounting period is the same. In

10% Royalty	Oil Price $20/BBL
No Cost Recovery Limit	Costs $5.65/BBL
60% Tax (first layer)	
30% Tax (second layer)	

	Cumulative Gross Revenues	
Company Share	**$20.00**	**Government Share**
	Royalty 10%	**$2.00**
	$18.00	
$5.65	**Deductions**	
Assumed Costs		Taxable Income
	$12.35	
$4.94	**Special Oil Tax** 60%	**$7.41**
($1.48)	**Income Tax** 30%	**$1.48**
$3.46		
$9.11	Division of Gross Revenues	**$10.89**
$3.46	Division of Cash Flow	**$10.89**
24%	**Take**	**76%**
$3.46/($20.00−5.65)		$10.89/($20.00−5.65)
90%	**Lifting Entitlement**	**10%**
($20−$2)/$20.00		($2.00)/$20.00

Figure 3.2   Royalty/Tax System Flow Diagram One Barrel of Oil (Full Cycle).

this particular case $20/barrel (BBL) is assumed to represent average gross revenue per barrel over the life of the field (full cycle).

In this example of an R/T system, I calculate Government Take over the full cycle of the project, which includes exploration and early development through to field decline and abandonment. Here I use a simplified form of the Government Take measure for the purposes of illustration. I use one barrel of oil at $20 to represent average full cycle revenues (per barrel) and show how that barrel of oil is divided between the government and the contractor.

Of the $20, the government gets a 10 percent royalty equal to $2. Assumed costs are deducted from the $18 left after the royalty is taken, leaving a taxable income of $12.35. Two layers of taxes are levied against the taxable income; first a 60 percent tax on the $12.35 gives the government $7.41, leaving $4.94. The second layer of tax, 30 percent, is levied against the $4.94, giving the government an additional $1.48 and leaving the contractor with $3.46.

Take statistics are a function of cash flow (gross revenue–costs). In this particular example, Government Take equals government cash flow divided by total cash flow, or $10.89/($20–$5.65) = 76 percent.

PRODUCTION-SHARING CONTRACTS

The concept of production sharing is ancient and widespread. Farmers in the United States have been familiar with the concept for decades. The concept of the production-sharing contract (PSC), as far as the oil and gas industry is concerned, was conceived in Venezuela in the mid-1960s.[4] The first modern PSC was signed in 1966 between the Independent Indonesia American Petroleum Company (IIAPCO) and Permina, Indonesia's National Oil Company at the time. The characteristic features of this pioneering agreement, which can still be found in most PSC arrangements worldwide, included the following:

- The title to the hydrocarbons remained with the state (Indonesia).
- Permina maintained management control (indeed, putting management control in the hands of Permina is what really distinguished the PSC from the Indonesian predecessors).
- The contractor submitted work programs and budgets for government approval.
- The profit oil (PO) split—the amount of oil remaining after allocation of royalty oil and cost oil—was 65 percent/35 percent in favor of Permina.

- The contractor bore the risk.
- The cost recovery limit (the limit to the amount of deductions that can be taken for cost recovery purposes) was 40 percent.
- Taxes paid "in lieu" (i.e., taxes paid for and on behalf of the IOC by Permina).
- Purchased equipment became property of Permina.
- Company entitlement equals cost oil (oil or revenue used to reimburse the contractor for exploration and development) plus profit oil.

Sample calculation. The example in figure 3.3 demonstrates the arithmetic performed to calculate contractor and Government Take, and entitlement. In this case, like the example R/T system above, I use the revenue from one barrel of oil—$20 to represent average (per barrel) gross revenue over the life of the field (full cycle).

10% Royalty	Oil Price $20.00/BBL
50% Cost Recovery Limit	Costs $5.65/BBL
60% Government P/O Share	
30% Corporate Income Tax (CIT)	

	Cumulative Gross Revenues	
Contractor Share	**$20.00**	**Government Share**
	Royalty 10%	**$2.00**
	$18.00	
$5.65	**Cost Recovery** 50% Limit	
Assumed Costs		
	$12.35 **Profit Oil**	
$4.94	**Profit Oil Split** 40/60%	**$7.41**
($1.48)	**Tax Rate** 30%	**$1.48**
$3.46		
$9.11	Division of Gross Revenues	**$10.89**
$3.46	Division of Cash Flow	**$10.89**
24%	**Take**	**76%**
$3.46/($20.00−5.65)		$10.89/($20.00−5.65)
53%	**Lifting Entitlement**	**47%**
($5.65+4.94)/$20.00		($2.00+7.41)/$20.00

Figure 3.3 Typical PSC–Flow Diagram One Barrel of Oil (Full Cycle).

This example is mathematically identical to the previous R/T system example—with the obvious exception of lifting entitlement—the share of production to which the various parties are allowed to take physical and legal possession—here the company cannot claim to book as many barrels. The terminology, however, is different. The R/T System employs the term "deductions" whereas with PSCs the term "cost recovery" is used. Also, instead of a 60 percent tax, there is a 60/40 PO split in favor of the government. Aside from these differences, the mathematics is the same and government and contractor take calculations are identical to the R/T system take calculations. This illustrates that from a mathematical/mechanical aspect the differences between R/T systems and PSCs are far outweighed by the similarities.

Note that from a mechanical aspect the cost recovery limit is the only difference between R/Ts and PSCs. In this case the difference did not matter because the cost recovery limit was not reached. Note also, as signaled previously, the difference between the entitlements in the two systems is dramatic.

SERVICE AGREEMENTS

Service contracts or service agreements (SAs) generally use a simple formula: the contractor is paid a cash fee for performing the service of producing mineral resources. All production belongs to the state. The contractor is usually responsible for providing all capital associated with exploration and development (just like with R/T systems and PSCs). In return, if exploration efforts are successful, the contractor recovers costs through the sale of oil or gas plus a fee. The fee is often taxable. These agreements can be quite similar to PSCs or R/T systems except for the issue of entitlement (entitlements are not granted and fees are paid instead). Thus, for example, except on the issue of entitlement, the 1996 round of oil negotiations in Venezuela contain the features of an R/T system because it has royalties and taxes. The Philippine SA, however, uses the terminology and structure of a PSC with a cost recovery limit and profit oil split. Examples of various Service Agreement fee structures follow.

Fixed fee—$/BBL

"Fixed fee" formulas that take revenue as a fixed ratio to BBL are used in joint ventures in Nigeria, a few contracts in Abu Dhabi, and as part of Kuwait's proposed Operating Service Agreement (OSA). A simplified example is as follows. First, the IOC conducts operations in much the same

Table 3.2   Government Take and Company Take Under $/BBL Fixed Fee Systems

		Scenario 1 ($20/BBL)	Scenario 2 ($60/BBL)
A	Gross revenues ($/BBL)	$20	$60
B	Fee $2/BBL	$2	$2
C	Net revenue	$18	$58
D	Assumed costs	$4	$4
E	Government profit (cash flow)	$14	$54
	Company cash flow [B]	$2	$2
	Government Take [E/(A−D)]	87.5%	96.4%
	Company Take [B/(A−D)]	12.5%	3.6%

way it would in virtually any fiscal system. For performing these services (in this example) the IOC is able to recover its costs (assumed to average $4/BBL) out of revenues and is also paid a $2/BBL fee for conducting operations. The example in table 3.2 shows how this simple arrangement looks at $20/BBL and $60/BBL oil prices. Notice with this structure the system is progressive—as oil prices go up (or as profitability goes up) Government Take also goes up.

Fixed fee as a percentage of costs (uplift)

Another type of fee-based approach—like that found in Iran under the "buy-backs" and proposed in Iraq under what is called a "squeeze PSC"—provides the IOC a means of recovering costs plus a fixed fee that is a function of the anticipated costs. The example in table 3.3 assumes the IOC will be reimbursed for costs of $4/BBL plus an "uplift" of 50 percent of those costs, an "uplift" being a fiscal incentive for the company in which the government allows the contractor to recover an additional percentage of capital expenditure costs. This is a simple example but it

Table 3.3   Government Take and Company Take for Systems with Fixed Fees as a Percentage of Costs

		Scenario 1 ($20/BBL)	Scenario 2 ($60/BBL)
A	Gross revenues ($/BBL)	$20	$60
B	IOC cost recovery (reimbursement)	$4	$4
C	IOC fee 50% of costs (remuneration)	$2	$2
D	Government profit (Cash Flow)	$14	$54
	Company cash flow	$2	$2
	Government Take [D/(A−B)]	87.5%	96.4%
	Company Take [C/(A−B)]	12.5%	3.6%

serves our purposes. The IOC would conduct operations in much the same way as with other petroleum operations. The example here shows how this arrangement would look with oil prices of $20/BBL and $60/BBL. A difference is that for a given percentage, higher costs translate into a higher percentage for the oil company. Notice this system is also progressive—as oil prices go up (or as profitability goes up), Government Take goes up.

Variable fee—percentage of gross revenues

Another type of fee-based approach (used very rarely) provides the IOC with a direct share of revenues from which, hopefully, it would be able to recover its costs and make a profit. This type of arrangement in its classic form is referred to as the "Peruvian model." Another variation is the Filipino Participation Incentive Allowance (FPIA; Clad 1988), which allows the contractor group a 7.5 percent "incentive" if there is sufficient participation (discussed further in the section on "The Government Participation Figure") by the Filipino government. This 7.5 percent allowance is based on gross revenues. A simple example here assumes the IOC will receive 25 percent of gross revenues. The IOC conducts operations in much the same way it would under almost all petroleum systems. Table 3.4 shows how this simple arrangement looks at $20/BBL and $60/BBL oil prices.

Notice that with this structure the system is regressive. As oil price or profitability goes up, Government Take goes down. This is because, while the IOC is guaranteed 25 percent of gross revenues (almost like a negative royalty), the government is guaranteed 75 percent (like a large royalty). Royalties, especially large ones, are notoriously regressive.

Table 3.4   Government Take and Company Take for Service Agreements with Variable Fees

		Scenario 1 ($20/BBL)	Scenario 2 ($60/BBL)
A	Gross revenues ($/BBL)	$20	$60
B	IOC fee 25% of gross revenues	$5	$15
C	Government profit (cash flow)	$15	$45
D	Assumed costs	$4	$4
	Company cash flow (B−D)	$1	$11
	Government Take [C/(A−D)]	93.75%	80.4%
	Company Take [(B−D)/(A−D)]	6.25%	19.6%

COMPARING SYSTEMS

Difference in ownership structure—where, when, and if ownership of the hydrocarbons is transferred to the IOC—is one of the distinguishing characteristics of petroleum fiscal systems. With an R/T system, title transfers to the IOC at the wellhead; the IOC takes title to gross production less royalty oil. For a PSC, title transfers at the export point or *fiscalization* point. The IOC takes title to cost oil and profit oil. With Service Agreements (by definition) there is no transfer of title to hydrocarbons and so this has direct implications for the IOC's ability to book barrels. While these systems are not fundamentally fiscally different for reasons discussed earlier, some other notable variations exist that merit mention.

Title to facilities remains with the oil company under R/T Systems, but, under PSCs and Service Agreements, title to facilities transfers to the NOC or government. There is some variation regarding *when* title to facilities (including production facilities, pipelines, and other associated facilities) transfers to the NOC or government but usually it transfers at the time of commissioning them. For example, in Nigeria, title to facilities transfers to the Nigerian National Oil Corporation (NNPC) when the equipment lands in-country. Some countries will wait until the facilities have achieved "payout," at which point title transfers to the NOC. From a financial point of view, as far as normal production operations are concerned, there is little difference to the IOC whether they or the government owns the facilities. The significant difference involves who is responsible for managing and restoring the site after production has concluded (the abandonment/site-restoration liability). In other words, the important legal implication is that the obligation for site restoration, abandonment, and cleanup is held by the *owner* in the absence of clear and well-crafted abandonment provisions.

Entitlement is handled in different ways. In the above examples we saw how a PSC and an R/T system over the full cycle can be financially identical, yet contractor entitlement in the PSC system may be about half that of the R/T system and, of course, is absent in the SA agreements.

Project costs may also differ across systems. Government Take is likely to be much higher for a PSC for low profitability projects. To see this, consider figure 3.4, which shows how the PSC's payoff in this particular case is more front-end loaded than that in the R/T example. It is the cost recovery limit that makes the PSC more front-end loaded (or regressive) than the R/T system. In early years, government revenue is guaranteed for both systems because of the royalty. The PSC, however, also has the cost recovery limit, which guarantees the government additional revenue. In fact, the Government Take for sub-marginal fields can be extremely high.[5] Note that once the costs are lower the two systems are the same.

These differences between systems are summarized in table 3.5, while the statistics in table 3.6 summarize the fiscal terms associated with the different systems. Features such as government participation, the ERR, and ringfencing in table 3.6 are discussed in next section ("Beneath the Surface: Evaluating Key Elements of an Oil Contract"). Data was collected in 2001 and therefore does not take into consideration the recent oil price increases. Keep in mind, however, that most fiscal systems in the world are moderately regressive. The revenue the governments receive will go up, but Government Take will go down on average (discussed more later). Finally, it is important to remember that the differences in fiscal terms across systems is not necessarily due to the different families being used—as already discussed, similar terms can be achieved across all of these systems. Rather, differences reflect varying conditions in the diverse environments in which these systems are employed.

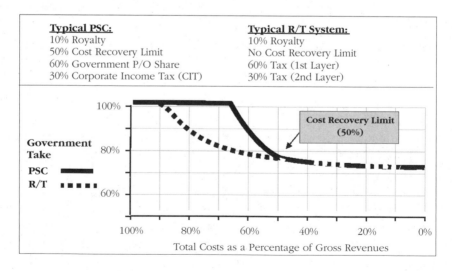

Figure 3.4   Government Take vs. Project Profitability.

Table 3.5 Comparison of Fiscal Systems

	Royalty/Tax Systems	Production-Sharing Contracts	Service Agreements
Global frequency (% of systems)	44%	48%	8%
Type of projects	All types: exploration, development, EOR	All types: exploration, development, EOR	All types but often non-exploration
Ownership of facilities	IOC	Government NOC	Government NOC
Facilities title transfer	No transfer	"When landed" or upon commissioning	"When landed" or upon commissioning
IOC ownership of hydrocarbons (lifting entitlement)	Gross production less royalty oil	Cost oil + profit oil	None
Hydrocarbon title transfer	At the wellhead	Delivery point, fiscalization point or export point	None
Financial obligation	Contractor 100%	Contractor 100%	Contractor 100%
Government participation	Yes but not common	Yes, common	Yes, very common
Cost recovery limit	No	Usually	Sometimes
Government control	Low typically	High	High
IOC lifting entitlement	Typically around 90%	Usually 50–60%	None (by definition)
IOC control	High	Low to moderate	Low

EOR, enhanced oil recovery; IOC, international oil company; NOC, national oil company.

Source: International Petroleum Fiscal Systems Data Base, © 2001 Daniel Johnston. Tulsa: PennWell.

Table 3.6 World Average Fiscal Terms

	Global Sample		Sample of Top 20th Percentile (Based on Prospectivity)	
	PSC	R/T	PSC	R/T
Number of systems	72	64	19	6
Government Take (%)	70	59	78	80
Government participation	36 countries	29 countries	12 countries	5 countries
Royalty rate (%)	5	8	5	11
Effective royalty rate (%)	23	8	29	11
Ringfenced systems (%)	75	30	90	33
Lifting entitlement (%)	63	92	55	89
Savings index (%)	39	56	30	37
Cost recovery limit (%)	65	N/A	62	N/A
Systems with ROR or "R" factors (%)	17	25	26	16

PSC, production-sharing contract; ROR, rate of return; R/T, Royalty/Tax system.

Source: International Petroleum Fiscal Systems Data Base, © 2001 Daniel Johnston. Tulsa: PennWell.

BENEATH THE SURFACE: EVALUATING KEY ELEMENTS
OF AN OIL CONTRACT

With the exception of the United States, Canada, and a very few old Spanish land grants in Colombia, mineral rights belong to the state. Indeed in many countries, managing a country's mineral wealth is seen as a sacred trust (even though, in practice, a nation's mineral wealth often benefits only a few people).

Countries with limited proven mineral wealth seek exploration activity and have limited leeway attracting it. Still, they want the best contract terms they can get given their unique boundary conditions, concerns, and objectives. Needs, traditions, perspectives, perceptions, and politics differ as well. Now that we have discussed the general families of oil contracts, we turn our attention to examining how the key elements of an oil contract reflect these aspirations. In particular, the major concerns facing a country government are:

1. Getting a large (and fair) share of the profits (Take) while keeping costs down

2. Guaranteeing a certain share *each accounting period* (ERR and/or Minimum Government Take)

3. Obtaining but not exceeding the Maximum Efficient Production Rate (MEPR)—the rate at which oil from an oil field can optimally be extracted

4. Maintaining a high degree of control over the country's resources

5. Attracting investment and the right *kind* of company even if the financial conditions appear not as good

Oil companies meanwhile want to explore in regions where there is a reasonable chance of finding oil and gas. They want to deal with stable governments, and prefer contract terms that will provide a potential return-on-investment that is commensurate with the associated risks. As already mentioned, companies are also interested in booking barrels. Indeed, in the eyes of Wall Street, oil companies are measured by their ability to replace the barrels pumped as well as by their finding and lifting costs. If they can book more barrels their "reserve-replacement-ratio"—a key measure of successful performance in the oil industry—benefits and their finding costs go down. This can be confusing and frustrating since the ability to book barrels and the amount of barrels a company can book strongly depends on the type of system and various other peripheral elements. I look at some determinants of a company's ability to book barrels toward the end of this section.

As mentioned earlier, there is no single clause or number in an oil contract that conveys whether the country or company (or neither or both) got a good deal. Evaluating the contract requires examining a series of conditions, the most important of which are summarized in table 3.7. Despite the multiplicity of goals on the part of governments and contractors, and the range of issues to be negotiated, a number of attempts have been made to create single measures to summarize the value of a contract. Chief among these is the "Government Take" statistic. I discuss this next.

THE "GOVERNMENT TAKE" STATISTIC

As mentioned earlier, the most common statistic used for evaluating contracts is the Government Take: the government's share of economic profits including almost all income sources (namely: bonuses, royalties, profit oil, taxes and government working interest—see table 3.8). While the Government Take statistic includes most revenues accruing to government it does not include "crypto taxes" or benefits such as employment benefits and skills transfers, items which are collectively included under "gross benefits."

While a widely used measure, Government Take as commonly calculated has numerous shortcomings that can undermine its usefulness (Johnston 2002). It is often calculated based on unrealistic assumptions; it cannot adequately capture risk; it does not take timing of payments into account; and it leaves out other key elements altogether. Each of these shortcomings is discussed in turn below.

Government Take is calculated using a number of assumptions about oil prices, costs, escalation rates, production rates, cumulative production, etc. Variations in these assumptions can affect the anticipated profitability of a field or project. Moreover, as can be seen from figure 3.4, Government Take can vary quite dramatically with the profitability of a project. Government Take also does not adequately capture risk.

In principle, the Government Take statistic represents the division of profits "full cycle"—over the full life of a field or fields. In other words, Government Take represents the government's share of total net profits. This includes years when profits are low (sometimes zero) and years when profits are high—assuming there are profits to begin with. In principle, however, at the beginning of a project, multiple Take statistics can be calculated, each conditional upon different possible outcomes.

Table 3.7 What's in an Oil Contract? Typical Contract Conditions

Condition	Description
Area	Block sizes range from extremely small for development/EOR projects to very large blocks for exploration. Typical exploration block sizes are on the order of 250,000 acres (1,000 km²) to more than a million acres (>4,000 km²).
Duration	Exploration: typically three phases totaling 6–8 years. Production: 20–30 years (typically at least 25 years)
Relinquishment	Exploration 25% after the first phase, 25% of "original" area after the second phase. This is most common but there is wide variation.
Exploration	Includes seismic data acquisition and drilling.
Obligations	Sometimes contract requirements can be very aggressive in terms of money and timing, depending on the situation.
Royalty	World average is around 7%. Most systems have either a royalty or an effective royalty (ERR) due to the effect of a cost recovery limit.
Profit oil split	Unique to PSCs and some SAs. Most profit oil splits (approximately 55–60%) are based upon a production-based sliding scale. Others (around 20–25%) are based upon an "R" factor or ROR system.
Cost recovery limit	Unique to PSCs and some SAs. Average 65%. Typically PSCs have a limit and most are based on gross revenues. Some (perhaps around 20%) are based on net production or net revenues (net of royalty). Over 20% have no limit (i.e., 100%). Approximately half of the world's PSCs have no depreciation for cost recovery purposes (but almost all do for tax calculation purposes).
Taxation	World average corporate income tax (CIT) is probably between 30% and 35%. However, many PSCs have taxes paid "in lieu" by the NOC.
Depreciation	World average is 5-year straight-line decline (SLD)—a constant percent decrease—for capital costs. Usually depreciation begins when equipment is placed in service or when production begins, whichever occurs later.
Ringfencing	Most countries (55%) erect a "ringfence" or a modified ringfence (13%) around the contract area and do not allow costs from one block to be recovered from another, nor do they allow costs to "cross the fence" for tax calculation purposes.
Government participation	Typically the NOC (or equivalent) is "carried" through exploration. Approximately half of the countries with the option to participate do not reimburse past costs.
Crypto taxes	Crypto taxes are those costs and obligations the contractor must take on that are not readily captured in the Take calculations.

EOR, enhanced oil recovery; NOC, national oil company; PSC, production-sharing contract; ROR, rate of return; SA, service agreement.

Source: Johnston, D. 2001. *International Petroleum Fiscal Systems.* Tulsa: PennWell Books.

Table 3.8   Government Take: Key Definitions

Economic Profit ($)	Cumulative gross revenues less cumulative gross costs over life of the project (full cycle). [Also referred to as cash flow.]
Government Take (%)	Government receipts from royalties, taxes, bonuses, production or profit sharing and government participation, divided by total economic profit
Contractor Take (%)	1–Government Take Contractor net cash flow divided by economic profit
Company Take (%)	1–Government Take (excluding government participation) Company net cash flow divided by economic profit

Note: In the past, most Take statistics were based on undiscounted cash flow. More recently, Take statistics are being quoted from a present value point of view (i.e., the division of discounted cash flow).

The Government Take statistic fails to provide information about the *timing* of payments. Yet, timing can be an issue of central concern to governments. For example, after Bolivia's first Gas War in 2003, a new fiscal system was proposed (Chávez 2004). The new system was intended to increase the share of revenue accruing to the Bolivian government in the early years of production from their newly discovered gas fields. Bolivia needed money sooner rather than later. The proposed system attempted to keep the revolutionaries happy without completely alienating the oil companies that risked capital exploring for and finding Bolivia's vast gas reservoirs. While a notable change to the timing of payments, the proposed system left the calculation of Government Take virtually unchanged: a comparison of the proposed system with the previously designed systems using undiscounted Government Take would not have shown a difference.

Few developing countries are able or willing to wait for profits to be generated from a developing field before they get a share. That is why we see signature bonuses and other front-end loaded elements, like royalties and cost recovery limits. As discussed in chapters 2 and 5, the decision to front-end load payments may or may not be wise in different circumstances. Regardless of the wisdom of the decision, the Government Take statistic does not provide guidance on how front-end loaded a payment schedule is. In fact, unless it incorporates discounting, it may not say anything at all about the time value of money. Taking timing into account requires companion statistics, such as the ERR (discussed later).

The Government Take measure excludes other key elements altogether. For example, the Take statistic says nothing about ringfencing—the practice of disallowing companies to consolidate their operations among more than one license area. In addition, it does not measure contract or system stability; remains silent on reserve/lifting entitlements; and does not account for ownership.

Overall, what the Government Take statistic does and does not include makes cross-national comparisons based on Take statistics especially difficult, all the more so since a country's fiscal system is often compared to those of neighboring countries. In one example, Chad's Government Take is often compared to those of other West African countries. Consider, for example, figure 3.5. The figure appears to indicate that the government of Chad got a raw deal, owing (according to some industry accounts) to its lack of experience in negotiation. This comparison is misleading, however. Low rates in the Chad case are likely to be due at least in part to other factors, such as risk, the quality of the oil, or transportation costs.[6]

In figure 3.6, I give another indication of Take rates around the world. This figure, however, shows how the Take figure depends on the price of oil. The figure represents fairly well the universe of systems that existed during the late 1990s and also includes the results of the recent feeding

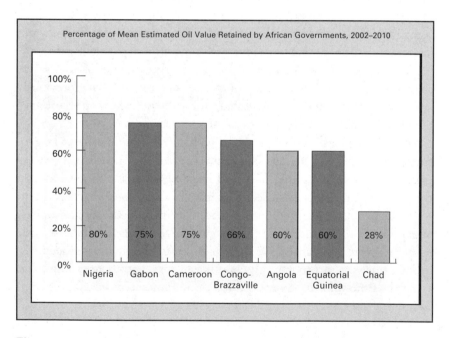

Figure 3.5   Chad's Take in Comparison to That of Other African Oil Producers.

Source: PFC Energy, *West Africa Petroleum Sector: Oil Value Forecast and Distribution,* December 2003.

frenzy in the January 2005 EPSA IV license round in Libya, which featured a new generation of PSC contract (Johnston 2005). For each country the white bar indicates the Take statistic when oil prices are at $20 a barrel. Some of the bars on the figure are wider than others because some countries have fixed terms (narrow bars) but many countries have terms that were either bid or negotiated, and there is more variation and diversity found in the country's agreements. Also, systems with "R" factors (tax rates based on predetermined payout thresholds, where the 'R' is typically the ratio of the company's cumulative receipts divided by its cumulative expenditures factor) or a "rate-of-return" (ROR) feature (where the higher is the rate of return the greater is the tax rate facing corporations) can have a greater range of financial outcomes than more conventional systems. The universe of systems represented in the figure were forged in an era when oil prices averaged slightly more than $18/BBL and around 90 percent of the time ranged between $16 and $20/BBL.

The natural question is: "How do terms change with $60/BBL oil?" The answer is given by the shaded bars that are marked for each country. Note that in some cases the shaded bars are to the right of the white bars, indicating that the systems are regressive—Government Take decreases. Notice that with most of these systems the Take changes only by a few points (2 to 3 percent). Cases in which the shaded bars are to the left of the white bars, such as in Azerbaijan or Malaysia, are progressive. In these countries, the Government Take goes up and typically by more than just a few points. The progressive systems are typically those with either an "R" feature; an ROR feature, or a price-cap formula. Right now many countries around the world wish they had structured their systems to adjust their Take upward. In fact, the scope for increasing the Take as prices go up is dramatic. The dotted line on the lefthand side gives an indication of the Take, at $60/BBL, that would in fact yield the same economic benefits to oil companies as the term's original $20/BBL Take would. The figure shows that, for an international oil company to achieve the same economic benefits or values, Government Take can be quite high. For example, from an international oil company point of view an average Government Take of 67 percent during the late 1990s at $20/BBL is roughly equivalent to a Government Take of 92 percent at $60/BBL.

EFFECTIVE ROYALTY RATE

ERR is a companion statistic to Government Take that helps to show how front-end loaded the system is (although, as we will see, it does not measure

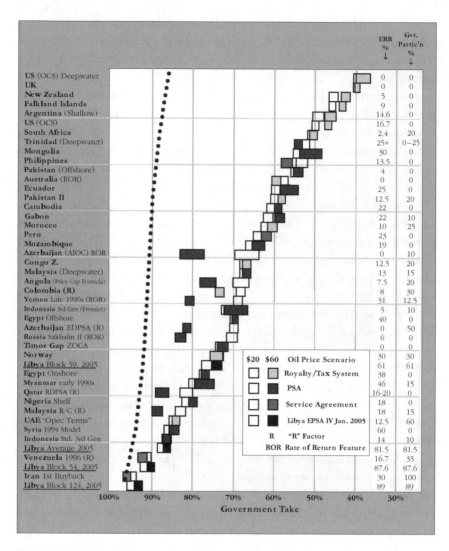

Figure 3.6   Government Take Around the World $20/BBL and $60/BBL.

Source: Based on figures in *Oil & Gas Journal*, 18 April 2005 / Daniel Johnston and Co. Inc.

all aspects of "front-end loadedness"). It gives a feel for how quickly a contractor can get its money back.

ERR is the *minimum* share of gross revenues a government will receive in any given accounting period for a field. It typically does not include the National Oil Company (NOC) or oil minister's working interest share of production. This index, developed by Daniel Johnston in the mid-1990s, has become a standard metric in the industry (and is sometimes referred to in the industry as "Minimum Government Take"). It is an important index that adds dimension to the Take statistics.

A complement to ERR—Access to Gross Revenues (AGR)—provides an important international oil company perspective. AGR is the *maximum* share of revenue a company or consortium can receive relative to its working interest in any given accounting period. It is limited by government royalties, and/or cost recovery limits and profit oil split (i.e., the ERR).

In an R/T system with no cost recovery limit, the royalty is the only government guarantee. The ERR *is* the royalty rate. AGR is limited only by the royalty. In most R/T systems in any given accounting period there is no limit to the amount of deductions a company may take and companies can be in a no-tax-paying position (although this can occur with a PSC as well).

PSCs with cost recovery limits guarantee the NOC a share of profit oil because a certain percentage of production is always forced through the profit oil split. Thus both royalties and cost recovery limits guarantee the government a share of production or revenues regardless of whether or not true economic profits are generated.

The ERR/AGR calculations require a simple assumption—that expenditures and/or deductions in a given accounting period, relative to gross revenues, are unlimited. Therefore cost recovery is at its maximum (saturation) and deductions for tax calculation purposes yield zero taxable income. Situations like this can occur in the early stages of production, with marginal or submarginal fields, or at the end of the life of a field. The object of the exercise is to test the limits of the system. This provides the ERR/AGR indices.

One key weakness of the ERR index is that it does not measure the effects of depreciation or amortization. It also does not include the effects of the guarantee provided by government participation if and where it exists. Huge problems can arise if the ERR is not taken into consideration when designing a fiscal system. Depending on costs and production, contractors could be in a no-tax-paying position for years. This can cause cash flow problems for governments as well as lopsided misperceptions. This was the case in Ecuador in the mid-1990s because the ERR under their service agreement was zero (0 percent). In fact, although it may seem surprising, it is not hard to create a situation where contractors do not pay taxes for many years. Consider the example shown in figure 3.7, which shows an accounting period early in the development phase of a project where costs are high. As a result of tax deductions on operating expenses, exploration costs, and depreciation, the contractor pays no taxes in the fourth and possibly also in the fifth years.[7]

Kazakhstan's Kashagan PSA has a Government Take of around 83 percent or more (depending on various factors), but only a 2 percent ERR. The contract is said to be extremely complex and back-end loaded. So even though the Take is high, in fact the government does not receive the bulk of it until the later years. It is estimated that in the first five to seven years of production, the government will receive only 2 percent of gross revenues. In many places such a deal could cause major problems. Imagine being the government or NOC official of a democratic country that

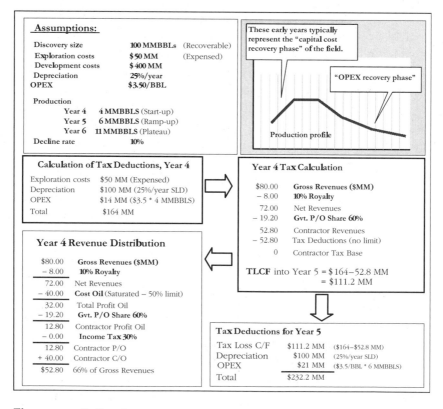

Figure 3.7   No Taxes?

Table 3.9   Sample Calculation of ERR

10% royalty		Oil price $20/BBL
50% Cost recovery limit		Costs assumed to be
60% Government P/O share		unlimited
30% Corporate income tax (CIT)		

Character Share	Gross Revenues $20.00	Government Share
	Royalty 10%	→ $2.00
	$18.00	
$10.00 ←	Cost recovery 50% limit	
	$8.00	Profit oil
$3.20 ←	Profit oil split 40/60%	→ $4.80
($0.00) →	Tax rate 30%	→ $0.00
$3.20		
$13.20 ←	Division of gross revenues	→ $6.80
	Effective royalty rate	34% $6.80/$20.00

has to paint the merits of back-end loaded contracts for legislatures, the press, or the citizens.

How is the ERR calculated? The ERR of an Indonesian-type PSC is calculated in table 3.9. Again, one barrel of oil is used to represent revenues for a single accounting period. Typically this would be an early accounting period following production start-up when accumulated costs are high and production is relatively low.

In this example the contractor is in a no-tax-paying position but the government receives a 10 percent royalty, and, because of the Cost Recovery Limit, the government is also guaranteed a percentage of the profit oil. The 34 percent ERR in this example is high by world standards.

THE GOVERNMENT PARTICIPATION FIGURE

Many systems provide an option for the national oil company to participate in development projects. Under most government participation arrangements, the contractor bears the cost and risk of exploration. The government then "backs in" for a percentage on discovery. Government participation typically is the result of a government option (through the National Oil Company) to take up a working interest in the event of a commercial discovery. In other words, the government is "carried" through the exploration and appraisal phase in that the government as a working interest partner plays a disproportionately lower share of costs and expenses in the exploration phase than its working interest share. Technically the government through the NOC is carried up to the commerciality point—usually downstream by a well or two from the actual discovery well. The contract clause that deals with the requirement for delineation/appraisal wells following a discovery is referred to as the "commerciality clause." The government agent, usually the NOC, must decide whether to exercise its right to back in once the commerciality point has been reached. Once the government exercises the option it then "pays its way" for development and operating costs from the commerciality point forward just like any other working interest partner.

More than half of all countries worldwide have this option. Contractors prefer no government participation, in part owing to efficiency considerations: Joint operations of any sort, especially between actors from different cultures, can have a negative impact on operational efficiency. On the other hand, if done the right way, such joint operations can be beneficial for governments, both because of the financial benefits (more on this later) and for building capacity. Government participation clauses vary in terms of how they are structured. The key aspects of government participation are:

- What percentage participation? Most range from 10 percent to 50 percent. In Colombia the government has the right to take up to 50 percent working interest and will reimburse the contractor up to 50 percent of any successful exploratory wells. In China, the government participation is 51 percent. This usually defines the upper limit of direct government working interest involvement. The average is around 30 percent.
- *When* does the government back in? This normally happens at commerciality.
- How much does the government participate? This varies considerably from case to case.
- What costs will the government bear? Usually the government bears its pro rata share of costs. There is variation, however, in whether governments reimburse "past costs"—the costs incurred by the IOC after the effective date of the contract up to the commerciality date

when the NOC backs in. About half of the contracts have a "past costs" clause.

- How does government fund its share of costs? Often this comes from a certain percentage of the government's share of production.

The financial effect of a government partner is similar to that of any working interest partner, with a few important exceptions. First, as noted earlier, the government is usually *carried* through the exploration phase and may or may not reimburse the contractor for past exploration costs. Second, the government contribution to capital and operating costs is often paid out of production. Finally, the government is seldom a silent partner.

A key question surrounding the calculation of government benefits from a contract is whether or not government participation should be included in the Take calculation. That is, is this process truly a way by which governments extract rents? Some analysts believe it is not appropriate to view this element of a system as a rent extraction mechanism on the grounds that such returns are just standard economic returns on investments made. However, this approach contradicts some basic economic laws. And it is easy to check by asking a simple question: "Does the 'back-in' cause the foreign investor financial pain?" The answer is a certain "Yes." And the pain is multidimensional. First of all, the value of a discovery to an explorer will be reduced by almost exactly the amount of the "carry"; second, the companies will not be able to book as many barrels.

A back-in option of 50 percent is not as costly to the company as a 50 percent tax on profits (both of which will guarantee the government an added 50 percent share of profits); but just *how* different the financial impact depends on profitability and timing. As profitability increases, the back-in or participation element takes on more of the characteristics of a pure tax or a royalty, depending on the point at which the government takes its share of production. While it is conceptually a bit abstract, as costs relative to gross revenues approach zero (the ultimate in profitability) the back-in begins to take on all of the characteristics of a tax. Thus, the less profitable a venture is, the less painful the government participation element is. Either way, both taxes and/or participation options cause the contractor various degrees of financial pain.[8]

As we saw, comparing two fiscal systems on the basis of Government Take alone is not a perfect comparison if one system has participation and the other does not. To simply ignore the participation element, however, would be a greater misrepresentation. When comparing fiscal terms for exploration rights it is not appropriate to exclude or ignore the participation element. Participation should be considered as a part of the Take for governments.

THE SAVINGS INDEX: A MEASURE OF CONTRACTOR INCENTIVE TO SAVE

The savings index is a measure (from an undiscounted point of view) of how much a company gets to keep if it saves $1. Because of the great concern on the part of both governments and companies about reducing costs, this statistic can be used to quantify to some extent the incentives companies have to keep costs down. Only the profits-based fiscal elements influence this statistic. Royalties (based on production not profits) have no influence.

The example given in figure 3.2 of an R/T system has two profit-based mechanisms: a 60 percent special petroleum tax and a 30 percent income tax. Therefore, if the company saves $1 there will be an added dollar of taxable income. The government gets 60 percent of that. The company therefore has 40¢ on the dollar saved prior to collecting the income tax. With a 30 percent income tax the company gets to keep only 70 percent of the 40¢. The savings index then is 28¢ on the dollar (saved), or 28 percent. Under a PSC a dollar saved means an extra dollar of profit oil and hence a saving that corresponds to the contractor's share of profit oil. Note that the savings index described above does not take into account present value discounting. The present value effect can be interesting and it often magnifies the IOC's incentive to keep costs down.

RESPONSIVENESS TO CHANGING CONDITIONS: REGRESSIVE SYSTEMS AND SLIDING SCALES

A regressive system is one in which Government Take goes down as profitability goes up. For a system to be regressive, it must have at least one regressive fiscal element. Conversely, for a system to be progressive it must have at least one progressive element. Today, oil prices are more than double what they were when most of the existing fiscal systems were designed or negotiated. With the higher oil prices comes higher profitability, but

Table 3.10   The Progressiveness of Different Provisions of an Oil Contract

Element	Effect
Bonuses	Extremely regressive
Royalties	Very regressive
Taxes	Neutral
Government participation	Neutral
"R" factors	Progressive
Rate-of-return systems	Progressive
Depletion allowances	Very progressive
Uplifts and investment credits	Slightly progressive

with most systems, a lower Government Take. In other words, governments are benefiting from higher oil prices as total revenue does increase; it is their percentage share of net profit that decreases (as seen in figure 3.6). This is simply a function of system design.

Many systems have built-in sliding scales to take advantage of the possibility of increased production ("production-based sliding scales"), but few systems were designed to take advantage of the increased oil prices. The elements of a fiscal system that determine whether the system will be regressive or progressive are described in table 3.10. Given the great volatility of oil prices, it would be wise for countries negotiating contracts to estimate the returns to them (and to private sector partners) under a range of different price scenarios.

FACTORS THAT AFFECT EXPOSURE TO EXPLORATION RISK (BLOCK SIZE, RELINQUISHMENT, AND RINGFENCING)

Most governments go to a great deal of effort to distance themselves as much as possible from exploration risk. This can be done through management of block sizes, relinquishment, and ringfencing, discussed in turn in the following paragraphs.

Block size and configurations. Block size refers to the size of the territory demarcated for exploration. Block sizes can range dramatically. Typically, block sizes will be smaller in proven geological provinces and much larger in frontier regions. The choice of block size and configuration is an important consideration. A challenge is to configure the blocks or licenses in order to provide interesting tracts instead of having just a few highly prospective blocks and others that will attract little interest. The larger regions can require considerable exploration expense. The IOC, however, may be able to recover dry hole and other exploration costs in one part of a block against a production in another part of the block.

From the government's perspective, with larger blocks there is the likelihood of a greater accumulation of exploration sunk costs prior to discovery. These expenses are typically cost recoverable and/or tax deductible, leading to larger accumulations of sunk costs and resulting in less income in taxes for governments. With smaller blocks governments can minimize or mitigate their exposure.

Relinquishment provisions. Relinquishment refers to a contract term that requires a certain percentage of the original contract area to be returned to the government at the end of the first phase of the exploration period. Relinquishment options are diverse and there is a full spectrum of methods employed, ranging from almost no relinquishment (in the ordinary sense) to very aggressive relinquishment requirements like those we see in the Middle East. For example, in some of these countries only a discovery will be retained and all other acreage will be surrendered at the end of the final exploration stage. In Indonesia, for many years oil companies could keep more than just development areas (discoveries) at the end of the final official stage of exploration. This meant that if a company made an economic discovery it could enjoy the opportunity to continue exploration in its *remaining* acreage while pursuing development of its discovery.

Ringfencing. Ringfencing is the practice of disallowing companies to "consolidate" their operations from one license area to another. It means that each license (typically) is treated as a separate cost center for cost recovery and tax calculation purposes. Thus, ringfencing limits cost recovery or deductions that can be taken against production to the activity inside the ringfence. A number of countries will automatically ringfence a discovery once it is made, which disallows deductions for exploration activity outside the initial discovery area. This kind of treatment is becoming more and more common.

Ringfencing can protect a government from what might otherwise be a marginal or submarginal discovery, by limiting the costs that can be cost recovered and/or deducted against revenues generated by the discovery. However, it can be a negative incentive to the exploration companies.

BOOKING BARRELS: LIFTING ENTITLEMENT AND RESERVES REPORTING

As described previously, "booking barrels" is the practice of counting oil among the assets of a company. As a general rule, oil companies will book barrels primarily according to their working interest and to their lifting entitlement. However, there are some less obvious ways in which barrels are often booked.

Under R/T systems, entitlement equals gross production less royalty oil. However, many governments take their royalty "in cash" instead of "in kind." In this case many companies are booking those barrels as well.

In PSCs, entitlement equals profit oil plus cost oil. However, in systems in which taxes are "in lieu," companies calculate what their profit oil share would have been (dividing their share by 1 minus the tax rate) and book the barrels they would have been entitled to lift had they paid taxes directly in cash (also called "grossing-up"). This is common with Egyptian-type PSCs. R/T systems would be much preferred by IOCs wanting to book barrels because they can typically book about twice as many barrels as they would with a PSC.

Finally, some companies book gas or oil consumed on-site as well as fuel for operations; and, even though, by definition, there is no entitlement under a service agreement, companies do sometimes book barrels in these cases also.

In general, PSC entitlements typically go up with falling oil prices and down with increasing oil prices. Because a company's entitlement with a PSC is based on its share of cost oil and profit oil when oil prices went from $20/BBL to $60/BBL the typical entitlement under a PSC went down by around 15 percent. The reason is that with higher prices, it does not take as much cost oil to recover costs and thus entitlement goes down. This is not an issue for R/T systems.

CONCLUSION

I conclude with some comments about how deals between governments and contractors should be made, issues that are taken up again in chapters 4 and 5. Fiscal design elements discussed in this chapter are important, but so are the means by which governments choose to *allocate* acreage or projects.

As in the past, there is significant competition for a limited amount of exploration capital. At the same time, exciting acreage is hard to come by. If governments want to increase exploration activity in their countries, they have to offer terms commensurate with their geological potential, location, and political situation. Acreage has begun to take on more of the characteristics of a global commodity. There is more than three times as much acreage available today as there was 25 years ago. In the past two decades, the Soviet Union split into multiple producers and many African and Eastern-bloc countries have opened up. Further, with more aggressive and specific relinquishment provisions in contracts, the market for acreage or projects is more dynamic and robust.

The means by which governments determine how to award licenses are extremely varied. Some governments (approximately 30 to 40 each year) have official "block offerings" or "license rounds" in which blocks are awarded on the basis of competitive bids.

In competitive systems there can be much variation over what in fact is bid on (elements that become part of a contract or a system are usually either negotiated, statutory, or bid items; working out which way to do it is of huge concern to many governments). Libya, for example, let companies bid the terms (Johnston 2005). By allocating licenses in a competitive bid round, the IOC ultimately determines what the market could bear for the Libyan blocks. This takes the burden of fiscal design off of the NOC personnel and places it on the IOCs. This is possible—and profitable—because oil companies will suffer just about anything for highly prospective acreage or projects (referring back to figure 3.6, we see that in the Libyan license rounds companies appear to have bid terms consistent with nearly $50/BBL expectations). Venezuela used a somewhat different approach. Venezuela launched its exploration round in 1996, putting 10 blocks up for bid. For all practical purposes, however, Venezuela had 10 separate license rounds, block by block. On a Monday morning, January 22, 1996, bids were opened for the first block only (the La Ceiba block). These licenses were awarded on the basis of a single-parameter bid—a profits-based tax known as the "PEG." Companies were to bid from zero to a maximum of 50 percent. Royalty and other fiscal elements were "fixed" (i.e., neither biddable nor negotiable). Ties were to be broken by a subsequent bonus bid round to follow the opening of the PEG bids within a few hours. On the first block, La Ceiba, 11 companies bid and 9 tied with a full 50 percent PEG bid. The tie was broken with a bonus of $103,999,999 from the Mobil/Veba/Nippon consortium. That afternoon the next license (Paria West) was awarded to

Conoco under the same rules. This kind of approach magnified the already intense competition by awarding licenses individually—one at a time. With each "round" the pool of bidders would potentially be reduced by perhaps only one group if any at all. This approach greatly reduced the chance that less prospective blocks would receive no bid (ultimately, two blocks did not receive a bid). The resulting Government Takes were around 92 percent. Finally, on the other end of the spectrum, in the Gulf of Mexico, licenses are awarded by the United States solely on the basis of a bonus bid (in practice, however, few countries worldwide extract such a large portion of rent through bonuses).

These are examples of competitive bidding systems. But other countries negotiate exploration rights one on one with companies. While companies typically prefer negotiated deals, these situations can be just as competitive as an official tender. It all depends, however, on the prospectivity of a block or area. When governments have good geology they are more likely able to allow companies to bid the terms. Sealed bid license rounds (auctions) can be very beneficial for a government with highly-sought-after acreage or projects.

These days there is considerable pressure from the World Bank, the International Monetary Fund, and bodies such as the Extractive Industry Transparency Initiative (EITI) for oil companies and governments to be more transparent. With these initiatives there is a strong push for governments to allocate acreage on the basis of public auctions similar to the highly publicized recent EPSA IV rounds in Libya. This likely makes sense for acreage where there is high potential for profit. The problem remains, however, that unless acreage is particularly interesting, the industry has been relatively unwilling to face the kind of magnified, head-on competition that a sealed bid type license round (like Libya) provokes. It is somewhat unrealistic to expect *all* governments to allocate *all* acreage and projects on the basis of sealed bids. Many countries, even Nigeria and Kazakhstan, have some acreage and some projects that are not quite as exciting as others. When it comes to attracting IOC investment, allocation of such acreage becomes much more important with less than exciting prospects. One of the most difficult things for IOCs to contemplate is a direct heads-on competitive sealed-bid license round for nonspectacular acreage or projects. Countries are also likely to find that with less exciting prospectivity they will have to design terms themselves and allocate licenses in a user-friendly way. In such cases, a government may have no choice—negotiated deals may be the only option. Otherwise it is likely to be disappointed with the level of exploration activity—a common complaint. In such cases, allocating licenses through negotiated deals can have its own advantages. Government officials (Energy Ministry or NOC) become aware of what the market can bear as they entertain various proposals and offers. Likewise, the lack of interest provides information too. There is nothing worse than a failed license round for a NOC official.

These considerations, however, tend to differ somewhat for different types of project. As summarized in table 3.11, competitive bidding tends to be more viable for frontier or exploration acreage than for development projects or enhanced oil recovery projects. The greater the risk the greater the range of bids possible; as risk diminishes, such as in the case of development projects, the terms tend to be fairly fixed.

Beyond this, which method is best depends to a large extent on the bargaining power of countries and what they can expect IOCs to accept. IOCs most prefer negotiated deals (such as are employed in Colombia, Trinidad and Tobago, or Indonesia), followed by fixed term contracts with work program bidding (as in the United Kingdom, Norway, Australia, or New Zealand). Fixed term contracts with bonus bidding (as in the United States, Nigeria, or Burma) cause more pain to IOCs. The least preferred form of bidding is the sealed bid round with terms bid (as in Venezuela, Libya). As described in chapter 5, in situations in which prospects are good, competitive bidding may be optimal and much care should go into auction design.

Table 3.11   Different Situations—Different Considerations

	Enhanced Oil Recovery	Development Projects	Exploration Acreage	Frontier Acreage
Degree of risk	Med–High	Low	High	Highest
Block size Acres (km²)	Field 4,000 or so (16)	Smaller 3,000–5,000 (12–20)	Large 1–2 MM+ (8,000)	Very large 3–4 MM+ (16,000)
Work program(s)	1. Feasibility study 2. Pilot program 3. Development	1. Appraisal 2. Development	Exploration program	Exploration program
Focus of negotiations/ analysis	IRR	IRR	Take	Take
Most common allocation strategy	Negotiated deals	Negotiated deals	Competitive bidding and other means	Competitive bidding and other means

In situations in which governments are in a weak bargaining position, however, negotiated deals may be required. Negotiated deals raise special challenges for negotiators, as discussed in chapter 4. They also risk raising political economy concerns. In the context of negotiated deals, it can be hard for governments to keep both oil companies and citizens happy simultaneously, leading to suspicions of foul play. This is where transparency can have a dramatic impact. Overall, transparency is a vital part of the education process for both states and citizens, and remains one of the best ways not only to control expectations at the outset but also to promote a healthy business environment over the life of the oil extraction relationship.

ACKNOWLEDGMENT

This chapter draws substantially on previously published work by David Johnston and Daniel Johnston (see references at end of chapter).

NOTES

1. Gas is simply much more difficult to transport than oil and is still "flared" (a process by which waste gases produced in the course of processing oil are disposed of through combustion) in many parts of the world. In fact, nearly 10 billion cubic feet of gas is flared per day. Nigeria flares almost 2 billion cubic feet per day in the Niger Delta oil fields—not far from some of the poorest people in the world. And in many other parts of the world gas discoveries are simply "shut in."

2. These distinctions are not always clear. Some risk service agreements (agreements in which fees are paid for services rendered) appear to have more of the characteristics of a royalty/tax system (Venezuela; with royalties and taxes), while some look more like a PSC (Philippines; with a cost recovery limit and profit oil split).

3. Region also plays an important role in determining what a contract is called. Hence, in some areas, R/T systems are often simply referred to as "concessions." In other parts of the world, however, the term "concession" has a negative connotation; in other words, it lacks political correctness. Political correctness also helps to explain why Production Sharing Contracts are sometimes called Production Sharing Agreements (PSAs). For instance, in Russia the word "agreement" is favored over the word "contract" because "contract" has a negative connotation when translated into Russian. Yet, a PSC and a PSA are virtually identical and I hereafter use the term PSC to refer to both.

4. According to a Permina brochure from 2000 (author's personal file).

5. Graphs like this are therefore usually capped at 101 percent—showing Takes beyond the 100 percent range is relatively meaningless.

6. One additional noteworthy feature in figure 3.5 is the time frame used: 2002–2010. Since Chad did not start shipping oil until 2003, the time frame represents

only the early years of production, when taxes would be minimal. It suggests that the Take calculation has not been "full cycle." If so, then the comparison in the preceding text is probably more of a representation of Chad's Effective Royalty Rate than overall Government Take, insofar as the Effective Royalty Rate measures the extent to which the system is front-end loaded.

7. This does not, however, mean the government is not receiving revenue as the government can still receive royalties and shares of profit oil.

8. Note, however, that from a project cash flow aspect, companies will certainly prefer 50 percent government participation to a 50 percent tax because at least with participation, after the NOC backs in, it "pays its way."

REFERENCES

Chávez, F. 2004. "Energy-Bolivia: Foreign Firms at Center of Natural Gas Bill Dispute." Global Information Network. New York: November 9: 1.

Clad, J. 1988. "Simply Striking: Manila Is Set to Offer an Even Better Deal." *Far Eastern Economic Review*. September 15.

Johnston, D. 1994. *International Petroleum Fiscal Systems and Production Sharing Contracts*. Tulsa: PennWell Books.

Johnston, D. 2001. "Current Developments of Production Sharing Contracts and International Petroleum Concerns." *Petroleum Accounting and Financial Management Journal* 20(2): 118–26.

Johnston, D. 2002. "Current Developments in Production Sharing Contracts and International Concerns: Retrospective Government Take—Not a Perfect Statistic." *Petroleum Accounting and Financial Management Journal* 21(2): 101–9.

Johnston, D. 2003. *International Exploration Economics, Risk, and Contract Analysis*. Tulsa: PennWell Books.

Johnston, D. 2005. "Impressive Libya Licensing Round Contained Tough Terms, No Surprises." *Oil and Gas Journal* 103(15): 29–38.

CHAPTER 4

How to Negotiate an Oil Agreement

Jenik Radon

ABSTRACT

Discoveries of oil and gas generate much excitement, and both governments and companies put great effort into understanding technical and commercial aspects of field development. In fact, however, the first challenges for governments are negotiation challenges. This chapter identifies the key areas on which governments should focus during their negotiations and provides guidance regarding who should be negotiating, over what issues, with what informational environment, and with what time horizon. Features such as contract structure are also examined and a set of especially tricky issues are discussed, including accounting standards, the role of social projects, health and environment concerns, stabilization clauses, and contract termination provisions.

INTRODUCTION

The mere mention of a natural resource discovery, especially of oil and increasingly of gas, ignites personal and national dreams of riches and hopes of prosperous times, fueled more than ever by recent dramatic increases in oil prices. Bolivia, Kazakhstan, Mexico, and other developing nations view their natural resources as an asset not belonging to any private party. Irrespective of who may own the surface land and rights, the nation owns the assets, and this position is often enshrined in a state's most fundamental law, its constitution (see also chapter 7). The "emerging" players, such as Mauritania, Equatorial Guinea, and Azerbaijan, optimistically view such a valuable treasure as a fast track to development. Their vision of tomorrow is the oil-rich nations of Kuwait and the United Arab Emirates of today. But the emotional euphoria of a beautiful tomorrow often runs into reality—namely, the financial, commercial, and political challenge of transforming locked underground assets into a usable liquid asset—cash. And dashed emotions can turn to anger; witness the recent popular protests in Bolivia, Ecuador, and Venezuela. Ruined dreams pose significant political and economic risks for the energy industry, for the consuming nations, as well as for the producing nations. Hence the hurdle: how can the challenge of rising expectations, desires, and demands be satisfied?[1]

The challenges involve overcoming technical engineering and related commercial hurdles in exploration and development. Indeed, from the viewpoint of many producing nations, the key hurdles center on management issues, as evidenced by the renewed desire to establish state-owned energy companies. In fact, however, the *first* challenges are typically negotiation challenges.

In most cases, resource-rich nations will seek to attract the participation of international companies with the resources and expertise to help them exploit and market their energy resources. Yet, once they start negotiating, they find that major oil and gas companies often possess greater financial resources, superior knowledge of the oil or mining fields, and more experience in negotiating contracts. Indeed, most countries where oil companies operate have far fewer resources than the oil companies themselves; for example, Exxon Mobil's income of $371 billion far outstripped even oil-rich Saudi Arabia's entire GDP of $281 billion.[2] Negotiations can thus become heated affairs.

Oil companies are highly motivated during negotiations. They resent the costly and speculative exploration investments and the number of dry wells encountered, and will seek to recover rapidly such out-of-pocket costs in any negotiations. They also lament that they have to deal in extremely difficult and corrupt situations, even if the home government—where oil companies are domiciled—at times provides "political support" (Radon 2005). Or as the president of an independent oil company told me: "We have to deal in chaos . . . but [then smiling] we make money in chaos." Oil companies often tailor their negotiation style to their interpretations of the political environments in which they operate. Accustomed to dealing with authoritarian regimes or in countries plagued by civil strife, oil companies often bring a self-protective, uncompromising, and feisty attitude toward negotiation.

This approach takes on a life of its own. As emphasized by one former international oil company executive, Donal O'Neill (see figure 4.1), too little time and effort gets spent on the "people" side of the oil development

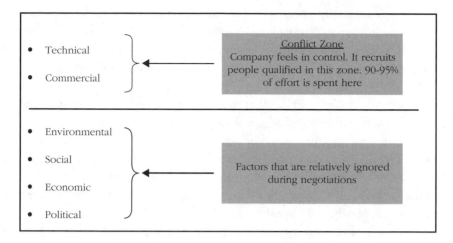

Figure 4.1   What Are the Key Issues During Negotiations?

Source: Based on figure provided by Donal O'Neill, Lansdowne Consulting.

process, with the result that many of the most important risks of the negotiations and the consequent agreements are ignored.

Negotiating a fair distribution of wealth with these companies is a major challenge and requires a significant investment of time and money in assembling a team of experts to conduct negotiations. These considerations are discussed in this chapter, and contractual issues and options of which government negotiators need to be aware are highlighted.

SETTING THE PARAMETERS

THE SETTING

Many eyes are on oil negotiations, not just those of the two principal parties. Affected landowners—often indigenous communities—demand compensation for the use and disturbance of their property. This will have to be taken into account, even if such groups are not part of the formal negotiation process. Local communities that, until recently, were on no one's checklist of factors to take into consideration now often demand their part of the spoils in the form of jobs and compensation payments. These demands will have to be handled, and ideally resolved, through the domestic political process, and, preferably, as part of the overall oil contract negotiations. Oil companies will thus often make specific commitments to train and engage domestic labor, as well as to support community development and cohesion—the ultimate in so-called soft (or social) issues. More broadly, political discussions on how to spend the not-yet-realized fortunes will quickly monopolize a nation's airwaves and the public discourse, bringing its own unrealistic momentum and pressure for fast action to bring the oil onstream. Political pressures in particular tend to undermine prospective negotiations with international oil companies by subtly establishing an artificial time schedule, namely a fast one. Negotiations will, however—if history is a guide—be intense and invariably time-consuming. They are also likely to be heated, if not acrimonious, as the differences of opinion, goals, and objectives among the many participants and affected actors are typically quite significant.

Despite the keen interests and the size of the stakes, the negotiation process itself is nonetheless all too often given insufficient attention by government parties. Negotiation is often not viewed as a real skill, but rather as something that anyone can do. Even when, for complex matters, parties engage an expert—such as a lawyer, for their legal knowledge, or an engineer, for his technical knowledge—the negotiation itself is frequently handled by the government, which will still tend to regard negotiating as a straightforward activity not deserving of much preparation or focus. Moreover, too often there is a refusal or reluctance to engage the necessary expertise, let alone pay for it. With oil contracts, however, too much is at stake—especially for the producer nation—to permit such a simplistic and narrow approach (see chapter 2).

Oil contracts are a direct result of negotiations. This is true even in bidding situations, which are often wrongly perceived as "negotiation neutral." The issues in an oil contract are many, varied, and complex. There is no model result that can or should be achieved. The result is the inevitable give-and-take as each line is negotiated.

Negotiations assume, and can be said to thrive on *uncertainty*, whether stemming from a lack of knowledge of the potential of the oil find, the break point of the negotiating partner, or the obvious inability to predict the future. Good negotiators know that, in every situation, there is an element of poker—a weak hand, if played well, can win, and even win big. But oil negotiations do not have the simplicity of poker, even if steadfastness, focus, and other lessons can be applied. There are too many issues to consider: the cost of exploration and development; the ever-changing market conditions; the possible field size, including the possibility of dry holes; and the difficulty of recovery. The list goes on.

Judgment is required to determine the importance and priority of each issue and, ultimately, to strike an ever-changing balance among them, with the result that no two contracts are identical. Moreover, there is the element of time, a powerful tool. There is a time to be patient and a time to rush. Time is an element to use and to control to achieve the desired end: maximization of returns for a country with the lowest economic and societal cost, including minimization of the potential for environmental damage. Overall, this means withstanding political, corporate, and other pressures.

WHO DOES IT?

The first issue a government faces is selecting who will be on a negotiating team. Selecting the right team requires recognizing the demands of the job. Negotiation is an art that weaves a host of elements into a coherent strategy. It demands the creation of a plan, well-conceived tactics, and the separation of negotiable factors (such as compensation) from non-negotiable factors (such as regulatory matters), all the while taking into consideration and addressing the valid concerns of the investor—the oil company.

Investors everywhere want and require legal and institutional stability, and seek to avoid instability from political, institutional, and societal inexperience in handling resource wealth. They also aim to avoid the conflict and development challenges that tend to prevail in many nations where natural resources are located. It is not surprising that oil companies, focused only on profits and operating worldwide in conflict zones and difficult-to-access terrain, are better prepared, skilled, and financed in their negotiations with officials from natural resource nations.

In contrast, emerging nations normally do not have sufficient domestic know-how or expertise, whether technical, financial, or legal, for development, implementation, and management. These shortcomings are compounded by private–public sector competition for skilled negotiators; the best educated and ambitious often turn to the more lucrative and professionally challenging private sector.

A solution for national counterparts is to treat the negotiation phase as an investment and seek to hire skilled, dedicated, and independent negotiators to counter the vastly superior experience and funds that oil companies bring to bear. In short, the negotiation process and the engagement of expert negotiators are the unheralded and often overlooked means for a developing country to successfully, profitably, and at relatively low cost, exploit its natural resources for national advancement.

Unfortunately, however, from the point of view of these governments, the value of outside negotiation experts is not obvious; the skills not appreciated and the advice suspect, especially if it comes from foreign advisers. Sometimes outside advice can be inadequate, poor, and even counterproductive. Nevertheless, oil contract negotiations demand expert advice as oil agreements cover a wide range of complex factors, from technical construction standards to equipment depreciation schedules, not to mention commercial and legal matters. In the end, a reasonable and mutually acceptable balance between the interests and concerns of an investor and those of a nation, as represented by its government, must be achieved. Simply put, expert advisers are the motor of successful negotiations.

Beyond the complexity of the issues and the asymmetry of negotiating skills, there is another often overlooked reason for engaging external independent negotiators: the problem of conflicts of interest. On one hand, a government is expected to use its regulatory power to protect the public interest.[3] Moreover, a government is increasingly called upon to create and foster a positive investment climate and provide economic freedom to attract investors, thereby promoting economic growth, increasing employment, and creating opportunities. On the other hand, as a signatory—a contractual party to a commercial oil development contract—a government assumes, often unwittingly, the role of a businessperson seeking to maximize its profits. In other words, the government seeks to maximize its income from oil wealth while simultaneously finding itself an object of its own regulations. It should be noted that this employment–regulation–profit maximization conflict is also inherent in state-owned energy companies. In addition, a government is also obligated to regulate its partners, namely the oil companies, in the conduct of their activities while still working with them on a day-to-day basis. This public–private conflict of interest may be manageable in a developed nation—such as Canada or Norway, with their well-established rule of law practices—but in a developing or an emerging nation, it is a daunting challenge at best and an unmanageable one at worst. Nigeria is a poster-child example of such a challenge. Notwithstanding its considerable oil wealth and its inherited British established institutions and legal system, Nigeria has been bedeviled by the natural resource curse and has witnessed a significant decrease in living standards, unfathomable corruption, and societal strife.

WITH WHAT TIME HORIZON?

In the case of oil contract negotiations, it should never be forgotten—though it frequently is—that these negotiations are dependent on time-sensitive factors, notably on current market conditions (especially the price of oil); the host country's current political and economic situation; and on present expectations of how these factors will change in the future. These expectations need to find expression in a contract that can withstand the challenge of time by anticipating and providing for foreseeable and unforeseeable changes or demands.

For example, the government of Norway, the model of stability, initially had to entice oil companies with a favorable tax regime of ordinary or standard taxes (i.e., no higher or super profits tax), and only a 10 percent royalty and license fee, so that it would invest in the geologically challenging and still uncertain North Sea oil development. Yet, the government of Norway did not mortgage the country's future by making an initial introductory concession a permanent lifetime one; indeed, it was able nearly to double the maximum royalty rate to 18 percent just 3 years after the discovery (see also chapter 2). Bolivia, with its enactment in the 1990s of a low energy tax rate, appeared not to have learned from the Norwegian experience. As a result, the Bolivian political storm of 2006, which led to the nationalization of Bolivian oil fields, was, if not inevitable, largely predictable.

Of course, in hindsight, such initial terms can look like giveaways if market conditions have changed. Current energy history, with its record high prices, is illustrative. Any agreement or tax regime that did not contemplate and provide for producing nations to receive a (greater) share in higher prices through a special profits tax is, in retrospect, found wanting (see figure 3.2 in chapter 3). The solution to the problem of inadequate arrangements under changing conditions is simple: make sure that contracts are more responsive to changing conditions. In particular, as prices rise, the proportionate gains to a government should also rise, in order to meet the certain political challenges of tomorrow, judged by the standards of tomorrow.

There is another way in which time matters. As prices change over time, so too do domestic conditions. Since most developing nations do not yet have established practices and stability in the rule of law and its application, oil companies seek to create a stable working environment through contractual means. In the process, they also try to eliminate contractually the normal dynamic changes that take place within a society, especially in regulatory matters, by insisting on so-called *stability clauses*. These provisions effectively freeze the "chaotic" present, not for a few short years (e.g., five to seven years) to permit recovery of an oil company's investment, but for the life of the contract. They do so by making tax, financial, and commercial concessions; environmental regulations; as well as other contractual provisions, permanent for a 20-, if not a 40- to 60-year period.

Stability clauses require a government to compensate an oil company for any change in a nation's laws, rules, or regulations that adversely affect a company or its operations. If, for example, a new environmental law—even if it is of general applicability to all companies and is adopted to bring the country into compliance with international treaty obligations—would increase the cost of oil development or operations, then the oil companies would automatically be exempt from complying with such a law. Or, a government would have to compensate the oil companies for the cost of compliance. Through stability clauses, oil companies limit the normal prerogatives of any legislature and government, such as their right to enact and issue protective environmental, labor, and other regulatory laws. These clauses are immune even to judicial challenge by the host country's domestic courts. In fact, a nation's domestic courts are often disempowered in an oil contract.

This type of contractual permanency should be examined very carefully by host governments since it restricts a country's freedoms in the future and implies great future costs. It can also be a source of distraction during negotiations, with the result that the size and scope of the government's Take, whether in the form of taxes, license fees, royalties, or other rents, is relegated in negotiations to simply being "a" factor rather than "the" factor. A government finds itself in the position of having to bargain with the oil companies for the right to modernize its legal system with the enactment of new safety standards, to maintain national fiscal stability by increasing its tax rates, and to adopt international treaties in the future. There is no equivalent to such clauses in states such as Canada or Norway, despite their extensive oil resources and similar need to strike deals with foreign actors. Stability clauses are too often "contractual colonialism," the modern world's legal answer to a discredited system.

The more unstable the legal environment is, the more likely companies are to make such demands. Their ability to make such demands, however, depends in part on their relative bargaining power, a power that may be waning. With rising energy security concerns stemming from a feared energy shortage (the new preoccupation of China and India, as well as of the United States), producing nations are competitively in the driver's seat in any current negotiations. The contracts of yesterday (as recently as 2000), negotiated in periods of assumed energy surplus, are again found wanting.

A fair question is how this private–public conflict can be reconciled in an oil contract, especially the need of the oil companies for rule-of-law stability; the government's need to be compensated well for its national asset; and the government's need to develop a dynamic, time-responsive legal system. There is no silver bullet answer, especially as the negotiated result, the oil contract, requires acceptance and must therefore withstand the force of time. Oil companies and their host nations are in reality long-term partners bound together in the same geographical space. That imposes a premium on achieving sustainable long-term acceptance.

WHAT IS THE INFORMATION ENVIRONMENT?

Transparency is the key to achieving public acceptance of a contract. It is a necessary condition to allow civil society to provide an informal mechanism of checks and balances where formal mechanisms do not operate; it is the motor for an institutionalized system, even a weak one. Transparency, defined here as disclosure of the terms of an oil contract and the payments to be made thereunder, is a *sine qua non*, notwithstanding that certain contractual matters may need to remain confidential for a specified period of time (notably company business information, such as exploration data derived and paid for by the oil company). Moreover, transparency is the only way to dispel the constant concerns of greed and corruption so often associated with oil contracts. Further, transparency is no longer a revolutionary, and therefore risky, concept, with the steady and widening acceptance of the principles embodied in the Extractive Industry Transparency Initiative (EITI), publicly launched by Tony Blair at the September 2002 World Summit on Sustainable Development in Johannesburg.[4]

Transparency prevents government officials from agreeing to terms that the citizenry cannot politically accept and will be wont to criticize, if not attack. Open public forums permit buy-in on the part of a public that firmly believes the oil is an asset that belongs to the nation. Transparency is long-term risk management for both the government and the oil companies, which are under increasing pressure to focus on long-term risk by such investors as pension funds, mutual funds, and hedge funds (an ironic switch for financial investors accustomed to analyzing and reacting to company quarterly reports). Publish What You Pay, a movement spearheaded by an international coalition of NGOs by the same name, serves not only to lessen corruption but also to provide resolve to government negotiators who know that they will need to publicly justify, explain, and defend the contractual terms.[5]

In this way, a transparency requirement can in fact strengthen the hand of a negotiator.

The oil companies have a need and an obligation to their shareholders to secure their significant investment through time, including against possible future negative public reaction that can take the form of violence, disruptive civil disobedience, and calls for nationalization. In fact, openness or public disclosure, notwithstanding that it lengthens the period of negotiation, benefits the oil companies with increased long-term stability as the public becomes a stakeholder, an integral part of the negotiation process. Transparency thus provides a useful public participatory mechanism, one often achieved only by pursuing a more flexible negotiation process than is normally favored by oil companies.

Reasonable people may nonetheless differ over what constitutes transparency. Full disclosure of an agreement, including all of its exhibits, would invariably include proprietary technical data and business know-how that ought to remain secret. Thus, complete disclosure is an illusion. Nevertheless, in their effort to achieve greater stability, oil companies sometimes effectively require and permit fuller disclosure of oil agreements by demanding that host country parliaments enact oil contracts, such as production-sharing agreements (PSAs), into law. Each contract thereby becomes a law unto itself. The ad hoc nature of this tendency, however, prevents a country from developing a coherent functioning legal system. It also does not necessarily withstand the test of time as there will always be the suspicion about such one-off tailor-made laws, with the public sooner or later demanding adjustment or "renegotiation" of such a law. In short, one-off disclosures, by not being embedded in a comprehensive legal system, are not sufficient.

Moreover, the terms of a published agreement will become, for better or worse, the psychological as well as the practical starting point, if not the model, for future negotiations and agreements. Existing agreements are precedents and therefore, color the future. If a government should, for whatever reason, determine to give more liberal terms in the future, there will invariably be public criticism or questioning. In addition, companies that have already signed agreements will demand equal treatment on the basis of nondiscrimination, arguing that the more favorable terms granted to other companies in the future also be granted automatically to them.

In short, transparency is a necessity, but as reasonable people can differ on what should be published, a debate is unavoidable in order to establish a consensus.

USING WHICH CONTRACTUAL FORM?

A critical decision for a government is to select the type of contractual system it will use in particular a concession or license agreement, a PSA, a joint venture (JV), or a service agreement. Although each type of contract has traditional advantages and disadvantages, as discussed in chapter 3, the provisions of concessionary systems and PSAs have converged and have come to resemble each other in substance.

License agreements

Concession or license agreements (see the discussion of "Royalty/Tax systems" in chapter 3) grant an oil company a right to explore, develop, sell, and export the oil extracted in a specified area for which the company has received exclusive development and production rights for a prescribed period of time. The degree of professional support and expertise required is not (necessarily) as extensive or as encompassing as in the case of JVs and PSAs (but only if an acceptable and reliable legal infrastructure is in place, which is often in reality a major "if"). Financial or economic advisers, not to mention lawyers, are of course needed to structure the bidding system. The financial and other terms of a license are drafted by a host government in compliance with applicable law. In a bidding situation, these terms are published and opened to bid. The successful party, selected by the host government, pays the asking price (i.e., a license fee and/or signing bonus) which is retained by the host government irrespective of whether production takes place. If commercial production occurs, the host government will earn additional compensation through royalties on gross revenues as well as from the income tax. All risks of exploration and development are borne by the successful party in the bid. The license is a relatively risk-free form for a government and the only serious shortcoming is the expense and loss of time if a bidding round does not attract an acceptable, financially strong, and technically competent bidder. There are commercial disadvantages of licenses, particularly if there is a reliance on up-front payments. If there is a lack of sufficient knowledge about the concession area, companies will have to take calculated risks about the price to bid; taking risk into account, they will be conservative in the amount they offer.

Production-sharing agreement

The PSA was originally conceived as a nationalistic response to the colonial originated license-concession method.[6] The virtue of the PSA for oil-producing nations, is that it forthrightly recognizes that ownership of the oil rests with the citizens of that country and not with private parties (see chapter 3). But like the license agreement, oil companies manage and operate the development of an oil field and bear the financial and operational risks. Despite the philosophical differences, the financial terms of the PSAs are in concept comparable to those of the license, although the structure may, at times, lead to different commercial results. The host government can earn a signing bonus, although this is often waived—or preferably traded—for a greater share of any future profits, the determination of which is a matter of negotiation. The oil company will first be entitled to cost recovery for both operating expenses and capital investment, but the agreed depreciation period for the latter is always a matter of hard negotiation. Simply put, the longer the period of depreciation, the better for the host government; not only because the government earns a greater share of oil proceeds early but also because it creates incentives for an oil company to keep producing until it recovers its investment. The balance after deducting expenses (i.e., the net profits) is then shared with the host government according to agreed percentages, with the oil company obligated to pay taxes on its share. The taxes are often waived and included in the agreed percentage profit split, however. Although PSAs follow a historical structure, today the details of PSAs can be so different and varied that the commonality of PSAs has basically been reduced to the concept of sharing. This flexibility is not surprising, as PSAs result from intense line-by-line negotiations. Also, the complexity of the PSAs are inversely related to the solidity and reliability of a nation's legal infrastructure. The less reliable the legal system, the more issues need to be addressed in the PSA, as this contract effectively becomes a self-contained law unto itself. The flexibility of the PSA masks many challenges. It demands skilled negotiators. It requires expertise in technical, environmental, financial, commercial, and legal areas, all of which are taken for granted in a licensing regime even if in practice they are absent. It demands judgment in balancing these conflicting matters. These are daunting challenges for a host government, which, as already mentioned, has considerably less data and information—as well as less technical and commercial knowledge and expertise—than oil companies.

Most important, as the host government earns a share of the profits, the PSA puts the government in direct and immediate conflict with itself as it is confronted with determining whether to offset profit making with the enforcement of environment and other regulations. As the PSA structure does not have the institutional checks and balances normally associated with a licensing regime, the PSA finds the government directly negotiating with itself, causing a conflict of interest. Moreover, as mentioned earlier, the PSA has given the oil companies a voice, if not a modified veto, over regulatory enforcement by the inclusion of regulations as contractual provisions. Contract terms can be more easily contested by the oil companies than statutes, with the further result that administrative prerogatives of the government have in part been transferred to the oil companies. Accordingly, the PSA provides a host government with a ready excuse for regulatory inaction.

Joint ventures

Joint ventures (JVs) defy ready explanation because there is no commonly accepted definition anywhere in the world. A JV arises if two or more parties wish to pursue a joint undertaking. There are a lot of questions to be answered when trying to evaluate a JV. What is its purpose—for example, exploration, development, and/or operation? What is each side's contribution and responsibility? How long is the venture to remain in existence? How are profits to be shared? How and by whom are decisions to be made? The JV is a double-edged sword as it is based on partnership. Therefore, it requires an allocation of operation, management, and financial risks and responsibilities, which means that the government is an interested and involved participant in the natural resource exploitation. As the question remains over where to draw the line in respect to these issues, and, as everything is accordingly subject to negotiation, JVs are a negotiator's dream (or nightmare) because they take notoriously long to negotiate. Further, in a JV, it is necessary to focus from the outset on termination. Unless there are clear, specific, and complementary (i.e., noncompeting or nonduplicative) contributions by the partners, JVs generally end in divorce (Radon 1989). Moreover, the negotiation is even more intense if the host nation lacks adequate laws. In short, JVs have little intrinsic merit, notwithstanding that there is or can be a transfer of technology, skills, and expertise to a host country.

Service agreements

In addition to these arrangements, service agreements can be employed, which in essence provide payments for specified tasks or services (see also chapter 3). In this case the contractor may receive a fixed payment independent of the discoveries or the price of oil. Key management decisions tend to stay within the hands of government. This type of agreement will likely gain increasing currency as Bolivia and other nations take direct control over their natural resources and increasingly rely on their state-owned energy companies. The major companies, such as Exxon, however, have no incentive to enter into such agreements (at least, not unless their compensation schemes are dramatically changed, so that in effect they resemble licenses or PSAs). Since, in the short run, the impact of this option will be limited, the merits of this arrangement have received relatively little attention.

OVER WHAT ISSUES?

As negotiation is an integral part of the process in all oil agreements, the major issue—from a national or public perspective—is to separate the negotiable from the nonnegotiable issues: what should and should not be the subject matter of a contract. In the latter category, there should be traditional regulatory matters, such as environment, health and safety, which are embedded in and governed by applicable domestic law, rules, and regulations. If such laws are inadequate or ambiguous, reference can be made in the contract for guidance—or even for determination—to a settled body of law, such as that of an EU member state. These domestic laws should be universal in application, without discrimination or favoritism, and not amenable to self-interest adjustment as the result of lobbying by or pressure from oil companies. They should not be the subject of negotiation with individual oil companies.

In the former category—the negotiable items—there are commercial or compensation matters, namely what a nation receives as rents. The question of Government Take, however it is measured, should always be at the heart of the negotiations. As discussed in the next section, compensation can be structured in diverse and multiple ways: in the form of income taxes; royalties or licensee fees; and bonus payments or profit-sharing arrangements, which can be recast as taxes. Of course, compensation parameters or principles can be set forth in a law, as they often are. If overly detailed, however, the required flexibility necessary in the negotiation process—especially where the geological data are still speculative—will be severely hampered.

Without such a division of issues into the negotiable and the non-negotiable, there will be the invariable horse-trading, with oil companies seeking to lower the amount of compensation to be paid to a state in return for having to comply with and maintain, for example, "expensive" state-of-the-art environmental standards set forth in a contract. Such separation is best achieved in the context of a strong rule-of-law system. Moreover, a contract should be flexible enough to foresee the development of such a system, but, in any event, a contract should not hinder a legal system's development through a stability clause or other cast-in-stone provisions.

HOW TO STRUCTURE PAYMENTS

In creating an oil compensation system in a developing nation, certain fundamental concepts are, at times, overlooked. Of central importance is the fact that income taxes are in and of themselves not sufficient for the host government. Every company, including an oil company, is subject to a corporate income tax at established (normally progressive) rates. This tax, however, does not take account of the fact that the state, as distinguished from a private party, is in many nations the owner of the oil.[7] A profits tax is, effectively, only a tax on the profits earned from the services and equipment utilized in converting the oil into a liquid or cash asset. Therefore, the state still needs to be compensated for any "transfer" of the oil from the state to a private party, which obviously occurs over an extended period of time as oil fields are developed. Moreover, to the extent that a profits tax system is used, a "windfall" profits tax, in which the rate increases when company profits exceed a certain threshold, is a reasonable mechanism. The price of the asset (oil) changes over time; without such a tax, the state would not receive its equitable share of any increased price for its asset while the costs to the oil company remain more or less constant. In short, the state, without such a tax, would have "sold" its asset at an initially set contractually low price and would not reap any benefit from a substantial increase in the price of the oil, which would instead inure solely to the oil companies. Nevertheless, a windfall profits tax should not be suddenly sprung, it is a mechanism that must be embedded in a legal system or contractually foreseen in order to underscore the goal of stability.

Mongolia has recognized this and recently enacted a novel statute by imposing a super profits tax in the event the market price of the natural resource in question (gold) exceeds a predetermined specified amount.[8] Even in such a case, a host government has to ensure through the agreement that production levels are maintained by the companies. This is especially important because, under some conditions, it may well be in their interest to decrease production and preserve the asset for future production, on the hope that the market price drops and the super profits tax is no longer applicable (discussed further below).

Royalties are normally levied on the value of the oil production, although they can also be based on quantities produced. Royalties have the virtue that they are simple to administer and can be levied with the very first production. As they are not affected by profit, however, corporations dislike them because they are a direct and immediate expense that (at a minimum) slows the recovery of capital expenditure and accordingly increases the uncertainty and risk of a project. It may even make the development of otherwise profitable fields unprofitable. Nevertheless, from the public perspective, royalties can be viewed as a (partial) payment to the government for the transfer of its asset to the oil companies, or even as a sales or excise tax. Yet, given the sharply different public–private perspectives, there is considerable room to negotiate, including the amount of royalties, the timing of payments; the degree of progressive structuring; and the tax structure and treatment, whether as an expense or a credit.

Bonuses, especially signing bonuses, are one way for the government to secure for itself some minimum compensation, even if, for example, the exploration does not result in sufficient recoverable oil. Without a signing bonus, a government has no assured means to secure any earnings, let alone cover its administrative expenses or the costs of its advisers. Bonuses can also be charged on discovery and during the course of production as different levels of production are reached. Bonuses are usually a fixed amount and do not take into account the profitability of a project. From the oil company's point of view, they are another expense that increases the uncertainty and risks of a project and therefore adversely affects the profitability of a project. Again, bonuses with their flexible structuring are another negotiable item.

The use of profit-sharing arrangements is conceptually similar to a progressive income profits tax combined with a windfall profits tax. In fact, it is often structured as a tax by a host country in order for oil companies to be able to preserve their benefits under double taxation treaties. Such an arrangement is quite complex, as agreement has to be reached on what constitutes an expense, reasonable depreciation schedules, and related or intercompany transfer pricing (among other matters). In addition, agreement has to be reached on the calculus of how different levels, as expressed in a percentage, of profit sharing are reached. Normally as increased profits are made the government share increases. In sum, a profit-sharing mechanism offers many issues for negotiation and sufficient flexibility to withstand the pressures of time, but puts a premium on getting it right initially.

One question remains unanswered: What should the compensation rates be? What companies pay under other agreements is not readily available, although one can examine public bidding situations for guidance. One can research the partner splits inserted in PSAs that have been enacted into law as they then become public information. Yet, as discussed in chapter 3, different tracts, different locations, and other differing factors complicate the comparability of such analyses, even if the data are available. One can take a working approach, however—namely viewing the oil companies as regulated utilities—by starting with the normal proposition that profits are oil sales less expenses and that all profits belong to the state, other than an agreed rate of return for the oil companies. This approach is akin to the approach underpinning a service contract. This admittedly simplistic method has the virtue that the oil companies have the burden of justifying and proving their demand for compensation, namely by disclosing their internal rate of return (a jealously guarded secret), rather than making the government shoulder the burden of justifying its claim to a higher share.

WHAT CONSTITUTES A FAIR OUTCOME?

Oil contracts are, by business custom, necessity, and tradition, private documents. Even oil contracts with governments are traditionally not public instruments, except in the unusual cases where the contracts have been enacted into law (this has its own complications, not the least being that it hinders the development of a national rule of law system). In the absence of contract transparency and availability, any analysis to determine whether a nation is receiving a contractually "fair," or competitive, return cannot be determined comparatively or objectively. The consequence of this lack of information is that any negotiator will have to rely almost exclusively on his judgment, experience, and analysis, which will always be based on incomplete information. Economists, however, could provide benchmark studies and analyses that support a nation's negotiator's position, especially as data on national oil production and corresponding export data are readily available.

Notwithstanding that Norway, with its state-owned oil company, Statoil, can be dismissed as an ideal national case, the Norwegian situation can provide data on the practical maximum return for a state from oil development. Norwegian data, and that from comparable nations or areas, can be used as a benchmark to extrapolate what a nation can presumably earn, what normal or standard operational expenses are, and what adjustments have to be made over time as an oil area matures. From this so-called ideal situation, adjustments need to be made for perceived and actual risks in any producing nation, whether political, exploratory, technical, or other, all of which would have to be quantified. The objective would be to develop data that provides state negotiators (and the public) with an ambitious target rate of return on oil development, deviations from which would have to be explained and justified, preferably publicly. These data could make it possible to switch the burden of proof to oil companies to justify their commercial positions and agree contractually to a "reasonable" maximum rate of return, with excess rate of returns accruing to the state. Such data could also support publish-what-you-pay efforts as it would establish upper limits of what a government or nation is presumably earning from its oil production.

THE DEVIL IN THE DETAILS: SAMPLE CONTRACTUAL PROVISIONS

No matter what contractual form is selected, the number of provisions that must be negotiated and the number of exhibits that must be agreed upon is extensive (see also chapter 3). Moreover, the truism that the devil is in the details is never more apposite than in oil and gas negotiations. The heart of the contract is the provision setting forth the compensation to be received by the government, and the factors that need to be considered have already been analyzed. Other contract clauses also have a direct impact on compensation—including oil price, details of the tax regime, development plans, cost and expenses, and stabilization—and are therefore critical. Further contract sections, such as those affecting health and environment, have an indirect but significant impact on compensation and cannot be overlooked. Social project commitments, often set forth in separate agreements or public pronouncements, actually can have a hidden negative impact. And the status of the contractual partner is critical to ensure that the contract is binding on a real party, with assets and technical competence, and does not simply morally oblige an oil company. A termination provision for noncompliance of the oil contract, especially for repeated violations, is a necessary enforcement tool. The list can, and does, go on.

OIL PRICE

Host government compensation, whether in the form of taxes, royalties, or profit-sharing arrangements, and irrespective of the contractual form of an agreement, is directly determined by the oil company's selling price for oil. But the challenge is to apply an objective, independent, and verifiable price. Governments should, for example, never accept the price paid between related or affiliated companies because that price is determined internally by a company's managers and will not reflect market rates (chapter 2), except by accident. The only objective method to calculate the selling price of oil is by reference to, for example, the applicable spot market price for the region, notwithstanding its volatility and the need for constant monitoring. This calculation method should be specified in the contract.

TAXATION, COSTS, AND EXPENSES

Irrespective of the percentage of compensation a host government is to receive, its compensation, other than off-the-top royalties, is decreased by the expenses incurred by the oil company.

The administration of a tax system requires skilled accountants and other personnel, which are often lacking in an emerging nation, certainly in adequate numbers. A tax system also demands agreement on applicable accounting standards. Monitoring an oil company's tax payments requires sophistication and a proper understanding of what constitutes a project expense. This is a fact that is frequently overlooked: countries should not rely heavily on self-reporting by companies but should instead invest in engaging sophisticated accounting services—the returns for doing so could be significant. For example, one particularly difficult area to monitor is payments made between affiliate companies having a common ownership. In these cases, it is difficult to determine the reasonability or accuracy of such transfers.

Determining what constitutes an expense is an unavoidable challenge. It starts with choosing the applicable accounting principles, often drawing on internationally acceptable accounting systems (such as those of the United States or the United Kingdom). But such principles will not help in deciding whether certain types of costs—ranging from first-class air tickets to five-star hotels for company employees to so-called hardship bonus payments for foreign workers posted in a developing country to fines for violating the law—are properly to be treated as business expenses with the consequent effect of decreasing profits, all the while countering the refrain of oil companies that such expenses are standard industry practice. A particular area of contention is payment for services of affiliate oil companies, the fairness and accuracy of which are almost impossible to determine. In addition, what constitutes an appropriate depreciation period for capital investments can produce reasonable disagreements. Micro-financial management is therefore an unavoidable necessity for a government. Accordingly, a list of items that are not to count as expenses must be agreed upon and set forth in the contract.

Simplicity in the creation and administration of a compensation system can be a benefit in an emerging nation. It permits easier verification, lessens disagreements, creates transparency and reduces public transaction costs. Yet, achieving simplicity is not easy, particularly as companies have an understandable interest in recapturing their substantial capital costs as quickly as possible, as well as covering the ongoing costs of extraction and operation and, of course, making a profit. Hence, companies will prefer a detailed tax regime. If there is no reasonable perspective for a company to recapture its capital costs from early oil or otherwise within a reasonable period of time, a company may well not undertake an investment, particularly in light of the uncertainty of the size of a prospective field. Even with the recent high market price of oil, investment is still of great concern because more costly exploration and development investments are being undertaken in traditionally unprofitable fields.

Consequently, sophisticated accounting and financial expertise will be required to determine, among other things, the total or full cost of capital investments and the appropriate recovery or depreciation periods, the latter especially being subject to differing reasonable opinions and, therefore, intense negotiation. From a state's perspective, the longer the depreciation period the better, as a state will receive more compensation early. A company, of course, takes the opposite viewpoint.

DEVELOPMENT PLANS

The challenge for any government is to balance the need to maximize rents with the need to incentivize a company to invest in exploration and development of a field, which in turn will provide future earnings for the government as well as the company. If the Government Take is too high, an oil company may well determine not to continue to develop or slow the development of a particular tract. This is especially true since oil companies have "competitive" fields or projects throughout the world, which are operated as a group for maximum return for an oil company, even if each project is a separate profit center. A well-structured agreement, however, can provide for the loss or termination of development rights if a field is not exploited in accordance with a detailed development plan. This requires the government to approve the plan and, accordingly, the government must have the expertise to negotiate the plan, monitor it, and supervise its implementation.

HEALTH AND ENVIRONMENT

Oil development is a "dirty" business. It affects the health of the workers themselves as well as the people and the communities living close to a field, even if a direct causal relationship between any particular activity—such as flaring—and health is still disputed by the oil industry. It also affects the environment, whether through flaring, escaped gases, explosions, or spills. To the extent that externalities or hidden costs—in particular health and environment costs, including the restoration of a development area to its original condition—are not fully borne by the oil companies, the oil company effectively receives public subsidies. The extent to which there should be such a subsidy is a matter of public concern that needs to be discussed, debated, and addressed in the legislature as well as in open public forums, but it clearly should not be relegated to a negotiable contractual issue. In the absence of adequate domestic legislation, a host government should consider incorporating by reference the applicable laws of a nation experienced in legislating such matters, such as Norway or the United Kingdom. Even these nations, however, have still not fully addressed the issue of mandating the corporatization of public external costs caused by a company, leaving many matters to be resolved by the vagaries of tort laws. Although it is common practice to apply the laws of England as the governing law of an oil agreement, there is a reluctance in many countries to incorporate directly the laws of another nation on such matters as health and environment on the grounds that this is a violation of national sovereignty. In essence, however, this means simply that the oil companies—in the absence of good local legislation—do not bear the true cost of compliance.

STABILIZATION

Oil companies, as already noted, require rule of law stability, which offers predictability and certainty for planning and commitment of significant investment. The possibility of annual or periodic changes in the tax rate increases uncertainty and risk—still an acute problem in developing nations where legislative and institutional systems are not well established. Also, the risk of creeping nationalization of an investor's assets (and therefore its future stream of revenue) through confiscatory tax rates is an additional risk that oil companies have confronted. Such concerns do validate the oil companies' need for a limited stability provision for a commercially justifiable period of time, such as five to seven years, and a clause negating nationalization in all its forms.

SOCIAL PROJECTS

Often oil companies, during the course of negotiations, will be asked to—or will offer to—underwrite social projects to demonstrate that they are good corporate citizens. These projects may include building schools, playgrounds, or hospitals, or sponsoring scholars and students. Supporting such projects is honorable and public-spirited. The building of a school, moreover, certainly provides favorable press, a good image, and cements community relations for a company. It also recognizes the government official negotiating an oil contract as a doer, a leader who can deliver public benefits. Too often, however, these visible and immediate charitable contributions become at best a distraction that deflects a government from vigorously negotiating the hard issues, in particular compensation, and at worst an expensive "trade" for the payment of lower compensation by the oil company. The government's goal should be to maximize receiving "real" compensation and not charity, and this can be attained only if social projects are not tied to contractual negotiations, whether in the oil contract or in simultaneously executed agreements.

OIL CONTRACT PARTIES

Oil companies normally operate through special purpose and country specific subsidiaries, which have limited capitalization and no separate technical expertise. Money and skills reside with parent companies and other affiliate entities on which these subsidiaries rely. Further, the structure is designed to minimize taxes—with a subsidiary frequently established in a tax haven—and to protect the parent company against potential liability from the actions of its subsidiary, including environmental pollution. Thus, if an oil contract is not guaranteed by a subsidiary's ultimate parent, a host government has literally no protection, no assurance of performance, and is subject to the "goodwill" of an oil company. The only appropriate and rightful contractual partner is the ultimate parent, and therefore a parent company guarantee (without any qualifications) of the performance and payment of all the obligations of its direct or indirect subsidiary is a sine qua non. In fact, such a requirement is no more than bank and other lenders regularly receive and secure from oil companies, and host governments should be treated no differently.

TERMINATION

A termination provision that does not provide for the possibility of the loss of all exploration and development rights is a contract with no teeth. Although reasonable people can differ on what constitutes grounds for the permanent loss of such rights—including, for example, the use of substandard construction material in violation of agreed specifications, the failure (or repeated failure) to pay the amounts due a government or the abandonment of development for a period of time—the lack of an effective and encompassing termination provision denies a government a valuable tool in policing and ensuring compliance of the oil contract.

CONCLUSION

With the ever-increasing global competition for the acquisition and control of energy resources—particularly from state oil companies, which readily offer state aid as an inducement for securing an oil supply agreement and therefore oil supplies—and with the heightened concern for energy security, especially in Europe and the United States, it is more critical than ever for emerging oil-producing nations to have the professional know-how to negotiate oil contracts with multinational oil companies that will be accepted and honored over time by the future governments of such nations. This new competitive environment will also require more, rather than less, openness from the multinationals in the negotiation process. Otherwise, oil-producing nations will have no way to determine whether they are being treated fairly. Delivering a sense of fair treatment, and fair return—which builds trust, the foundation of a long-term partnership—can therefore prove to be a competitive advantage for a multinational oil company in the ever more competitive game of securing new exploration and development rights and, therefore, reserves. So let the "great game" not continue to be a modern version of colonialism but become the "great fair game."

NOTES

1. Oil companies do need to be concerned about how the compensation paid to host governments pursuant to an energy agreement is in fact spent; or they may well (unwittingly) be accused of complicity in the actions of the host government and will, accordingly, not only have failed to manage future rising expectations but may well have been complicit in a human rights violation (see Radon 2005).

2. "At Exxon Mobil, a record profit but no fanfare," *New York Times*, January 31, 2006.

3. Such principles are laid out in documents approved by the United Nations General Assembly, like the International Covenant on Economic, Social and Cultural Rights (available at http://www.publishwhatyoupay.org/english/) and the Declaration on the Right to Development (available at http://www.unhchr.ch/html/menu3/b/74.htm).

4. For more on this initiative, visit the EITI homepage at http://www.eitransparency.org/.

5. http://www.publishwhatyoupay.org/english/.

6. See chapter 2 for a discussion of the relation between production-sharing contracts (PSCs) and production-sharing agreements (PSAs).

7. The United States, where assets are owned privately, is an important exception to this rule.

8. For background, see "Mongolian tax on copper and gold likely to 'kill exploration efforts'" *Financial Times* (London), May 17, 2006.

REFERENCES

Radon, J. 1989. "Negotiating and Financing Joint Venture Abroad." In *Joint Venturing Abroad*, N. Lacasse and L. Perret, eds. Montreal: Wilson & Lafleur Itee.

Radon, J. 2005. "'Hear No Evil, Speak No Evil, See No Evil' Spells Complicity." *The Compact Quarterly* 2. United Nations. Available at http://www.enewsbuilder .net/globalcompact/index000075845.cfm.

CHAPTER 5

How Best to Auction Oil Rights

Peter Cramton

ABSTRACT

A good auction design promotes both an efficient assignment of rights and competitive revenues for the seller. The two key factors that determine the best design are the structure of bidder preferences and the degree of competition. With weak competition and "additive values," a simultaneous first-price sealed-bid auction may suffice. With more complex value structures, a dynamic auction with package bids, such as the clock-proxy auction, is likely needed to increase efficiency and maximize revenues. Bidding on production shares, rather than bonuses, typically increases Government Take by reducing oil company risk.

INTRODUCTION

There are many ways for states to assign oil rights. Rights are sometimes assigned via informal processes, such as first-come-first-serve, or other processes, such as "beauty contests," in which companies submit exploration and development plans. In this chapter, however, I examine the design of auctions for oil rights, focusing especially on issues faced in developing countries. For the purposes of this chapter, I assume that revenue maximization is the overriding objective. While certainly there can be other objectives, such as the timing of the revenues and country employment and investment (see chapter 3), in what follows, I assume that revenue is the main objective. In this context, the advantage of an auction is that it is a transparent method of assignment, which if well designed is capable of maximizing the revenues that a developing country can receive from its oil and gas endowments. Nonetheless, there are advantages and disadvantages of different auction designs for oil- and gas-producing developing countries, which render the design of auctions especially important.

Design and process issues are in fact especially important with developing countries. While it is always necessary to tailor a design to a particular setting, we can draw a number of general insights from recent auction theory and practice, both in oil rights auctions and in other sectors. The first step is defining the product: the term of the license, the block size, royalties and tax obligations, and so on. Next, a number of basic design issues must be resolved: whether to sell rights sequentially or simultaneously, whether to use a dynamic or a static auction, what information policy should be used, and whether and how reserve prices should be set. In considering these questions, risks of collusion and corruption must also be examined.

Much depends on the structure of bidder preferences (or "values"). Two aspects of bidder preferences are especially important. The first is that the values to a bidder of a particular item might depend on what other items he already owns. Items for sale—the right to explore and develop oil and gas on a particular geographic block—are sometimes "substitutes" and sometimes "complements," in the sense that sometimes possessing one right (a block for instance) makes other rights less valuable for a particular bidder, but sometimes possessing one right makes other rights more valuable. If for a particular bidder, the value of one block is independent of ownership of another, then we say that the values are additive. The second is that, unlike in many settings, the *values* that the bidders place on oil and gas rights may be interdependent across the different bidders, since each bidder has private information, from surveys and seismic tests, that is relevant in determining the overall value of a block. Bidders have "common values" if it is the case that the ex post value of the block is the same for all bidders. This ex post value is unknown at the time of the auction; bidders have only estimates of the common value from the surveys, seismic tests, and expert analysis they have conducted.

Auction theory suggests that when bidders have preference structures like this—viewing blocks as substitutes or as complements and having common values with private information, then some version of a *simultaneous ascending auction* is best, since this will promote efficient pricing and packaging of the blocks. In brief, a simultaneous ascending auction is characterized by the simultaneous sale of many related blocks using an ascending price process in which bidders can improve their bids for the blocks. The auction ends when no bidder is willing to bid higher for any block.

There are a number of different types of simultaneous ascending auctions. At one extreme is the clock-proxy auction (Ausubel et al. 2006), a sophisticated version of the simultaneous ascending auction often used in the auction of radio spectrum. The mechanics of the clock-proxy auction are discussed in greater detail later. The clock-proxy auction is a method of auctioning many related items over multiple bidding rounds, allowing bids on packages of items. The auction begins with a clock phase. The auctioneer names a price for each block and the bidders respond with the set of blocks they desire at the specified prices. Prices increase on blocks with more than one bid. The process continues until there are no blocks with more than one bid. After this, there is a final proxy round in which bidders express values for any desired packages of blocks. An efficient assignment of blocks is found based on the proxy bids and all the bids in the clock phase; prices are determined, and an efficient assignment of blocks is found.

The clock-proxy auction encourages effective price discovery in the clock phase and the proxy round promotes an efficient assignment and competitive revenues. Although this approach may appear complex, it is actually simpler for bidders than common alternatives. The reason is that, although the rules may appear complex, the best strategies for bidders are simple. The price discovery reduces guesswork and focuses the bidders' attention on the relevant part of the price space; then the proxy round gives the bidders a means to further express package preferences and fine-tune the assignment of blocks. The approach is well suited for excellent prospects, with complex value structures, like those described in the preceding text.

At the other extreme is the first-price sealed-bid auction used in the United States for offshore leases. The bidders simultaneously submit bids for each desired block. Each block is awarded to the highest bidder at the winning bid price. This simple format is suitable for marginal blocks with nearly *additive* value structures (the value of a package is equal to the sum of the values of the individual blocks) and *small value interdependencies* across bidders.

Still other designs between these two extremes are appropriate when the bidder preferences are not so complex that package bidding is essential and not so simple as additive values. In the remainder of this chapter, I develop the logic of these different types of auction in more detail and discuss when one type of design is likely to work better than another. I begin with some motivating insights from auction theory and practice. I then consider bidder preferences and some of the basic design issues in oil rights auctions. The following three sections address problems specific to developing countries and the experience with oil rights auctions and auctions in other sectors. I then describe the clock-proxy auction and in the final section consider a number of alternative auction formats and make recommendations based on the particular setting.

KEY INSIGHTS FROM AUCTION THEORY AND PRACTICE

WHY AUCTION?

Auctions allocate and price scarce resources in settings of uncertainty. Every auction asks and answers the basic question: who should get the items and at what prices? Auctions are a formal and transparent method of assignment. Clear rules are established for the auction process. Transparency benefits both the bidders and the country. It mitigates potential corruption and encourages competition through a fair and open process.

A primary advantage of an auction is its tendency to assign the blocks to those best able to use them. Although this does not always occur (a number of features that limit the efficiency of auctions are discussed later), the competitive character of auctions makes it more likely: Companies with the highest estimates of value for the blocks are likely to be willing to bid higher than the others, and hence tend to win the blocks.

Informal processes, such as negotiation on a first-come-first-serve basis, lack transparency and are vulnerable to favoritism and corruption, which undermines competition. The reduced competition inherent in an informal process reduces both the efficiency of the assignment and the country's revenues. Informal processes also tend to be more vulnerable to expropriation, further discouraging competition.

A leading alternative to auctions is an administrative process, often called "beauty contests," in which oil companies present plans for exploration and development according to a formal process. This approach may be more flexible than auctions, but it makes the assignment less transparent and more vulnerable to favoritism and corruption.

DOES AUCTION DESIGN MATTER?

One of the most important results of auction theory is the "revenue equivalence theorem." The revenue equivalence theorem makes a remarkable claim: under particular assumptions, the four standard methods for auctioning a single item (first-price sealed-bid, second-price sealed-bid, English ascending, and Dutch descending)[1] all result in exactly the same expected revenue for the seller. In each case, the expected revenue is equal to the expected value placed on the item by the bidder who values it the second most. Further, when the seller sets an appropriate reserve price, these four methods all result in revenues that are at least as large as those that can be achieved from any other trading mechanism. From this striking result, one might conclude that auction design is of little importance—that all standard auctions perform well.

This, however, is the wrong conclusion. The assumptions required for the revenue equivalence theorem are quite special; notably the theory assumes that sellers are auctioning a single item, that bidders have independent private values, that bidders are risk neutral, that the number of bidders is independent of the type of auction used and that there is no collusion or corruption, and except for their different valuations of the good, bidders are otherwise identical to each other. In practice, none of these assumptions holds: many related items are for sale; bidder values depend at least in part on value estimates of other bidders and these estimates are correlated; bidder participation decisions are of paramount importance; bidders care about risk; there are ex ante differences among the bidders (e.g., some are large and some are small); and mitigating collusion and corruption are important. Each of these features impacts the performance of alternative auction designs. The choice of the best auction design depends on which of these different features are most salient.

PRODUCT DEFINITION

The first step is product definition—what is being sold. There are two key elements: (1) the contract terms of the license (duration, royalties, tax obligations) and (2) the geographic scope of the blocks. The first of these is discussed in more detail in chapter 3. The determination of the second depends to a large extent on local context and I do not discuss it at length here. In general, however, blocks are defined as rectangular blocks, as specified by a pair of longitude and latitude coordinates. The appropriate size of the blocks depends on the quality of the prospect. More promising regions support smaller blocks. In the United States, blocks are nominated by the oil companies. This is a sensible approach in most cases because it guarantees at least some interest in the auctioned blocks.

AUCTION PROCESS

As important as the auction design itself is the process through which the auction takes place. To promote transparency, the auction process must be specified well in advance of the tender. The process should be open to all oil companies on a nondiscriminatory basis. The process should begin with a public advertisement of the tender and a complete description of the procedure for awarding a license should be provided, including bidder qualification procedures and the auction rules. Such a clear and complete statement of the auction process is essential to bidder participation. The country should be committed to the process. Finally, the process should allow for and encourage input from the oil companies in a transparent setting with "sunshine" rules that require public announcement of the content of meetings between the country and the oil companies. At a minimum, this would include the nomination of blocks, but allowing comments on all aspects of the rule making is generally worthwhile. Bidder participation and bids are enhanced if legitimate bidder concerns and preferences are addressed.

BIDDER PREFERENCES AND AUCTION DESIGN

THE STRUCTURE OF BIDDER PREFERENCES

Before considering design issues, it is helpful to think first about the bidders' preferences. We consider two aspects of bidder preferences that affect the optimal design of auctions: the interdependence of valuations across bidders and the interdependence of valuations across blocks.

Interdependence of valuations across bidders

In the study of auctions there are three standard models for describing the valuations of bidders: private values, common values, and interdependent values.

If there are *private values* then this means that each bidder's value does not depend on the private information of the other bidders. Each bidder has its own valuation of the expected worth (to it) of the different packages of items on sale.

If there are *common values*, then packages of items have the same value to all bidders. But these values are unknown. The value can be written as a function of the individual bidder's private information, as well as the information held by all other bidders. The more a given bidder knows about other bidders' valuations, the better is that bidder able to estimate the worth of the item.

If there are *interdependent values*, then each bidder's value of a package depends on his private information as well as the private information of the other bidders. This is a more general formulation and both private and common values can be written as special cases of interdependent values. With interdependent values, each bidder has its own estimates of the value which is a function of the bidder's own information and may also be a function of the other bidders' information. In this situation, a bidder's value depends on the values assigned by other bidders.

The oil rights setting is the textbook example of a common values auction. All companies value the oil at about the same amount (the world price of oil), but there is enormous uncertainty about the quantity of oil and the cost of extracting it. Before bidding, each company estimates these uncertainties from geological surveys, seismic tests, and analysis of petroleum engineers. Yet each company would like to have the private information of the other bidders to further reduce uncertainty. The common value depends not just on the bidder's estimate of value, but on all the other estimates. In practice, there are also some private value elements—the company's exploration and development capacity, its reserves, its expertise in the particular type of prospect, its ability to manage exploration and political risks—but these elements typically are of secondary importance. Thus, the oil rights setting has interdependent values with strong common value elements.

In situations in which there are common values, the strategies chosen by bidders are conditioned by a phenomenon known as the *winner's curse*. This is the insight that winning an item in an auction is actually bad news for the winner about the item's true value, because winning implies that no other bidder was willing to bid as much for the item. Hence, it is likely that the winner's estimate of value is an overestimate. Since a bidder's bid is relevant only in the event that the bidder wins, the bidder should condition the bid on the negative information winning conveys about value. Bidders that fail to condition their bids on the bad news winning conveys suffer from the winner's curse in the sense that they often pay more for an item than it is worth. In oil rights auctions, adjusting bids in light of the winner's curse is a key element of strategy. In contrast, in private values auctions, there is no winner's curse: each bidder knows what value he or she places on the object and this value does not depend on the values of the others.

Interdependence of valuations across blocks

Thus far, we have focused on how package values depend on private information. A second important dimension is the structure of *package* values. How does the bidder value a package of blocks?

The simplest valuation model is *additive values*: the value of a package is the sum of the values of the individual blocks. In oil rights auctions, additive values are a good first approximation. The primary determinant of value is the quantity of oil, and the quantity of oil in a package of blocks is simply the *sum* of the quantities in each block. However, sometimes values may also be either *sub*additive or *super*additive.

With *subadditive values*, the value of a package is less than the sum of the individual values. One source of subadditive values is capacity constraints on exploration and refining. Additional blocks have less value if the company lacks the resources to efficiently exploit that value. Another source is risk, holding many blocks within the same region where values are highly correlated is riskier than holding a few blocks in each of many dispersed regions. Values for substitute goods are subadditive.

With *superadditive values*, the value of a package is greater than the sum of the individual values. Superadditive values arise if there are synergies or blocks act as complements. One source of complements is exploration and production efficiencies that arise from holding many neighboring blocks. Traditional economies of scale may arise in drilling from sharing staff and equipment. A more subtle form of complements comes from more efficient exploration. For example, if two neighboring blocks are owned by different companies, each may have an incentive to free ride on the exploration efforts of the other—waiting to see if the other's drilling is successful. As a result, the exploration of both tracts may be inefficiently delayed. Hendricks and Porter (1996) provide both a theoretical model and empirical support for this behavior in the U.S. offshore oil lease auctions. If instead, the two blocks are held by the same company, there is no information externality and the blocks are explored efficiently. A related synergy comes from the common pool problem, in which neighboring blocks are drawing oil from the same pool. When the blocks are held by the same company, the exploitation of the pool is efficient; whereas, with separately held blocks, the companies would need to negotiate a unitization agreement to coordinate the development. Ideally, blocks are defined to avoid this problem, but the country may not have sufficient information to avoid it entirely.

In the oil rights setting, additive values may be a good first approximation. Nonetheless, complements (superadditivity) and substitutes (subadditivity) likely are important in at least some applications. If this is the case, then the auction design needs to allow for efficient packaging. Otherwise, if values are largely additive, then packaging issues can be safely ignored, resulting in a much simpler auction design.

BASIC DESIGN ISSUES

Given this characterization of the different ways that bidders might value a set of blocks I now address several key issues of auction design in the oil rights setting.

OPEN BIDDING OR SEALED BIDDING?

Especially in contexts where there is interdependence of valuations across bidders, open bidding is generally better than a single sealed bid. An essential advantage of open bidding is that the bidding process reveals information about individual valuations. This information promotes the efficient assignment of licenses, since bidders can condition their bids on more information. Moreover, since bidders' private information is likely to be positively correlated, open bidding may raise auction revenues (Milgrom and Weber 1982). Intuitively, bidders are able to bid more aggressively in an open auction, since they have better information about the item's value. The open bidding reveals information about the other bidders' estimates of value. This information reduces the bidder's uncertainty about value, and thus mitigates the winner's curse—the possibility of paying more than the value of the item. Thus, bidders are able to bid more aggressively, and this translates into high revenues for the seller. That turns out to be a strong argument in favor of open rather than sealed bidding.

Sealed bidding has some advantages. Most importantly, a sealed-bid design is less susceptible to collusion, such as agreements among oil companies not to compete against each other (Milgrom 1987). Open bidding allows bidders to signal through their bids and establish tacit agreements. With open bidding, these tacit agreements can be enforced, since a bidder can immediately punish another that has deviated from the collusive agreement. Signaling and punishments are not possible with a single sealed bid. So in situations in which collusion is a major concern, sealed bidding may make more sense.

A second advantage of sealed bidding is that if there are ex ante differences among the bidders, it may yield higher revenues (Klemperer 2002; Maskin and Riley 2000). This is especially the case if the bidders are *risk averse* and have *independent private values*. The reason is that in a sealed-bid auction, a strong bidder can guarantee victory only by placing a high bid; even if a strong bidder who expects to win has a good sense of what the next most likely winner is willing to bid, he is likely to bid some margin above this to avoid the risk of losing the block. In an open auction on the other hand, the strong bidder never needs to bid higher than the second highest value.

In the oil rights auctions, an open auction probably is best, provided the design adequately addresses potential collusion. The reason is that values have a strong common value element and so the benefits of sealed bids are not so great but the benefits of an open auction are substantial.[2]

SHOULD AUCTIONS OF MULTIPLE BLOCKS BE RUN SIMULTANEOUSLY OR SEQUENTIALLY?

Generally, simultaneous open bidding is better for the seller than sequential auctions. A disadvantage of sequential auctions is that they limit the information available to bidders and limit how the bidders can respond to information. With sequential auctions, bidders must guess what prices will be in future auctions when determining bids in the current auction. Incorrect guesses may result in an inefficient assignment when item values are interdependent. A sequential auction also eliminates many strategies. A bidder cannot switch back to an earlier item if prices go too high in a later auction. Bidders are likely to regret having purchased early at high prices, or not having purchased early at low prices. The guesswork about future auction outcomes makes strategies in sequential auctions complex, and the outcomes less efficient.

In a simultaneous ascending auction, a large collection of related items is up for auction at the same time. Hence, the bidders get information about prices on all the items as the auction proceeds. Bidders can switch among items based on this information. Hence, there is less of a need to anticipate where prices are likely to go. Moreover, the auction generates market prices. Similar items sell for similar prices. Bidders do not regret having bought too early or too late and with less fear of such regrets are willing to bid more.

Proponents of sequential auctions argue that the relevant information for the bidders is the final prices and assignments. They argue that simultaneous auctions do not reveal final outcomes until the auction is over. In contrast, the sequential auction gives final information about prices and assignments for all prior auctions. This final information may be more useful to bidders than the preliminary information revealed in a simultaneous auction. However, empirical analysis of simultaneous ascending auctions indicates that the preliminary information is highly correlated with final outcomes (Cramton 1997).

Supporters of sequential auctions also point out that the great flexibility of a simultaneous auction makes it more susceptible to collusive strategies. Since nothing is assigned until the end in a simultaneous auction, bidders can punish aggressive bidding by raising the bids on those items desired by the aggressive bidder. In a sequential auction, collusion is more difficult. A bidder that is supposed to win a later item at a low price is vulnerable to competition from another that won an earlier item at a low price. The early winner no longer has an incentive to hold back in the later auctions. This potential problem, however, can be mitigated through an effective information policy, which determines what information is made public during the auction.

In oil rights auctions, the virtues of the simultaneous auction—greater information release and greater bidder flexibility in responding to information— would improve efficiency. But as with our arguments for adopting open bidding over sealed bidding, this depends in part on how well concerns about bidder collusion can be addressed.

SHOULD BIDDERS BID FOR INDIVIDUAL BLOCKS SEPARATELY OR FOR PACKAGES OF BLOCKS?

In general, it is a good idea for the seller to allow bidders to give different bids for different packages. Package bidding is desirable when a bidder's value of a block depends on what other blocks it wins. Package bidding also has advantages when bidders have budget constraints or other constraints that depend on the package of blocks won. Then bidders may prefer being able to bid on a combination of blocks, rather than having to place a number of individual bids. With a package bid, the bidder either gets the entire combination or nothing. There is no possibility that the bidder will end up winning just some of what it needs or that it wins more than it wishes to pay for.

With individual bids, bidding for a synergistic combination is risky. The bidder may fail to acquire key pieces of the desired combination, but may pay prices based on the synergistic gain. Alternatively, the bidder may be forced to bid beyond its valuation to secure the synergies and reduce its loss from being stuck with some low-value blocks. This is called the *exposure problem*. Individual bidding exposes bidders seeking synergistic combinations to aggregation risk.

To see how not allowing package bids can create inefficiencies, consider the following example of two bidders bidding for two adjacent parking spaces. One bidder with a car and a trailer requires both spaces. She values the two spots together at $100 and a single spot is worth nothing; the spots are perfect complements. The second bidder has a car, but no trailer. Either spot is worth $75, as is the combination; the spots are perfect substitutes. Note that the efficient outcome is for the first bidder to get both spots for a social gain of $100, rather than $75 if the second bidder gets a spot. Yet any attempt by the first bidder to win the spaces is foolhardy. The first bidder would have to pay at least $150 for the spaces, since the second bidder will bid up to $75 for either one. Alternatively, if the first bidder drops out early, she will "win" one license, losing an amount equal to her highest bid. The only equilibrium is for the second bidder to win a single spot by placing the minimum bid. The outcome is inefficient, and fails to generate *any* revenue. In contrast, if package bids are allowed, then the outcome is efficient. The first bidder wins both spots with a bid of $75 for the pair of spots.

This example is somewhat extreme but it illustrates well the exposure problem. The inefficiency involves large bidder-specific complementarities and a lack of competition. In practice, the complementarities in oil rights auctions are likely to be less extreme and the competition is likely to be greater.

Unfortunately, allowing package bids creates other problems. Package bids may favor bidders seeking large aggregations as a result of a variant of the free-rider problem, called the *threshold problem*. Continuing with the last example, suppose that there is a third bidder who values either spot at $40. Then the efficient outcome is for the individual bidders to win both spots for a social gain of $75 + $40 = $115. But this outcome may not occur when values are privately known. Suppose that the second and third bidders have placed individual bids of $35 on the two licenses, but these bids are topped by a package bid of $90 from the first bidder. Each bidder hopes that the other will bid higher to top the package bid. The second bidder has an incentive to understate his willingness to push the bidding higher. He may refrain from bidding, counting on the third bidder to break the threshold of $90. Since the third bidder cannot come through, the auction ends with the first bidder winning both spaces for $90.

A second problem with allowing package bids is complexity. If all combinations are allowed, even identifying the revenue maximizing assignment is a difficult integer programming problem when there are many bidders and items. Nonetheless, our understanding of and experience with package auctions has advanced considerably in recent years (Cramton et al. 2006). Package bids should therefore now be considered a viable option. Whether package bids are the best option will depend somewhat on the details of the setting.

HOW SHOULD RESERVE PRICES BE USED?

Reserve prices in oil rights auctions have two main purposes: (1) to guarantee substantial revenue in auctions where competition is weak but the reserve is met and (2) to limit the incentive for—and the impact of—collusive bidding. Reserve prices mitigate collusive bidding by reducing the maximum gain of the collusive bidding. In effect, this heightens the competition between bidders by increasing the importance of the gains they can make unilaterally relative to the gains they can make through collusion. Setting reserve prices for oil rights auctions is difficult given the enormous uncertainty of values. There is, however, an alternative to posting a reserve price that can be considered and that has, for example, been used in the United States. It is possible for the seller to place a low minimum bid that applies to all blocks, and then accept or reject winning bids *ex post* (note the idea is to decide ex post whether to accept or reject a *winning* bid not to pick and choose between bidders ex post). Under such a system a reserve price exists but it is secret and can in fact depend on the observed bidding behavior.

BONUS BID, ROYALTIES, AND PRODUCTION SHARING

Oil rights auctions commonly involve bonus bids and either royalties or production sharing (see chapters 2 and 3 for further discussions of the merits of these different approaches). The bonus bid or signature bonus is the upfront payment determined in auction for the right to explore and develop the block during the license period. If exploitable reserves are found, the license is renewed for a nominal fee as long as development continues. The royalty is the share of the oil and gas revenues that goes to the government. Royalty rates vary country to country and even within countries. For example, in the U.S. offshore oil lease auctions, the royalty rate is 1/6, where one-sixth of revenues for any oil extracted is paid as a royalty, whereas the onshore rate typically is 1/8. The motivation for royalties is to have the oil company payment more closely reflect ex post realized value. This reduces the risk of the oil company. The disadvantage of royalties is that, like a tax, it distorts investment decisions. A larger royalty rate reduces the incentive for the oil company to invest in exploration and development activities. In contrast, the signature bonus is a sunk cost after the auction and does not distort subsequent investments. In a setting where there is no uncertainty about values, then only a bonus bid is needed (a zero royalty rate); in a setting where exploration and development are costless, then a 100 percent royalty rate is optimal. In practice, oil rights auctions have large uncertainty about values as well as large exploration and development costs. Thus, an intermediate rate is generally best.

Production-sharing contracts (PSCs) attempt to further reduce oil company risk and better manage investment incentives by specifying the terms of cost sharing and profit sharing throughout exploration and development. The contract can allow the oil company to recover exploration and development capital costs before the country shares in the revenues. Then the government's profit share increases with the success of the project, allowing the terms to handle both marginal and windfall economics. The contracts often are made immune to tax changes by having the government counterparty, typically the national oil company, liable for all taxes. Work programs specify a minimum level of exploration effort. This is an important constraint on more marginal blocks, where high government profit shares might otherwise discourage exploration.

With PSCs, it is common for bidding to be over the government's highest profit share, rather than the signature bonus. Thus, bidders compete on their willingness to share profits in the most favorable circumstances. This approach, used recently in Libya and Venezuela, reduces oil company risk without upsetting development incentives, since the bid share only applies for blocks that are highly successful. Development incentives are further maintained by having the government share in the development capital costs and the operating costs. If the government's share of development capital and operating costs is the same as its production share, then post-exploration the project essentially is a joint venture with first-best incentives for development.

PROBLEMS SPECIFIC TO DEVELOPING COUNTRIES

Developing countries face additional challenges in establishing an effective auction program. These include political risk, risk for companies of expropriation, favoritism, and corruption. All of these challenges tend to discourage participation in auctions and so reduce competition. In fact, the strongest indicator of success of the auction program is the presence of robust competition. The geological prospect of the region is a primary factor in attracting oil companies, but political, legal, and process factors are also key.

There is little a country can do in the short term to reduce perceptions of political risk. Legal risks can be reduced through choice of contract law. And over the medium term, institutions can be developed that provide the ground rules for oil exploration and development.

Companies' fear of expropriation or adverse renegotiation can be mitigated somewhat through the cash flow structure of the contract terms. For example, a pure bonus bid system (zero royalty) is problematic in light of expropriation risks. This would force the oil company to sink most funds upfront, making the company vulnerable to expropriation. Even developed countries, such as the United Kingdom and the United States, have a tendency to adjust tax rates after companies have begun production to capture a larger share of "windfall" profits. As a result, companies heavily discount bonus bids. Some reliance on royalties or production sharing is better, since these payments are not due until after revenues or profits have been received by the oil company. Another option is share bidding in which oil companies offer equity shares in the venture (the highest offered share wins the block). In this case, the country and the oil company are partners. Each makes investments and reaps rewards according to its share. This approach shifts risks from the oil companies to the country. More importantly, it aligns the interests of the company and the country, reducing expropriation risks for the company.

Such approaches are mutually beneficial but sometimes appear unattractive for developing countries. Developing countries, especially small ones, may have important constraints with respect to cash flows. For example, a country may be unable to make upfront outlays and so have strong preferences for early payments. However, too much focus on early revenues may greatly reduce total revenues, especially in an environment where renegotiation risk is high. For this reason, in the medium to long run, countries often are better off with PSCs with small upfront payments and large government shares in the event of successful finds.

Finally, favoritism and corruption can be addressed in the auction process. A transparent, nondiscriminatory process is the key to mitigating favoritism and corruption. Independent third-party auction managers can help as well. Likewise, a trustee observing and commenting on all aspects of the auction process can further reduce the possibility of corruption. This approach is commonly used in developed countries. For example, electricity auctions in restructured electricity markets in North America and Europe are typically conducted by independent third parties, often with a further independent review and certification of the entire process by an auditor or trustee.

EXPERIENCE WITH OIL RIGHTS AUCTIONS

Oil rights have been auctioned in many countries throughout the world. Much can be learned from these experiences. Here, I focus on the experiences of a wealthy nation, the United States, and compare this with recent experiences elsewhere, notably in Venezuela and Libya.

THE U.S. EXPERIENCE

The most studied program is the U.S. offshore oil lease auctions. The discussion that follows draws largely on Porter's excellent survey of this research (Porter 1995). These oil lease auctions began in 1954. The product auctioned is a lease granting the right to explore and develop a particular tract for a period of five years (U.S. auctions use the terms "lease" and "tract," rather than "license" and "block"). If oil is found and developed, the lease is renewed for a nominal fee as long as production continues. The process begins with the oil companies nominating tracts for auction. The government then makes a list of tracts to be auctioned. The auction is a simultaneous first-price sealed-bid auction. Each bidder simultaneously submits a bid on each of the tracts it desires. The bid must meet or exceed the minimum bid, which is stated as a dollar amount per acre. The per-acre minimum depends only on the type of tract. A tract is either awarded to the high bidder or all bids on the tract are rejected; thus, the reserve price is secret and determined after the bids are observed by the government. A winning bidder pays its bid, which is referred to as the *bonus*. In addition, the company pays a royalty of 1/6 of revenues for any oil extracted.

Bidders are allowed to bid jointly; however, after 1975, none of the top eight oil companies could combine in a joint bid with another top eight company.

Tracts are of three types. Wildcat tracts are new offerings that are not adjacent to developed tracts; drainage tracts are adjacent to developed tracts; and development tracts are a reoffering. There is an important economic difference between wildcat tracts and drainage tracts and these differences are reflected in the types of auctions used. With a drainage tract, bidders holding leases on adjacent tracts may have a much better estimate of value than those without adjacent tracts. Thus, the drainage tract sales may have large asymmetries among the bidders, whereas in the wildcat sales bidders are more symmetric. This difference has important implications for both bidding behavior and auction design. In particular, one would expect that a simultaneous ascending auction would be best for the wildcat tracts and a simultaneous sealed-bid auction would be best for the drainage tracts. However, the United States, perhaps for reasons of inertia, uses the same sealed-bid auction method for all tracts.

From 1954 to 1990, there were 98 auctions. On average, 125 leases sold per auction. Eight percent of the high bids were rejected. The auctions raised $55.8 billion from bonus bids and $40 billion from royalties (1972 dollars). Hendricks et al. (1987) estimate from ex post price and quantity data that the government share of value (revenue net of costs) was 77 percent with the oil companies receiving the remaining 23 percent.

Porter (1995) concludes that the U.S. auction program in many respects is well designed. Certainly the government is getting the lion's share of the value. On drainage tracts, informed bidders (those with leases on adjacent tracts), reap informational rents. The government could consider using a higher royalty rate on these tracts to the extent that the informational rents are not capitalized in the earlier wildcat sales.

One potentially troubling feature of the U.S. offshore program is the use of the simultaneous first-price sealed-bid format. This is easy for the government to implement, but poses challenges to bidders, which may reduce efficiency and revenues. In particular, the format prevents the bidders from expressing preferences for packages of tracts and it provides no price discovery. In addition, a bidder's budget constraints or other package-based constraints either cannot be satisfied or can be satisfied only by greatly distorting one's bids.

Onshore auctions in the United States are conducted at the state level. These auctions often are done as sequential open outcry auctions: each tract is sold in sequence using an English auction. This approach allows for some price discovery and better handles budget constraints, but it still forces bidders to guess auction prices for leases sold later.

EXPERIENCE OUTSIDE THE UNITED STATES

Unfortunately, there is little publicly available information about oil rights auctions in developing countries, and little research on the topic (although one important exception is Sunley et al. [2002], who provide a study of government revenue sources from oil and gas in developing countries). Typically, however, countries employ a range of revenue methods: bonus bids, royalties, production sharing, income taxes, and state equity. Not surprisingly, the terms vary widely across countries, reflecting at least in part differences in political risks and geological uncertainty. A reasonable conclusion from the experiences of these countries is that auctions are a desirable method of allocating the rights among companies, but multiple revenue sources should be used to best manage risks and incentives.

Recent auctions conducted in an environment of high oil prices have been highly competitive, especially in regions with known reserves. For example, in the Libyan auction of 15 blocks on January 29, 2005, some blocks received as many as 15 bids.

Johnston (2005) examined the contract terms and bidding in the 2005 Libyan auction. This case study offers insights into modern contract terms and bidder competition in a major auction of excellent prospects during a period of high price expectations. The 15 blocks were offered in a simultaneous sealed-bid auction, in which oil companies bid a production share and a signature bonus for each desired block. Each license was awarded to the company with the highest production share (share of gross revenues going to the government). In the event of a tie, the signature bonus was used as a tiebreaker.

The contract terms fully specify the split of revenues and costs between the government and the oil company. Companies bid only on the production share and the signature bonuses. Hence, for example, on block 54, the winning bid offered a production share of 87.6 percent. In effect this means that the government gets 87.6 percent of the gross revenues, for which it pays none of the exploration costs, 50 percent of the development capital, and 87.6 percent of the operating costs. The oil company uses the remaining 12.4 percent of the gross revenues to recover its costs (100 percent of exploration costs, 50 percent of development capital, and 12.4 percent of operating costs). Once these costs are recovered from the 12.4 percent, the excess ("profit oil") is split between the government and the oil company according to a sliding scale based on a revenue/cost index. The government's share of this excess increases from 10 percent to 50 percent as the company's revenue/cost index increases from 1.5 to 3. Under these terms, the initial up-front capital expense is limited to the exploration cost and a modest signature bonus. Since development capital costs are split 50/50, the high production share does mean that some profitable fields may go undeveloped. However, once development capital is sunk, the 87.6/12.4 split of operating costs results in first-best incentives for extraction.

Competition in the Libyan round was intense, with an average of seven bidders per block. The winning production shares ranged from 61.1 to 89.2 percent with a mean of 80.5 percent. The Government Take (share of project profits) depends on the assumptions one makes on costs and revenues. Johnston (2005) estimated the Government Take to range from 77.0 to 97.7 percent with a mean of 89.9 percent, well above the 80 percent that is more typically captured for good prospects or the 77 percent realized in the U.S. auctions before 1990.

The 1996 Venezuela auction of 10 blocks had similar contract terms and also was highly successful. There were, however, some important differences. The 10 blocks were offered in sequence. Also, to maintain better development incentives, the production share bids were capped at 50 percent. First, the bidders bid production shares, and then in the event of a tie (e.g., two or more bid 50 percent) the bidders bid signature bonuses to break the tie. This resulted in large signature bonuses for desirable blocks, shifting risk to the winning oil companies. However, the Venezuelan terms were more favorable than the Libyan terms with respect to cost recovery, so it is unclear which terms were riskier. Indeed, the Government Take estimate of 92 percent remains a landmark figure (Johnston 2005).[3]

Both of these examples illustrate the success of first-price sealed-bid auctions. In light of the revenue equivalence theorem, this is not surprising. All competitive auctions, regardless of design, should generate substantial government revenues for excellent prospects. However, these examples do not show that the chosen approach was best. Indeed, revenues would be even higher if a simultaneous ascending auction was used.

RECENT EXPERIENCE WITH AUCTIONS
IN OTHER INDUSTRIES

Over the last 10 years, there has been a great advance in the development of methods for auctioning many related items. Innovative auction designs have been proposed and applied to allocation problems in several industries. The auction of radio spectrum is one important example, but these methods have been adopted in several industries, such as energy and transportation.

SIMULTANEOUS ASCENDING AUCTION

The simultaneous ascending auction is one of the most successful methods for auctioning many related items. It was first introduced in U.S. spectrum auctions in July 1994, and later used in dozens of spectrum auctions worldwide, resulting in revenues in excess of $200 billion (Cramton 2002).

The simultaneous ascending auction is a natural generalization of the English auction when selling many items. The key features are that all the items are up for auction at the same time, each with a price associated with it, and the bidders can bid on any of the items. The bidding continues until no bidder is willing to raise the bid on any of the items. Then the auction ends with each bidder winning the items on which it has the high bid, and paying its bid for any items won.

The reason for the success of this simple procedure is the excellent "price discovery" it affords.[4] As the auction progresses bidders see the tentative price information and condition subsequent bids on this new information. Over the course of the auction, bidders are able to develop a sense of what the final prices are likely to be, and can adjust their purchases in response to this price information. To the extent price information is sufficiently good and the bidders retain sufficient flexibility to shift toward their best package, the exposure problem is mitigated—bidders are able to piece together a desirable package of items, despite the constraint of bidding on individual items rather than packages. Moreover, the price information helps the bidders focus their valuation efforts in the relevant range of the price space.

Auctions have become the preferred method of assigning spectrum and most have been simultaneous ascending auctions. (See Cramton 1997 and Milgrom 2004 for a history of the auctions.) There is now substantial evidence that this auction design has been successful (Cramton 1997; McAfee and McMillan 1996), with revenues often exceeding industry and government estimates. The simultaneous ascending auction may be partially responsible for the large revenues. By revealing information in the auction process, bidder uncertainty is reduced, and the bidders safely can bid more aggressively. Also, revenues may increase to the extent the design enables bidders to piece together more efficient packages of items.

Despite the general success, the simultaneous ascending auctions have experienced a few problems from which one can draw important lessons (Cramton and Schwartz 2002). One basic problem is the simultaneous ascending auction's vulnerability to revenue-reducing strategies in situations where competition is weak. Bidders have an incentive to try to work together to reduce their demands in order to keep prices low, and to use bid signaling strategies to coordinate on a split of the items.

A second problem in the early U.S. auctions arose from overly generous installment payment terms for small businesses. This led to speculative bidding. Winning prices were well above subsequent market prices, and most firms defaulted on the installments and went into bankruptcy. The end result was that substantial portions of the mobile wireless capacity lay fallow for nearly 10 years. Some 3G auctions in Europe (notably the U.K. and German auctions) also ended at prices well in excess of subsequent market prices. However, the European auctions did not allow installment payments, so the outcome was simply a wealth transfer from the shareholders of the telecommunications companies to the taxpayers.

SIMULTANEOUS CLOCK AUCTION

A variation of the simultaneous ascending auction is the simultaneous clock auction. The critical difference is that bidders simply respond with *quantities* desired at prices specified by the auctioneer. Clock auctions are especially effective in auctioning many divisible goods, like electricity, but the approach also works well for indivisible items like oil licenses. There is a price "clock" for each item indicating its tentative price. Bidders express the blocks desired at the current prices. For those blocks with excess demand the price is raised and bidders again express their desired blocks at the new prices. This process continues until supply just equals demand. The tentative prices and assignments then become final.

Clock auctions have been used with great success in many countries to auction electricity, gas, pollution allowances, and radio spectrum. Participants value the simplicity and price discovery of the auction. Further, auction theory suggests that in a competitive setting, if bidding is continuous, then the clock auction is efficient with prices equal to the competitive equilibrium (Ausubel and Cramton 2004). This provides a strong rationale to adopt this auction format.

If bidding is not continuous (in the sense that there are discrete rounds) then issues of bid increments, ties, and rationing are important. But there is an easy solution to these problems in which bidders are allowed to express their demands for all points along the line segment between the start of round prices and the end of round prices. Allowing a rich expression of preferences within a round makes bid increments, ties, and rationing less important. Since preferences for intermediate prices can be expressed, the efficiency loss associated with the discrete increment is less, so the auctioneer can choose a larger bid increment, resulting in a faster and less costly auction process.

The problem of noncompetitive settings is more difficult to handle, but there are some things that can be done. Although some auction settings approximate the ideal of perfect competition, most do not. In the U.S. oil auctions, especially in recent years when more marginal tracts have been offered, it is common for tracts to receive one or zero bids. In such a setting, tacit collusion is a real concern with the dynamic auction. One solution is to limit the amount of information that the bidders receive after each round of the auction. In doing this, the auctioneer can enhance the desirable properties of price and assignment discovery, while limiting the scope for collusive bidding. In the clock auction, this is done by only reporting the total quantity demanded for each block, rather than all the bids and bidder identities, as is commonly done in the simultaneous ascending auction.

DETAILS MATTER

Not all auctions are successful. The most common source of failure is a lack of participation. Sometimes this is because what is being sold has little value. Other times the lack of competition is the result of a poor auction process, for example, the product is ill defined, the marketing is inadequate, or the political risks are too great. Recognition of the needs of the bidders is critical in getting participation. An important lesson is that careful planning and design are essential to maximizing results and that this can often be achieved through a prior process of consultation with prospective bidders. These efforts can translate into billions of dollars in higher revenues.

A PRACTICAL PACKAGE AUCTION

We have seen that there are theoretical reasons to expect that some version of a simultaneous ascending auction will make sense for auctioning oil rights; we have seen, further, that this type of auction design has been very successful in other industries. In this section, I describe a practical method for auctioning many related items. The version I describe—the clock-proxy auction (Ausubel et al. 2006)—also allows for package bids and so is especially appropriate to some oil and gas settings. I then turn to discuss variations for situations where packaging issues are less important. All methods are described with oil rights auctions in mind. The items sold are licenses to explore and develop specified geographic blocks. The bidder expresses quantities of either 0 ("No") or 1 ("Yes") for each block offered. The method combines two auction formats—the clock auction and the proxy auction—to produce a hybrid with the benefits of both.

The *clock auction*, as described earlier, is an iterative auction procedure in which the auctioneer announces prices, one for each of the items being sold. The bidders then indicate the licenses desired at the current prices. Prices for items with excess demand then increase, and the bidders again express quantities at the new prices. This process is repeated until there are no items with excess demand.

The *ascending proxy auction* is a particular package bidding procedure with desirable properties (Ausubel and Milgrom 2002). The bidders report values to their respective proxy agents. The proxies are in fact algorithms that receive information from the bidders just once and are then programmed to bid in the interests of the bidder. They iteratively submit package bids on behalf of the bidders, selecting the best profit opportunity for a bidder given the bidder's inputted values. For example, if the proxy is told by a bidder that a block is worth $100M, the proxy will bid up to $100M in order to get the block but will never bid more than is needed to secure the block. The auctioneer then selects the provisionally winning bids that maximize revenues. This process continues until the proxy agents have no new bids to submit.

The clock-proxy auction begins with a clock phase and ends with a final proxy round. All bids are kept live throughout the auction. There are no bid withdrawals and the bids of a particular bidder are mutually exclusive. Finally, there is an activity rule throughout the clock phase and between the clock phase and the proxy round.

CLOCK PHASE

The clock phase has several important benefits. First, it is simple for the bidders. At each round, the bidder simply expresses the set of licenses desired at the current prices. Additive pricing means that it is trivial to evaluate the cost of any package—it is just the sum of the prices for the selected licenses. Limiting the bidders' information to a reporting of the excess demand for each item removes much strategizing. Complex bid signaling and collusive strategies are eliminated, as the bidders cannot see individual bids, but only aggregate information. Second, the clock phase produces highly useable price discovery, because of the item prices. With each bidding round, the bidders get a better understanding of the likely prices for relevant packages. This is essential information in guiding the bidders' decision making. Bidders are able to focus their valuation efforts on the most relevant portion of the price space. As a result, the valuation efforts are more productive. Bidder participation costs fall and efficiency improves.

The weakness of the clock auction is its use of additive pricing at the end of the auction. This means that, to the extent that there is market power, bidders will have an incentive to engage in demand reduction to favorably impact prices. This demand reduction implies that the auction outcome will not be fully efficient (Ausubel and Cramton 2002). The proxy phase will however eliminate this inefficiency.

There are several design choices that will improve the performance of the clock phase, when packaging issues are important. Good choices can avoid the exposure problem, improve price discovery, and handle discrete rounds.

Avoiding the exposure problem

To avoid the exposure problem, the clock phase can allow a bidder to drop a license so long as the price has increased on some license the bidder was demanding. This flexibility is needed in the case of complements. The bidder may want to drop a license when the price of a complementary license increases. With this rule, the clock auction becomes a package auction. For each price vector, the bidder expresses the package of licenses desired without committing itself to demanding any smaller package. The disadvantage of this rule is that the clock phase may end with a substantial number of unsold licenses. However, this undersell will be resolved in the proxy phase.

Improving price discovery

In auctions with more than a few items, the sheer number of packages that a bidder might buy makes it impossible for bidders to determine all their values in advance. Bidders adapt to this problem by focusing most of their attention on the packages that are likely to be valuable relative to their forecast prices. A common heuristic to forecast package prices is to estimate the prices of individual items and to sum these up over the elements in the package. Clock auctions with individual prices assist bidders in this *price discovery* process.

Price discovery is undermined to the extent that bidders misrepresent their demands early in the auction. One possibility is that bidders will choose to underbid in the clock phase, hiding as a "snake in the grass" to conceal their true interests from their opponents. To limit this form of insincere bidding, the U.S. Federal Communications Commission (FCC) introduced the Milgrom-Wilson activity rule, and similar activity rules have since become standard in both clock auctions and simultaneous ascending auctions. In its most typical form, a bidder desiring large quantities at the end of the auction must bid for quantities at least as large early in the auction, when prices are lower.

The most common activity rule in clock auctions is monotonicity in quantity. As prices rise, quantities cannot increase. This means that bidders must bid in a way that is consistent with a weakly downward sloping demand curve. This works well when auctioning a single product, but is overly restrictive when there are many different products. If the products are substitutes, it is natural for a bidder to want to shift quantity from one product to another as prices change, effectively arbitraging the price differences between substitute products.

A weaker activity requirement is a monotonicity of a bidder's *aggregate* quantity. This allows flexibility in shifting among licenses. This is the basis for the FCC's activity rule. A weakness of this rule is that it assumes that quantities are readily comparable. Oil licenses, however, are not comparable. For example, the area of the block is a poor measure of quantity.

Ausubel et al. (2006) propose an alternative activity rule based on revealed preference that does not require any aggregate quantity measure. This rule is suitable for bonus bidding, but not for bidding on production shares. The rule is derived from standard consumer theory and works as follows. Consider any two times, denoted s and t $(s < t)$. Let p^s and p^t be the price vectors at these times. Let x^s and x^t be the associated demands of some bidder at these two points in time, and assume that x^s is different from x^t. Finally, let $v(x)$ be the bidder's value of a given package x. Unfortunately $v(x)$ is not known; nonetheless, we can derive a very simple condition on the relationship between the prices and the quantities if x^s and x^t reflect the demands of a sincere bidder, even though v is not known. With a price vector p^s and a vector of demands for blocks x^s (x^s is in this case a set of 0's and 1's), the amount that a buyer pays is given by $p^s \cdot x^s$. Similarly the total cost of a vector x^t at prices p^s is given by $p^s \cdot x^t$. Now, a sincere bidder prefers x^s to x^t when prices are p^s and prefers x^t to x^s when prices are p^t. This means that:

$$v(x^s) - p^s \cdot x^s \geq v(x^t) - p^s \cdot x^t$$

and

$$v(x^t) - p^t \cdot x^t \geq v(x^s) - p^t \cdot x^s.$$

Adding these two inequalities together yields the *revealed preference activity rule*:

$$(p^t - p^s) \cdot (x^t - x^s) \leq 0.$$

This inequality gives a condition on the prices and quantities that should hold for a sincere bidder without using any information about v. This condition can be used as a rule in auction design: At every time t, the bidder's demand x^t must satisfy this condition for all times $t > s$. Straightforward bidding—bidding on the most profitable package at every instant—will always satisfy the condition.

Handling discrete rounds

As described in the preceding text, discrete bidding rounds are handled with intra-round bidding, enabling the bidder to express quantity reductions at any prices between the start-of-round price and the end-of-round price. This allows the use of much larger bid increments without much loss in efficiency. In this way, the auctioneer can better control the pace of the auction, which is important here given the large uncertainty in block values.

PROXY PHASE

Like the clock auction, the proxy auction is based on package bids. However, the incentives are quite different. The main difference is the absence of additive prices on individual items. Only packages are priced—and the prices may be bidder specific. This weakens price discovery, but the proxy phase is not about price discovery. It is about providing the incentives for efficient assignment. All the price discovery occurs in the clock phase. The second main difference is that the bidders do not bid directly in the proxy phase. Rather, they submit values to the proxy agents, who then bid on their behalf using a specific bidding rule. The proxy agents bid straightforwardly to maximize profits. The proxy phase is a last and final opportunity to bid.

The proxy auction works as follows (see Ausubel and Milgrom 2002). Each bidder reports his values to a proxy agent for all packages that the bidder is interested in. Budget constraints can also be reported. The proxy agent then bids in an ascending package auction on behalf of the real bidder, iteratively submitting the allowable bid that, if accepted, would maximize the real bidder's profit (value minus price), based on the reported values. The auction in theory is conducted with infinitesimally small bid increments. After each round, provisionally winning bids are determined that maximize seller revenue from compatible bids. All of a bidder's bids are kept live throughout the auction and are treated as mutually exclusive. The auction ends after a round with no new bids. For more information on the practicalities of how to implement the proxy phase, see the description in Day and Raghavan (2004).

The advantage of this format is that it produces an outcome for which there is no *other* allocation that the seller and any collection of bidders all prefer (where "preference" is given in terms of the reported preferences of the bidders). In economic theory, we say that such an outcome is in the "core." In principle there can be many outcomes in the core, but every outcome that is in the core has the property that the seller would not be able to find an alternative group of buyers that would be willing, collectively, to pay more for the goods on sale (see Ausubel and Milgrom 2002; Parkes and Ungar 2000). Hence under this method, the seller earns competitive revenues. The fact that the outcome is in the core also implies that it is *efficient*. In particular this means that the proxy auction is not subject to the inefficiency of demand reduction: no bidder can ever reduce the price it pays for the package it wins by withholding some of its losing bids for other packages.

THE CLOCK-PROXY AUCTION

The clock-proxy auction is a recent innovation in auction design. Although it has been used successfully in a spectrum auction in a developing country (Trinidad and Tobago, June 2005), it has not yet been applied to oil rights auctions. The clock-proxy auction begins with a clock auction for price discovery and concludes with the proxy auction to promote efficiency.

The clock auction is conducted with the revealed-preference activity rule until there is no excess demand on any item. The market-clearing item prices determine the initial minimum bids for all packages for all bidders. Bidders then submit values to proxy agents, who bid to maximize profits, subject to a relaxed revealed-preference activity rule (see Ausubel [2006] for details). The relaxed revealed-preference activity rule operates also between the rounds and so bidders that failed to bid aggressively in the clock stage are constrained on how aggressively they can behave in the proxy stage. The bids from the clock phase are kept live as package bids in the proxy phase. All of a bidder's bids, both clock and proxy, are treated as mutually exclusive. Thus, the auctioneer obtains the provisional winning bids after each round of the proxy phase by including all bids—those submitted in the clock phase as well as those submitted in the proxy phase— in the winner determination problem and by selecting at most one provisional winning bid from every bidder. As usual, the proxy phase ends after a round with no new bids.

WHY INCLUDE THE CLOCK PHASE?

The clock phase provides price discovery that bidders can use to guide their calculations in the complex package auction. At each round, bidders are faced with the simple and familiar problem of expressing demands at specified prices. Moreover, because there is no exposure problem, bidders can bid for synergistic gains without fear. Prices then adjust in response to excess demand. As the bidding continues, bidders get a better understanding of what they may win and where their best opportunities lie.

The case for the clock phase relies on the idea that it is costly for bidders to determine their preferences. The clock phase, by providing tentative price information, helps focus a bidder's decision problem. Rather than consider all possibilities from the outset, the bidder can instead focus on cases that are important given the tentative price and assignment information. Although the idea that bidders can make information processing decisions in auctions is valid even in auctions for a single good (Compte and Jehiel 2002), its importance is magnified when there are many goods for sale, because the bidder's decision problem is then much more complicated. Rather than simply decide whether to buy at a given price, the bidder must decide which goods to buy and how many of each. The number of possibilities grows exponentially with the number of goods. Price discovery can play an extremely valuable role in guiding the bidder through the valuation process.

Price discovery in the clock phase makes bidding in the proxy phase vastly simpler. Without the clock phase, bidders would be forced either to determine values for all possible packages or to make uninformed guesses about which packages were likely to be most attractive. My experience with dozens of bidders suggests that the second outcome is much more likely; determining the values of exponentially many packages becomes quickly impractical with even a modest number of items for sale. Using the clock phase to make informed guesses about prices, bidders can focus their decision making on the most relevant packages. The bidders see that they do not need to consider the vast majority of options, because the options are excluded by the prices established in the clock phase. The bidders also get a sense of what packages are most promising, and how their demands fit in the aggregate with those of the other bidders.

In competitive auctions where the items are substitutes and competition is strong, we can expect the clock phase to do most of the work in establishing prices and assignments—the proxy phase would play a limited role. When competition is weak, demand reduction may lead the clock phase to end prematurely, but this problem is corrected at the proxy stage, which eliminates incentives for demand reduction. If the clock auction gives the bidders a good idea of likely package prices, then expressing a simple approximate valuation to the proxy is made easier.

WHY INCLUDE THE PROXY PHASE?

The main advantage of the proxy phase is that it pushes the outcome toward the core, that is, toward an efficient allocation with competitive payoffs for the bidders and competitive revenues for the seller. In the proxy phase, there are no incentives for demand reduction. A large bidder can bid for large quantities without the fear that doing so will adversely impact the price the bidder pays. The proxy phase also mitigates collusion. Any collusive split of the items established in the clock phase can be undone in the proxy phase.

done in the proxy phase. The relaxed activity rule means that the bidders can expand demands in the proxy phase. The allocation is still up for grabs in the proxy phase.

A natural concern with the proxy phase is that it may discourage bidding in the clock phase. The activity rule that operates between the two phases is essential in mitigating this possibility. Bidders bid aggressively in the clock phase, knowing that a failure to do so will limit their options in the proxy phase.

IMPLEMENTATION ISSUES

We briefly discuss three important implementation issues.

Confidentiality of values

One practical issue with the proxy phase is confidentiality of values. Bidders may be hesitant to bid true values in the proxy phase, fearing that the auctioneer would somehow manipulate the prices with a "seller shill"[5] to push prices all the way to the bidders' reported values. Steps need to be taken to assure that this cannot happen. A highly transparent auction process helps to assure that the auction rules are followed. In fact, there is no reason that the auctioneer needs to be given access to the high values. Only the computer need know. Auction software can be tested and certified to be consistent with the auction rules. At the end of the auction, the auctioneer can report all the bids. The bidders can then confirm that the outcome was consistent with the rules.

Price increments in the clock phase

When auctioning many items, one must take care in defining the price adjustment process. This is especially true when some goods are complements. Intuitively, the clock phase performs best when each item clears at roughly the same time. Thus, the goal should be to come up with a price adjustment process that reflects relative values as well as excess demand. Moreover, the price adjustment process effectively is resolving the "threshold problem" by specifying who should contribute what as the clock ticks higher.[6] To the extent that prices adjust with relative values, the resolution of the threshold problem will be more successful.

One simple approach is to build the relative value information into the initial starting prices. Then use a *percentage* increase rather than a fixed increment increase, based on the extent of excess demand. For example, the percentage increment could vary linearly with the excess demand, subject to a lower and upper limit. This will make it more likely that the demand for the different items clears at about the same time.

Expression of proxy values

Even with the benefit of the price discovery in the clock phase, expressing a valuation function in the proxy phase may be difficult for bidders. When many items are being sold, the bidder will need a tool to facilitate translating preferences into proxy values. The best tool will depend on the circumstances. The seller can lower bidder participation costs by providing a useful tool to express valuations.

At a minimum, the tool will allow an additive valuation function. The bidder submits its maximum willingness to pay for each license. The value of a package is then found by adding up the values on each item in the package. This additive model ignores all value interdependencies across items; it assumes that the value for one item is independent of what other items are won. Although globally (across a wide range of packages) this might be a bad assumption, locally (across a narrow range of packages) this might be a reasonable approximation, especially in the setting of oil rights. Hence, provided the clock phase has taken us close to the equilibrium, so the proxy phase is only doing some fine-tuning of the clock outcome, then such a simplistic tool may perform reasonably well. And of course it performs very well when bidders actually have additive values.

The bidders' business plans are a useful guide to determine how best to structure the valuation tool in a particular setting. Business plans are an expression of value to investors. Although the details of the business plans are not available to the auctioneer, one can construct a useful valuation tool from understanding the basic structure of these business plans.

ALTERNATIVE AUCTION FORMATS AND RECOMMENDATIONS

It is not possible to specify one "best" design—the best approach depends on the setting. The clock-proxy auction as described above is an excellent choice in settings where packaging issues are important. In other settings, variations are worth considering. The variations depend on how four features are handled (table 5.1).

The standard clock-proxy auction is defined by the first option (a) for each issue in table 5.1: clock bidding for packages with the revealed prefer-

Table 5.1   Designing a Clock-Proxy Auction

Feature:	1. Clock bidding	2. Activity rule	3. Proxy bidding	4. Pricing in proxy phase
Options:	a. Package bids	a. Revealed preference	a. Package bids	a. Bidder-optimal core
	b. Individual license bids	b. License-by-license monotonicity	b. Individual license bids	b. Pay-as-bid
	c. None		c. None	

Note: This table lists the main options available to auction designers for four key components of the clock-proxy auction.

ence activity rule, followed by a final proxy round with package bids and bidder-optimal core pricing. This is a sensible choice when packaging issues, value interdependencies and price discovery are important aspects of the setting. This approach is the most difficult to implement, but accommodates the richest set of bidder valuations.

At the other extreme is the U.S. offshore approach, which is simultaneous seal-bid for individual licenses with pay-as-bid pricing (1c, 3b, 4b). This approach makes sense if there are no packaging issues (e.g., additive values), little value interdependencies, weak competition, and potentially large asymmetries among the bidders. Although this method is easy to implement, it is problematic for bidders unless values really are additive.

Another variation, close to the U.S. approach, has clock bidding on individual licenses, a license-by-license activity rule, and no proxy bidding (1b, 2b, 3c). This effectively is a simultaneous ascending auction version of the U.S. approach. This is sensible in settings where packaging is of only minor importance (nearly additive values), but value interdependencies make price discovery important. This approach also works best when competition is not too weak and bidder asymmetries are not too large.

A similar variation, close to the U.S. spectrum auctions, is clock bidding on individual licenses, a revealed preference activity rule, and no proxy round (1b, 2a, 3c). This works well when there are moderate packaging issues and value interdependencies. The approach has good price discovery and does allow bidders to piece together desirable packages of licenses. The format improves on the U.S. spectrum auctions in two respects. Tacit collusion is mitigated with the use of clocks and only reporting excess demand, rather than all bids. Efficient packaging is facilitated with the revealed preference activity rule. This method is easy to implement and yet accommodates a richer set of valuations.

A final variation, related to the Anglo-Dutch format[7] (Klemperer 2002), has clock bidding on individual licenses, a revealed preference activity rule, and a proxy round with individual license bids and pay-as-bid pricing (1b, 2a, 3b, 4b). However, in this variation, the price clock stops when demand falls to two on the license, so there is still excess demand. The excess demand is then resolved in the simultaneous pay-as-bid proxy round. This approach is well suited to situations where packaging is of minor importance (nearly additive values), but value interdependencies make price discovery valuable, and competition is weak with potentially large bidder asymmetries. The approach enjoys some of the price discovery benefits of the dynamic methods, but handles weak competition and bidder asymmetries better than the approach without a last-and-final round. The approaches are summarized in table 5.2.

For settings in which there are sets of licenses with substantially different value structures, it makes sense to use different formats with different sets of licenses. For example, a country may have 12 wildcat blocks that are excellent prospects, 36 drainage blocks that are good to excellent prospects, and 200 blocks that are marginal prospects. The excellent prospects could be done as a standard clock-proxy, the drainage blocks as an Anglo-Dutch, and the marginal prospects as a first-price sealed-bid. With this approach the clock-proxy auction is not complicated by the great number of drainage and marginal blocks. Moreover, the drainage blocks may have large asymmetries among the bidders as a result of private drilling information from neighboring blocks. The Anglo-Dutch design handles these asymmetries well. Finally, additive values are probably a good assumption on marginal prospects and in any event, the economic loss from the less efficient first-price sealed-bid approach is not great when auctioning marginal licenses. Alternatively, since implementing three different formats is probably too much, the country could split the blocks into two sets: those with high prospects and those with low prospects. The first-price sealed-bid format could be used for the low-prospect blocks and one of the dynamic formats could be used for the high-prospect blocks.

LIBYA AND VENEZUELA RECONSIDERED

Although the 2005 Libya auction and 1996 Venezuela auction were successful, they could probably be improved. The Libya auction, using simultaneous sealed-bids, prevented both price discovery and efficient

Table 5.2 Alternative Auction Approaches

Interdependence of Valuations Across Bidders	Interdependence of Valuations Across Blocks			
	Additive values	**Nearly additive values**	**Substitutes and mild complements**	**Complex structure of substitutes and complements**
Private values	**First-Price Sealed-Bid** Simultaneous sealed-bid Pay-as-bid pricing **Notes:** Easiest to implement. No price discovery. Handles weak competition. Handles bidder asymmetries.	**Anglo-Dutch Clock** (see below)	**Clock with Switching** (see below)	**Clock-Proxy** (see below)
Mostly private values	**Anglo-Dutch Clock** (see right)	**Anglo-Dutch Clock** Clock individual bids (stops with demand = 2) Revealed preference activity rule Proxy with individual bids Pay-as-bid pricing **Notes:** Harder to implement. Some price discovery. Handles weak competition. Handles bidder asymmetries.	**Clock with Switching** (see below)	**Clock-Proxy** (see below)
Interdependent values	**Clock No Switching** (see right)	**Clock No Switching** Clock individual bids License-by-license activity rule **Notes:** Easy to implement. Good price discovery with nearly additive values. Handles production shares.	**Clock with Switching** Clock individual bids Revealed preference activity rule No final proxy round **Notes:** Harder to implement. Very good price discovery.	**Clock-Proxy** Clock package bids Revealed preference activity rule Proxy package bids Bidder-optimal core pricing **Notes:** Hardest to implement. Excellent price discovery. Excellent efficiency. Competitive revenues.

packaging. The Venezuela auction, using sequential sealed-bids, allowed only minimal price discovery and packaging. In both auctions, competition was anticipated to be strong. Values included both private and common elements, although the common elements were more important. Values probably were nearly additive, although bidders likely faced budget and risk constraints given the size of the commitment.

In such a setting, a simultaneous clock auction is desirable, and especially simple given the small number of blocks. Bids would be over the production share. In the case of Venezuela, the 50 percent cap on production share could be dropped and the terms could be adjusted so that the government has a share in the development capital expense, thereby improving the development incentives without limiting the production share. A license-by-license activity rule (no switching) is desirable given the bidding is on production shares. Under this rule, once a bidder stops bidding on a block, the bidder cannot return to the block at higher production shares. This simple rule allows price discovery and some degree of packaging.

CONCLUSION

Auctions are a desirable method of assigning and pricing scarce oil rights. A well-designed auction encourages participation through a transparent competitive process. The design promotes both an efficient assignment of the rights and competitive revenues for the seller.

I find that a variety of auction formats are suitable for auctioning oil rights. The best auction format depends on the particular setting, especially the structure of bidder preferences and the degree of competition. When bidders have additive values and competition is weak, a simultaneous first-price sealed-bid auction may be best, especially if the blocks are marginal prospects (relatively low value). When bidders have nearly additive values and competition is stronger, then one of the clock auctions should be considered. This approach will improve price discovery and reduce bidder uncertainty, improving efficiency and revenues. Finally, for high-value blocks in which packaging issues are important (bidders care about the particular package of blocks won), a clock-proxy auction is appropriate. The clock-proxy auction has excellent price discovery and handles complex bidder preferences involving substitutes and complements. The clock-proxy auction does well on both efficiency and revenue grounds.

In closing, I emphasize a theme raised elsewhere in this volume (see especially chapters 2 and 3): Regardless of the auction format, a critical element of the design is defining *what* is being bid. The *what* element is just as important as the *how* element. Possibilities include bonus bids, royalty rates, or production shares. Bidding on production shares, rather than bonuses, for example, typically increases Government Take by reducing oil company risk and fears of expropriation. More generally, these contract terms determine key features such as the allocation of risk between country and oil company, the cash flows over time, and the incentives for exploration and development.

ACKNOWLEDGMENT

I gratefully acknowledge the support of National Science Foundation Grants SES-01-12906, IIS-02-05489, and SES-05-31254.

NOTES

1. Sealed-bid auctions are static auctions in which the bidders simultaneously submit bids in sealed envelopes to the auctioneer. The auctioneer then orders the bids from highest to lowest. The highest bidder wins the item. In a first-price auction, the highest bidder pays its bid. In a second-price auction, the highest bidder pays the second-highest bid for the item. The English ascending and Dutch descending are dynamic auctions that occur in a series of rounds or with a continuous price "clock." In the English auction, the bidders have the opportunity to improve their bids until no bidder is willing to bid any higher; the high bidder then pays its bid. In the Dutch auction, the auctioneer begins with a high price that no bidder is willing to accept; the auctioneer then reduces the price until a bidder indicates acceptance; this bidder wins the item and pays the last price called out by the auctioneer.

2. However, a likely exception to this recommendation is for drainage blocks in which one bidder has much better information about value.

3. Government Take is a calculated estimate of the government's share in the project profits, given all the contract terms. Production share is simply the split of the oil revenue between government and the oil company. Thus, it is perfectly reasonable for Government Take to be 92 percent even though the production share is 50 percent.

4. Price discovery is a feature of dynamic auctions in which tentative price information is reported to bidders, giving bidders the opportunity to adjust subsequent bids based on the price information.

5. A seller shill is a fake bidder created by the seller. The shill bids in a way to increase auction revenues. Shills are especially a problem in ascending auctions and second-price auctions.

6. The threshold problem is the problem that allowing package bids may favor bidders seeking larger packages, because small bidders do not have the incentive or capability to unilaterally top the tentative winning bids of a large bidder.

7. The Anglo-Dutch format is an ascending clock auction that stops while there is still excess demand, at which point a final first-price sealed-bid round is conducted among those bidders that are still active at the end of the clock phase.

REFERENCES

Ausubel, L. M. and P. Cramton. 2004. "Auctioning Many Divisible Goods." *Journal of the European Economic Association* 2: 480–93.

Ausubel, L. M., P. Cramton, and P. Milgrom. 2006. "The Clock-Proxy Auction: A Practical Combinatorial Auction Design." In *Combinatorial Auctions*, P. Cramton, Y. Shoham, and R. Steinberg, eds. Cambridge: MIT Press, pp. 115–38.

Ausubel, L. M. and P. Milgrom. 2002. "Ascending Auctions with Package Bidding." *Frontiers of Theoretical Economics* 1: 1–45. http://www.bepress.com/bejte/frontiers/vol1/iss1/art1.

Compte, O. and P. Jehiel. 2002. "Auctions and Information Acquisition: Sealed-Bid or Dynamic Formats?" Working Paper, CERAS-ENPC.

Cramton, P. 1997. "The FCC Spectrum Auctions: An Early Assessment." *Journal of Economics and Management Strategy* 6: 431–95.

Cramton, P. 2002. "Spectrum Auctions." In *Handbook of Telecommunications Economics*, M. Cave, S. Majumdar, and I. Vogelsang, eds. Amsterdam: Elsevier Science, pp. 605–39.

Cramton, P. and J. Schwartz. 2002. "Collusive Bidding in the FCC Spectrum Auctions." *Contributions to Economic Analysis & Policy* 1: 1. http://www.bepress.com/bejeap/contributions/vol1/iss1/art11.

Cramton, P., Y. Shoham, and R. Steinberg. 2006. *Combinatorial Auctions*. Cambridge, MA: MIT Press.

Day, R. W. and S. Raghavan. 2004. "Generation and Selection of Core Outcomes in Sealed-Bid Combinatorial Auctions." Working Paper, University of Maryland.

Hendricks, K. and R. H. Porter. 1996. "The Timing and Incidence of Exploratory Drilling on Offshore Wildcat Tracts." *American Economic Review* 86: 388–407.

Hendricks, K., R. H. Porter, and B. Boudreau. 1987. "Information, Returns, and Bidding Behavior in OCS Auctions: 1954–1969." *Journal of Industrial Economics* 35: 517–42.

Johnston, D. 2005. "Tough Terms—No Surprises: Libya EPSA IV License Round, 29 January 2005." White Paper, Daniel Johnston & Co.

Johnston, D. and D. Johnston. 2001. "Kashagan and Tengiz—Castor and Plux." White Paper, Daniel Johnston & Co.

Klemperer, P. 2002. "What Really Matters in Auction Design." *Journal of Economic Perspectives* 16: 169–89.

Maskin, E. and J. Riley. 2000. "Asymmetric Auctions." *Review of Economic Studies* 67: 439–54.

McAfee, R. P. and J. McMillan. 1996. "Analyzing the Airwaves Auction." *Journal of Economic Perspectives* 10: 159–76.

Milgrom, P. 1987. "Auction Theory." In *Advances in Economic Theory—Fifth World Congress*, T. Bewley, ed. Cambridge, UK: Cambridge University Press, pp. 1–31.

Milgrom, P. 2004. *Putting Auction Theory to Work*. Cambridge, UK: Cambridge University Press.

Milgrom, P. and R. J. Weber. 1982. "A Theory of Auctions and Competitive Bidding." *Econometrica* 50: 1089–122.

Parkes, D. C. and L. H. Ungar. 2000. "Iterative Combinatorial Auctions: Theory and Practice." Proceedings of the 17th National Conference on Artificial Intelligence (AAAI-00), pp. 74–81.

Porter, R. H. 1995. "The Role of Information in U.S. Offshore Oil and Gas Lease Auctions." *Econometrica* 63: 1–28.

Sunley, E. M., T. Baunsgaard, and D. Simard. 2002. "Revenue from the Oil and Gas Sector: Issues and Country Experience." IMF Conference Paper.

PART II

MANAGING
THE MACROECONOMY

CHAPTER 6

Are Oil Producers Rich?

Geoffrey Heal

ABSTRACT

What can national income accounting tell us about whether resource-depleting nations are rich or poor? I argue that most conventional statements of national income overestimate the incomes of such countries by failing to account for resource depletion. Perhaps more importantly, they typically overestimate investment. I derive here a correct measure of trends in sustainable welfare which takes account of the changes in all capital stocks, including stocks of natural capital. This chapter also demonstrates how this measure can be calculated for individual countries and used to ascertain whether oil-exporting countries are consuming too much too quickly.

INTRODUCTION

There is a popular image of an oil-producing country, a real stereotype: It is of a very rich land where no one needs to work and everything is provided by the state. True, some other aspects of the image are typically less attractive, but the essential popular image relates to extreme abundance. Yet, in sharp contrast to this we find a vast and growing literature on the "resource curse" that documents how and why an abundance of natural resources, in fact, leads to social and economic problems. How can we reconcile these conflicting images? How can we reconcile the seemingly obvious fact that oil makes a country rich with the equally undeniable fact that few countries heavily dependent on the production of oil are as rich, in terms of per capita income, as many developed countries (Norway is an obvious exception), and, moreover, rarely even appear to be moving toward that goal?

This chapter focuses on features of this paradox that can be illuminated by thinking clearly about the basic ideas of income and wealth, and about how these ideas relate to accounts of national income and national wealth; that is, to national income statements and national balance sheets. The role of capital markets proves to be central to the apparent paradox of poor resource-exporting countries. I shall argue that the exhaustibility of oil makes income generated from oil quite different from income generated by other sources in terms of its implications for the country's underlying wealth, and that a failure to see this explains much of the apparent paradox.

Before developing these arguments in detail, some facts may shed light on the problem. Take Saudi Arabia, an extreme case and for some a poster child for the oil producer as economic utopia: Its proven reserves of oil are 262.7 billion barrels, and its population is 25 million.[1] So, at $30 per barrel—a typical oil price for 2003 and 2004—its oil wealth per capita is $315,240. Does this make Saudi Arabia rich? Imagine that Saudi Arabia truly were a country where oil wealth meant that no one needed to work. If the wealth were to be invested at a 4 percent real return, this would provide a typical family of four with about $50,000 per year (that is, assuming an equal division of the wealth or income; we know, however, that for reasons discussed in this book, oil wealth is usually spread very unequally). This would be a very comfortable income indeed, but would not qualify as rich by Western standards. Doing the same calculation for all oil-producing countries in the Middle East, the number for a family of four is closer to $8,000. If we move the oil price up to its present level in 2006, say $60, then we double these numbers, implying that an average Saudi family—if it could invest its share of the country's oil wealth—could earn $100,000 per year; an average family in a typical Middle Eastern oil producer would make about $16,000 per year. So, even at current elevated oil prices, while oil wealth could dramatically increase the quality of living for a family of four, these numbers are not necessarily consistent with the images of 'extreme' abundance.

But there is a second way of looking at the data that makes oil wealth seem even less abundant. Saudi Arabia produces about 8 million barrels of oil daily for an annual oil revenue of $175 billion. Expressed per family of four, this is $28,000 per year—barely above the U.S. poverty line, even at $60 per barrel. At the average oil price for the last decade, the figure is well below the U.S. poverty level—even for Saudi Arabia, one of

ARE OIL PRODUCERS RICH? 157

the richest oil-producing countries in the world. Further, and most importantly, this income, if used for consumption, is *not sustainable* since it depends on the depletion of a finite stock. As discussed below, the real income, taking into account the depletion of stocks, is considerably lower still and may be near zero. This second way of calculating oil revenues is in fact the more realistic of the two approaches since Saudi Arabia is not in a position to invest its oil wealth: Most of this wealth lies in the ground earning no income.

The contrast between these two calculations foreshadows a point I shall be emphasizing in the sections that follow. To summarize briefly, if Saudi Arabia could sell all its oil now and invest the proceeds at 4 percent then a typical family could earn about $100,000 per year. (Selling all that oil, however, would surely force the price down dramatically given the inelasticity of demand.) But, if Saudi Arabia just extracts as much oil as it can—about 8 million barrels daily—then the per-family income is just over a quarter of this, at $28,000. Why the difference? The important point to learn from this is that capital markets matter to oil-producing countries. Their access to these markets, and how well they use them, is a major factor in determining their living standards. In fact, they depend on capital markets as much as they depend on their natural resources. Oil in the ground earns no income and contributes nothing to welfare, however envious the rest of the world may be of this asset. Envy, however, does not pay interest, whereas money in an investment fund does, so it clearly pays (from a financial point of view) to turn oil in the ground into money in a bank account. But this involves huge transactions and assumptions about future oil prices (for more political economy arguments on why keeping wealth in the ground may be safer, see chapter 2). In other words, it involves access to a comprehensive set of capital markets.

One message of this chapter is that if we think clearly about what we mean by income and wealth, then a resource-rich country such as Saudi Arabia is not necessarily "rich" in the conventional sense (see also chapter 7). Its income as properly measured may be near zero, and whether it owns wealth and can convert some of this into income depends entirely on its access to capital markets. Thus, the central role of capital markets in the welfare of resource-rich countries, which has perhaps not been adequately highlighted elsewhere, is another message of this chapter.

A third point that I emphasize is that *any measure of income or of wealth change must allow for the depletion of the natural resource stock.* Conventional measures of national income such as gross national income

(GNI) and gross domestic product (GDP) do not do this and therefore overstate, probably quite significantly, the real income of these countries. From the perspective of understanding the evolution of long-run welfare—the "sustainability" perspective—the important measure is what Heal and Kriström (2005) call national wealth, the change in which can be captured by the World Bank's (1997) "genuine savings" measure. This is the value *at shadow prices* of the changes in all capital stocks, including changes in natural resource stocks. The shadow price of a good is the social value of an extra increment of the good: If there is a market price, it equals the market price corrected for external costs or benefits associated with the use of the good. Depletion of natural resources has, of course, to be included in calculating the value of the change in capital stocks. In the last section of the chapter I review some recent calculations (from Arrow et al. 2004) of trends in total capital stock per capita for a range of countries, including some oil producers. Incorporating the changes in natural capital stocks makes a big difference to our perception of a country's sustainability if it is a resource exporter. All resource exporters appear to be depleting natural capital faster than they are building up other forms of capital, and so are becoming poorer, whatever their income levels.

The next section of the chapter sets out a rather general model and uses it to draw some broad conclusions about welfare. It also provides a framework for a series of applications to more specific models that capture key aspects of resource-rich but otherwise underdeveloped countries. A final section summarizes the arguments and suggests some policy implications. Central to these sections is to understand that savings and investment as reported by conventional national income accounts are grossly overstated: Real investment is less than measured investment by the amount of resource depletion. Hence, very high rates of savings and investment as conventionally measured are needed if there is to be real accumulation of capital to sustain future welfare.

GENERAL WELFARE RESULTS AND APPLICATIONS

We begin with a general mathematical proposition and a result on welfare in dynamic economic models. We define a *state valuation function*, $V(S)$ that tells us the present value of the benefits that can be obtained from a current level of capital stock (the "state"), S. It is a measure of the maximum amount of welfare that an economy can produce now and in the future. This is found by using a welfare function $u(C_t)$ that records welfare from consuming C_t at each instant t, and then summing (integrating) this value from time $t = 0$ up to $t = \infty$, placing lower weights on more distant periods. Using the framework and notation in Heal and Kriström (2005), the intertemporal optimization problem of maximizing the present value of welfare given some initial state S_0 is given by:

$$V(S_0) = \text{Max} \int_0^\infty u(C_t)e^{-\delta t}dt$$

subject to a set of constraints imposed by technology, institutions, and resource availability.

This is the classical optimal growth problem of which special cases are well known.[2] From an analysis of the solutions to such problems one can prove that:

- The rate of change of the state valuation function, V, equals the value of investment at shadow prices.
- Both of these are equal to the rate of change of national income, where national income is defined as the present value of consumption at shadow prices.

These features are summarized in the following proposition (note that in this example national income refers to the present discounted value of consumption at all dates, calculated at shadow prices):

Proposition 1. (Heal and Kriström 2005): The change in welfare over time is exactly equal to "genuine savings" which is itself exactly equal to the change in national income over time. Formally we have:

$$\frac{dV}{dt} = \sum_i \lambda_i \frac{dS_i}{dt} = \frac{d}{dt}(\text{National Income}) = \frac{d}{dt}\left(\int_0^\infty \sum \lambda_i c_i e^{-\delta t}dt\right)$$

Here λ_i is the shadow price of capital good i, the stock of which is S_i. Consumption of good i is given by c_i. The term $\sum_i \lambda_i \frac{dS_i}{dt}$ represents "genuine savings" and records the total value of investment (including resource depletion). This quantity has recently been the subject of extensive study by the World Bank (2005). Proposition 1 is critical in what follows: It tells us that both the value of investment and the change in the value of

national income are good measures of future welfare changes. The more invested today, the higher future welfare. It is important to emphasize that welfare changes are given by the value of investment *at shadow prices,*
$\sum_i \lambda_i \dfrac{dS_i}{dt}$, and not by the total change in wealth, $\dfrac{d}{dt}\left(\sum_i \lambda_i S_i\right)$ which would, in addition, contain a term in capital gains.[3] It is important to note that capital gains have no role to play in accounting for natural resources. The next issue is to investigate these measures in particular contexts that relate directly to the resource curse.

MODELS OF RESOURCE DEPLETION

THE HOTELLING CASE

Hotelling's model (1931) provides a simple and well understood framework for beginning this process. There is an initial stock S_0 of an exhaustible resource (such as oil), consumption of which at time t is C_t, and the rate of depletion of the resource stock is given simply by the rate at which

it is consumed or $\dfrac{dS}{dt} = -C$, conditional on $S_t \geq 0$.

The usual way to measure net national product (NNP) is consumption plus investment. But in this framework, since consumption equals the rate of depletion, net income (consumption plus investment) is always zero by definition. Formally:

$$\text{NNP} = \frac{dS}{dt} + C = 0$$

In an economy that lives purely by resource depletion, income in the sense of NNP is always zero, even though wealth is positive. In other words, there is no *sustainable* positive level of spending in this framework. This makes intuitive sense: The economy has a fixed resource base that can only change in one way, downwards. So, potential welfare must drop as the resource is consumed.

Access to capital markets makes a big difference to this conclusion, and, in fact, overturns it: With access to capital markets, it is possible to get a sustainable spending level and a nonzero income. Imagine that, instead of producing the resource gradually over time, the country sells the *entire* stock of the resource S_0 at one go and invests the proceeds: Now the interest on this investment gives a sustainable consumption level. Indeed it is precisely what Hicks (1939) called *income*: That is, income is the return on capital. Formally, if r is the interest rate and Y_0 is income, we have:

$$Y_0 = rS_0$$

In this modified framework with overseas investment, the depletion of the capital stock is now $\frac{dS}{dt} = rS - C$, where the first term is income and the second is expenditure, and so NNP, which is investment plus consumption, is now given by:

$$\text{NNP} = \frac{dS}{dt} + C = rS \neq 0$$

So access to capital markets transforms NNP from zero to a positive number: It allows the transformation of nonearning assets into earning assets, making a fundamental difference to income. This is the point that is reflected in the numerical example pertaining to Saudi Arabia in the introduction. Providing access to capital markets is like giving the economy a superior technology, a greater intertemporally feasible set: Even though the physical resource base is unchanged, its welfare potential is improved.

AN OPEN ECONOMY

The next move is to develop this insight about capital markets further. I no longer assume that the entire stock of the resource is sold up front. I shall assume that a flow of the resource can be extracted and then either consumed at home or sold abroad and the revenues from this invested overseas. So, at each date, the output of the resource is either consumed C or invested abroad I_f, and the economy's basic accounting identity is that the sum of consumption and overseas investment must equal the depletion of the resource plus any income earned on existing overseas investments:

$$C + I_f = -\frac{dS}{dt} + rK_f \tag{2}$$

where K_f is overseas capital and r is the interest rate on this, and I_f is overseas investment so that $I_f = \dfrac{dK_f}{dt}$. Consider a path that solves the maximization problem $Max \displaystyle\int_0^\infty u(C)e^{-\delta t}\,dt$ subject to Eq. (2). The two conditions that need to be satisfied at the solution are:

1. On the margin, investing overseas and consuming must be equally valuable ($u' = \lambda_s = \lambda_i = \lambda$); and

2. The percentage change in the (shadow) price of the resource over time is equal to the difference between the discount rate and the return on overseas investment $\left(\dfrac{d\lambda}{dt}\dfrac{1}{\lambda} = \delta - r \right)$. If the latter exceeds the former then the price of the resource will fall over time because the return to investment is so large that the resource is in effect becoming more abundant.

NNP is now $C + I_f + \dfrac{dS}{dt} = rK_f$ so it is equivalent to the interest on overseas investments, just as in the previous section. The change in the state valuation function, V, is $\lambda\left(I_f + \dfrac{dS}{dt} \right)$, the value of investment including capital investment and stock depletion. This represents the change in the present value of welfare as a result of investment and depletion: Welfare is increasing if the value of investment exceeds that of stock depletion.

A natural next step in extending the model is to let r be a function of overseas investment, K_f, reflecting diminishing returns to investment in overseas opportunities. Given the scale on which oil countries must invest, the possibility that they will move the market against them is real. In this case, the second condition above has to change to include a term reflecting the impact of investment on the return to capital:

$$\frac{d\lambda}{dt}\frac{1}{\lambda} = \delta - r - \frac{dr}{dK_f}K_f$$

A stationary solution (in which $\dfrac{d\lambda}{dt} = 0$) would then require: $\delta = r + \dfrac{dr}{dK_f}K_f$. With $\dfrac{d\lambda}{dt} = 0$, consumption is also constant. Over time, the resource stock S falls to zero and the overseas capital stock K rises to some constant value. In this case NNP is $r(K_f)K_f$ and the change in welfare as a result of investment and depletion is again $\lambda\left(I_f + \dfrac{dS_t}{dt}\right)$. The bottom line here is that, as the introduction to this chapter suggested, access to capital markets makes a huge difference to the economic constraints on a resource-rich country. Its income—even accounting for depreciation—goes from zero to a positive number, equal to interest on overseas investments; there is a positive consumption level that can now be sustained indefinitely.

AN OPEN ECONOMY WITH EXTRACTION CAPITAL

So far, we have assumed that the economy can extract any amount of the resource without incurring any costs. This is, however, somewhat unrealistic. Suppose instead that you have to invest in order to extract the resource, and that, as above, you can invest the proceeds from sale in overseas assets. Let I_d denote domestic investment in extraction capital K_d, and I_f denote investment in overseas interest-bearing assets K_f with interest rate r. The rate at which the resource can be extracted is bounded by the amount of investment in extraction capital, so that if R is the extraction rate, then $R \le \alpha K_d$. As before, we maximize the welfare from all future consumption where consumption is given by the output of the resource, minus investments in domestic and overseas capital, plus interest on existing overseas investments. Assuming that the output of the resource is proportional to the capital available for resource extraction (that is, $\dfrac{dS}{dt} = \alpha K_d$) we have:

$$C = \alpha Kd - I_f - I_d + rK_f$$

At any solution to this problem the values of both types of capital must be equal if there is investment in both (that is, $u' = \lambda_f = \lambda_d$ if both I_f and I_d are positive). At the optimum, however, λ_f and λ_d should change at different rates, since the change in λ_f should reflect the difference between the discount rate and the interest rate on foreign assets, while the change in λ_d should reflect the difference between the discount rate and the efficiency of the extraction technology (α). Hence, because they change at different rates but must be equal if both I_f and I_d are positive, it cannot be that the country invests both in foreign assets and in extraction for any length of time. Presumably countries start off by investing in positive capital extraction and later—once the stock of extraction capital is built up to an appropriate level—shift investment to foreign investment, leaving extraction capital constant.

In this model as in the earlier ones, all investment levels will feature in NNP:

$$\text{NNP} = C + r_f K_f + I_f + I_d - \alpha K_d$$

and the change in the state valuation function is $\lambda_f I_f + \lambda_d I_d - \lambda_s \alpha K_d$. Hence, again, the depletion of the resource needs to be taken into account in the measurement of welfare.

EXTRACTION CAPITAL AND USE IN PRODUCTION

As the final variant of the basic Hotelling model of resource depletion, I consider the case of a closed economy that extracts a resource and then uses it in domestic production. Extraction of the resource leads to domestic output, which can be invested. So the resource can, as in the previous sections, be transformed into a capital stock, this time through the domestic production process. Extraction of the resource is costly: To be precise, $X(R)$ is the cost of extracting at rate R. We assume that X is increasing in R. Domestic production depends on inputs of capital and the resource and is given by $Y = f(K,R)$, where the capital stock, K, depends on investment I. This time we aim to maximize the integral of the welfare from consumption conditional on the constraints that $\dfrac{dS}{dt} = R$ and the accounting identity: $Y = C + I + X$, or equivalently: $I = f(K,R) - C - X(R)$.

A solution to this problem requires that the shadow price of the resource equals its marginal productivity in the domestic economy ($\partial F/\partial R$); that consumption and investment are valued equally on the margin; that the resource price follows Hotelling's Rule (the percentage change in the price of the good is exactly equal to the discount rate) and remains constant in present value terms; and, finally, that the accumulation of capital follows the well-known Keynes-Ramsey rule. This rule—which states that the percentage change in the shadow price of the capital good must be equal to the difference between the discount rate and the marginal return to capital in the economy (see, e.g., Heal 1973)—simply specifies that the country's capital assets be efficiently used, and that the breakdown of income between consumption and investment is such that the returns to each are equal on the margin.

NNP in this case should be:

$$NNP = C + I - R$$

and the change in welfare is $I - R$. Once again, the possibility of transforming the resource into a capital stock means that, in spite of its exhaustibility, the economy can attain a positive income level. Indeed, a positive level may even be sustainable, depending on whether the resource is "essential" or not, as shown in Dasgupta and Heal (1979).

THEORETICAL SUMMARY

The theoretical models developed so far, which certainly capture what is unique about resource-based economies, imply very clearly that accounting for the changes in capital stocks is a prerequisite for understanding the evolution of welfare in an economy. As the natural resource stock is an important capital stock—often the most important (see World Bank 2005)—this means that depletion of this stock *must be measured and recorded in national income accounts if these are to have any predictive value for welfare.* In plain English, resource depletion must be deducted from national income. This is not conventionally done and, as a result, national income figures are too high and the growth of national income is overstated. But national income in the conventional sense is not the best measure if we are interested in the long-run welfare potential of the economy. The right measure instead is $\sum_i \lambda_i \frac{dS_i}{dt}$, the value of investment at current shadow prices. Again, stock depletion will feature in this.

This is not the only point to emerge from this discussion: Another related point is that a resource-rich country's relationship with capital markets is important in determining its living standards. Oil in the ground brings in no income and is inherently depletable. Through trade and capital markets, however, or through use as an input into domestic production, it can be converted to a stock of wealth of another sort, which generates income and can in principle be preserved indefinitely.

In the next section we show the practical applicability of this framework, summarizing recent work by Arrow et al. (2004). This work attempts to compute the value of investment at current shadow prices $\sum_i \lambda_i \dfrac{dS_i}{dt}$ for a wide range of countries, from rich industrialized to poor developing and oil-producing. The calculation of trends in genuine wealth per capita, allowing for technical change, allows us to rank countries by their long-run welfare trends. A striking conclusion is that *most oil-exporting countries have a negative trend in long-run welfare*. The conclusions of Arrow et al. are supported by a recent study just released by the World Bank (2005), which presents more recent results for a wide range of countries and also shows that resource-rich countries are depleting their overall capital stocks and facing declining welfare levels, and will continue to do so unless they substantially change their policies (the World Bank study does not allow for technical progress).

APPLICATIONS

Table 6.1 shows the results that Arrow et al. (2004) find when we compute the value of investment at current shadow prices $\sum_i \lambda_i \dfrac{dS_i}{dt}$ for a wide range of countries, including two rich industrial countries, the United States and the United Kingdom; two rapidly growing developing countries, India and China; two very poor developing countries/regions, Bangladesh and Sub-Saharan Africa; and one oil-exporting region, the Middle East and North Africa. The data cover the period 1970 to 2001 and are taken from the World Bank (1997).[4] The first numerical column shows domestic net investment, the starting point of the calculations and an estimate of investment in physical capital. To this is added expenditure on education as an indicator of investment in human capital. We then add investment (usually disinvestment) in various types of environmental capital. The third numerical column shows an estimate of the social cost of CO_2 emissions; the fourth column the depletion of energy resources (particularly large for the Middle East and North Africa). The next column represents forest depletion, large for Nepal and zero for the United States where there has actually been regrowth of forests over the period of interest. The final column gives the sum, an estimate of genuine investment as a percent of national income. This is an estimate of the value of investment

Table 6.1 Estimates of Genuine Investment as Percentage of GDP for a Sample of Countries

	Domestic Net I	Education	CO_2	Energy	Mineral	Forest	GI
Bangladesh	7.89	1.53	−0.25	−0.61	0.00	−1.41	7.14
India	11.74	3.29	−1.17	−2.89	−0.46	−1.05	9.47
Nepal	14.82	2.65	−0.20	−0.00	−0.30	−3.67	13.31
Pakistan	10.92	2.02	−0.75	−2.60	−0.00	−0.84	8.75
China	30.06	1.96	−2.48	−6.11	−0.50	−0.22	22.72
Sub-Saharan Africa	3.49	4.78	−0.81	−7.31	−1.71	−0.52	−2.09
Middle East and North Africa	14.72	4.70	−0.80	−25.54	−0.12	−0.06	−7.09
United Kingdom	3.70	5.21	−0.32	−1.20	0.00	0.00	7.38
United States	5.73	5.62	−0.42	−1.95	−0.05	0.00	8.94

at current shadow prices $\sum_i \lambda_i \frac{dS_i}{dt}$. Full details of the data and the calculations are in Arrow et al. (2004).

Clearly there are many shortcomings here, and I shall talk about correcting some of them shortly. Among the shortcomings that we do not correct are the inadequacy of educational expenditure as a measure of investment in human capital, and the incompleteness of the list of categories of environmental capital for whose depletion we allow. Both could be serious sources of error, but it has so far not been possible to obtain data to take this process further. Nonetheless the numbers that emerge make some intuitive sense. For example, for the Middle East and North Africa, a domestic net investment of +14.72 percent turns into a genuine savings of −7.09 percent after allowing for the depletion of energy resources, drawing attention to the fact that this part of the world lives unsustainably by depleting an exhaustible resource, as in the Hotelling models reviewed earlier. Sub-Saharan Africa is also shown to be living unsustainably, a tragic and not surprising result. Allowance for the impact of HIV/AIDS on human capital would probably make their genuine investment number even worse. The remaining countries all appear from these numbers to have positive genuine investment and thus meet one of the criteria for sustainability, namely that the present value of future welfare obtainable from capital stocks be nondecreasing.

All of these numbers omit two factors that could be important, however: one is population change, omitted from the earlier discussion but a real issue in several countries; the other is technical change. A higher rate of population growth will presumably increase the level of investment required to maintain living standards constant so that the numbers in table 6.1 will overstate the extent of sustainability with a growing population and vice versa. Technological progress will act in the opposite direction, allowing humans to extract more welfare from a given set of resources. So, we make two more modifications to the data in table 6.1, adjusting for population growth and for technological progress. Neither factor was part of the theory developed earlier in this chapter and, to my knowledge, there is little to no discussion of either of these issues in the literature on sustainability or on optimal growth with environmental resources. Yet, intuition suggests that they are important, and the numbers in Arrow et al. confirm this, indicating a lacuna in the theory developed so far.

Table 6.2 shows the results of these modifications. The first column is the last column from table 6.1, our preliminary estimates of genuine savings. The second column gives an estimate of the growth rate of genuine wealth derived from the previous column using an assumed GDP/wealth ratio (see Arrow et al. 2004 for details). The fourth gives the growth rate of genuine wealth per capita, using the population growth rate given in the third numerical column. This is followed by an estimate of the growth rate of total factor productivity and then the growth rate of per capita

Table 6.2   Genuine Investment as Percentage of GDP Adjusted for Population and Technical Change

	GI	Growth of Genuine Wealth	Population Growth	Growth of Genuine Wealth p.c.	Growth of Total Factor Productivity	Growth of Genuine Wealth p.c. (adjusted for total factor productivity growth)	Standard GDP p.c. Growth Rate
Bangladesh	7.14	1.07	2.16	−1.09	0.81	0.30	1.88
India	9.47	1.42	1.99	−0.57	0.64	0.54	2.96
Nepal	13.31	2.00	2.24	−0.24	0.51	0.63	1.86
Pakistan	8.75	1.31	2.66	2.06	1.13	0.59	2.21
China	22.72	3.41	1.35	−3.05	3.64	8.33	7.77
Sub-Saharan Africa	−2.09	−0.31	2.74	−3.05	0.28	−2.58	−0.01
Middle East and North Africa	−7.09	−1.06	2.37	−3.43	−0.23	−3.82	0.74
United Kingdom	7.38	1.48	0.18	1.30	0.58	2.29	2.19
United States	8.94	1.79	1.07	0.72	0.02	0.75	1.99

genuine wealth adjusted for total factor productivity growth. For comparison purposes, the last column gives the conventional figure for growth of GDP per capita.

Only two estimates of the growth of genuine wealth per capita are negative, the same two as before, but many others are probably not significantly positive. The high population growth rates of Bangladesh, Nepal, and Sub-Saharan Africa all act to reduce their countries' rates of genuine savings.

Although the methodology differs in some technical details, and does not allow for technical progress, our results are very consistent with those of the World Bank (2005), which cover a much greater range of countries. The World Bank concludes that most resource-dependent countries are not replacing the capital that they deplete in extracting their resources and are therefore reducing their long-run welfare potential.

A clear implication of this work is that we are measuring the income of oil producers wrongly. We know how to measure it better: the issue is now to ensure that the data needed are collected and incorporated into the accounts. For oil producers, the most important data are the depletion of oil and gas reserves. In addition, we need data on the changes in other forms of capital stocks—other natural resources (such as water and soil), environmental impacts (such as pollution and CO_2 emission), and on the accumulation or decumulation of overseas assets. As some overseas assets are privately held, measuring these might not always be straightforward.

CONCLUSION

I began this chapter by referring to the paradox of resource-rich countries—if they are resource rich they should be rich financially too, but it seems that they rarely are. Some of the paradox can be resolved just by looking at the numbers, as I did in the introduction. This shows that even the richest of oil-rich countries are not that rich. Even Saudi Arabia with oil at $60 per barrel could barely lift its population above the U.S. poverty level if it were to spread its oil earnings equally. The numbers in the introduction also suggested something else that the more formal analysis corroborated: Access to capital markets matters and is a part of the resolution of the paradox. A country with modest oil reserves and no access to capital markets is not rich in any real sense.

The analytical models established two further points. One is that national income is measured wrongly in resource-rich countries, as they do not subtract depreciation of their asset base from their income figures. In failing to do so, they omit from their calculations the fact that their income from resource use is generated by the depletion of a nonaugmentable asset. It is like augmenting the family income by selling the family silver: It cannot last and is really a form of asset disposal—not a source of income. Indeed, in U.S. corporate accounting conventions, the sale of oil or gas is recognized as asset disposal. A proper measure of income allows for resource depletion. Conventional measures of investment will greatly overstate the real investment rate in resource-based economies. And a measure of the sustainability of welfare is based on the value of the changes in all forms of capital, natural and other. This fact emphasizes the importance to resource-rich countries of a conscious policy of investing some of the income from resource sales, as noted also by the World Bank 2005. A commonly suggested rule of thumb is to invest the revenues from resource production net of production costs, a rule known as Hartwick's Rule (1977).[5] While this rule may not be optimal under all circumstances, the fact that conventional measures overstate investment does suggest the need for very high apparent investment rates to provide a firm basis for future welfare. The figures suggest that no resource-rich countries are attaining appropriate investment levels: All are depleting their natural capital and not replacing it with any other form of capital, a sure road to poverty in the long run (see also chapters 2 and 7).

The second key lesson is that the value of resources depends on access to capital markets so that income from sales can be invested. Indeed, in an ideal world, resource-rich countries would be able to borrow responsibly on the security of their resources and invest the proceeds, although the pitfalls of irresponsible borrowing are large and discussed in chapters 1, 2, and 11. Or, they would be able to sell their oil forward (although again, as discussed in chapter 8, there are political challenges that accompany this solution). In either case, if used wisely, capital markets can transform the possibilities open to a resource-based economy and governments need to act on this basis.

There is still work to be done in this area. Foremost is the need for better data on capital accumulation or decumulation (for all forms of capital) for resource-rich countries. Then we need to understand better the obstacles to better access to capital markets on the part of oil-producing countries, particularly those that are underdeveloped. They would benefit from being able to sell their resources forward to a much greater degree than is now possible. It may be that this is impossible because countries cannot always be legally bound to uphold their agreements in these types of arrangements, so that counterparties have no redress in the event of default. But there may be remedies for this, through clever institutional arrangements that exploit cooperative strategies from game theoretic work on repeated interactions. And an obvious fact in most poor, oil-rich countries is that the income from oil wealth is usually spread very unevenly through the country. Thus, while we need a greater appreciation for those factors that can increase income in oil-rich countries, such as making use of capital markets, further investigation needs to proceed in tandem with efforts to understand better how to prevent the emergence of the usual syndrome linking oil, corruption, and inequality.

ACKNOWLEDGMENT

I am grateful to Macartan Humphreys for valuable comments on an earlier draft.

NOTES

1. Figures come from the BP Statistical Review of World Energy (available at http://www.bp.com), and from the CIA Factbook.

2. Special cases include the Hotelling model (1931); the Solow model (1956); and the Dasgupta-Heal-Solow model (see Dasgupta and Heal 1974; Solow 1974).

3. Since $\dfrac{d}{dt}\left(\sum_i \lambda_i S_i\right) = \sum_i \lambda_i \dfrac{dS_i}{dt} + \sum_i \dfrac{d\lambda_i}{dt} S_i$

4. To be precise, the coverage is as follows: Bangladesh 1973–2001; India 1970–2001; Nepal 1970–2001; China 1982–2001 (without 1994); Sub-Saharan Africa 1974–1982 and 1986–2001; Middle East and North Africa 1976–89 and 1991–2001; United Kingdom 1971–2001; and United States 1970–2001.

5. For a critique of this rule, see Asheim et al. (2002).

REFERENCES

Arrow, K., P. Dasgupta, L. Goulder, G. Daily, P. Ehrlich, G. Heal, S. Levin, K.-G. Mäler, S. Schneider, D. Starrett, and B. Walker. 2004. "Are We Consuming Too Much?" *Journal of Economic Perspectives* Summer 18(3): 147–72.

Asheim, G., W. Buchholz, and C. Withagen. 2002. "The Hartwick Rule: Myths and Facts." Discussion Paper. No. 2002 52, CentER (available at http://greywww .kub.nl:2080/greyfiles/center/2002/doc/52.pdf).

Dasgupta, P. and G. Heal. 1974. "The Optimal Depletion of Exhaustible Resources." *Review of Economic Studies* 41 (Symposium): 3–28.

Dasgupta, P. and G. Heal. 1979. *Economic Theory and Exhaustible Resources.* Cambridge, UK: Cambridge University Press.

Hartwick, J. 1977. "Intergenerational Equity and Investing the Rents from Exhaustible Resources." *American Economic Review* 66: 9072–74.

Heal, G. 1973. *The Theory of Economic Planning.* Amsterdam: North Holland Publishing.

Heal, G. and B. Kriström. 2005. "National Income and the Environment." In *Handbook of Environmental Economics,* Vol. 3, K.-G. Mäler and J. Vincent, eds. Amsterdam: Elsevier, pp. 1147–1217.

Hicks, J. 1939. *Value and Capital: An Inquiry Into Some Fundamental Principles of Economic Theory.* Oxford: Oxford University Press.

Hotelling, H. 1931. "The Economics of Exhaustible Resources." *Journal of Political Economy* 39(2): 137–75.

Solow, R. 1956. "A Contribution to the Theory of Economic Growth." *Quarterly Journal of Economics* 70(1): 65–94.

Solow, R. 1974. "Intergenerational Equity and Exhaustible Resources." *Review of Economic Studies* 41 (Symposium): 29–45.

World Bank. 1997. *Expanding the Measure of Wealth: Indicators of Environmentally Sustainable Development.* Washington, DC: World Bank.

World Bank. 2005. *Where Is the Wealth of Nations? Measuring Capital for the 21st Century.* Washington, DC: World Bank.

CHAPTER 7

How to Handle the Macroeconomics of Oil Wealth

Jeffrey D. Sachs

ABSTRACT

The idea that oil is a "curse" is only partly true. On many measures, oil-rich states are doing well. Nonetheless, the economic performance of oil economies has fallen far short of potential, and sometimes disastrously so. One reason is that large earnings from oil and other natural resources can have adverse effects on other sectors of economies, particularly those that can be motors for sustained economic growth. The problem arises when oil earnings are used for consumption rather than for public investment. The solution lies in a long-run growth-focused investment strategy. With the correct investment strategy nonresource export sectors can benefit from increased natural resource earnings, and indeed it is possible to reverse the infamous "Dutch Disease" by generating growth in sectors that are central for poverty alleviation but that are in practice nontradable (including food production) alongside real exchange rate depreciation.

INTRODUCTION

The idea that oil is a "curse" is only partly true. Oil is, of course, an enormously valuable resource that can bring economic benefits to an economy. Oil-rich states have often outperformed their neighbors that lack oil, as illustrated in table 7.1, showing regional comparisons using the most recent available data. Generally, oil-rich countries, region by region, tend to have higher per capita income levels (in purchasing power terms). This often corresponds to higher levels of private consumption as well. In many other categories of well-being—life expectancies, child mortality rates, electricity use per capita, paved roads—oil producers are better off than their oil-poor counterparts. Sometimes the gap is statistically significant, though

Table 7.1   Indicators of Welfare Across Regions

	CIS		Latin America		Middle East		Sub-Saharan Africa	
	Oil	Non-Oil	Oil	Non-Oil	Oil	Non-Oil	Oil	Non-Oil
Oil production (barrels/cap/year)	19.2	0.7	31.6	2.5	161.7	1.4	46.0	0.1
Life expectancy	63.7	66.5	72.3	68.7	71.7	70.7	51.3	45.1
Child mortality (deaths per 1,000 live births)	71.8	63.0	22.7	40.3	27.1	32.7	149.3	173.5
GDP per capita (PPP)	6012	2384	6086	4581	9959	4202	5109	1178
Net primary school enrollment (%)	85.5	86.5	94.0	94.0	81.4	90.7	72.3	62.0
Roads (km paved/1000 pop)	4.2	4.0	3.4	5.0	5.2	1.4	5.2	3.2
Electricity (KWh produced/cap)	3705	2586	3029	781	7147	1681	304	283

Source: Author's calculations based on World Bank data.

often not. There is no generalized tendency, to be sure, for oil-rich countries to perform economically less well than oil-poor counterparts in terms of *levels* of economic performance.

The "curse" is real, however, in one important sense: economic performance of oil economies has fallen far short of potential, and sometimes disastrously so. Oil earnings have rarely lived up to the plausible expectation that they should be a stimulus to long-term economic development (Sachs and Warner 1999, 2000, 2001; Sachs and Rodriguez 1999). Many oil-rich countries experienced declines in per capita income between 1970 and 2000, and quite a few fell into deep debt crises. The curse—that oil earnings often do not translate into long-term development—is not a matter of fate, however. Oil can be a springboard to development. This chapter discusses ways to turn oil and gas holdings to the advantage of long-term economic development.

OIL IN THE CONTEXT OF NATIONAL DEVELOPMENT STRATEGIES

Despite the checkered history, oil in principle should offer three huge benefits for poor oil-producing states. First, the oil income itself can boost real living standards by financing higher levels of public and private consumption.

This has typically been the case. Second, oil can finance higher levels of investment, both out of oil income itself and out of borrowing made possible by the oil income. Third, since the oil income typically accrues largely to the public sector, and indeed to the public budget, the oil can obviate one huge barrier to development: the lack of fiscal resources needed to finance core public goods, including infrastructure. The point, of course, is that oil is part of national income not only but also of *fiscal* income, with the potential advantage of financing *public* investments that are inevitably a key part of any coherent development strategy.

The starting point of managing oil, therefore, is taking a long-term view of national development. While volumes can and have been written on appropriate development strategies, and while circumstances necessarily differ across countries, some general principles are helpful.

First, development depends on a *mixed* economy, in which both public and private investments contribute to economic growth. Public investments are needed to finance two kinds of goods: public and merit. Public goods are goods that are *underprovided* by the private sector in a market economy, generally because the goods are nonrival or nonexcludable or both.[1] Public goods include national defense, the rule of law, environmental protection, scientific research, infectious disease control, and basic infrastructure networks (roads, power, urban water, and sanitation). Even when some of these goods are technically excludable (e.g., access to roads can be rationed by toll booths or permits for use), it is often very inefficient to exclude potential users because marginal costs of new users are low. Merit goods are goods that on principle should be available for everyone in the society for the sake of social harmony and justice. Merit goods include basic health care, basic education, social insurance for unemployment and disability, safe drinking water and sanitation, adequate basic nutrition, and safe shelter. The provision of merit goods to the poorest members of society has spillover benefits for the entire society in the form of enhanced political and social stability.

Second, public investments should be based on a sound macroeconomic strategy, meaning a budgetary framework that preserves both short-run macroeconomic stability and long-term fiscal solvency. Macroeconomic stability entails overall price stability, and the absence of abrupt cuts in spending that result from a sudden worsening of credit terms. Fiscal solvency, of course, means the management of the public sector to maintain the ability to service public debts without crisis. The investment framework should take account of the inherent instability of oil earnings on a year-to-year basis, and the eventual depletion of oil reserves. Both because of volatility and depletion, it is useful to distinguish a "sustained" or "permanent" level of oil income flows as distinct from the oil earnings in any particular year. Based on the long-term profile of oil income, a sound public investment profile should be adopted for incorporation into annual and medium-term (say five-year) budget frameworks.

Third, public investment spending should be seen as a complement rather than substitute for private investment spending. In practice, this means achieving a clear understanding of the respective roles of the public and private sectors in the economy. Public investments should be focused on public goods and merit goods, leaving the private sector free to build a private-owned economy alongside the public investments. The major public sector investments come down to infrastructure, health, education, social security, and knowledge creation (especially basic science). Private sector investments focus on the rest: agriculture, mining, manufacturing, and nonstate services.

Fourth, the public investment spending should be part of a development strategy with a time frame of a decade or more, since many public investments have long lead times. The Millennium Development Goals (MDGs) provide an enormously useful framework for such a development strategy, because the MDGs set bold but achievable poverty-reduction goals that have been endorsed by all of the world's governments. The MDGs therefore offer the practical advantage to poor countries that they can appeal for help to the rich donor "development partners." Of course, "stretch goals" raise special challenges. If public investment projects are scaled up too quickly, inefficiencies are bound to multiply because of limited absorptive capacity in the domestic economy. For example, increased physical investments in health and agriculture (e.g., clinics, irrigation systems) are far more effective when they are combined with multiyear training programs for workers in those sectors, to avoid skill shortages and other bottlenecks. The MDGs are achievable in all parts of the impoverished world (see the UN Millennium Project Report, 2005), but it will require sophisticated intersectoral planning on a decade-long timetable to do so.

OIL AND PUBLIC INVESTMENTS

The key recommendation of this chapter is that oil earnings in low-income countries should be turned into public investments rather than into increased private consumption. Most poor countries are severely constrained in their development by the underprovision of public goods. Economic development, though undoubtedly requiring a predominance of the private sector in agriculture, industry, and services, also depends on core public goods. These are generally deficient, sometimes so much so that their absence impedes investments by the private sector and leaves countries in a poverty trap. The poverty trap works as follows. The profitability of private investment depends on complementary public investments (in key infrastructure, health, education, etc.). Public investments, however, require budgetary outlays. In impoverished countries, those outlays are constrained by poverty itself. Typically, the government is not creditworthy, and therefore cannot borrow the needed investment funding from private capital markets. Thus, poverty leads to underinvestments in public goods, which in turn lead to underinvestments in the private sector, and poverty continues or worsens (e.g., because of continued population growth). The causal chain, and vicious circle, is therefore as follows:

Poverty → Lack of public finance → Lack of public goods → Lack of private investment → Poverty

Oil earnings, at least in principle, allow countries to break out of this trap. The key is to use the oil earnings in a responsible manner to finance outlays on public goods that serve as the platform for private investment and long-term growth. When oil earnings rise and are successfully invested in public goods of various sorts, the resulting economic activity and stimulus to private investment should lead to higher incomes, improved budgetary resources *including non-oil income*, and therefore increased possibilities of financing public goods through an overall rise in economic activity. Even as oil resources are depleted, or diminished by declines in world oil prices, a strengthened private sector economy should be able to compensate.

In this view, the popular idea of dividing the oil earnings into "citizen shares" and distributing the purchasing power to the public, as has been done in Alaska, is generally the wrong answer in poor countries, where public investment outlays rather than private consumption spending are typically needed to break out of a poverty trap. Even when increased private consumption is an urgent short-run objective for vulnerable groups (e.g., for the elderly or for people in extreme hunger), targeted public outlays rather than a general distribution of oil income is preferable. Some of the outlays may be direct cash transfers (e.g., for the elderly), but more often they should be in the form of public services (such as health care) or the provision of inputs for private producers (such as fertilizers and improved seeds for smallholder farmers, or the extension of microcredit).

In any event, there is a strong case against transferring a depleting resource solely to the current generation, rather than spreading the benefits across the current and future generations. Intergenerational sharing is best accomplished through fiscal means. Norway, for example, invests its hydrocarbon income in the Government Pension Fund to spread consumption benefits to future generations, mainly by accumulating assets that will help indirectly to fund future pension benefits to be paid by the government's social security system (see chapter 8).

PUBLIC INVESTMENTS WITHIN AN OVERALL DEVELOPMENT STRATEGY

A successful development strategy should include three components:

1. A time path of public investments suited to the national circumstances
2. An economic policy framework to support private-sector economic activity
3. A political framework to ensure the rule of law and macroeconomic stability

The detailed sequence of public investments must of course be based on the context of each country. For the poorest oil countries, the overriding goal is to use oil income to enable the economy to meet basic needs (food, safe drinking water, essential health services, basic education) and to put in place the infrastructure (power, irrigation, roads, ports, telecoms, the Internet) for private-sector-led economic growth. For middle-income oil countries, the overriding goal is typically to promote the transition from a resource-based rural economy (including agriculture, oil, and other mining) to a human-capital and knowledge-based urban economy. Key investments typically need to be made in knowledge creation and diffusion (higher education, scientific institutions) as well as in infrastructure in fast-growing urban areas. For high-income oil countries (e.g., Norway), which already have extensive physical infrastructure in addition to well-endowed systems of higher education and science, a priority for oil earnings may be to support the budget burdens of social insurance (e.g., pensions, low-income support, public-sector insurance).

In the poorest oil-exporting countries, for example, Sao Tome and Principe and Nigeria, the prevailing conditions are characterized by a rural economy in extreme poverty and an absence of basic infrastructure (power, water and sanitation, roads, rail, telecoms, primary education, primary health care). Generally, these countries have long ago developed public investment strategies for each of these key sectors, but have been unable to fund those strategies because of a lack of fiscal resources and an inability to tap into private capital markets for project financing. A key priority for the poorest countries should be the power sector itself. Many impoverished oil economies export their oil and gas without developing their own modern energy system. Yet exporting the hydrocarbons without a strategy for expanding access to electricity and refined products can be a major lost opportunity, one exemplified by the situation in Chad, which is exporting its limited oil reserves while depending for the vast majority of its energy needs on burning biomass. Other investment priorities are likely to include the construction of a road system, port facilities, access to safe drinking water and sanitation, a fiber optic network for telecoms and the Internet, primary schools, and primary health services (including community health workers, village-based dispensaries, local clinics, and hospitals).

The MDGs, as previously noted, offer a useful "checklist" and organizing structure for public investments in poor countries. The eight MDGs call for decisive progress against extreme poverty in all its major dimensions—low income, high disease burden, hunger, lack of schooling, lack of safe childbirth (and attendant high maternal mortality), environmental degradation, and lack of access to basic amenities including safe drinking water and sanitation. Many middle-income countries are on track to achieve most or all of the MDGs (with maternal mortality and environmental goals being the most frequent exceptions), while the poorest countries are often far off course from achieving most or even any of the goals. The most glaring gaps between the MDGs and current trajectories are found in Sub-Saharan Africa. The UN Millennium Project has emphasized the centrality of increased public investments needed to achieve the MDGs, in key sectors including agriculture, education, health, and infrastructure.

SOME DISTINCTIVE ASPECTS OF DEVELOPMENT
STRATEGIES IN HYDROCARBON ECONOMIES

Oil is different from other sources of national income, in that the preponderance of the income stream is a natural resource *rent* rather than the returns to reproducible capital (such as factories, machinery) or human capital (education, health). For this reason alone, it is easy for the state to appropriate the natural resource income (e.g., through nationalization), if it does not own the resource base in the first place. In fact, public ownership of hydrocarbon reserves is the norm. Major fields are often located on public lands or in public waters in the first place. Public ownership of hydrocarbon resources is often required by the national constitution. And where private owners are in control of oil fields, they often must transfer licit and illicit shares of oil earnings to governments and political leaders in order to maintain their share of the rents.

Treating the oil earnings as a simple rental income, however, is misleading in two important ways. First, a considerable investment of reproducible capital is required to produce the hydrocarbons, both for exploration and development of fields, and of course storage and transport. By "overtaxing" the oil flows, and thereby reducing or eliminating the returns to reproducible capital, the amount and value of the oil ultimately produced from a given field may be adversely affected. Second, since oil is a depleting commodity, the flow of oil income is in fact a conversion of natural capital (oil in the ground) into financial capital, and from there into consumption or into other kinds of capital such as human capital or reproducible physical capital. A sound investment strategy must take into account the time paths of oil production and depletion, so that the time paths of investment and consumption will be smoothed over time (see chapter 6).

Oil is distinctive for other reasons as well. The world price of oil is highly unpredictable and subject to large swings. Therefore, to the extent that the government relies on oil income for a significant part of budget revenues, policy makers must anticipate unpredictable and variable budgetary revenues. These pose enormous risks to macroeconomic stability. Three basic approaches have been taken to address these risks. The first is hedging against future price changes (e.g., in the futures markets, but hedging possibilities are generally limited to the near term of a year or so). The second is to budget based on estimates of "permanent" oil flows based on predictions of long-term average prices and quantities, rather than on short-term income based on current prices and current production levels.

The third is diversification, through privatization of public-sector holdings of oil, and investment of the cash value from privatization in a diversified portfolio. This third option depends on the ability of the government to carry out a privatization program that secures a market bid for the oil fields reflective of their actual present value. As argued by Stiglitz in chapter 2 of this book, such returns might be difficult if not impossible to achieve because of problems of asymmetric information and lack of enforcement of property rights subsequent to privatization (both of which lead prospective bidders to underbid the expected net present value of the oil income).

Another aspect of oil revenues is that they often can serve as a kind of collateral or security for international borrowing by the government. As a result, it is possible that following an oil boom (caused either by rising international prices or increased production) a government will be able to increase spending more than one for one with the increased oil earnings, by borrowing in international capital markets against the increased future flow of oil income. Many oil-exporting countries in the midst of an oil export boom have actually ended up deeply in debt, since they spent more than 100 percent of the increased oil income. If future oil incomes were wholly predictable, borrowing against future oil earnings to raise public investment spending might indeed make good sense. Given the enormous uncertainties of oil income flows, however, borrowing against future oil earnings can be treacherous.

THE EXAGGERATED FEAR OF "DUTCH DISEASE"

One of the possible harms of an oil export boom is that the rise in oil earnings leads to increased public and private spending, which in turn leads to a sharp appreciation of the real exchange rate, and then to a decline in non-oil exports and to slower economic growth. This pattern is called the "Dutch Disease," and is named after the overvaluation of the Dutch guilder in the wake of a boom in the Netherlands' natural gas earnings in the 1960s. The frequent counsel given to oil states is therefore to refrain from spending much of the increased oil earnings, and rather build up financial assets, in order to minimize real exchange rate appreciation.

The proposed mechanism is understood in an economic framework that draws the distinction between internationally traded goods on the one hand, and nontraded goods and services on the other. When spending increases following an oil boom, the increased spending falls both on traded and nontraded goods. Traded goods include sectors such as cash agriculture (coffee, tea, cocoa) and manufactures (processed foods, textiles, apparel), which are traded in world markets. Nontraded goods include food production for local use (maize, cassava) or local services.

The dollar price of traded goods is set in international markets. The dollar price of nontraded goods, on the other hand, adjusts to clear supply and demand of nontraded goods at home. The increased demand for traded goods can be met through increased imports. The increased demand for nontraded goods, however, must be met by increased local supply. The price of nontraded goods rises relative to the price of traded goods in order to equilibrate increased supply with increased demand. The rise in the relative price of nontraded goods to traded goods (or equivalently, the fall in the relative price of traded goods) is termed a real exchange rate appreciation.

All of this is illustrated by the famous traded–nontraded goods model shown in figure 7.1. The figure in the first panel shows the production possibility frontier (PPF) of the economy before the oil boom, with possible combinations of (non-oil) traded goods production (horizontal axis) and nontraded goods production (vertical axis). Curve II (marked with a dotted line) shows the consumer indifference curve. The initial equilibrium is at point E, at a point of tangency of the PPF and the II curve. On the horizontal axis we find E_T, the level of non-oil traded goods production, and on the vertical axis we find E_N, the level of nontraded goods production. The slope of the PPF at point E is equal to the real exchange rate (or the relative price of traded goods to nontraded goods). The steeper is the curve, the more depreciated is the exchange rate.

Now, suppose that there is an oil boom, which raises the total output of traded goods, equal to the sum of non-oil traded goods plus the oil

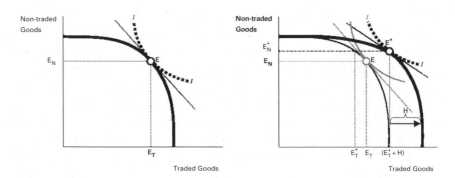

Figure 7.1   The Geometry of the Dutch Disease.

production. The entire PPF shifts to the right by the amount of the oil boom, H. The new equilibrium is shown in the right-hand panel as point E^*. Notice that nontraded production has risen to E_N^*. The total amount of traded goods (both oil and non-oil) has also risen, in this case to the level $E_T^* + H$. But importantly, the amount of *non-oil* traded goods production has actually declined to E_T^*. We can see that the real exchange rate has appreciated since the slope at point E^* is less steep than at point E, signifying a rise in the relative price of nontraded goods (i.e., a real-exchange-rate appreciation).

The real exchange rate appreciation, we see clearly, has induced a re-adjustment of output in the non-oil part of the economy. With a rising relative price of nontraded goods, workers and capital shift into nontraded goods production. Those workers and capital arrive in the nontraded goods sector by leaving the non-oil traded goods sector. In short, the rise in oil spending induces a shift of production away from traded goods (e.g., cash agricultural and manufactured export goods) and toward nontraded goods and services.

These adjustments are not really a "disease" per se. The rise in non-traded production at the expense of (non-oil) traded production does not by itself constitute a "mistake" of market forces, but rather the only way that the economy can enjoy more of *both* traded and nontraded goods. The increase in traded goods is met through increased imports. The increase in nontraded goods and services can be met only through an increased domestic output of those goods and services.

These resource shifts can become a true "disease" or market failure if there is something special about the traded goods sector that is being squeezed. Suppose, for purposes of illustration, that the economy is exporting apparel before oil is discovered. Once oil is discovered, workers and capital goods are induced to leave the international apparel sector and to migrate to the nontraded goods sector. If the apparel sector were making a special contribution to growth (e.g., by spreading international best practices in computerization and logistics), the decline of the apparel sector could spell trouble for the economy at large. The oil boom would therefore induce a decline in a technologically leading sector of the economy, with adverse consequences for long-term growth. One solution would be to limit the boom in oil spending, and thereby limit the spillover of workers from apparel to nontraded goods. Another possibility, however, would be to provide special targeted subsidies for the apparel sector, to support the transfer of technologies taking place in that sector. A squeeze of the non-oil tradable sector might, under some circumstances, also have special adverse consequences for income distribution, particularly hurting the poorest of the poor. That is less likely than often supposed, however, since the poorest of the poor are often economically isolated rather than in tradable goods production. Moreover, the advice to save rather than invest the oil income in order to protect the poorest of the poor would not make sense in any case if the public investments have direct benefits for the income-earning opportunities of the poorest (e.g., by expanding the road and power grids into impoverished regions).

The real fear of the Dutch Disease, in short, is that the non-oil export sector will be squeezed, thereby squeezing a major source of technological progress in the economy. *But this fear is vastly overblown if the oil proceeds are being properly invested as part of a national development strategy.* Suppose that the proceeds of the oil earnings are being invested in infrastructure (roads, power, telecoms) that raise the productivity of workers in both the traded and nontraded goods sectors. Assume for the moment that all of the investment goods are directly imported by the government using the oil proceeds. There is no direct spending effect of the oil income. Consumption rises to the extent that the non-oil sectors (both traded and nontraded) expand following the increased public investments financed with the oil income. In the right panel of figure 7.2, this is represented as an outward (that is, upward and rightward, rather than simply rightward) shift in the PPF. Production and consumption of both non-oil traded goods and nontraded goods increase. The real exchange rate at E^{**} may or may not appreciate relative to the initial equilibrium at E, but it does not matter very much, since the non-oil traded goods sector expands in any event. It expands as a result of the increased productivity due to public investments.

If the increased spending on public investments falls partly on nontraded goods (rather than entirely on imported capital goods), there can be a minor Dutch Disease effect emanating not from a consumption boom but from the investment boom itself. In this case, the rise of investment spending will tend to lead to an appreciation of the real exchange rate and a short-term squeeze on tradable goods, at least until the productivity-enhancing effects on tradable production kick in. This can be quite fast, however, since the benefits of roads, power, and other infrastructure investment spending can come on line very rapidly. Any squeeze on tradables production is likely to be very short lived.

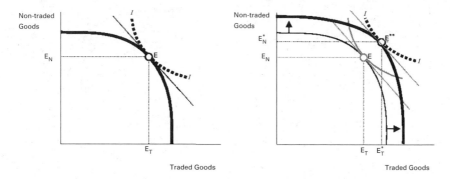

Figure 7.2   The Effects of Public Investments via an Oil Boom.

It is also quite possible, especially in the poorest countries, that the oil boom leads to a real exchange rate *depreciation* if the public investment financed by the oil substantially raises the productivity of nontraded sector, as shown in figure 7.3. This can be a very important and likely outcome. In the poorest countries, staple food production (e.g., maize) is the most important nontraded good in the consumption basket. Although we often think of these staples as internationally traded goods, in fact—because of very high transport costs in the rural areas of impoverished countries—staple food is consumed mainly on the premises of the farm household, rather than being marketed and traded for other goods. Food also constitutes by far the largest single item of household consumption of the poor. If the oil earnings are invested in raising the productivity of smallholder farmers (e.g., by financing improved seed varieties for local production), then the production possibility frontiers shift upward, as indicated by the vertical arrow in figure 7.3. The overall effect of the oil export boom may be a *reduction* of the relative price of nontradable foodstuffs and therefore a real depreciation (the slope at E^{***} is steeper than at E). Moreover, it is clear that the production of both nontraded and (non-oil) traded goods increase. There is, once again, no squeeze of non-oil traded goods.

In summary, the Dutch Disease is a worry mainly if the oil boom is used to finance consumption rather than investment. In that case, the non-oil traded sector might well be squeezed on a sustained basis, with adverse consequences for long-term growth. This is very unlikely if the oil earnings are properly used for public investments in economies largely bereft of public goods, especially infrastructure. In that case, the positive benefits of increased public investments on the non-oil traded sector are

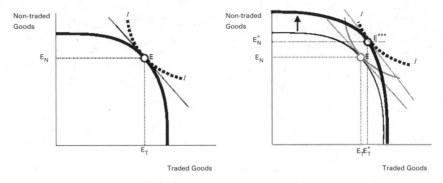

Figure 7.3   Real Depreciation Following a Rise in Non-traded Food Yields.

very likely to outweigh any negative consequences of real exchange rate appreciation.

A final note on public investment is warranted here. Even when public infrastructure (roads, ports, power) is highly productive, and when financing is available, the actual physical investments will necessarily take time to put in place, and the optimum pace is itself an economic calculation. Many investment projects impose adjustment costs (e.g., disruptions of other economic activities or congestion due to the investment projects) that increase in proportion to the rate of investment. The optimum response in that case is to spread the investments over time, to maximize the benefits of the investments net of the adjustment costs themselves. This pacing of investments is sometimes described as investing according to the "absorptive capacity" of the economy. Perhaps the most famous example of an investment boom gone awry was the massive and costly congestion in Nigeria's ports in the spending boom that followed the oil price increases in the early 1970s. The optimum pacing of investment spending is not motivated by the Dutch Disease per se, or by any automatic desire to spread oil spending over time, but rather by the adjustment costs imposed by the investment projects themselves.

EXCHANGE RATE POLICY

In the "normal" case that the real exchange rate tends to appreciate following an increase of oil earnings, government policy makers can "engineer" that appreciation in two ways. In the first case, the central bank maintains a floating exchange rate. The oil proceeds lead to an appreciation of the nominal exchange rate vis-à-vis the dollar and euro. This puts downward pressure on the local currency prices of non-oil traded goods, and thereby leads to a fall in the price of traded goods relative to non-traded goods (i.e., a real appreciation). In the second case, the nominal exchange rate of the national currency is pegged to the U.S. dollar, or euro, or basket. Now the increase in domestic spending that follows the oil boom leads to a rise in the prices of nontraded goods, while traded goods prices are kept constant because of the constancy of the nominal exchange rate. Once again, there is a fall in the price of traded goods relative to non-traded goods (i.e., a real appreciation). There is no decisive case as to which of these exchange rate mechanisms is to be preferred. For small countries facing large structural transformations, instability in the demand for the local currency, and the uncertainties of oil and capital flows, there is probably a preference for maintaining an "adjustable peg" exchange rate, wherein the central bank keeps the nominal exchange rate stable, but reserves the option to make discrete devaluations or revaluations in the future. (If oil prices fall sharply, for example, the central bank might undertake a devaluation to reduce the relative price of nontraded goods). The pegged rate adds predictability to the price level, and makes monetary policy subordinate to the exchange rate target. Of course a successful peg requires substantial foreign exchange reserves, the avoidance of excessive domestic credit expansion, and the avoidance of high levels of short-term external indebtedness that can lead to panicked withdrawals of foreign capital and self-fulfilling speculative attacks on the domestic currency.

As described in the preceding text, a real appreciation is not the same as a squeeze on production of the traditional tradable sector (e.g., agriculture). It is perfectly possible that the exchange rate appreciates, and also that the non-oil tradable production expands. This is the case when the oil earnings are used to finance public investments that boost the productivity of the non-oil tradable sector. In poor countries with extremely deficient infrastructure, the productivity gains in the non-oil tradable sector that result from new infrastructure investments (especially in power, roads, telecoms, and port facilities) are likely to outweigh any negative effects on production caused by exchange rate appreciation due to the public investment spending. This conclusion will at least apply over a period of a few years (enough time for the infrastructure to get into place), if not immediately at the start of an oil boom. The idea, therefore, that the government should withhold investment spending in order to prevent real appreciation of the exchange rate, in order to "protect" the non-oil tradable sector, is very likely to be wrong in practice. (Of course, even if the non-oil tradable sector production is actually squeezed, whether or not that is a "disease" depends very much on whether there are special externalities, or income distributional consequences, associated with the traditional tradable sector, as explained earlier).

CASH TRANSFERS OF OIL EARNINGS TO THE PUBLIC

Among free-market advocates, there is a repeated call on the state to distribute oil earnings directly to households in a lump-sum transfer. The free-market analysts base their arguments on three positions. First, they tend to reject the idea that investments in infrastructure (including roads, power, telecoms, water, and sanitation) should be provided by the public sector in the first place. The private sector, they claim, will supply the needed investments, but only if government is truly pursuing the rule of law. Second, they distrust the political leaders of the state to manage large income flows on behalf of the general population as opposed to their own behalf. By forcing the state sector to disgorge the oil earnings in direct payments to the public, the argument holds, the abuses of public spending can be avoided. Third, they believe that social safety net spending should be carried out through direct transfers from the state to the poor. This has been done, with some apparent success, in Brazil and Mexico, where direct cash transfers to poor households are linked to a "good performance" by the households in sending the children to school and to health checkups.

These positions are not generally persuasive, especially for the poorest countries. For example, the experience on private financing of infrastructure in low-income settings has been very disappointing. There is an increasing skepticism that private investments will finance the basic infrastructure network, especially roads and power. Both sectors are subject to important increasing returns to scale, suggesting the need for a public supplier of the infrastructure or at least a publicly regulated monopoly. In addition, some of the most urgent investments (such as for primary health and education) are beyond the financial reach of the poorest households. Direct public financing of these services is needed to ensure the universal access to such services by those in need. Finally, Brazilian or Mexican private transfer schemes to households work in large part because the basic rural infrastructure (schools, clinics, transport, and power) is already in place in those countries. That is not the case in rural areas of many low-income oil-exporting countries.

Note that even the Brazil and Mexico programs are far from the proposals for a general handout of a fixed share of oil earnings to each household, a proposal repeatedly made by free-market advocates in the United States, and modeled on the distribution in Alaska. The transfers in the Brazil and Mexico programs are targeted to low-income households, and are conditional on certain actions of the households in support of their children's well-being. Thus, the transfers are providing social welfare services. In Norway, the gas earnings are also distributed to the public, but as pension benefits. As such, the gas earnings are first accumulating in national pension accounts, which will then be used to service pension obligations for decades in the future. As in Brazil and Mexico, the gas earnings are thereby satisfying a core public function of social insurance, rather than serving as a mere transfer of income to households.

SAVING OIL INCOME FOR THE FUTURE THROUGH FINANCIAL ASSETS

Oil-rich low-income countries have sometimes been advised to accumulate their oil income into a national financial pool or fund (perhaps held in foreign stocks and bonds), and to spend only the "income" or "earnings" on the financial assets in that fund. The idea is to create a financial endowment that can be used to fund public outlays into the indefinite future, for example, pension benefits over the course of generations. This kind of advice rightly recognizes that with a depleting asset like oil, there is a powerful case for smoothing consumption over a much longer time horizon than the depleting income flow from the oil itself. Still, the idea of spending only the income from accumulated financial assets makes little sense as a general rule on the timing of oil-backed outlays. To the extent that the oil income is used for public investments, the oil is turned into long-lived physical assets and human capital rather than financial capital, but the intertemporal benefits of the oil income are similarly spread across time.

In essence, policy makers face a choice among four kinds of long-lasting assets: oil in the ground, financial assets (e.g., foreign exchange reserves), physical assets (e.g., roads), and human capital (e.g., a better educated labor force). For an oil-rich country like Norway, with extensive physical and human capital already in place, the best choice might well be to accumulate financial assets to cover the long-term costs of the public pension system. This is indeed the policy of the National Pension Fund. For poor countries, however, it is likely to make much more sense to turn oil earnings quickly into physical assets and human capital. It may even make sense in these countries to borrow against *future* oil earnings for the sake of increasing investment outlays on high-return public investments. Still, this latter option requires great prudence because of the volatility of capital markets and world oil prices. Attempts to mortgage future oil earnings for the sake of increased public outlays have repeatedly led to eventual budget and debt crises.

GOOD GOVERNANCE AND OIL INCOME

Many chapters in this book detail aspects of good governance of oil income, from the initial exploration, to auctions and contracting, to long-term fiscal transparency. Here it will suffice to stress some of the elements of good governance as they relate specifically to the linkage of oil earnings and national development strategies. First, there is an urgent need for each government to prepare specific assessments of national income and fiscal revenues that can be expected from the oil and gas sector. These assessments should take account of costs of production, world prices, and depletion, with all of the uncertainties attached to each of these items. The expected income flows should be public information, and subject to regular revision given the enormous uncertainties involved. Second, the specific fiscal flows associated with these earnings should be explained and made public. Fiscal implications of oil earnings typically come in many forms: production sharing, royalties, corporate taxation, and other ways. These should be detailed clearly and consistently, again with stress put on the uncertainties as well as the main forecasts.

As previously noted, transparent means should be used to manage the high risks of volatile international prices and uncertain national production. The budget should be based on a cautious assessment of the future path of world prices. Great caution should be used in pledging future oil revenues to secure current borrowing. Aggressive borrowing, often pushed by international banks, has repeatedly proven to be the bane of commodity exporters. Ways to hedge oil price risks should be repeatedly sought.

The government should be explicit about converting the limited and depleting oil resources into long-term and sustainable benefits for society. Rather than transferring the oil earnings as current income to the current generation, the bulk of the earnings should be invested, not only to provide the foundations for long-term growth, but also to ensure that the benefits are spread across generations. That can be accomplished financially (e.g., by investing the oil earnings in international assets to be used for future pension payments, as in Norway), or physically, by building the infrastructure (road, power networks) and human capital that will last for decades.

In a recent publication, the International Monetary Fund summarized five prudent ways for a low-income country to manage increased foreign aid flows. The same basic principles apply to managing increased oil flows as well. Indeed, aid and oil have similar economic implications. Both are revenues that accrue to the state. Both are volatile. Both are tradable. And both are "depleting" resources, since aid flows, like oil flows, are likely to be temporary. Here are the five IMF recommendations (recommendations italicized) with regard to aid, with brief comments on each regarding how they apply to oil.

1. *Minimize the risks of Dutch Disease.* This can be done by ensuring that the oil earnings are invested in ways that enhance productivity, and thereby raise rather than lower production in the non-oil traded good sector.

2. *Seek to enhance growth in the short to medium term.* The oil earnings can be invested in some high-return "quick win" areas, such as improved food production, strengthened infrastructure (especially roads, power, and ports), and increased educational outlays.

3. *Promote good governance and reduce corruption.* The key here is transparency and reliable public information on the sources and uses of oil earnings, and the expected flow of oil earnings in the future.

4. *Prepare an exit strategy.* Just as increased foreign aid flows are temporary (by design), so that a recipient government must plan to substitute its own revenue base in the future as aid flows decline, so too an oil-exporting country must prepare for the depletion of oil income flows.

5. *Regularly reassess the appropriate policy mix.* Oil earnings are highly volatile and the specific mix of appropriate fiscal, monetary, and exchange rate policies will change over time along with fluctuations in international prices, oil flows, and changes in productivity in the non-oil sectors. Evidence of serious overvaluation of the real exchange rate (e.g., an intense squeeze of profits in non-oil export sectors) should prompt policies to depreciate the nominal exchange rate, either through an outright movement

of a pegged exchange rate, or a change in the monetary–fiscal mix consistent with exchange rate depreciation.

TOWARD A QUANTITATIVE ASSESSMENT OF OIL REVENUES AND NATIONAL DEVELOPMENT

All that has been said here is, of course, general. To move beyond these generalizations requires quantitative modeling of a country's specific circumstances, modeling that is beyond the scope of this chapter. A typical formal analytical approach would be to maximize intergenerational well-being subject to the production possibilities of the economy, the time path of oil earnings, the uncertainties about world prices of oil, and the investment opportunities at hand, considering both physical investments in productive capacity and financial investments in overseas assets. The formal analysis can show how a temporary and depleting path of oil earnings can best be extended into a long-term benefit for succeeding generations. The rate at which the policy planner "discounts" the future will determine much about the time path of using oil revenues.

CONCLUSION

Oil revenues need not be a curse. When properly managed, they can play a special and important role in overall economic development in low-income countries, especially by providing the public financing for critical investments in key public goods. As long as this is done, the fears about the Dutch Disease are likely to be exaggerated. The specific nature of the goods will vary by country and region, notably according to the stage of economic development. For the poorest of the poor, priorities will lie in meeting basic needs and basic infrastructure. For middle-income countries, priorities will lie in expanding access to higher education, science, and advanced technologies. For high-income countries, priorities will most likely lie in meeting the commitments of social welfare spending, especially on pensions and health care. In all of these cases, there will be a likely advantage in using the oil earnings to cover priority *public* spending, rather than viewing the oil earnings as an income flow to be transferred back to households. (Of course such a conclusion begs the question of the transparency and honesty of the public sector.) Given the volatility of world oil prices and the depletion of oil over time, considerable care must be given to managing the large macroeconomic risks of oil income flows, as well as to spread the benefits of the oil earnings across generations. This is best accomplished by converting oil flows into long-lasting financial, physical, and human capital.

NOTE

1. By "nonrival" I mean that one person's consumption of the good does not take away the potential for another person to enjoy the good. By "nonexcludable" I mean that it is difficult to *prevent* people from making use of the good once it is produced.

REFERENCES

Sachs, J. D. and F. Rodriguez. 1999. "Why Do Resource-Abundant Economies Grow More Slowly?" *Journal for Economic Growth* 4: 277–303.

Sachs, J. D. and A. Warner. 1999. "The Big Push, Natural Resource Booms and Growth." *Journal of Development Economics* 59: 43–76.

Sachs, J. D. and A. Warner. 2000. "Natural Resources Abundance and Economic Growth." HIID Development Discussion Paper 517a, October 1995. Later published in *Leading Issues in Economic Development*. New York: Oxford University Press.

Sachs, J. D. and A. Warner. 2001. "The Curse of Natural Resources." *European Economic Review* 45: 827–38.

UN Millennium Project. 2005. *Investing in Development: A Practical Plan to Achieve the Millennium Development Goals*. New York: Earthscan.

CHAPTER 8

The Political Economy of Natural Resource Funds

Macartan Humphreys and Martin E. Sandbu

ABSTRACT

The economic case for natural resource funds is surprisingly weak. There is, however, an important political rationale for resource funds. In this chapter, we show theoretically that the importance of natural resource funds (NRFs) lies in the effects that they have on the incentives facing political actors. Our theoretical analysis is supported by empirical work on institutions and expenditure decisions. If, as is sometimes the case, NRFs do not substantially affect political incentives then they can be ignored or bypassed by governments and have no beneficial effect. To be effective, we argue that (1) withdrawal decisions should be regulated in part by clear rules rather than general guidelines, (2) key decisions should be made by bodies representing the interests of diverse political constituencies, and (3) there should be high levels of transparency regarding their status and operation—in particular there should be a unified budgetary process and public reporting of payments, holdings, and investments. However, we emphasize that in all cases the impact of the institutional details will depend on the extent to which they alter the incentives facing political actors. We identify a series of ways to ensure that these provisions are correctly aligned with political incentives, including ways in which institutional strength can be "imported" from third parties.

INTRODUCTION

Despite popular belief in their utility, research on natural resource funds does not find evidence that funds lead to better management of natural resources (Davis et al. 2003; Fasano 2000). Natural Resource Funds (NRFs) are employed in countries that use revenues well, but they are also employed in countries that use them badly. While they may restrain government overexpenditure in some cases, in other cases, fund rules are changed or the NRFs themselves are raided when governments wish to increase expenditure. In cases where there appears to be a positive relationship between the presence of NRFs and expenditure smoothing, it is not clear that the NRFs themselves, rather than other features of a country's political system, are responsible for the policy choices. Norway, for example, is often cited as a country with a highly effective NRF, yet inferring a causal effect for the Norwegian case is difficult: the restrictions imposed upon policy makers by the Norwegian fund are extremely weak.[1] In contrast, much effort went into ensuring that Chad put in place a fund for future generations, as a precondition for World Bank financing of the Doba oilfield developments and the Chad–Cameroon pipeline. But despite the fund, Chad remains one of the most corrupt and least democratic countries in the world, and as recent experience has shown, the government felt free to simply change the rules when it wanted greater access to the oil revenues. These facts then create a puzzle: what features, if any, of a natural resource fund might lead to beneficial changes in economic policy choices?

To confront this puzzle, we draw on recent research in the political economy of policy making. This research studies the incentives that face policy makers in different institutional environments and examines how these incentives affect the choices that policy makers take. Our analysis suggests that one reason for the poor empirical relationship between NRFs and effective policy is that the economic logic used to justify the use of NRFs does not, by itself, show that NRFs are necessary. Good expenditure policies can be adopted with or without formal NRFs. More important than the economic rationale are political economy considerations. We address the question of whether resource funds are useful by analyzing how political incentives influence key decisions regarding how much to accumulate. Setting up a natural resource fund does not automatically change the political economy incentives for "misbehavior." The potential value of an NRF lies instead in the details of a fund's institutional procedures and on *how these affect the political incentives facing policy makers*. An NRF is useful only insofar as it improves these incentives; if incentives remain unchanged the NRF will not contribute to better fiscal management and might even make matters worse by adding complexity and reducing transparency.

The crux of our argument is the following. A crucial reason for the inability of policy makers to save windfall revenues for the future is that they risk losing control over how money will be spent at a later time. If a new government can come to power and dramatically alter the way the money is spent, an incumbent policy maker has an incentive to spend more money now, *even if he himself* would also prefer to smooth spending out over future time periods. This means that some compromises that benefit all political factions are in principle possible although in practice they do not get made. These compromises would require potential future governments to desist from changing policy too much, and this would induce incumbent governments to save more for the future. The problem is in getting policy makers to commit now to implementing more moderate policies in the future. Such commitments are made possible by political institutions. If Norway manages to save most of its oil revenues, it is because the general institutional environment (and not just the oil fund) endows the politics with a high degree of predictability (below we present more general empirical findings to this effect). In countries with weaker governing systems, the challenge is to build institutional mechanisms for commitment and predictability. This point is certainly much more general than the question of whether or not to have an NRF; it goes to the heart of state-building. Our more modest focus is on whether and how the occasion of setting up an NRF can be used to make incremental improvements to the institutional structure of a country's political economy. In doing so, we emphasize the risk that the goals that an NRF is set up to achieve may come to naught if the political incentives work against them.

We argue, therefore, that it is crucial for designers of natural resource funds to take into account the political economy context within which the resource fund is to be set up. Although this context is unique to every country, we aim to illustrate various types of political economy effects that are likely to operate quite generally, and show how they create incentives against the prudent management of natural resource wealth. How these effects play out "on the ground," as well as their relative importance, is something that can be determined only with local knowledge. Our aim is to show policy makers an inventory of effects that could be at work, and encourage them to identify the specifics of these effects in their local context.

In the final section of this chapter, we suggest a series of ways to mitigate such harmful incentives. We emphasize a role for joint decision-making or separation of powers in withdrawal or spending decisions, and a high level of transparency in fund operations. A number of these solutions, for which we provide a social-scientific rationale in this chapter, are taken up again in chapter 11, which provides further detail on the legal aspects of achieving the goals we set out here.

ECONOMIC CASE FOR ACCUMULATION AND NATURAL RESOURCE FUNDS

The economic arguments usually advanced for natural resource funds (NRFs) do not, in fact, provide a rationale for new government institutions. Instead, they provide an argument for the principle of *expenditure smoothing*. The argument runs as follows. In low- or middle-income countries (and a small number of high-income countries) whose main exports consist of fuel or mineral resources, governments often face revenues that are both large (as a share of the country's economy or compared to the government's other sources of public revenues) and extremely unstable. The instability of natural resource rents derives in the short run from the high volatility of world commodity prices, and in the longer run from the fact that natural resources are depletable and therefore cannot be exploited in perpetuity. These features create a special problem for fiscal policy,[2] as volatility in expenditures is generally suboptimal. Public spending yields "diminishing marginal benefit"—the social gain from spending more than the long-term average in some years is not great enough to outweigh the social cost of having to reduce spending below the average in other years.[3] Such boom–bust patterns, however, are a nearly universal experience in commodity-dependent economies.

This has several important implications. One is that spending should be stabilized and should not track revenues closely. Another is that temporarily large revenues—such as those deriving from depletable natural resources—ought to be saved so as to also benefit future generations. Natural resource funds are often set up with one or the other of these as the main goal, and the detailed accumulation and spending rules designed accordingly. Indeed, NRFs are often labeled "stabilization funds," "savings funds," or "future generations funds." The general principle behind both stabilization and saving is the same. When revenues are front loaded, as is usually the case with natural resource revenue streams, a policy of constant public expenditures does double duty, as it fulfills both a savings function and a stabilization function.

This is not the place to debate the details of the economically optimal spending path, about which there can be reasonable disagreements (see chapter 7 and Engel and Valdés 2000 for several views). The main point to note is that the optimal pattern of public spending is *independent* of the shape of the revenue stream. The implication is that the public administration in such situations must manage the mismatch between incomes and expenses: It must, so to speak, save in plentiful years to compensate for meager years. The difficulty of this challenge is illustrated by the dramatic failures of most natural resource-rich countries once the meager years set in.

The need to separate the pattern of spending from the pattern of income means that good fiscal policy in countries with large natural resource wealth typically involves accumulating large amounts of revenues for future use. In a notional sense, therefore, natural resource-rich countries should always have a "fund," meaning simply that they should have a stock of accumulated savings, to be drawn down when the natural resource revenues dry up. Nothing in this economics argument, however, requires that the natural resource monies be administratively separated in any way from other government assets, as a formal NRF does. In other words, there is no *economic* need for new institutions or rules governing the accumulation of revenues—there is just a need for accumulation according to some optimal policy.[4]

Nevertheless, several countries have sought to tackle the fiscal policy difficulties precisely by establishing formal NRFs. The experience with NRFs goes quite far back; Kuwait's General Resource Fund for example was established in 1960, and Kiribati's Revenue Equalization Reserve Fund for phosphate revenues was established in 1956. Many currently active NRFs have been in existence for several decades—two examples considered relatively successful are the Alaska Permanent Fund (established in 1976) and the Norwegian State Petroleum Fund (established in 1990, although it did not receive any inflows until 1995). In the past few years, there has been quite a scramble among natural resource producers to set up NRFs. Some of these are new producers such as Sao Tome and Principe, which passed legislation establishing a permanent fund in December of 2004,[5] while others are established producers, many of which have experienced political transitions in the recent past (e.g., Azerbaijan established its State Oil Fund in 1999, Kazakhstan set up its National Fund in 2001,[6] and East Timor has set up a Petroleum Fund after the Norwegian model).[7]

The stated purpose of these NRFs is to facilitate the accumulation of large, volatile, and temporary revenues when times are good; stabilize public spending; and finance public spending when natural resource revenues are no longer flowing in. The reality, however, is more worrisome. Studies show that it is difficult to detect a consistent improvement of fiscal policy in countries with NRFs relative to those without them. Fasano (2000) examined the NRFs of Norway, Chile, Alaska, Venezuela, Kuwait, and Oman, and found that the outcome is "mixed," which reflects in part "the challenges in *adhering* to the operational rules" (emphasis added) and the "overall fiscal discipline in the country." Davis et al. (2003) carried out an econometric analysis of the effect of NRFs on the link between changes in public expenditures and variations in revenue. They found that while some countries with NRFs exhibit a lesser sensitivity of government expenditure to natural resource revenues than countries without NRFs, that advantage was already present before the countries set up their respective NRFs. There is therefore no evidence that adopting NRFs in these countries contributed to the soundness of their fiscal policies.

The experience of African states with the primary commodity marketing boards of the 1970s and 1980s also provides grounds for caution. These institutions were similar in principle to natural resource funds in many ways. The marketing boards, established with the purpose of smoothing income fluctuations, building up savings and facilitating local investment, became a tool for governments to generate private gains at a cost to economic producers (Bates 1981). The failure of these boards lay in part in the fact that their design ignored the incentives facing the political leaders who controlled them.

We see that in practice, NRFs and similar institutions rarely make it any easier to accumulate large amounts of money in the orderly fashion the normative economic model calls for, reflecting the fact that the incentives surrounding the choices of politicians do not conform to this idealized model. For fiscal policy to be correct, it is not sufficient to get the economics right. One must also get the political economy right, and as much as possible align the political economy incentives of decision makers with what is good policy for the country.

POLITICAL ECONOMY INCENTIVES
AGAINST ACCUMULATION

In this section we analyze the political economy incentives that may face politicians in countries with accumulated revenues—whether or not these revenues are formally a "fund." To set up institutional solutions to make it more likely that a beneficial spending path will be followed, it is necessary to understand the incentives that make it unlikely in the first place. Why do decision makers tend to be impatient—why are they so likely to spend too much of the money that is available instead of saving it for harder times and for future generations?

Our main analysis concentrates on the nature of *interest-group politics with power rivalry*. Most of politics involves a struggle between competing interests, and we show in what follows that the competition for power among different groups can create perverse incentives to overspend in early time periods (with less left for later), even when there exists a more stable time path of spending that all groups would prefer. After this main case, we extend the basic analysis to discuss how overspending can be affected by the following possibilities.

- Politicians may gain political support through higher public expenditures.
- Conversely, an informed citizenry might punish politicians who imprudently overspend.
- Increased public spending may be privately valuable for the politician (independently of any political support it buys him).
- Accumulated revenues may provide an incentive to undermine the "rules of the game" embodied in the country's governing institutions.

Before turning to these specific possibilities, we now describe our basic model of power rivalry.

INTEREST-GROUP POLITICS WITH POWER RIVALRY

Political competition often consists of the contest between representatives of different interest groups to control the public purse and use it to the benefit of their own group. The nature of the different groups varies across different countries. The dividing lines can be based on class, ideology, ethnicity, language, religion, or other traits. The severity of the divisions, and the extent to which political competition follows interest-group lines, are also different in every country.

The degree to which politicians compete for the opportunity to favor their own group at the expense of others will affect the fiscal policies of the state. Dixit et al. (2000) show how the division of the budget in an electoral period depends on the nature of the political competition, in particular the likelihood of a change in government in the next period.

When the sitting government decides how much of the budget to allocate to its own group, it must take into account how the opposition will behave as a result if they take power next. A similar dynamic can affect the *total* amount of spending of natural resource-generated wealth. A government may ideally want to spread spending evenly across all periods, but the possibility that another group takes power in the next period, and one's own group loses out as a result, creates an incentive to spend too much now. The incumbent government can choose its own preferred spending patterns with today's expenditures, whereas if another group takes power tomorrow, it will allocate tomorrow's expenditure according to *its* preference. This makes it preferable for an incumbent government to shift expenditure from the future to today.

We consider the following setting[8]: Suppose a country has an amount of accumulated past natural resource revenues—that is, it has a "fund," at least in the notional sense, of past earnings. We assume that there is no other income or wealth. To keep it simple, we assume that the population is divided into two equally sized groups (*a* and *b*). The politicians must select some share of the total "fund" to allocate to projects benefiting each of the two groups in each of two periods (1 and 2). Hence they must choose both the division of *aggregate* expenditures in the two periods and the allocation of resources to projects benefiting each of the two groups within each period.

Suppose now there are two potential policy makers that we also call *a* and *b,* with divergent preferences over the welfare of two different constituencies. We assume that each of them cares about both groups, but they care relatively more about their own group than about the other.[9] In addition, we impose some technical constraints on the preferences of the policy makers. In particular, we assume that benefits delivered today are considered better than the same benefits delivered tomorrow (that is, policy makers are impatient), that there are *positive but diminishing marginal benefits* from spending on each group (i.e., each additional dollar spent on the same group adds progressively less benefit), and that the elasticity of substitution of benefits across groups is constant.

Now, suppose policy maker *a* is in power in period 1 (so she is the "incumbent," and policy maker *b* is the "challenger"). Consider first the situation where she knows for certain that she will still be in government in period 2. In this case, we can show that her preferred choice is very simple and can be thought of as consisting of two components: a decision regarding how much to spend in each period, and a decision about how to divide a given period's expenditure across the two groups.

Under the assumptions of the model, we can show that for the second decision, she simply allocates a fixed share of whatever amount of money is available for spending in that period to her own group, and the remaining fraction to group *b*. The share is independent of the *total* amount spent in each period. The same is true for the challenger, although obviously the shares will be different from those of the incumbent.

Finding 1

Once the aggregate amount of spending for a period is set, the policy maker gives a fixed share to each group. The policy maker's own group gets the largest share, and the share increases the more biased the policy maker is. Moreover, the more slowly diminishing marginal benefit sets in, the more unequal is the allocation. This suggests that if marginal utility diminishes more slowly in poorer societies, then poverty will be associated with deeper disagreements.

Since we know how the policy makers want to "divide the pie" between groups in each period, we need now only work out how they would choose to divide the total fund across the two periods. Policy maker *a*'s choice can be simplified to choosing the amount to be spent in the first period and therefore implicitly the amount for the second period (whatever is left unspent from period 1). We consider first a situation where she *knows* that she will be in power next period as well, and show that she will smooth aggregate spending across periods, with any change from period 1 to period 2 caused by the impatience inherent in the preferences—the more patient she is, the closer the division is to a 50:50 split across the two periods.[10] (*Within* each period the division between the two groups can be far from a 50:50 split; that will depend on how biased the incumbent is toward her own group.)

This choice has several appealing properties:

Finding 2

When the incumbent knows she will be in power in both periods, she chooses a time path of aggregate spending that is *efficient* in the sense that there is no allocation that can allow any one group to do better without making the other group worse off. Furthermore, it is *optimal* for the incumbent in the sense that there is no other allocation across groups and over time that would make *her* better off, even at the cost of making the other policy maker worse off.

One implication of this is that the policy is *time consistent*—it does not matter whether the incumbent makes her decisions regarding both periods right away, or decides on the allocations one period at a time. The sequentially decided policy is the same she would choose if she could commit to the entire time path of spending allocations (i.e., for both periods) at the beginning of period 1. This is not true for all types of economic policy choices,[11] but it is true here: with correct anticipation of her own choices in the second period, the staggering of the decision-making process has no impact on the policy maker's choices.

Now consider the more realistic situation in which the policy maker is uncertain over the choices that will be made in future periods. There is some probability q that she will be turned out of office and be replaced by policy maker b. In this case, she will choose a different allocation of expenditure across time. Her best choice, given that she expects b to favor his group, now depends not just on her impatience, but also on the size of q—the probability that she will be turned out of office—and the degree to which her priorities differ from those of a potential rival.

From this simple result, we can draw certain immediate lessons:

Finding 3

The less stable the government—in the sense that there is a higher likelihood of an imminent change in government—the stronger the incentive for spending a lot today. Period 1 spending is higher the larger is q, which shows that as policy maker a's power becomes more precarious, she is tempted to spend more.

Finding 4

The deeper is the division among the groups—the more pronounced is the tendency of politicians to favor only their own group at the expense of others—the greater will be the incentive to spend too much while one is in power.

The model also shows that these last two effects—the instability effect and the conflict effect—reinforce each other. Instability has a more adverse effect in more divided societies.

Disagreement and instability, then, cause overspending and inefficient fiscal policy. This should *not* be interpreted as a claim that dictatorships are more efficient than democracies; rather, what matters is the *horizon* of regimes. Governments or rulers who expect to be in power for a long time have an incentive (out of their self-interest) to smooth spending over time. This incentive disappears when power is precarious, for example, because of frequent coups or revolutions (as is in fact empirically more likely in nondemocratic systems). As we shall see below, electoral politics can modify this finding in several ways. Moreover, if in democracies, government changes do not produce as large shifts in spending allocations, the incentive to overspend is weaker in them.[12]

Since distributive conflicts can lead to overspending of accumulated funds, we should not be surprised that the resulting front loading of spending has distributive effects:

Finding 5

The distortion has distributive implications. It redistributes to the incumbent's group (*a*) from the other group (*b*), thereby partly compensating for the lower welfare the incumbent has due to the probability of losing office. Given that the incumbent *a* prioritizes her own group within each period, *b* would prefer aggregate expenditure to be shifted toward period 2, when policy maker *b* has some likelihood of deciding the allocation, and away from period 1, when it is certain policy maker *a* decides. The challenger *b*, then, would prefer a *reduction* in first-period expenditure relative to the baseline efficient time path, rather than an increase. Thus, as policy maker *a* protects herself against the eventuality that *b* gains power, she makes *b* worse off. Only if $q = 0$ and there is no chance that *b* will gain office is *b*'s ideal intertemporal expenditure the same as *a*'s.

An important finding of the model is that the loss that the incumbent inflicts on the challenger by shifting expenditure to period 1 is *greater* than her own gain. As a consequence:

Finding 6

There exist of expenditure intertemporal profiles that are not chosen but that would make *all* groups better off.[13]

The challenge for institutional designers in countries where this is a big problem is to find ways to solve this problem and realize the efficiency gain that could in principle benefit all parts of society. Two types of improvements are possible. One involves *risk sharing*. Since the policy makers in this model are risk averse, they dislike the uncertainty of what the spending pattern across groups will be in period 2. Both will therefore, *ex ante*, prefer outcomes that minimize the variation in the expected second period expenditure.[14] This could be achieved in all cases by both parties committing *ex ante*—were this possible—to implementing the same compromise allocation in period 2, the value of which would exceed the expected, risk-adjusted, value of the policies that may be implemented by the uncertain winner of the power contest. Such risk sharing can be beneficial even without any change in the *intertemporal* allocation of aggregate resources and is a feature that has been studied elsewhere in settings in which total per period allocations are fixed (see, e.g., Alesina 1988; Dixit et al. 2000). Of course, the big obstacle to such joint commitments is the difficulty of making a credible commitment that one will not exploit an advantageous position once it has been determined who is in power.

The second type of improvement involves intertemporal smoothing of aggregate expenditure. From the point of view of our examination of NRFs, these concerns are especially interesting. Inefficiency arises in part because the first period government increases the expenditure beyond her own optimum; this rise in expenditure implies a loss for her relative to the situation in which her return to office is guaranteed. But as noted earlier, this loss for the first government does not imply a gain to the second period government since the increase is in the direction of distributive allocations favored by the incumbent only. To see how an improvement in this case is possible, imagine a situation in which player b could commit, in the event that he takes office in the second period, to allocate shares that are more favorable to a relative to what he would normally like to allocate. With such a commitment, a would find it advantageous to shift more spending from period 1 to period 2, making herself better off and more than compensating b for his reduced share, should he gain office. Again, the downside of such a solution is the commitment problem—a promise by player b not to take full advantage of being in power in period 2 is not necessarily credible.[15]

Here we reach the heart of the matter. Inefficient overspending occurs because of incentives created by diverging interests and competition for power to advance those interests. The inefficiency can be overcome if policy makers can commit not to take full advantage of their power when they are in government. If such commitments could be credibly made, incumbents would have fewer incentives to spend everything before losing power. Everybody would benefit from the resulting change: The challenger would benefit from having the prospect of more money to spend once he gains power, and the incumbent from the more efficient time path of spending on her group, as well as a more favorable treatment than her group would otherwise receive at the hands of b should he gain power.

This point is really a special case of the more general idea that efficiency can be improved by the predictability made possible by the rule of law and checks and balances in government.

Can a natural resource fund provide the kind of commitment device needed here? An NRF could place a cap on expenditures in each period, which, if implemented, could return the society to an efficient expenditure profile. This profile, however, *would not necessarily make both players better off than in the situation which would otherwise obtain* (that is, the fund may not constitute a "Pareto improvement" on what would prevail in its absence). Imposing a limit on how much *a* is allowed to spend in the first period will reduce *her* expected welfare, and she therefore has a strong incentive to resist compliance with such a rule. As we saw earlier, she needs to expect a compensation in period 2 (in the form of a less biased allocation by policy maker *b* should he gain power) for what she gives up by shifting expenditure to a time during which it is uncertain that she would control how it is spent. An NRF design that did not take account of this would run a serious risk of being ignored, violated, or changed, with the possible further harmful effect of reducing the respect for policy commitments or the force of law.

A Pareto-superior time path would require some form of implicit contract compliance *across* governments, in which present governments that cap present expenditure are compensated by actions of future governments. The implication is that expenditure stability might require not simply caps on *how much* can be spent, but also guarantees regarding *on what* the saved money is to be spent. Also implicit in our analysis is the fact that the problem is likely to be worse if a sitting government faces fewer and lesser constraints on what it can do. If the opposition, say, can prevent the worst excesses of the sitting government, the latter would be forced to take into account the interests of the former. Further, if the incumbent knows that she can prevent a new government's excesses in the case she loses power, she will be more willing to delay spending.

SPENDING AND POLITICAL SUPPORT

In the analysis so far, we have ignored one very important fact: The government's spending decisions can affect the incumbent's likelihood of remaining in power. As the incumbent foresees these consequences, she will modify her behavior. There are myriad mechanisms through which such effects may be mediated—some mechanisms will make matters worse, others might alleviate the problem. We first survey some of the former type: mechanisms that are likely to exacerbate the incentives for overspending.

Why may a politician be rewarded for a policy that deviates from the one that is best for the population? One reason is that citizens themselves may be myopic, and therefore ignore the long-term consequences of a policy that is satisfying in the short term. There is strong evidence from social psychology that such impatience (or "hyperbolic preferences") is a common trait (Ainslie and Haslam 1992). Another situation in which politicians' fortunes might be better served by spending more is when a political system gives disproportionate influence to the support of a small part of the population (see chapter 2). In such circumstances, that small part of the population might expect always to be favored by the spending policies of the government without having to pay the burden of future spending cuts, which may be more evenly spread across the population. Put differently, the future negative consequences of profligate spending today may be insufficiently internalized by the politically most powerful group. A third and important mechanism by which spending affects support is that larger budgets allow a government to employ more civil servants, which may lead directly to a rise in political support. We refer to Robinson et al. (2005) for an analysis of the effect of natural resource booms on the incentives for bloating the public sector with inefficient patronage jobs. Their model produces a general pattern similar to that described here: The ability to strengthen one's political support by expanding the public sector leads to an inefficiently high level of extraction of the depletable natural resources. The more the power prospects can be manipulated in this way, of course, the higher the extraction/depletion rate.

Our simple model also sheds light on these cases. The findings discussed in the preceding text were generated for cases where the probability of a power change is independent of policy choices. If the likelihood of remaining in power is instead *improved* by expansionary policies, as suggested by the literature on political business cycles and public debt,[16] then the problem is exacerbated. Suppose that instead of a fixed q, the probability of a power change depends on the amount of aggregate spending in period 1:

Finding 7

If the probability that a government is removed decreases when incumbents spend more, then the distortion effects are even greater than in the baseline case. Moreover, the more sensitive to first-period spending is the probability that power will change, the more inefficiently high is first-period spending. Conversely, if the probability of a power change depends positively on spending in the first period, then the level of aggregate spending in period 1 is lower than it would be with a fixed probability, and consequently closer to the socially efficient level.

As the second part of the finding says, the need for political support can also encourage *more prudent* fiscal policy. Overspending, after all, can considerably reduce the welfare of the population, relative to the policies prescribed by the economic analyses we discussed in the previous section. In a well-functioning democracy, informed voters could impose discipline on the government by throwing the incumbent out of office if she overspends by too much in the first period. This type of mechanism will be affected by how well the citizenry can observe the fiscal policies of the government, in particular the magnitude of natural resource revenues and the rate at which they are spent. Even in a country where the citizens are both motivated and have the ability to discipline the government, this cannot happen easily if they do not know what the government is doing.

TRANSPARENCY

We now proceed to identify the effect of transparency on the political incentives we have discussed. To do so, we draw on the analysis of government choices and political support found in Ferejohn (1986). This analysis assumes that the public observes the actions of politicians with some error. It may be, for example, that the public observes aggregate government expenditure but does not know the precise origin of such funds. In this extension of our simple model, citizens are, on average, correct about how much is left for spending in period 2, but they do not all get it right. The less transparency there is, the more the estimates of individual citizens vary. Those who think too little is left for period 2 punish the incumbent by supporting the challenger. Under such circumstances, we obtain the following result:

Finding 8

Greater levels of transparency result in more efficient monitoring and disciplining of the government by civilians and result in more efficient expenditure profiles.

We complete this section by considering two other mechanisms that may generate perverse incentives.

PRIVATE GAIN FROM PUBLIC SPENDING

Public spending may give politicians benefits other than stronger political support. There may, for example, be private benefits to spending more. Larger budgets—and consequently higher public employment—may give the members of the government social status and prestige, and greater opportunity for patronage. This could be seen as a personal investment for a policy maker, since it could result in a return of favors once he or she is out of office. This would create a separate incentive for spending even when there is little political competition and the officeholder is certain that his or her successor will be from the same party or represent the same interest group.

This effect is likely to be especially important when the end of the politician's term in office is imminent. More generally, the shorter is the average tenure of office, the stronger will be the incentive to boost the rate of public spending. The incentive is also likely to be stronger in societies where patronage positions and favors are important parts of the social fabric, and where meritocracy is weak, so that a politician's future welfare more strongly depends on the friendships and relationships he has established while in office.

INCENTIVES TO CHANGE THE RULES OF THE GAME

In institutionally weak environments, the presence of large resource rents can also provide a "prize value" to state capture (Fearon and Laitin 2003). In cases in which violence or extraconstitutional means can be used to overturn a sitting government, the holding of valuable assets by weak political actors can be an especially risky enterprise. In terms of our model in the preceding text, this effect can be captured (as we did for the case of endogenous reelection probabilities) simply by treating the probability of termination of office (now by constitutional *or* extraconstitutional means) at the end of the first period as an increasing function of the remaining assets.[17] As before, this would lead to a rise in first-period expenditure. Note, however, that this should occur only if coup-makers can expect to have easy access to government revenues upon overthrowing the sitting government.

SUMMARY OF RESULTS

Our simple model of policy choices provides insight into the factors affecting government decision in the presence of accumulated revenues. We find that the tendency to spend too much too quickly, far from being irrational, follows a simple logic. The incentives to overspend produce outcomes that have distributional as well as efficiency implications. These incentives cannot be changed simply by placing caps on expenditure. Instead, they require some form of coordination between governments at different time periods regarding not simply *how much* is spent, but *how* it is spent.

The adverse effects that we identify are likely to be more pronounced in some places than they are in others. The incentives are greatest in societies in which there are deep social divisions and in which political instability is high. They will be exacerbated in contexts in which current spending increases the chances of retaining power; a feature that is likely to prevail when (1) a large part of the population lives in poverty and has very high discount rates; (2) due to horizontal or vertical income inequality (see chapter 9), small but politically pivotal groups can affect policy choices disproportionately; (3) governments have greater freedom to use expenditure decisions to fund patronage networks that increase their support base; or finally (4) due to low education levels or a lack of transparency about the implications of government choices, the population is less able to exert control over policy makers.

We developed these results within a simple model of policy choice over two periods. In a more realistic environment, the decision-making processes described in the preceding text are repeated many times. In such a case, the effects we identify can still be observed, but other outcomes are also possible. In particular, it is possible that if players are sufficiently patient, a form of *tacit coordination* across policy makers can emerge, in which each policy maker voluntarily moderates expenditure from fear of retaliatory action by future policy makers should she overspend. Such tacit coordination does not *require* the existence of formal institutions to ensure compliance. It does, however, depend on some of the same conditions that we argued can help ameliorate the problem even in the two-period setting. In particular, it depends on a minimal degree of transparency that allows future governments to observe the actions of past governments and condition their behavior on these actions.

POLITICAL ECONOMY CHALLENGES TO PRUDENT POLICY: EMPIRICAL RESULTS

A key result in our analysis above is that a high degree of discretion by a single political constituency creates incentives to use up windfall revenues as soon as they come in instead of accumulating them. Here we present some empirical results which suggest that this relationship holds in practice as well as in theory. As discussed in the preceding text, the optimal economic policies should not let year-to-year government expenditures vary much in response to oil revenue fluctuation. To examine whether natural resource-rich countries follow such policies, we consider a simple econometric model of government consumption in a sample of oil producing countries. In this model we relate change in government consumption (as recorded in the World Bank's World Development Indicators 2002) to an indicator of the value of receipts earned annually from a country's oil industry, as recorded by published sources.[18] The results of the model are presented in table 8.1. The first column in the table shows that on average, there is no discernible pass-through of year-to-year oil revenue changes to aggregate government consumption. The coefficient on year-to-year changes in oil revenues is statistically indistinguishable from zero.

The picture changes, however, when we differentiate between countries with weak and strong divisions of power in the governance systems. The variable used, CHECKS, is drawn from the Database of Political Institutions (Beck et al. 2000) and measures the degree to which political

Table 8.1   Empirical Results

	Year-to-Year Change in Government Consumption	Year-to-Year Change in Government Consumption
Year-to-year change in GDP, %	0.663 (0.000)***	0.644 (0.000)***
Year-to-year change in oil revenues (dOIL), %	0.009 (0.411)	0.092 (0.003)***
CHECKS × dOIL		−0.090 (0.003)***
Checks and balances (CHECKS)		0.001 (0.957)
Constant	0.013 (0.631)	−0.031 (0.199)
Observations	2118	1284
Number of countries	94	91
R-squared	0.12	0.14

Fixed effects regression (country fixed effects). Yearly change variables measured with one-year lag. Controls not reported: Year dummies. p-values in parentheses.
*significant at 10%; **significant at 5%; ***significant at 1%

power in a country is subject to checks and balances.[19] The data show a strong relationship between the strength of the institutional environment and the effect of oil revenues on spending. The importance of the institutional environment for how oil revenues are managed is vividly illustrated by a simple scatterplot of the change in government consumption against the change in oil sales, drawn separately for countries with weak and strong checks and balances (figure 8.1).

The graphs bring out the essential finding of the second regression. In countries with strong checks and balances, government consumption bears little relationship to oil sales volatility. However, there is a strong effect in countries with worse governing systems. The elasticity of the change in government consumption with respect to the change in oil sales is 0.092 in countries with few checks and balances, meaning that for a doubling of oil sales, government consumption in such countries increases on average by 9.2 percent. This implies a high rate of pass-through of oil revenue changes. Suppose that 20 percent of government consumption is financed by oil and oil sales double. Then we have that oil earnings in-

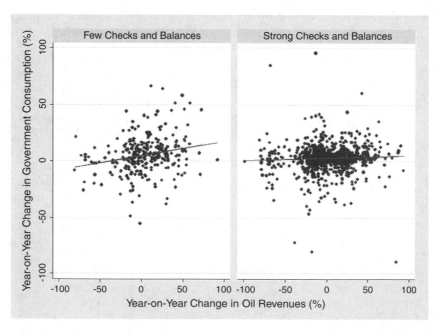

Figure 8.1   Sensitivity of Government Expenditure to Annual Changes in Oil Revenues in Countries with Many and Few Checks and Balances.

Source: Authors' calculations.

crease by 20 percent of baseline government consumption, and expenditure increases by 9.2 percent of baseline government consumption, implying that 46 percent (that is, 9.2 percent/20 percent) of the additional money is consumed within a year.[20]

POLICY IMPLICATIONS

Our analysis makes plain that policy makers have strong *political* incentives not to follow what economists might describe as the economically best policy. We should therefore not be very surprised to find that economic logic is rarely followed in natural resource-rich countries. But our analysis also shows that it can be in the interest of *all* parties, including incumbents, to find institutional arrangements that help discipline expenditure. The model described shows how overspending can result from the fact that individual policy makers cannot commit to undertake a given set of actions in the future. The practical issue is, then, how to overcome this problem. In particular, what kind of institutional reforms might improve the ability of policy makers to make mutually advantageous, credible commitments?

It is in light of this question that the decision whether or not to establish an NRF—and what kind of fund to design—should be resolved. Since an NRF is not necessary for strictly economic reasons, the rationale for it has to be as a vehicle for institutional solutions to the political economy problem. If that is impossible, an NRF is at best useless—and if designed without a view to its effect on political incentives, may even make such incentives worse—and should be eschewed. Designers of prospective NRFs, therefore, must determine whether an NRF can realign local incentives. As we have emphasized, this is different from answering the basic economic question of what the optimal time path of natural resource–financed expenditure would be.[21] Instead, the analysis we recommend would focus on what the agents entrusted with carrying out the expenditure policy are likely to do, and how different NRF designs may change their behavior. Such analysis could conceivably prefer an NRF that encouraged a less-than-perfect expenditure path, but a path that policy makers would in fact implement, to one which called for policy makers to implement the optimal policy but gave them no incentive to comply.

We emphasize that the best design will be different in different countries. It has to take account of the local political economy, which is best understood by experienced practitioners with intimate knowledge of local political conditions. What we can do at a general level is to list types of institutional mechanisms that could be implemented through an NRF, and that may work in some local settings, if not in all. What we aim to provide in this section, then, is an inventory of potential institutional "fixes," which designers of NRFs can use as a roadmap to identify solutions that are most likely to work in their local political setting.

The ways in which NRFs could embody institutional solutions to the incentive problem fall, very roughly, into three categories:

1. The NRF can be set up with *rules* that govern the *magnitude* and *composition* of spending from it. The use of rules rather than discretionary decisions can provide one way of improving the regularity of policy across governments and help solve the commitment problem identified above.

2. An NRF can impose a *separation* or *sharing* of decision-making authority between different political constituencies. For example, the preceding discussion suggests that one way to remedy the commitment problem is to *separate the authority to decide how much is to be spent from the authority to decide on what it is spent.*

3. An NRF can have an *informational* role. We have shown that under certain conditions, transparency increases the ability of the citizenry to hold the government accountable. In addition, it is well known from the economics of information that when information is scarce and asymmetric, efficient outcomes are more difficult to sustain. An NRF could alleviate this problem by facilitating the flow of information within the government system and between it and the population or the international public.

We now survey a range of more specific institutional mechanisms an NRF could use to implement these three principles. Chapter 11 discusses some of these mechanisms in further detail, in particular with a view to the legal issues they raise.

RULES

One possible solution to the problem of overspending is to remove the government's discretion over how natural resource wealth is spent. Most NRFs are set up with conditions on how and when money can be withdrawn from them, with the intention of making the money in the NRF less easy to mismanage than revenues that are at the government's free disposal in the normal budget. We discuss three types of rules institutional designers will wish to consider.

Quantitative constraints: Rules governing *how much* can be spent.

An NRF can limit the government's discretion over how much of natural resource wealth is spent by a rule or formula indicating the maximum expenditure allowed (or conceivably, the exact amount to be spent). In practical terms, the rules can express how much is available for spending either as a function of that year's revenues, or as a function of total wealth, or some combination. Often rules are expressed as a function of the commodity's price and its deviation from some benchmark level. Other times, rules limit spending to a proportion (typically the expected investment return) of the money already accumulated in the NRF, that is, a function of financial wealth rather than total natural resource wealth (i.e., excluding the resources not yet extracted).[22]

Regardless of how the ceiling on yearly aggregate spending is specified, the legal status of the rule can vary considerably. In fact, "rules" are situated on a continuum between discretion and rigid formulas. On one end of the spectrum there are "rules" that have no legal force and only reflect the government's intended policies or policy "guidelines" or "commitments" (an example is the Norwegian State Petroleum Fund, and to a lesser degree the Petroleum Fund of East Timor). At the other end are formulas for expenditure ceilings enshrined in law (such as in Sao Tome and Principe), or with constitutional force (as in Alaska). Table 8.2 lists some countries with NRFs and describes the legal force of the rules governing in- and outflows from their funds, situating the "rules" from the almost discretionary to the constitutionally mandatory.

Depending on how mandatory a rule really is, restricting policy makers' discretion comes at a cost of flexibility. Governments can respond less easily to crisis situations or unforeseen changes that change the optimal policy, but it can also give current governments confidence that the results of prudent expenditure in one period will not be squandered through lavish expenditures in future periods. Nevertheless, quantitative caps are probably not a sufficient solution to the basic commitment problem that affects policy choices in resource-rich countries. The core problem, as our analysis suggests, is that policy makers will have an incentive to overturn or ignore these caps, because the incentives to spend too much too early derive in part from concerns about how, rather than simply how much, money will be spent.

Table 8.2   Rules Governing Inflows and Outflows from NRFs in Selected Countries

More Discretion	Inflows	Quantitative Constraints	Qualitative Constraints
Norway	All oil revenues enter the fund.	Parliament is unconstrained, but politicians have committed to an informal "handling rule" not to spend more than 4% of the balance of the fund per annum.	Outflows cover balance of government budget, decided by Parliament.
East Timor	All oil revenues enter the fund.	Parliament is unconstrained, but is supposed to stay within the highest amount that can be sustained in perpetuity (the permanent income from the oil wealth). The formula is given by law. Special reporting and justification procedures must be followed if amount exceeds the guideline.	Outflows cover balance of government budget, decided by Parliament.
Sao Tome and Principe	All oil revenues enter the fund.	Outflows cannot legally exceed the highest amount that can be sustained in perpetuity (except in the transition period before regular oil production starts). The formula is specified in the law on oil revenue management.	Outflows enter the government budget directly, but must be used for development purposes.
Alaska	A fixed proportion of oil revenues enters the fund.	A formula governs the amount of money that can be paid out from the fund. The rules are enshrined in state law and the state consitution.	Outflows can only go to citizens in the form of "permanent fund dividends." The rules are enshrined in state law and the state constitution.

Less Discretion

Qualitative constraints: Prededicated expenditures

In addition to codified rules for the amount of *aggregate* spending, an NRF could have rules for *how* the money is to be spent. Ecuador, for example, allocates excess oil revenues (above a budgeted oil price) to various funds with specific uses determined by law. For some of these, the decision of the aggregate amount to spend remains at the president's discretion, but the allocation to various uses must comply with the law.[23] Chad's oil revenue management law provides for fixed percentage allocations of oil revenues to special "priority sectors" such as health and education (we refer here to the law in vigor before the amendments announced in January 2006). Alaska state law specifies that 50 percent of the investment return on the principal of the Alaska Permanent Fund be distributed to all the state's residents on a per capita basis (the remainder has to be used to inflation-proof the principal before it can be spent on other uses). In other countries, fund rules state the general purposes for which the money should be spent, but in such a broad way that almost everything would seem to be allowed.[24] Again, the rules of existing NRFs vary widely in how legally binding they are (see table 8.2).

Proposals to impose such qualitative rules are commonly met with a concern that prededicated expenditures may occasion parallel budgets, which lead both to a loss in allocative efficiency and to a decline in transparency. As a practical matter, steps can and should be taken to ensure that this does not occur, by requiring that prededicated expenditures are entered into the general budget, or ideally, that qualitative constraints are referenced to the entire budget and not simply to the portions financed by an NRF. We return to this point when we discuss transparency below.

Rules governing inflows to the NRF

Many NRFs are set up with specific rules as to what should go *into* the NRF. This is not always necessary—money can be placed in the NRF by a discretionary act of the incumbent authorities when revenues are high. Discretion, however, allows governments to circumvent the rules the NRF imposes on *spending* by simply directing money straight to the budget without passing through the NRF. In the case of Chad, for example, signatory bonuses were not required to enter the fund with the result that initial expenditures of oil revenues in Chad were used for military rather than developmental purposes. Several countries accordingly channel *all* their natural resource revenues, including signatory bonuses, into their NRFs; others a fixed proportion (table 8.2). In some countries, NRFs receive some proportion of "excess" natural resource revenues, where the excess is defined relative to some budgeted price for the commodity in question (this is the case for Ecuador's oil revenues and Chile's copper revenues, for instance).

Benefits and drawbacks of rules

How likely are rules to improve the political economy challenges we have discussed? They may do so if breaking the rule imposes costs on the policy maker, or if policy makers recognize that when they follow these rules, other policy makers may also be more likely to follow them.[25] The nature, magnitude, and probability of such costs will however vary both with the legal status of the rule (abandoning a policy commitment is different from breaking the law) and with the local political and institutional context. Even the authority of the law is a real problem in many countries, and a law that the government has an incentive not to follow may not be complied with.[26]

This points to a deeper problem: Even if a rule stating that the government should not overspend changes the political calculation (because it is costly to break), it does not remove the original reason why the government wants to overspend—it merely counterbalances it. The original incentives may therefore prevail even in the presence of a legally enshrined rule. Just as we were earlier asking what incentives a policy maker had to deviate from the economically optimal policy, we may now ask what incentives a policy maker has to violate the rule (even one with legal force) that tells her to adopt that policy. Rules that implement spending paths that are not Pareto improvements on the *status quo ante* may be brittle, in the sense that they may be flouted at the first spike in commodity prices. Worse, they may also, by creating or reinforcing a precedent of rule-breaking, weaken the force of law overall. Designers of NRFs, therefore, must strike a compromise between creating incentives for the right policy *and* incentives to comply with the rules themselves.

Creating the incentives to comply with the rules is more than a legal issue or issue of institutional design. It also touches on aspects of investment policy, economic planning, and political communication. In some instances, for example, decisions regarding how monies in the fund are to be invested can affect the costs and benefits associated with ignoring, altering, or complying with rules. For example, fixed-term investments with a long term to maturity can in principle help enforce quantitative restrictions by reducing the liquidity of assets, although the impact of such investment policies on the incentives to alter or ignore the law will naturally depend on the country's access to debt financing. In many cases, we may expect that the political costs associated with ignoring rules, such as rules allocating expenditures to key development areas or to particular regions, to be greater the more embedded the rules are in the longer term development planning within the country and the greater is the information available to the beneficiaries of those rules regarding the targeted funding.

SEPARATION OF POWERS

A reliance on rules, then, is vulnerable to the possibility that policy makers have incentives to break them. In polities where the costs of breaking rules are low, therefore, other mechanisms are needed to change policy makers' incentives. An alternative to (or reinforcement of) attempts to reduce discretion through rules is to change the incentives of decision makers by *spreading* or *dividing* decision-making authority. If several political actors (including potentially nongovernment actors) participate in spending decisions, it can become necessary for each party to take the interests of the others into account in each period, thus altering the types of policies that emerge. An NRF whose institutional structure spreads decision-making authority across several constituencies with partly overlapping and partly divergent interests may encourage compromise solutions that are to the benefit of all and reduce the intertemporal disagreements that can give rise to inefficient expenditure.

The degree to which power is shared can range from granting an equal standing to several constituencies in the decision-making process, through giving some constituencies veto rights over the decisions made by the executive, to merely affording other constituencies a monitoring and supervisory role. We now survey some concrete possibilities and examples.

Political power-sharing

The NRF can be set up so that it vests the authority to make (or approve) spending decisions across multiple political constituencies. In Norway, for example, transfers from the State Petroleum fund must be approved by the parliament, even though the fund itself is managed by the Bank of Norway and therefore ultimately by the Ministry of Finance. Since the political opposition is typically strong in Norway, and the electoral system often produces minority governments, this constitutes a real (if not very deep) division of decision-making authority. Nevertheless, this particular mechanism is unlikely to work as well in countries where the opposition may be too small or too weak to influence parliamentary decisions. In such countries, one can envisage other forms that the division of power could take, such as

- requiring the assent of a supermajority of the legislature for spending decisions.
- requiring the main opposition party, or some share of the opposition, to sign off on spending decisions every year before the NRF can disburse.[27]
- dividing the decisions about *how much* to spend and *on what* to spend across different levels of government. For example, the national executive could decide on the aggregate amount, while the allocation to different projects could be decided by local governments.[28] Alternatively, in bicameral legislatures, the two decisions can be vested in separate chambers.

Independence

So far we have considered dividing discretionary decision authority between different political constituencies (or removing discretion altogether by rules, if they can be made to work). Another "separation" of powers would be to *shift* either the discretionary decision making power or at least the power to *approve* or *supervise* decision making to a constituency that does not have incentives for overspending. An NRF could do this by vesting the authority to make spending decisions in independent or technical bodies (if such exist) or civil society representatives. Examples of such mechanisms for institutional independence include the following:

- Giving the NRF itself legal personality and institutional independence. Alaska's Permanent Fund, for example, is a separate public corporation, although its trustees are appointed by the governor.
- Giving courts the authority to review compliance with the spending rules/funds.
- Creating a new technical body not beholden to the executive, and giving this the authority to determine a spending cap. This solution has been chosen in Sao Tome and Principe, which is in the process of creating a "Petroleum Oversight Committee." Alternatively, the Central Bank, if sufficiently independent, could be given such a role.
- Giving civil society representatives decision-making power or supervisory authority over how much to spend, how to spend it, or both. This has been done in both Sao Tome and Principe and Chad,

where civil society representatives belong to the Petroleum Oversight Committee and the Collège de Contrôle, respectively.

- Writing spending rules into the contract with the bank holding the NRF. The bank has incentives to comply with its contract, and does not have the same incentives for overspending as the executive.[29]

The establishment of an NRF is an opportunity to vest decision-making authority in institutions that are independent of the executive. In countries with strong executive branches, however, that opportunity might sometimes not be very attractive to rulers. The regulations governing the recently established oil funds of Kazakhstan and Azerbaijan, for instance, eschew a use of this opportunity. In both of these funds, the supervisory board is controlled by the president of the country, and spending decisions are determined by presidential decrees. As before, in countries with weak institutional capacity the formal separation of powers might not be sufficient to produce genuine counterbalancing forces. Among the weaknesses identified in the case of the Collège de Contrôle in Chad, for example, are that the institution has been under-resourced, particularly in terms of skilled personnel and information; this has limited it in its ability to act as a counterbalancing force.[30]

Again, the aim should be to ensure not just that the right institutions are formally in place but that the incentives are properly aligned so that these institutions can function as intended. A number of legal and other mechanisms could be used to strengthen such bodies. Companies could be required to provide information directly to such bodies (in the case of Chad information is passed from companies to the executive and the Collège then relies on the executive to receive this information in a timely manner); or the agreement of such bodies could be treated as a requirement for access to fresh funds from an NRF or indeed from development partners.

Contracting out

A problem with using NRFs to implement a separation of powers is that in many poor countries, truly independent institutions are rare. Even private actors, such as banks, may be exposed to pressure from the executive. Again there are possibilities here for governments of developing countries to draw on the institutional strength of other actors. A country with weak institutions could *in extremis* consider "contracting out" some of its political economy through an NRF, in the following sense. If the institutional resources at home do not prevent overspending, a foreign institution might be better suited to enforce commitments by politicians. For example, spending rules could be written into a contract with foreign financial institutions in which the fund's account would be held.[31] More far-reaching institutional reforms could include the following:

- Rich countries could finance a "global clearinghouse" for natural resource revenue funds. This clearinghouse could deal with the logistical issues, but far more importantly, with the commitment issues. It could, for example, accept only accounts that come with strict rules on the magnitude of funds that could be withdrawn every year (as in the first subsection in this section) and only implement changes to such rules subject to some predetermined lag.
- Alternatively, the contract with the global clearinghouse might stipulate that disbursements be made only with the required signatures of several branches of government, or only pursuant to the assent of an independent control/oversight committee (as discussed in the previous section).
- To discourage the temptation to use unconstitutional means to take over the state, discussed above, the global clearinghouse could also commit to not disbursing a country's NRF monies to the new rulers after a nonconstitutional power change. For example, the account could be frozen in the case of a coup, until the régime was recognized as legitimate by an appropriate international organization.

In sum, many of the solutions we have listed might be easier to implement with the help of a foreign institution such as the suggested global clearinghouse. Such an institution is better placed to stand firm in the face of attempts to circumvent the various possible constraints on spending. In the case of breach of contract, the global clearinghouse might be prosecuted under the laws of its home government, which could provide a stronger legal regime than that of the country owning the fund.[32]

TRANSPARENCY

The third class of institutional mechanisms that could be implemented through an NRF covers those that aim to promote transparency and the dissemination of information. It bears emphasizing that the mechanisms we discussed for dividing power are also, as a side effect, transparency-promoting. With a more balanced distribution of power, we can expect that the demand and pressure for information—in particular by those who are to participate in the shared expenditure decisions—will increase. Moreover, if it also leads to outcomes considered better by everyone, as we have suggested it may, there is plausibly less reason to be secretive about the policies that are adopted.

In addition to these effects, however, a natural resource fund can be used to put in place mechanisms that *directly* improve the flow of information in the society. For the reasons we outlined when discussing our model, transparency is likely to have salutary effects on the behavior of politicians who depend on popular support, at least if voters are prepared to punish incumbents for inefficiencies.[33] Of course transparency should not be limited to revenues originating from the natural resource sector. But in countries with low levels of transparency in general, the occasion of setting up an NRF may provide an opportunity to create a sphere with better practice than the rest of the public sector. Indeed a successfully transparent NRF could have spillover effects both on the government's technical capacity and on the pressure on it to increase transparency elsewhere.

Publication of transactions

These considerations suggest that all information about the decisions and transactions of NRFs should be public. In particular, all *payers* of natural resource revenue should publish their payments in detail, so that it is possible to certify that the NRF is in fact receiving what it should. In addition, the NRF itself should be required to publish details of all its transactions. Both of these are more easily said than done. Institutional provisions can, however, facilitate both goals. The requirement that payers publish payments, for example, can be introduced into contracts with corporations and other parties. If nonpublication thus constituted a possible cause for contract annulment by host countries, companies would have an incentive to publish the required information. To routinize publication of receipts by governments, on the other hand, one possibility is to contract with the agency that houses the fund—for example an international bank—to make information on holdings, deposits, and withdrawals available in real time online, much as is the case for private accounts with commercial banks.[34] Finally, information on the NRF's transactions should be audited by competent and independent auditors.

These suggested mechanisms for greater transparency draw on the strength of international contractual relations. Other mechanisms emphasize domestic oversight. One approach is to create institutions specifically for information dissemination and oversight that operate independently of the executive. Such agencies should in all cases be sufficiently financed to do their job properly and independently of the executive and represent a diversity of political actors. To give teeth to such institutions, they could eventually be provided with the power to halt transfers out of the NRF in case of insufficient information (or the standing to request courts to do so, provided there is sufficient judicial independence).

In practice, there have been many recent developments around initiatives to improve transparency. Some countries have gone very far in the use of legal mechanisms, requiring all information relating to natural resource exploitation and related revenues to be made public, to the point of voiding contracts that do not comply with this, such as in Sao Tome and Principe.[35] Others have relied on domestic institutions; in Chad, for example, much of the oversight depends on the Collège de Contrôle, an institution that by many accounts has not been given adequate resources to do the monitoring expected of it (Catholic Relief Services 2005).

Unified budgets

It is important to be aware that some of the other institutional devices we have recommended considering—in particular dividing the authority to make different spending decisions—carry the risk of confusing and obfuscating the overall budget process. This is as serious a threat to transparency and efficient information flows as imperfect publication. It is therefore essential that even as decisions are made by different entities, there is clarity as to what they are and how they affect each other. A minimum condition for this is that there be a single budget for public expenditures. To keep public finances orderly and transparent, it is vital that an NRF not have a separate budget for the spending of oil-derived revenues; instead, it should only transfer funds directly to the national budget. This is not to say that proceeds from the NRF may not be earmarked for such specified purposes as development spending or pension expenditures—on the contrary, we have suggested that such rules can be useful if designed judiciously. But such allocations should happen through the normal budget, rather than being kept off-budget. This will mean that there will be legal constraints on how the general government budget can allocate expenditures to different uses.

A unified budget facilitates transparency; it also helps address a core problem dogging the use of NRFs: that of "fungibility." The fungibility of monetary resources means that even if an NRF reins in overspending of natural resource-generated revenues, the overspending can reappear in other parts of government expenditures. Fungibility is sometimes taken as a reason to be skeptical of the ability of NRFs to change policy makers' incentives: Even if the NRF effectively limits overspending the resources *it* controls, the government may simply overspend in the part of the budget beyond the reach of the institutional constraints of the NRF. This argument is powerful; however, if an NRF can be made to work, fungibility is less of a problem precisely in those countries where overspending is more of a problem—that is, where accumulated natural resource revenues are very large relative to other government resources. This is because the larger the share of government resources that are subject to the types of constraints we have outlined, the less other resources are available to undo the overall restraining impact on spending. The more general implication of the fungibility problem is that ideally, the institutional solutions to the political economy problem (such as greater levels of transparency and oversight) should be applied to the *entire* system of government finances, and not just the part deriving from natural resource exploitation or that managed by an NRF. Insofar as the mechanisms that we have described in this section can be implemented across the public sector, they should be. Since in practice, local reform is often easier than general reform, the establishment of an NRF should be used as an opportunity to carve out a space within the public sector in which the appropriate mechanisms can be put to work in a highly visible manner.

We conclude by noting that some of these transparency conditions could also be well handled by a global clearing house or by a financial institution that houses the NRF. An international agency may simply be better equipped for such information-intensive tasks in purely logistical terms, compared to some of the poorest natural resource-exporting countries. And as with the power-sharing mechanisms, the transparency mechanisms could be included in the contract setting up the account for the NRF such that banks, as a matter of contractual obligation, are required to publicly report all transactions related to the management of an NRF.

CONCLUSION

There is a simple reason why natural resource revenue funds do not on average contribute to better fiscal policy in countries heavily dependent on natural resource exports. The reason is that the economic considerations that are usually used to motivate funds support only a certain optimal fiscal policy, and are silent on what is the right institutional framework for implementing that policy. However, the political economy of power rivalry can create incentives for rapid overspending of natural resource revenues relative to the ideal levels of expenditure of any given government.[36] We argue that these adverse effects are strongest when political divisions are deep, when institutions are otherwise weak, where political power is concentrated, where transparency is limited, and where there are risks of rapid changes of government. This analysis, we argue, is supported by the empirical evidence available on expenditure in resource-rich countries. The concerns we highlight, then, are very real.

An NRF is not a panacea for these problems and the incentives to spend too rapidly persist whether or not an NRF is established. The obvious difficulty is that NRFs are least needed when institutions are strong; but they are least likely to work in precisely those institutionally weak environments where they appear to be most needed. A fund that does not address the incentives of governments is subject to being abolished or ignored. The case of Chad is instructive in this respect. In the worst cases, if funds are designed such that they are under the control of a small number of actors, nontransparent and poorly linked with budgetary processes, they may render the problems we identify more severe (Davis et al. 2001).

The question then is whether NRFs can be used to realign incentives in a way that makes them self-enforcing. There appear to be a number of possibilities for this. We describe three families of responses. If the NRFs render discretionary uses of finances more difficult in the future this can reduce the incentives to spend too much now. A broadening of decision-making authority may have a similar effect if it leads to greater predictability and moderation in future spending. So too we may expect NRFs to have beneficial effects if they increase transparency by providing a simple summary to voters of the government's overall success at managing resource wealth and alerting them to misuses of revenue.

Which exact model is best for a given country will depend on the circumstances of that country. While the solutions we propose are a priori promising, future research can help deepen our understanding of why funds so often seem to fail. An important research question is exactly how funds interact with the overall institutional structure of the country.

More research is also needed on the possible institutional solutions to the political economy problems that we listed. We argued that in various contexts, some of these might encourage more cooperative behavior on the part of policy makers over time by dividing authority and increasing transparency and information. Both theoretical and empirical work would be needed to establish with more certainty the expected effects of each specific proposal. In particular, it would be informative to investigate in more detail our conjecture that many of the domestic incentive problems could be alleviated by a global clearinghouse that would take on the responsibility of running the fund, partly sheltered from the incentives prevailing in the domestic political economy of the country.

In all cases, the core message here is that designers of natural resource revenue funds should look first to the political incentives in their country, and attempt to design fund rules that not only approximate the optimal fiscal policy, but, more importantly, create political incentives (or at least mitigate political disincentives) for abiding by that policy. Unless they alter the incentives of political actors, resource funds will not help solve any of the economic problems facing resource-rich countries. For cases in which the domestic institutional environment is too weak to overcome the problems we identify in the short run, we argue that policy makers in natural resource-rich countries can consider a series of creative ways to draw on the strength of external institutions. Such innovations could include provisions to invest assets in fixed term investments, to require companies and banks to render information public or to provide it on request to multiple branches of government, or to freeze accounts under specified conditions such as in the event of an unconstitutional change of government. Engaged correctly, such innovations would not impinge on sovereignty but would rather help strengthen the state and its ability to engage in consistent long-term planning and protect it from abuse by small but powerful constituencies.

NOTES

1. For details about the Norwegian fund, see http://www.norges-bank.no/english/petroleum_fund/.

2. The *economic* challenges of fiscal policy in natural resource-rich countries have been analyzed in great detail. For a recent collection of insightful essays, see Davis et al. (2003); see also chapter 7 of this volume.

3. Formally, the argument can be made by considering the case of a benevolent "social planner" that seeks to maximize a social welfare function of the form:

$$V(X_1, X_2, ..., X_\infty) = \sum_{t=1}^{\infty} \delta^{t-1} u(X_t)$$

where X_t is public spending in period t, the social benefit of which is given by $u(X_t)$. This benefit is discounted by a discount factor δ less than 1. The present value of all future spending must not exceed the sum of current wealth, A_0, and the present value of future incomes, Y_t, given the interest rate r. This can be expressed as an intertemporal budget constraint of the form

$$\sum_{t=1}^{\infty} (1+r)^{1-t} X_t \leq A_0 + \sum_{t=1}^{\infty} (1+r)^{1-t} Y_t$$

The solution to this problem is expressed in what is known as the "Euler equation," which holds at all times t:

$$\frac{u'(X_t)}{u'(X_{t+1})} = \delta(1+r).$$

The Euler equation implies that the rate of change in spending should not vary from year to year (so long as the interest rate is unchanging). This could involve a falling or rising time path of expenditures, but in any case the adjustments from one year to the next are regular, and spending should not go up *and* down. If the prevailing interest rate accurately reflects the impatience, that is, where $\delta = 1/(1 + r)$, the optimal policy holds spending *constant* from year to year. This simple example is merely illustrative. A proper technical analysis of optimal fiscal strategy in natural resource exporting countries can be found for example in Engel and Valdés (2000).

4. Nor is there any obvious economic reason *not* to have a fund. Once the optimal policy is determined, it is relatively straightforward to design a fund with rules that in principle carry it out (see Engel and Valdés 2000, section 7, and the studies cited there). The relevant criteria for whether to have an NRF or not are therefore those of political economy, not of economics.

5. Information about oil revenue management in Sao Tome and Principe is available on http://www.earthinstitute.columbia.edu/cgsd/STP. See also chapter 11.

6. The International Monetary Fund's country reports on Azerbaijan and Kazakhstan (International Monetary Fund 2003, 2004) provide information on these funds.

7. The East Timorese law establishing a Petroleum Fund is available at http://www.transparency.gov.tl/PA/pf_act.htm.

8. A formal version of the model described in this chapter is available in an appendix available online at http://www.martinsandbu.net/docs/academic/funds. Here we describe the assumptions behind the model and the findings in words, and refer the reader interested in the technical derivations to the appendix.

9. Specifically, we assume that they want to maximize a weighted average of the benefits to the two groups, where the weight on one's own group is of course higher than that on the other group. See formal derivation.

10. More precisely, the division is given by $X_1 = \dfrac{1}{1+\delta^{1/1-\rho}}, X_2 = \dfrac{\delta^{1/1-\rho}}{1+\delta^{1/1-\rho}}.$

11. Some aspects of fiscal and monetary policy that rely on responses by the private sector or other actors may generate inconsistency over time (see, e.g., Dixit and Londregan 1995; Garfinkel and Lee 2000; Kydland and Prescott 1977).

12. To elaborate, there are at least three reasons why Findings 3 and 4 do not imply that democracies have less efficient spending patterns than dictatorship. First, as we suggest in the main text, dictatorships may well have a higher probability that power changes. Elections are not the only thing that can threaten an incumbent's hold on power, and dictators must typically worry more about extraconstitutional changes of power like *coups d'état*. Finding 3 is not about the *duration* of régimes, but about their expected planning horizon, where governments more secure in their power will plan for the longer term. Second, Finding 3 is based on the assumption that q is fixed, and in particular, that the probability of a change in government is not affected by the incumbent's spending decision. We relax this assumption below, where we show that when the incumbent's political support depends negatively on overspending in the first period, she will restrain spending. If this feedback in political support is stronger in democracies, as one may plausibly think, then democracies will see more efficient spending than dictatorships. Finally, in democratic countries where the rule of law is strong there may be less profound internal divisions and less biased policy makers, for example, because of the more predictable policy environment and the limits on what governments can do. As Finding 4 shows, less bias leads to less overspending.

13. In the language of political economists, the increase in first-period spending results in a Pareto-inefficient expenditure profile.

14. This is a consequence of diminishing marginal utility. The prospect of high spending in one state of the world is not enough to outweigh a correspondingly low level of spending in other states of the world. Policy makers would therefore prefer to secure similar levels of spending and benefit in all potential situations—they are averse to risk.

15. But note that this solution only requires the commitment on behalf on one player—the challenger—not both, as in the risk-sharing solution.

16. See section 13.3 of Persson and Tabellini (2000) for a discussion of conditions under which this is likely to hold.

17. Note that this is mathematically equivalent to treating the probability that a policy maker *remains* in office as an increasing function of the *spent* assets.

18. Note that the oil measure employed captures estimated total earnings from national oil production rather than government revenue from oil alone. For more information on the oil measure employed here, see Humphreys (2005).

19. It uses information on the presence of independent participants in the political process, including the number of different parties in a governing coalition and the extent to which there is a competitive legislature independent of the president or prime minister's party.

20. This calculation assumes that oil sales and oil revenues are proportional to each other.

21. This economic question is addressed in chapter 7.

22. Clearly, limiting spending to a function of revenues is inferior from an economic point of view to limiting it to a function of wealth, inasmuch as a purpose of the fund is to divorce spending patterns from year-to-year revenue fluctuations. Even on this question, however, one must take into consideration how political pressures may act differently on the two types of constraints.

23. This was true, for example, of the Fund for Stabilization, Social and Productive Investment and Reduction of the Public Debt (FEIREP) in 2002–2005, whose resources had to be spent on debt reduction (70 percent), public revenue and emergency spending (20 percent), and health and education (10 percent). The aggregate amount spent, however, was left to be determined by presidential decree. The same seems to be true for FEIREP's successor, although the exact allowed expenditures have been changed.

24. The Oil Revenue Management Law of Sao Tome and Principe states the following: "The allocation of the Annual Funding Amount shall be decentralized with respect to sectors and territory, and aimed at the elimination of poverty and the improvement of the quality of life of the Saotomean people, the promotion of good governance, and social and economic development. In addition, such allocation shall be used, namely, to strengthen the efficiency and effectiveness of the State Administration, to ensure a harmonious and integrated development of the Country, a fair sharing of the national wealth, the coordination between economic policy and social, educational and cultural policies, rural development, preservation of the ecological balance, environmental protection, the protection of human rights, and equality among citizens before the law."

25. Recall our discussion of tacit coordination at the end of the section "Political Economy Incentives Against Accumulation." When policy makers engage in repeated interactions over a lengthy period of time, a reciprocating attitude may arise. When this happens, an incumbent will refrain from overspending today in the expectation that challengers who gain power in the future will do the same, since this will benefit the today's incumbent when she at some point returns to power again. If such expectations take hold, they may become self-fulfilling. NRF rules, even if they do not by themselves create incentives for restraint, may help generate such expectations and serve as a benchmark for identifying when one or another party has failed on their side of the agreement.

26. A case in point is Chad, whose strict rules on how oil revenues from the Doha fields and the Chad–Cameroon pipeline could be spent were changed unilaterally in

early 2006. Before its demise Ecuador's FEIREP's website reported transactions that, while not in real time, remained very up to date.

27. The Alberta Heritage Savings Trust Fund Act provides that its standing committee include 3 members (out of 9) who are members of the Legislative Assembly but not members of the governing party. While a minority, this does give the opposition some influence on decisions concerning the fund. See http://www.qp.gov.ab.ca/Documents/acts/A23.CFM.

28. Colombia's 1995 law which regulates the Fund of Petroleum Saving and Stabilization imposes stabilizing rules for municipalities' aggregate spending of their share of oil royalties, without specifying on what the local authorities must spend the available amounts.

29. This possible mechanism is not restricted to the government's relationship with private banks. The Central Bank of Ecuador, for example, managed FEIREP (see footnote 22) as a legally contracted fiduciary, whose contractual terms explicitly allowed it not to disburse monies from the fund unless requested to do so in the legally prescribed manner.

30. See Catholic Relief Services (2005).

31. Sao Tome and Principe has attempted to set up such a relationship with the Federal Reserve Bank of New York (see chapter 11 for more detail).

32. We recognize, of course, that this proposal may run up against problems of sovereignty. But the idea is not to devolve sovereignty. The global clearing house would act as the agent and the sovereign country as the principal in this relationship, but it would permit the latter to solve commitment problems by using the agent as a proxy in certain short-term decisions. This is not too different from the way democratic governments devolve certain decision-making powers in monetary policy to independent central banks. The difference between devolving such authority to the domestic central bank and a foreign bank is that the former is subject to the country's own laws. The situation we are considering, in contrast, is one in which the rule of law is stronger in the country of the foreign bank than in the natural resource–exporting country itself. In a sense, making use of a stronger legal regime abroad might paradoxically increase the government's ability to exercise its sovereignty, as a wider range of policy options become achievable—in particular the desirable one of accumulating oil revenues.

33. This has been recognized by several recent international policy initiatives, in particular the intergovernmental Extractive Industries Transparency Initiative and the non-governmental Publish What You Pay coalition (see chapter 10).

34. Before its demise Ecuador's FEIREP's website reported transactions that, while not in real time, remained very up to date.

35. Information pertaining to "proprietary industrial property rights" can be exempted, but not financial information.

36. Again, it is very important to note that our analysis is silent on the economic question of what is the optimal amount to spend in any given year; rather it shows that once the optimal amount is identified from an economic point of view, there will be political incentives to spend beyond that amount.

REFERENCES

Ainslie, G. and N. Haslam. 1992. "Hyperbolic Discounting." In *Choice Over Time.* J. Elster and G. Loewenstein, eds. New York: Russell Sage Foundation.

Alesina, A. 1988. "Credibility and Policy Convergence in a Two-Party System with Rational Voters." *The American Economic Review* 78(4): 796–805.

Barro, R. 1973. "The Control of Politicians: An Economic Model." *Public Choice* 14: 19–42.

Bates, R. 1981. *Markets and States in Tropical Africa.* Berkeley: University of California Press.

Beck, T., G. Clarke, A. Groff, P. Keefer, and P. Walsh. 2000. "New Tools and New Tests in Comparative Political Economy." World Bank Working Paper. Washington, DC: World Bank.

Catholic Relief Services. 2005. *Chad's Oil: Miracle or Mirage? Following the Money in Africa's Newest Petro-State.* Baltimore: Catholic Relief Services and Bank Information Center.

Davis, J., R. Ossowski, J. Daniel, and S. Barnett. 2001. "Oil Funds: Problems Posing as Solutions?" *Finance and Development* 38: 4. Washington, DC: International Monetary Fund.

Davis, J., R. Ossowski, J. Daniel, and S. Barnett. 2003. "Stabilization and Savings Funds for Nonrenewable Resources." In *Fiscal Policy Formulation and Implementation in Oil-Producing Countries,* J. Davis, R. Ossowski, and O. Fedelino, eds. Washington, DC: International Monetary Fund.

Davis, J., R. Ossowski, and O. Fedelino, eds. 2003. *Fiscal Policy Formulation and Implementation in Oil-Producing Countries.* Washington, DC: International Monetary Fund.

Dixit, A., G. M. Grossman, and F. Gul. 2000. "The Dynamics of Political Compromise." *Journal of Political Economy* 108(3): 531–68.

Dixit, A. and J. Londregan. 1995. "Redistributive Politics and Economic Efficiency." *American Political Science Review* 89(4): 856–66.

Engel, E. and R. Valdés. 2000. "Optimal Fiscal Strategy for Oil Exporting Countries." IMF Working Paper WP/00/118. Washington, DC: International Monetary Fund.

Fasano, U. 2000. "Review of the Experience with Oil Stabilization and Savings Funds in Selected Countries." IMF Working Paper. Washington, DC: International Monetary Fund.

Fearon, J. D. and D. Laitin. 2003. "Ethnicity, Insurgency, and Civil War." *American Political Science Review* 97(1): 75–91.

Ferejohn, J. 1986. "Incumbent Performance and Electoral Control." *Public Choice* 50: 5–26.

Garfinkel, M. R. and J. Lee. 2000. "Political Influence and the Dynamic Consistency of Policy." *The American Economic Review* 90(3): 649–66.

Humphreys, M. 2005. "Natural Resources, Conflict and Conflict Resolution." *Journal of Conflict Resolution* 49(4): 508–37.

International Monetary Fund. 2003. *Azerbaijan Republic—Selected Issues and Statistical Appendix.* IMF Country Report No. 03/130. Washington, DC: International Monetary Fund.

International Monetary Fund. 2004. *Republic of Kazakhstan—Selected Issues.* IMF Country Report. Washington, DC: International Monetary Fund.

Kydland, F. and E. Prescott. 1977. "Rules Rather than Discretion: The Inconsistency of Optimal Plans." *Journal of Political Economy* 85: 473–90.

Persson, T. and G. Tabellini. 2000. *Political Economics: Explaining Economic Policy (Zeuthen Lectures).* Cambridge, MA: The MIT Press.

Robinson, J. A., R. Torvik, and T. Verdier. 2005. "Political Foundations of the Resource Curse." Unpublished manuscript.

PART III

———

HANDLING THE POLITICS

CHAPTER 9

How Mineral-Rich States Can Reduce Inequality

Michael L. Ross

ABSTRACT

What should governments in mineral-rich states do about the gap between rich and poor populations (vertical inequality), and the gap between mineral-rich and mineral-poor regions (horizontal inequality)? This chapter looks at how mineral wealth can affect vertical and horizontal inequality, and what governments can do about it. It also explores the advantages and disadvantages of the decentralization of mineral revenues, and offers a series of guidelines for states that seek to better manage the distributional problems caused by mineral booms.

INTRODUCTION

If we use a broad measure of development progress—changes in child mortality rates between 1970 and 2000—we find enormous variation in the performance of oil- and gas-exporting states (figure 9.1). Indeed, oil and gas exporters tend to have *more* varied outcomes than non-exporters: as the dependence of countries on oil, gas, and other mineral exports rises, so does the variation among states in development outcomes. Oil and gas revenues seem to magnify the ability of governments to do both good and bad things for their citizens.

One key to success is managing the impact that mineral rents have on the distribution of income—both the "vertical" (between rich and poor) and the "horizontal" (across regions of a country) distributions of income. Both kinds of inequality can be harmful: high levels of vertical inequality may retard development, and can reduce the poverty-alleviating powers of economic growth (Easterly 2002; World Bank 2001); horizontal

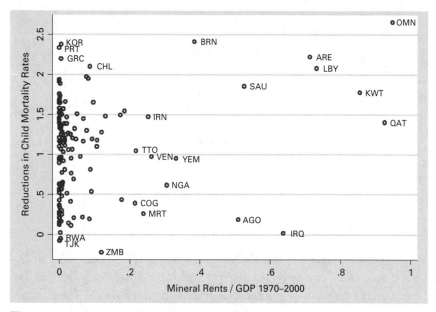

Figure 9.1   Mineral Wealth and Reductions in Child Mortality, 1970–2000.

Note: The vertical axis measures the difference between (the log of) child mortality in 1970 and (the log of) child mortality in 2000. Higher numbers indicate faster progress in reducing child mortality.

inequality—and sudden changes in horizontal inequality—can lead to violent conflict (Stewart 2000).

Surprisingly little is known about the relationship between mineral wealth and vertical income inequality. If one uses what is the perhaps the most common measure of income inequality—the "Gini" coefficient—one finds that a country's dependence on mineral wealth appears to be uncorrelated with inequality. Resource-rich countries appear to be neither more nor less unequal, on average.

But in fact there are good reasons not to draw strong conclusions from the lack of a simple relationship between inequality and mineral wealth. First, data on income inequality are missing for most of the world's oil-dependent countries. In fact, as can be seen in figure 9.2, there is a strong *negative* relationship between a country's dependence on mineral rents and the amount of data we have about its inequality levels.

Second, there are other dimensions of inequality that are not captured by standard inequality data and for which we also lack data—particularly income inequality between groups: such as between rural and urban workers, and between men and women. A great deal of research remains to be done.

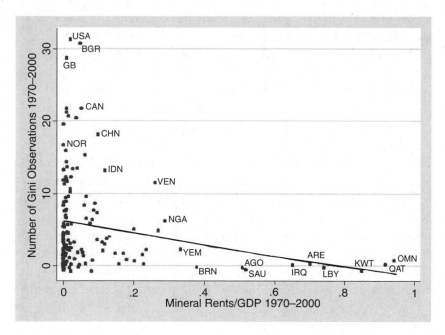

Figure 9.2   Mineral Wealth and Missing Gini Data, 1970–2000.

   This chapter discusses what we *do* know about inequality and mineral wealth, and what governments can do to promote better outcomes. The next section discusses the impact of mineral wealth on vertical inequality; it suggests that despite our poor state of knowledge, governments can take certain steps to foster better outcomes. The third section considers the influence of mineral wealth on horizontal inequality, noting that many mineral-rich states are plagued by secessionist movements. The fourth section explores one common approach to horizontal inequality: the decentralization of mineral revenues. It argues that decentralization has many drawbacks, but if it is unavoidable, governments can design policies to minimize these drawbacks. The fifth section discusses research priorities on this topic, and the sixth section concludes.

VERTICAL INEQUALITY

THE PROBLEM

Mineral booms have strong effects on the labor force; yet we know little about their ultimate impact on the vertical distribution of income. It may be useful, however, to describe how mineral booms typically affect the labor force and to highlight some concerns.

A mineral boom can affect the labor force through two mechanisms. The first is the Dutch Disease, described in chapter 1: a sharp rise in mineral exports will typically cause an appreciation in the real exchange rate, which in turn will reduce the international competitiveness of the country's agricultural and manufacturing exports and may reduce employment in these sectors (Corden and Neary 1982; van Wijnbergen 1984). Although governments can do much to offset the effects of the Dutch Disease, too frequently they do not. Nigeria's economy, for example, suffered because of the government's failure to act. A sharp rise in Nigeria's petroleum exports in the 1960s and early 1970s led to an appreciation of the exchange rate. The higher exchange rate made it virtually impossible for firms in the agriculture and manufacturing sectors to sell their goods profitably abroad. Instead of devaluing the currency, the government kept it overvalued, for fear of inflation. The result was that booming oil exports crowded out agriculture and manufacturing exports, and hence, jobs in these sectors.

The shift in exports from agriculture and manufacturing to oil leads to a shift in the sectoral composition of the labor force. Table 9.1 compares the sectoral employment patterns in two countries with large oil sectors (Nigeria and Saudi Arabia) to otherwise similar countries that lack oil (Ghana and Egypt).[1] In both cases we see that the oil exporters have considerably lower employment in agriculture relative to services.

Even though this sectoral shift is well understood by economists, it is unclear how it affects the distribution of income. In theory, the impact on employment levels should be neutral: if workers can easily move from one sector to another—for example, from agriculture to construction—then the sectoral shift could have modest effects on income distribution.

Table 9.1   Employment by Sector in Selected Countries

	Agriculture	Industry	Services
Middle East/North African Comparison			
Egypt (1995)	34	21.9	44.1
Saudi Arabia (1990)	19.2	19.8	61
West African Comparison			
Ghana (1990)	62.2	10.1	27.9
Nigeria (1995)	2.9	22	75.1

Source: World Development Indicators (online; accessed July 8, 2005).

If there are limits on intersectoral labor mobility, however—meaning some types of workers in agriculture and manufacturing are unable to move into services—it could cause a rise in unemployment for these types and a shift in income distribution. This could affect the distribution of income between men and women: if there is a shift away from sectors where women have good job opportunities (manufacturing) to ones where they have poor or no job opportunities (construction), then gender inequality may rise. Similar problems could arise for older workers, low-skill workers, and rural dwellers.

Mineral booms have a second effect on the labor force, by generating new government jobs that are funded from mineral revenues; this may have important consequences for income distribution. There is some evidence that inequality is lower in countries where a larger fraction of the labor force is employed by the government, since governments tend to compress the wages of their employees (Milanović 2001). If this is true, an oil boom may reduce inequality—at least in the middle quintiles of the income distribution—although policies intended to prevent a bloating of governments will attenuate this effect.

THE RESPONSES

It is difficult to predict how oil revenues will change the vertical distribution of income for any given country. Yet if the revenues have a strong impact, the social and economic consequences could be far reaching. A first implication is that any country that anticipates a substantial increase in oil and gas revenues should commission research on how growth in the oil and gas sector will affect the distribution of income. Failing to anticipate these effects will likely make it more difficult to respond to growing inequality when it occurs.

If research suggests that oil revenues will widen the gap between rich and poor, governments can take three types of measures: first, they can try to offset the hardships in the agriculture and manufacturing sectors by promoting productivity and export growth; second, they can provide new government jobs to displaced workers in these sectors; and third, they can adopt targeted pro-poor policies.

Indonesia's strategies offer a good illustration, and provide a sharp contrast to Nigeria's policies. In the 1960s and 1970s, the Indonesian government adopted many programs targeted toward the poor, including universal primary education, price controls on food and kerosene, and rural public

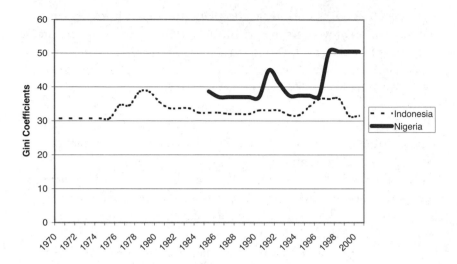

Figure 9.3   Inequality in Nigeria and Indonesia, 1970–2000.

works projects; the Nigerian government did nothing comparable. The Indonesian government also took measures to enhance agricultural production and to devalue the exchange rate, allowing exports to remain competitive and avoiding the collapse in agricultural exports that hurt the rural poor in Nigeria. Finally, Indonesia's exchange rate policies, and pro-export regulatory stance, led to sustained growth in Indonesia's manufacturing sector, unlike Nigeria's manufacturing sector, which declined sharply in the 1980s (Bevan et al. 1999). These policies helped Indonesia's gini coefficient remain low and stable between 1970 and 2000, while Nigeria's gini coefficient jumped by about one-third (figure 9.3).

FOCUS ON DIRECT DISTRIBUTION

Another way to promote equity is to dispense mining revenues directly to citizens, in the form of a cash payment. A uniform transfer to all citizens acts like a progressive tax (or more accurately a negative regressive tax) and produces a decline in the rich to poor income ratio and in this way reduces the level of vertical inequality.

Direct distribution arrangements are used in both the U.S. state of Alaska and the Canadian province of Alberta. The older of these—the Alaska Permanent Fund—has been in place since 1977 and is widely perceived as a success (although see also the discussions in chapters 7, 8, and 11). The Fund receives about 10 percent of the state's income from oil and annually distributes a share of the accrued interest to all citizens—both adults and children—as a dividend. Dividends fluctuate in size depending on the Fund's performance; since the first year of dividends, they have ranged from $526 to $2106 (2004 constant dollars). The Fund is managed by an independent corporation that invests the principal in stocks, bonds, and real estate, and whose mandate is to maximize earnings—not to invest in local development. It has grown so popular that politicians "virtually fall over one another to demonstrate to the public their efforts to defend the program" (Goldsmith 2001, 5).

Several recent articles have argued that other countries—notably Iraq—should adopt direct distribution plans (see, e.g., Birdsall and Subramanian 2004; Palley 2003; Sandbu 2006).[2] Advocates suggest such a plan would:

- distribute oil rents equitably;
- do a better job than the government of allocating rents in optimal ways;
- keep at least part of the state's oil revenues out of the hands of politicians, and hence reduce corruption, rent-seeking, and government inefficiency;
- create a second-best mechanism for hedging against price volatility;
- give citizens a more direct stake in the government's management of oil revenues, and hence force it to become less corrupt and more accountable;
- deepen financial systems in countries where they are weak; and
- become a powerful tool for achieving social goals if the distribution is made conditional on certain practices—such as immunizing children, or enrolling them in school.

There are, however, reasons to be skeptical about whether a direct distribution fund would work well in a developing country. Governments in developing states tend to be less bound by the rule of law, have less institutional stability, and are more susceptible to rent-seeking and corruption than in the advanced industrialized states.[3] A direct distribution plan would work only if it were managed in ways that are uncharacteristic of most oil-rich developing country governments: with strict adherence to the law, intertemporal stability, and immunity from political and rent-seeking pressures.[4] For many years, developing states have established other types of specialized commodity funds (for savings or stabilization); in general, these funds have not functioned well (Davis et al. 2001; Ross 2001; see also chapter 8, this volume).

Since the distributions would take the form of rents, a direct distribution plan could also encourage several types of rent-seeking. One danger could be rent-seeking through migration: new immigrants might enter the country until the rents available are largely dissipated.[5] Another problem could be the growth of coercive rent-seeking organizations at the local level, such as protection rackets, shakedown operations by the police or military, for-profit rebel armies, and similar mafia-type associations.

There may be other drawbacks to having a direct distribution plan:

- It could create a parallel budget with its own revenues and disbursements, which would complicate fiscal policies.
- It may not be viable in countries that lack well-developed financial systems, where people lack the ability to manage large infusions of cash.
- It may be complex to administer, since it requires the state to maintain a large, reliable database of all of its citizens. While many states keep citizen lists for voting, people would have a much larger incentive to fraudulently manipulate a direct distribution list.
- It is unclear how it would affect regional grievances, since those who live closer to the mineral's source would be likely to demand a larger share of the funds.

If direct distribution functioned well, it would certainly allocate mineral rents in an equitable way. But there are reasons why it might not work well, and governments should proceed with caution when considering this option. States that adopt direct distribution plans should be ready to avert fraud and rent-seeking, and may wish to consider using the distributions to encourage social goals such as child immunization and school enrollment.

HORIZONTAL INEQUALITY

THE PROBLEM

If the mineral-producing region is onshore, and concentrated in one or several parts of the country, a booming mineral sector may affect the geographical distribution of income.

The strength of this effect depends on four factors:

1. Initial incomes in the extractive region: if the region is poor, mineral wealth can help close any gap with the rest of the country; if it is relatively rich, it can widen the gap.

2. The difference between growth in the minerals sector and growth in the non-minerals sector.

3. The strength of linkages between the minerals sector and other economic activities.

4. The ability of the subnational government to capture income from the minerals sector.

If the mine operates as an enclave, and the regional government has no taxing authority, then a booming minerals sector may have little or no impact on the region's living standards. But if the extractive sector is well linked to the local economy, or the local government can tax minerals revenues directly or indirectly, a minerals boom can sharply boost employment and wages in the region.[6]

While a rise in the region's *actual* incomes may be good, a disproportionate rise in *expected* incomes may pose problems. People are dissatisfied with their income—no matter how large it is—if it falls short of their aspirations (Frey and Stützer 2002). A large gap between real and expected incomes can lead to political and social unrest. This is a special danger in regions that are geographically peripheral, have little influence over the central government, and are populated by citizens with a distinct ethnic or religious identity. In these cases, discoveries can lead to a rise in frustrations due to rising expectations even if there are no measurable adverse effects on income distribution.

Many recent econometric studies find a correlation between the production (or export) of oil and the risk of civil war.[7] Table 9.2 lists 10 cases of violent separatist movements in regions with significant oil, gas, or other mineral wealth. Although none of the movements were caused solely by mineral wealth, in each case separatists appeared to believe that mineral revenues would raise the benefits, or lower the costs, of independence. As Collier and Hoeffler (2002) suggest, the "allure of claiming ownership of a natural resource discovery" can encourage populations in peripheral regions to favor independence. The economic and social costs that result from such civil conflicts are extremely large; governments can avoid these costs by responding quickly to any rise in horizontal inequality.

Table 9.2   Oil/Mineral Resources and Secessionist Movements

Country	Region	Duration	Mineral Resources
Angola	Cabinda	1975–2002	Oil
Congo, Dem. Rep	Katanga/Shaba	1960–65	Copper
Indonesia	West Papua	1969–	Copper, gold
Indonesia	Aceh	1975–	Natural gas
Morocco	West Sahara	1975–88	Phosphates, oil
Myanmar	Hill tribes	1983–95	Tin, gems
Nigeria	Biafra	1967–70	Oil
Papua New Guinea	Bougainville	1988–97	Copper, gold
Sudan	South	1983–	Oil
Yemen	East and South	1994	Oil

THE RESPONSES

Changes in horizontal inequalities are easier to anticipate than changes in vertical inequality. Direct distribution, discussed in the preceding text, can also reduce horizontal inequality. Another strategy to offset any expected jump in regional inequality is to decentralize mineral revenues. I discuss this option in a separate section below.

Besides decentralization and direct distribution, governments can do much to narrow the gap between actual and expected incomes in the mineral-rich region. Options include:

- Giving mineral companies incentives to hire local workers and to purchase local products as part of their licensing agreement.
- Restricting the migration of workers into the extractive region. Resource booms often attract low-wage laborers from other parts of the country, or from other countries. Their presence can reduce the number of jobs for local peoples and introduce social tensions. In some countries, such as Indonesia and Papua New Guinea, tensions between locals and migrants around mining projects helped spark or accelerate separatist movements. Limiting migration—perhaps temporarily—can avert these tensions and raise the benefits of mineral extraction for local peoples.[8]
- Encouraging mineral firms to invest in local development. In southern Venezuela, for example, Placer Dome has allocated part of its concession to local, artisanal miners, and helped train them in mining techniques and business management. In the Philippines, WMC has helped indigenous communities gain official recognition from the government, so they can obtain royalty payments

and legal protection for their ancestral lands (for a more detailed treatment of such initiatives, see Switzer 2001).

- Encouraging nongovernmental organizations (NGOs) to mediate between local peoples and mineral firms. There is often a sharp divide between local citizens, who have complaints about the environmental, social, and economic consequences of mineral extraction, and large foreign firms, who have little understanding of local concerns and conditions. NGOs that specialize in environmental protection, social justice, and labor rights can help bridge this gap: they can help administer local development programs that are funded with mining revenues; monitor the activities of firms, government, and other actors; convene adversarial parties, making them more transparent and accountable; and provide early warnings about impending conflicts.

- Promoting full transparency for all mining revenues. Local peoples may develop inaccurate beliefs about the size and distribution of mining revenues when they lack accurate information, or when the government lacks credibility. In Aceh, Indonesia, the rebel movement fostered the widespread belief that if the region became independent, citizens would be 20 times richer—a wild exaggeration, but one that worked well for the rebel group. Had the government's revenue figures for Aceh been more transparent, and credible, citizens would have been less susceptible to this propaganda. Transparency would also reduce corruption and improve people's confidence that mineral revenues were not being squandered.

Finally, distributional issues are more likely to ignite violence when police or military forces engage in predatory behavior. Mineral projects often attract police, military, and paramilitary organizations that use extortion to gain a share of the available rents, either directly from the extractive firm and its contractors, or indirectly from the people who work for them. In some cases, military units have staged or facilitated attacks on mining firms in order to extort funds.[9] Local populations understandably resent such predatory behavior, which helps widen the rift between their actual and expected incomes from mining.

Both governments and firms can help curtail these activities. A recent project by BP in West Papua, Indonesia, has used innovative techniques to minimize the gap between real and expected incomes, and avoid predation by the Indonesian military. These include holding extensive consultations with local communities and NGOs since the early days of the project; developing a relocation agreement with a small village, which included plans for local hiring, restrictions on in-migration, sustainable economic development, cultural preservation, and biodiversity conservation; insisting that Indonesian security forces remain away from the project area, and creating instead a community-based security force; and agreeing to independent evaluations of its operation, which helps make its promises to the community more credible.

DECENTRALIZING REVENUES

Another response to risks of rising horizontal inequality is to divide mineral revenues between central and subnational governments. Indeed, there now appears to be a global trend toward the decentralization of petroleum and other mineral rents (Brosio 2003). While these arrangements may look like an easy way to manage regional tensions over mineral rents, they have serious drawbacks.

Most of the oil-rich countries in the Middle East are unitary states and have fully centralized revenue systems.[10] Outside the Middle East, however, many oil exporters divide mineral rents between central and subnational governments, regardless of whether they are unitary states (Colombia, Ecuador, Kazakhstan) or federal states (Mexico, Nigeria, Russia, Venezuela, and Indonesia[11]) (Ahmad and Mottu 2003).

There are three ways that subnational governments may receive mineral revenues: they may levy taxes directly on the mineral industry; they may receive direct transfers of a share of the central government's mineral revenues, based on some formula; and they may receive indirect transfers from the central government, once the revenues have been smoothed and allocated according to the national budgeting process. The first two approaches in particular—subnational taxing authority over minerals, and direct transfers of mineral revenues—have serious drawbacks:

- Since central governments have more diversified revenue bases than subnational governments, they are better insulated from the effects of mineral revenue volatility.
- The capacity of any subnational region to efficiently absorb new investments from windfall spending will be less than the national capacity to do so.

- Central governments are better able to implement countercyclical fiscal policies—that is, to expand the economy during a recession, or contract it when inflation becomes too high.
- While fiscal discipline is a problem for most central governments, the problem is often worse at the subnational level.[12]
- Allowing subnational governments to impose taxes creates special problems:
  - Subnational governments have less ability to administer complex types of taxes, and to tax large foreign firms, than central governments.
  - When subnational governments impose their own taxes or royalties, they may create inefficiencies by overlapping with national levies.

Subnational governments are clearly entitled to revenues that compensate them for the social, environmental, and infrastructure costs of oil and gas extraction. But beyond these, the arguments in favor of subnational petroleum taxes are political. Local governments find oil and gas taxes attractive, because they are taxing an immobile asset, and the costs are typically borne by those who reside in other jurisdictions. Regional governments often claim ownership of these resources, and may threaten secession if they get less than they seek. Moreover, the constitution may give them the right to levy certain kinds of taxes within their jurisdictions.

Ahmad and Mottu (2003) argue that the first-best arrangement is full centralization of all oil revenue, with carefully designed transfers to subnational governments. Recognizing that this is often politically untenable, their second-best recommendation is to allow subnational governments to levy relatively small, stable types of petroleum taxes—such as production excise taxes—while the national government levies taxes and royalties that capture the more volatile forms of revenue. They also suggest any subnational petroleum taxes be supplemented by more stable revenue sources. They prefer this to revenue-sharing arrangements, which they fear will allow subnational governments to avoid accountability, complicate the central government's macroeconomic planning, and fail to provide subnational governments with stable financing for local public services.

While Brosio (2003) agrees that full centralization is the first-best solution, he favors a revenue-sharing arrangement as the second-best alternative.

He argues that the process of collecting and administering taxes is too complex for most subnational governments to carry out, at least in developing states; that it makes it harder to equalize revenues across subnational jurisdictions; and that it impinges on national energy policies.

The case for giving subnational governments taxing authority, or a direct share of mineral revenues, would be strengthened if there was evidence that these measures could help avert secessionist movements. No systematic analyses have been done, however, leaving the issue unclear. On the one hand, bargaining with subnational governments can be an arduous process: the division of oil revenues is a zero-sum game in which every state and local government wants as much as it can get, and there is no magic allocation formula that everyone will think is just. On the other hand, revenue-sharing arrangements have sometimes been important components of broader policies to reduce secessionist pressures in resource-rich regions—for example, in Indonesia.

Local and regional governments should be compensated for the costs they bear when mineral extraction occurs in their jurisdiction. Local and indigenous peoples, who live on the land where extraction takes place, deserve special accommodations—beginning with their full recognition as stakeholders whose concerns must be addressed before any new project begins.[13] But giving subnational governments either the authority to levy mineral taxes or a fixed share of the nation's oil revenues should be avoided whenever possible. The best approach is for governments to collect revenues centrally, and make allocation decisions centrally, but with input from local and regional authorities.

If such an arrangement is unobtainable, the government should try to adopt a revenue system that

- minimizes the volatility of subnational revenues;
- minimizes any inefficiencies created by overlapping tax bases;
- does not exacerbate preexisting regional inequalities;
- encourages or requires subnational governments to coordinate their fiscal policies with the central government;
- encourages subnational governments to use any oil revenues to complement, not substitute for, their existing tax base;
- is accompanied by expenditure responsibilities, so that the added revenues are targeted toward some type of public good;
- is based on a formula that is stable over time, so that the issue of revenue or tax sharing will not be constantly revisited;

- is fully transparent and regularly audited; and
- does not encourage citizens to create new subnational jurisdictions in order to collect the rents provided by the central government.

RESEARCH PRIORITIES

There is much we do not know about inequality in mineral-rich developing states. Future research in this area could address five questions:

1. *How does mineral wealth influence vertical inequality?* Data on income inequality are almost nonexistent for mineral-rich countries. Finding ways to measure inequality in these countries would give us a better idea of the general relationship between mineral wealth and income inequality. Equally valuable would be studies that track the distribution of income over time in countries undergoing a mineral boom. To understand the links between mineral wealth and income inequality, gaining this baseline data is critical.

2. *Are there significant constraints on intersectoral mobility for certain groups in mineral-rich countries?* If certain groups—such as women, older workers, rural workers, or low-income workers—are less able to move from the tradable to the nontradable sector when an economy is faced with the Dutch Disease, then mineral booms will have important distributional consequences. It will also open the door to government remediation. There has been little or no research on this issue.

3. *What strategies have mitigated horizontal inequalities when a mining boom has strong local effects?* There are many cases of secessionist movements in minerals-rich regions; yet there are other countries where no such conflicts occur, even though the preconditions exist.[14] Careful studies of these successful cases may provide us with clues about ways that states can avert regional conflicts over mineral rents.

4. *How and why have decentralization strategies in mineral-rich states varied in their effectiveness?* Even though decentralization has many drawbacks, states continue to decentralize their mineral revenues. The more we know about these experiments, the more we can help governments improve outcomes. Studies that compare successful and unsuccessful decentralizers would be valuable, as would studies that compare regional outcomes in decentralizing states. It may be especially fruitful to study states (such as Indonesia) that have decentralized and have multiple mineral-rich regions, so we can observe variation in outcomes between these regions.

5. What are the conditions under which direct distribution is most likely to work? Direct distribution plans have only been implemented in wealthy states. Yet if there continues to be interest in these plans, it would be valuable to have a more precise theory about the conditions under which they are most likely to produce success.

CONCLUSION

Despite some claims to the contrary, in fact surprisingly little is known about the links between mineral wealth and vertical inequality. Many observers assume that mineral rents—in the presence of weak institutions—increase the gap between rich and poor. Yet it is possible that the opposite is true: growth in the government sector may lead to wage compression and less inequality. The data and analyses we have at the moment are just not good enough to tell us which scenario is more likely.

At a minimum, states facing mineral booms should focus their attention on the problem of vertical inequality, and pay special attention to the ability of workers to move from the "tradable" sector (typically agriculture and manufacturing) into the "nontradable" sector (generally services). If an intersectoral shift will leave behind certain groups—such as women, low-income workers, rural workers, and older workers—the government should consider countermeasures. Apart from equity considerations, governments should also adopt policies that can help prevent the economy from growing excessively dependent on a single commodity, including prudent exchange-rate policies, and measures to boost productivity and competitiveness in the manufacturing and agricultural sectors.

We have a much clearer picture about horizontal inequality. Mineral booms tend to exacerbate regional inequalities under certain conditions: when the extractive region was initially wealthy; when growth in the minerals sector outpaces growth in other sectors; when the minerals sector has strong forward or backward linkages to the local economy; and when the regional government can directly or indirectly tax mineral incomes. It can be especially destabilizing when, in the extractive regions, expected changes in income outpace real changes in income.

States have a large toolkit for addressing these problems. Unfortunately, one of the most common approaches—decentralizing mineral revenues—has many drawbacks, and should only be done when it is politically unavoidable. A second approach, the Alaska-type direct distribution plan, has not been tried in a developing state, where institutions tend to be weak. If successful, it would allocate mineral revenues in an admirably equitable way; if unsuccessful, it could promote widespread rent-seeking and fraud.

A less risky approach would be to adopt policies that narrow the income gap between the extractive region and the rest of the country, and, within the extractive region, policies that reduce the gap between real and expected incomes. These measures include full revenue transparency, promoting good corporate citizenship, restricting migration to the extractive region, fostering the role of NGOs, and curtailing predation by security forces.

NOTES

1. Note that under the ILO definition used by the World Bank, not all people working in a sector are considered "employed"; rather, in the definition used by these institutions, "[e]mployees are people who work for a public or private employer and receive remuneration in wages, salary, commission, tips, piece rates, or pay in kind."

2. Sandbu (2006) suggests a unique arrangement, whereby the government would distribute oil rents and simultaneously tax back a fraction of them.

3. Even in Alaska, the Permanent Fund has not been fully protected by the rule of law: since the early 1990s, the state legislature has used deficit spending to gain access to the Fund's revenues (Goldsmith 2001).

4. Several studies argue that when developing states have large rents available, their political leadership becomes subject to a type of adverse selection: the politicians most likely to gain office are the ones most willing and able to seize these rents and deploy them for political gain (Collier and Hoeffler 2005; Ross 2001). Hence even if such a fund were established under a wise government, it would create an incentive for more opportunistic leadership.

5. This does not occur in Alaska, for two reasons: the annual payment accounts for about six percent of total household income, meaning that the rents are fairly small; and the costs of migrating to Alaska—due to its harsh winter and physical isolation—are fairly large.

6. I am assuming that the local labor supply is not perfectly elastic.

7. See Buhaug and Rod (2005), Fearon (2004), Humphreys (2005), and Ross (2004).

8. Of course, restricting migration to a booming region may also have harmful effects that must be weighed against these benefits: it could reduce job growth (while raising wages) in the extractive region; if the region is relatively wealthy, it could heighten geographical inequalities; and if done without due consideration, it could exacerbate regional tensions. Still, under some conditions it may be a useful policy tool.

9. See, for example, "US Mining Company's Payments to Indonesia Trigger Probe," *New York Times,* January 18, 2006.

10. The United Arab Emirates is a notable exception.

11. Indonesia is a unitary state that has recently decentralized, and now bears many of the features of a federal state.

12. On these points, see Ahmad and Mottu (2003), Bahl (2001), Brosio (2003), and McLure (2003).

13. The World Bank, the International Council on Metals and Mining, and ES-MAP have recently developed a "Community Development Toolkit" to help firms and governments assess and respond to the needs of affected communities in extractive regions. It is available at http://www.icmm.com/library_pub_detail.php?rcd=183?

14. Malaysia—where there is substantial oil wealth off the coasts of the remote, ethnically distinct states of Sabah and Sarawak—is one example.

REFERENCES

Ahmad, E. and E. Mottu. 2003. "Oil Revenue Assignments: Country Experiences and Issues." In *Fiscal Policy Formulation and Implementation in Oil-Producing Countries,* J. Davis, R. Ossowski, and A. Fedelino, eds. Washington, DC: International Monetary Fund, pp. 216–42.

Bahl, R. 2001. "Equitable Vertical Sharing and Decentralizing Government Finance in South Africa." *International Studies Program Working Paper Series.* Atlanta.

Bevan, D. L., P. Collier, and J. W. Gunning. 1999. *Nigeria and Indonesia.* New York: Oxford University Press.

Birdsall, N. and A. Subramanian. 2004. "Saving Iraq from Its Oil." *Foreign Affairs* 83(4): 77–89.

Brosio, G. 2003. "Oil Revenue and Fiscal Federalism." In *Fiscal Policy Formulation and Implementation in Oil-Producing Countries,* J. Davis, R. Ossowski, and A. Fedelino, eds. Washington, DC: International Monetary Fund, pp. 243–72.

Buhaug, H. and J. K. Rod. 2005. "Local Determinants of African Civil Wars, 1970–2001." Working Paper. The Norwegian University of Science and Technology (NTNU), and the International Peace Research Institute, Oslo (PRIO).

Collier, P. and A. Hoeffler. 2002. "The Political Economy of Secession." 23 December. Available online at http://users.ox.ac.uk/~ball0144/self-det.pdf.

Collier, P. and A. Hoeffler. 2005. "Democracy and Resource Rents." ESRC Working Paper.

Corden, W. M. and P. J. Neary. 1982. "Booming Sector and De-industrialization in a Small Open Economy." *The Economic Journal* 92: 825–48.

Davis, J., R. Ossowski, J. Daniel, and S. Barnett. 2001. "Oil Funds: Problems Posing as Solutions?" *Finance and* Development 38(4): 56–59.

Easterly, W. 2002. *Inequality Does Cause Underdevelopment.* Washington, DC: Center for Global Development.

Fearon, J. D. 2005. "Primary Commodities and Civil War." *Journal of Conflict Resolution* 49(4): 483–507.

Frey, B. S. and Stützer, A. 2002. *Happiness and Economics: How the Economy and Institutions Affect Well-Being*. Princeton: Princeton University Press.

Goldsmith, S. 2001. "The Alaska Permanent Fund Dividend Program." Working Paper. University of Alberta, Edmonton, Alberta.

Humphreys, M. 2005. "Natural Resources, Conflict, and Conflict Resolution: Uncovering the Mechanisms." *Journal of Conflict Resolution* 49(4): 508–37.

McLure, C. E. 2003. "The Assignment of Oil Tax Revenue." In *Fiscal Policy Formulation and Implementation in Oil-Producing Countries*, J. Davis, R. Ossowski, and A. Fedelino, eds. Washington, DC: International Monetary Fund, pp. 204–15.

Milanovic, B. 2001. "Determinants of Cross-Country Income Inequality: An 'Augmented' Kuznets Hypothesis." *World Bank Policy Research Working Papers*.

Palley, T. 2003. "Combating the Natural Resource Curse with Citizen Revenue Distribution Funds." *Foreign Policy in Focus* (December): 1–12.

Ross, M. L. 2001. *Timber Booms and Institutional Breakdown in Southeast Asia*. New York: Cambridge University Press.

Ross, M. 2004. "What Do We Know About Natural Resources and Civil War?" *Journal of Peace Research* 41: 337–56.

Sandbu, M. E. 2006. "Taxable Resource Revenue Distributions: A Proposal for Alleviating the Natural Resource Curse." *World Development* 34(7): 1153–70.

Switzer, J. 2001. "Armed Conflict and Natural Resources: The Case of the Minerals Sector." London: International Institute for Environment and Development.

van Wijnbergen, S. 1984. "The 'Dutch Disease': A Disease After All?" *The Economic Journal* 94: 41–55.

World Bank. 2001. *World Development Report 2000/2001: Attacking Poverty*. New York: World Bank and Oxford University Press.

CHAPTER 10

Ensuring Fairness

The Case for a Transparent Fiscal Social Contract

Terry Lynn Karl

ABSTRACT

The "resource curse" is primarily a political and not an economic phenomenon. In this chapter I identify the key features of dependence on natural resource rents that produce the political problems. On the one hand, the exceptional value of their leading commodity has meant *unusually high levels of external intervention* in shaping their affairs and capturing their resources by dominant states and foreign private interests. On the other hand, petro-states are even *less subject to the types of internal countervailing pressures* that helped to produce bureaucratically efficacious, authoritative, liberal, and ultimately democratic states elsewhere *precisely because they are relieved of the burden of having to tax their own subjects.* Many of the solutions that are commonly proposed fail to take account of these basic dynamics. What is needed first and foremost is a far-reaching "fiscal social contract" based on transparency—one that creates incentives to change the rent-seeking behavior of all actors, both international and domestic, involved in the oil game.

INTRODUCTION

The "resource curse" in oil-exporting countries, a catchall phrase capturing the perverse development outcomes linked to natural resource wealth,[1] is primarily a political/institutional and not an economic phenomenon— a fact that most policy makers have been slow (or perhaps unwilling) to grasp.[2] For oil exporters, the resource curse cannot be attributed to oil itself, which is merely a black viscous material, but rather to the types of arrangements that have developed around its exploitation. Nor can it be attributed to the mere possession of petroleum; for the full panoply of resource curse consequences to appear, petroleum must be sold in the international market and not used solely for domestic purposes.[3] Moreover, the resource curse is due as much to the nature of the international oil regime—meaning the institutions shaped by multinational oil companies, their host governments, and foreign lenders—as it is to the structures of states and private actors in oil-exporting countries—another inconvenient reality that is often not addressed.

Simply stated, petroleum dependence turns oil states into "honey pots"— ones to be raided by all actors, foreign and domestic, regardless of the long-term consequences produced by this collective rent-seeking. In computer terminology, a honey pot is a trap that poses risks to an entire system if it is not appropriately contained. The analogy is appropriate: the pursuit of oil rents by both domestic and international actors has produced an "oil trap"—one that threatens not only the economic and political stability of petro-states but also the health of the international economy and the prospects for a more peaceful world. Because the roots of this trap are largely political and institutional, overcoming the perverse impacts of oil-led development must begin with political and institutional agreements. As we shall see, this requires a "big push" in the direction of a far-reaching "fiscal social contract" based on transparency—one that creates incentives to change the rent-seeking behavior of all actors, both international and domestic, involved in the oil game. The initial step in this fiscal social contract is in effect a broad-based agreement among nations and their citizens, companies, and international financial institutions to be more open about the allocation of oil rents so that their distribution can become fairer. This would also permit the eventual transition to alternative energy forms to be made in a more orderly and less conflict-laden fashion. Its outlines are already discernible in the emerging convergence over the importance of transparency as a first step in overcoming the resource curse.

Whatever the past benefits of relatively cheap energy, current arrangements in the oil sector are now associated with so many harmful outcomes that they must be changed. The list of costs to the oil exporters speaks for itself: slower than expected growth; barriers to economic diversification; poor social welfare indicators; high levels of poverty, inequality and unemployment; higher than average corruption; poor governance; outright authoritarian rule or its omnipresent threat, weak rule of law; a culture of rent-seeking; often devastating environmental damage; human rights violations; and greater risks of conflict and war.[4] These results are not confined to the world's hotspots such as Iraq, Indonesia, Sudan, Chad, the

Niger Delta, and Colombia but also extend to more peaceful countries attempting to manage serious domestic cleavages such as Venezuela, Iran, and Saudi Arabia. Today, at least 34 less developed countries rely on oil and natural gas for at least 30 percent of their export revenues, and more than one third of these countries have annual per capita incomes below $1500 (Birdsall and Subramanian 2004). Almost all of the latter group and many of the former are potential or actual failing states.

The imperative for reform is also underscored by the ever more obvious costs to the consuming countries. This is apparent not only through significantly higher prices at the pump and growing concerns about inflation and recession but also through the politically uncomfortable juxtaposition of these prices with skyrocketing company profit.[5] Further, with 2005 ranked as the hottest year on record and increases in the intensity of and damage caused by dramatically shifting weather patterns,[6] the fear of global warming linked to fossil fuels is more real every day. The concern with "peak oil"—the notion that the height of discovery will soon be (or has been) reached and will inevitably decline—exacerbates these worries. These trends are just now being felt, but there is certainly worse to come. The war in Iraq, a potential nuclear threat in Iran (for which sanctions might push up prices to $100 per barrel), and the growth of terrorism fueled by energy-related grievances or paid for by oil purchases are urgent signs of a brewing fossil fuel crisis. [7] If this crisis is not managed with planning and anticipation, it is likely to pose a grave threat to the entire world.

Still, even with these alarming prospects staring the petroleum sector in the face, arriving at a social contract for curtailing rent-seeking, the main cause of the resource curse, will not be easy. Nor can this be the province of technocrats alone. The efficacious use of petroleum wealth and the fair division of oil rents is, at heart, political—a question of power, bargaining, and social justice. As we shall see, the resource curse is the manifestation of such long-standing and institutionalized patterns that it cannot be undone without a huge coordinated effort by all the stakeholders involved—including the governments and citizens of producing and consuming countries, international oil companies, and international financial institutions—to design new norms and practices for energy production.

This chapter explores the need for what Moore (2004) has called a fiscal social contract and what I have elsewhere referred to as pact-making to improve governance in the petroleum sector (Karl 1987). To explain the roots of the resource curse, it focuses on an argument first presented in *The Paradox of Plenty* (Karl 1997) about the political and organizational consequences, both nationally and internationally, of relying upon petroleum revenues rather than direct taxation for the development of stateness in oil-exporting countries. It then reviews some of the proposals for ameliorating the resource curse showing that, whatever their strengths, *they can work only where rent-seeking has been identified, made transparent, and becomes an issue of monitoring and open political debate.* This is especially true in those countries where kleptocracy is most often the rule and not the exception, for example, in parts of West Africa and the Caspian Basin. Finally, this chapter highlights the outlines of the first essential step in overcoming the resource curse— what is becoming an emerging social contract involving transparency and the monitoring of oil revenues at the international and domestic levels.

DIAGNOSING THE PROBLEM: THE STATE AS "HONEY POT"[8]

"The revenue of the state is the state," said Edmund Burke, and this is precisely the dilemma of oil exporters.[9] Scholars of state-building, whatever their differences, agree that capable states are built through bargaining with other states, on the one hand, and bargaining with organized groups within their own territory, on the other. State authority is historically constructed and maintained through a series of exchanges of resources for institutions (Tilly 1975, 1992). Because oil states support themselves through *rents*, or what Adam Smith (1937) described as "activities of people who reap what they do not sow," these exchanges are significantly delayed and skewed, or they must occur through other mechanisms.

Dependence on rich mineral endowments, when aimed for export, generally makes for poor institutions, especially those that deal with state administration (e.g., civil services) or political representation (e.g., political parties). In effect, these institutions are the intermediate causal link between the exploitation of resources and the quality of economic performance. Petro-states suffer from a double perverse effect: their states, so often formed during the period of oil extraction, are skewed by the imperatives of resource extraction, but the intensification of the resource dependence that accompanies state-building subsequently produces even further decay in critical arenas such as non-mineral–based revenue raising, expenditure patterns, fiscal accountability, and citizen participation. A vicious cycle between mineral extraction and state making is set in motion. Even though many other factors unrelated to petroleum dependence affect state-building, these other factors are generally not strong enough to counteract this "oil effect." In the best cases, mineral dependence initially contributes to some form of state-building, but even here, the public sector eventually becomes a "honey pot" that lends itself to state capture to the detriment of the state's efficacy, representative capacity, and sustainability.

In the short to medium term, oil-based revenue raising and resource allocation tend to support whatever type of government is in power as petrodollars come on stream. This is why some stages of oil dependence have been marked by unusual regime longevity, some by uneven forms of state-building and stability; witness, for example, the rule of Iraq's Saddam Hussein, Indonesia's Suharto, or Saudi Arabia's royal family. But eventually (and often immediately in the worst cases), kleptocracy comes to rule, development possibilities are horrifically squandered, opposition rises and regimes eventually cannot be stabilized, producing a higher propensity in oil-exporting countries for conflict and war. In this respect, oil regimes as a whole are marked by an unusual "paradox of plenty:" they are simultaneously more stable and more prone to conflict.

A contrast with state development in Europe best makes the point. In the European experience, state-building[10] arose primarily from the long and violent struggle to define national borders—a struggle that ultimately required taxation (Tilly 1975, 1992). The development of the modern state paralleled the growth of permanent standing armies because any state that wished to survive had to increase its extractive capacity to pay for its protection; war generated an increased need for revenues that could be met only through taxation or borrowing. Because taxation often provoked costly and violent resistance, and borrowing depended on the ability to demonstrate a secure revenue base, regimes had to invest real political and organizational effort into developing linkages with their subjects in order to raise the revenues they needed. In this respect, states became motors of change. Rulers learned that using consensual mechanisms for extracting taxes was in their interest in the end, even if this meant increasing revenue transparency, submitting to oversight in the revenue-raising and public spending processes, and giving taxpayers a say in how their monies were spent. The net result was the construction of an administrative apparatus that could penetrate the national territory, the creation of merit-based civil services, the evolution of the rule of law to ensure compliance on all sides, and the facilitation of some type of representative institutions that could provide for some citizen input.

In effect, an eventual fiscal social contract was achieved between those who provided taxes or loans and those who had the power to give constitutional promises of consultation and respect for the rule of law.[11] This changed what could have become a catastrophic stalemate between rulers and their subjects into a win–win situation, producing a virtuous cycle between political institutions and economic patterns. Bureaucracies became repositories of knowledge that could facilitate better public policy and more informed political debate. Further, once a more routinized, predictable, and consensual state apparatus was in place, lending to the state became more attractive to financiers. This helped to increase state capacity since greater access to borrowing was tied to, and not disconnected from, performance. States with strong taxation mechanisms were able to depend on loan financing in addition to their tax revenues because they could leverage their revenue-raising capacity to borrow money, both domestically and abroad. Thus arose what Moore (2004) calls the first modern fiscal states.

States in the developing world, and especially petro-states, have had a very different experience. Not only have most been created with artificial borders or a prolonged history of direct or indirect external control, but they have also all emerged into an international environment already dominated by rich and powerful states driven by their own interests. Thus, the construction of state authority has been strongly shaped by international power asymmetries that were qualitatively different from those in Europe. Conquest may have facilitated the eventual drawing of boundaries, but it disrupted the tight cycle connecting state-making, war, taxation, and borrowing at the expense of the institutionalization of authority and the administrative differentiation of control. Because mineral states in particular were not built through direct taxation, the pressures for rule of law and more fair distribution, so present in Europe, were especially weak. Not only were such states bureaucratically anemic and lacking in transparency, but they were also especially vulnerable to state capture by private foreign and domestic interests. Under these circumstances, economic outcomes were marked by a continuing vicious cycle of poverty and inequality (Karl 2000).[12] That the resource-rich exporting countries of Latin America, the Middle East, and Africa historically lacked the "stateness" characteristic of their resource poor Asian "tiger" counterparts is another counterintuitive aspect of "the paradox of plenty."

Within the category of resource-rich exporting countries, petro-states are a special, and in this respect an especially unfortunate, subset. While they may share properties with other states in the developing world in that their revenues do not originate from taxing their subjects, oil states are different because of the qualitatively greater scale and duration of their "unearned income." They are "rentier" states *par excellence*—states that rely to an unusually great extent on externally generated revenues.[13] This has two broad developmental effects. On the one hand, the exceptional value of their leading commodity has meant *unusually high levels of external intervention* in shaping their affairs and capturing their resources by dominant states and foreign private interests. On the other hand, petro-states are even *less subject to the types of internal countervailing pressures* that helped to produce bureaucratically efficacious, authoritative, liberal, and ultimately democratic states elsewhere *precisely because they are relieved of the burden of having to tax their own subjects.*

The unusual degree of external pressure is most evident in the revenue imperative. The history of petroleum is the story of geopolitical maneuvering around the lifeblood of the industrialized world, and oil and war have been linked since the beginning of the twentieth century (Kaldor et al. 2006; Yergin 1992). This is not true to the same extent for any other commodity. The industrialized states have always pursued their own vital interests in securing supplies and ensuring that no single country can dominate the production of supplies, backing their own multinational energy companies to the hilt. The companies, in turn, wield their clout to maximize their own benefits, in large part by shaping the regulatory environment in their own interests rather than for the long-term benefit of people living in oil-exporting countries. At the same time, however, oil governments have always had a certain advantage when it came to international financial institutions. Because borrowing by petroleum-exporting countries is a type of "strategic rent"[14] in that it supports status quo rulers who can use future barrels as collateral, lending has most often taken place without strict conditionality and under more favorable circumstances than are available to other developing countries. Thus borrowing becomes an attractive substitute that permits politicians to avoid domestic taxation. The allocation of oil rents between countries and companies depends on the capacity of petro-states to redress this company/country balance of power. Observe, for example, the difference in the mere 7 percent of revenues that accrued to Chad in its earliest contracts compared to the approximately 90 percent of revenues going to the more experienced and capable petro-states.

This unusually high external profile encouraged a qualitatively different "resources for institutions" bargain, this time between rulers and international actors. External dominance and control of capital and technology

has meant that oil governments have engaged first and foremost in negotiations with foreign companies instead of bargaining with their own populations. For different reasons, both rulers and companies historically
favored strong centralized authority. The net result in most oil exporters
was a marriage of convenience between companies and rulers, based on extreme overcentralization and concentration of power—with little incentive
on either side to change the system. True, this marriage was filled with per-
petual tension, especially when oil states faced powerful demands from
their own citizens to capture and distribute more petrodollars or to nation-
alize foreign companies,[15] but, with few exceptions, rulers learned (sometimes by seeing their stubborn counterparts removed elsewhere)[16] that it
would be difficult to remain in power without some form of *modsus vi-
vendi* with multinational companies. While bargaining between companies and governments became increasingly more complicated as internal
constituencies became more mobilized and regimes more democratic (as
contemporary events in Nigeria, Venezuela, and Bolivia demonstrate), it
remains the decisive mechanism for revenue raising.

Not surprisingly, then, oil-based regimes eventually developed a differ-
entiated and efficient bureaucratic apparatus in the areas necessary to extract revenues from the international oil industry, especially in powerful
energy ministries and national oil companies. Propelled by their particular
form of revenue imperative, petro-states have been organizationally innovative in the international arena, especially through the formation of the
Organization of Petroleum Exporting Countries, sophisticated contracting arrangements, and other mechanisms to increase their take of oil
rents.[17] But these externally oriented bureaucracies, however capable, cannot play the same role as efficient and merit-based civil service organizations aimed at extracting revenues from their own population, managing
territorially comprehensive tax systems, and subsequently directing resources where they should go. While they may be important repositories of
skills and knowledge in some cases,[18] such bureaucracies are significantly
smaller in size and limited in their range of expertise and territorial reach.

The reliance on this unique revenue source also created especially
distributive expenditure patterns, producing the *ne plus ultra* of the "no
tax and spend" state. Because governments in petro-states have their own
guaranteed source of income, they have revenue autonomy from their subjects, an unusual degree of independence, and the power to decide who
gets what from oil rents inside the national territory. As long as oil revenues
are available in sufficient quantities (meaning that downward price trends

do not last overly long), it is most efficient to allocate petrodollars in a fairly predictable pattern: buying off powerful groups and individuals so that they do not become a threat, permitting some degree of trickle-down, and building powerful coercive apparatuses to ensure compliance from their subjects. This appears to be precisely what occurred until the late 1990s in the OPEC countries when approximately 65 to 75 percent of the post-1974 gross domestic product was for public and private consumption, largely through subsidies to friends, family, and political supporters of the government.[19] The remaining portion (25 to 35 percent of national output) was either invested or used to build sophisticated militaries for national defense or for the suppression of opposition movements.[20]

Such distributive patterns, so obviously detrimental to the economy, also have harmful impacts on state structures. They foster a widespread culture of rent-seeking as a wealth creation strategy, not only among public officials and private interests but also within the entire population. Moreover, since merit-based civil service and monitoring systems with their concomitant public service values were never firmly established, there is very little—apart from religious or ideological networks—to counteract widespread rent-seeking. Patronage and corruption become the name of the game, and when revenues are scarce, a type of "rentier borrowing" can fill the void. The result is evident. Because petrodollars are not "their" money, citizens are not motivated to ensure that state revenues are well spent; they are not engaged; and they seldom demand better monitoring of the utilization of revenues. Like their rulers, they too often become addicted to their share of oil rents even as a type of permanent disconnect between the state and its subjects sets in.

Thus, while petro-states may look strong, the impact of reliance on petroleum rents is gradually devastating. Because these states tend to substitute the distribution of rents for more enduring forms of statecraft, they appear large and powerful, but they are hollowed out. Not only do governments have strong political incentives to undertake inefficient distribution, they lose the potent brake of scarcity—one of the chief motors of innovation. This is especially the case during boom periods, ironically the most dangerous time for oil states.

Over time, petro-states suffer from at least three types of "stateness" deficits: information, monitoring, and participation.[21]

- The *information deficit* arises from the absence of a robust tax bureaucracy, the dearth of feedback mechanisms that are derived from citizen payment of taxes, and, as we shall see, the general opacity of the industry itself. This means that oil governments are denied crucial knowledge showing, for example, the types of successful businesses that should be promoted or how patterns of income distribution are changing; at the same time, without this sort of information, citizens have virtually no viable way of assessing whether their own demands on the state or the government's expenditure patterns are reasonable or effective.

- The *monitoring deficit* originates from the lack of a revenue incentive to develop or comply with regulations on the part of economic producers; it is exacerbated by the acute overcentralization of power within the executive that makes it difficult to construct meaningful checks and balances, and in the case of the energy sector, by the enormous capacity of multinational energy companies to prevent or circumvent regulations, both in their home and host countries.

- The *participation deficit* comes to pass in a myriad of ways but most especially from the lack of connection between subjects and the state, which breaks any sense of ownership of public resources or consequent citizen engagement. This fosters a rentier culture because citizens tend to track governments less when they are untaxed and rulers have less interest in the productivity of their subjects when they do not depend on these activities for raising revenues.

Together, these three deficits effectively remove any effective form of fiscal accountability in oil-exporting countries. They also weaken efforts to hold foreign and national energy corporations accountable for their activities inside petro-states, most especially with regard to environmental damage and impacts on local communities. Whatever the type of regime in place, building better governance both within oil states and in the international petroleum sector rests on addressing all three of these deficits.

MARKET FAILURE AND STATE FAILURE: THE COSTS OF BUSINESS AS USUAL

Opacity is the glue holding together the patterns of revenue extraction and distribution that characterize petro-states as well as the entire international petroleum sector. Companies do not publish what they pay to states, and states do not disclose what they earn and spend. Neither concessionary nor the more common contractual systems are transparent;

governments, for their part, do not even provide the most basic information about their revenues from their natural resources. There is no transparency regarding the amount of resources available to be exploited, their rate of exploitation, the funds that governments actually receive, and the uses to which these funds are put. Indeed, concealing information, hiding output plans and price objectives, refusing to be transparent about how governments interact with those involved in the extraction of oil, and using confidentiality clauses to obscure the content of signed contracts has been the name of the game. Thus huge amounts of money are virtually untraceable and not subject to any oversight.

The "marriage of convenience" between oil countries and companies means that obscuring information is not difficult. The short-term advantages of doing so are readily apparent. For the companies, for example, confidentiality shapes how they account for their costs, what profits they report, how much profit tax they must pay to governments, whether they can offer large signature bonuses or side payments to enhance their competitive advantage in a country, and even how they interpret or indeed whether they can veto environmental or human rights standards. For oil governments, opacity affects the kinds of contracts they enter into, the amount of revenues they receive and whether these funds are ultimately traceable, and the types of security or environmental standards they do or do not defend. But in the longer run, opacity is a formula for corruption and concomitant development disaster. As long as authorities have the power to permit one firm to enter their country ahead of others (for a price) or set up bonus bidding to require companies to compete on the basis of how large an up-front bonus they will pay, these practices ultimately discourage competition and result in lower revenues over time for the nation as a whole. Opacity simply means that enormous sums of money are passed around, both internationally and domestically, without the most basic forms of accountability.

The failure to recognize and remedy this problem may mean that all of those involved believe that the lack of transparency serves their interest (and this is certainly the case for a small number of actors), but the reality for most stakeholders is quite different. The information deficit, not only within petro-states but also in the entire industry, encourages increasingly problematic market failures and dangerous state failures, which in turn reinforce each other through feedback mechanisms. Thus, current arrangements in the oil sector are producing too many losers worldwide—and threaten to produce even more in the future.

The cost of oil price volatility, which is twice as variable as other commodities, is a case in point (Aizeman and Marion 1999; Karl 2004). Beginning in 1973, prices began to experience more rapid and greater fluctuations, and this volatility has accelerated exponentially (on the downside and the upside) after the collapse of OPEC's administered pricing in 1985.[22] Volatility is directly related to the lack of transparency, including OPEC's failure to publish field-by-field oil production data,[23] the extraordinary secrecy of the only swing producer, Saudi Arabia, and the extensive speculative activities encouraged by industry secrecy. The information available to economic agents, including the companies, countries, and traders, is so poor[24] that the responses to this information, which determines future price formation, often has little relationship to actual economic conditions.[25] When added to the reality that the actions of a small number of very powerful and sophisticated players can cause prices to move in different directions, economic fundamentals become only one determinant in the price equation, causing still higher volatility. In effect, *prices are robbed of their most basic function*—serving as signals of the demand/supply balance. While this price failure affects everyone, especially as the shifting cost of fuel works its way through a global economy, its impact is asymmetrical: a 50 percent increase in the price of oil might only cut the U.S. gross domestic product (GDP) by half a point, but the same changes will cause severe contractions or overheating inside oil-exporting countries. Volatility's boom–bust cycles exert a strong negative influence on planning, budgetary discipline and the control of public finances, meaning that economic performance may deviate from planned targets by as much as 30 percent. Price fluctuations are also detrimental to investment, income distribution, and, most important, the alleviation of poverty inside oil exporters.

Opacity has other severe costs. While policy failure is to be expected in states subject to very rapid, unpredictable, and often wild price fluctuations, their lack of information about projected revenues and their own past expenditures makes such failure even more likely. This is most evident in the loss of fiscal control manifest after the booms of 1973 and 1980 (and surely to be manifest in the current boom), which ultimately produced absorption problems, rampant rent-seeking, overheated economies, widespread inefficiencies, extensive waste, spiraling subsidies, and over-borrowing likened to that of "drunken sailors in a bar."[26] The result is the astonishing loss of a unique development opportunity. Petro-states, including Algeria, Angola, Ecuador, Gabon, Iran, Iraq, Kuwait, Libya, Nigeria, Qatar, Venezuela, and

Trinidad and Tobago, experienced real per capita income plunging back to levels of the 1960s and 1970s. In Saudi Arabia, where oil reserves are (reputedly) the greatest in the world, per capita income dropped from $28,600 in 1981 to $6800 in 2001 (Karl 2004).

Astounding heights of corruption (and widespread smaller levels that are difficult to entangle from "normal" rent-seeking) form the capstone of these economic outcomes. The stories are legendary: In Angola, where Global Witness (2004) reports that a billion dollars a year representing about a quarter of its oil revenues disappears, President Dos Santos keeps large sums of money in secret bank accounts while 70 percent of Angolans live on less than a dollar a day; in Kazakhstan, President Nazarbayev has hidden more than a billion dollars in a secret fund in Switzerland, and the largest foreign corruption investigation in U.S. legal history has uncovered kickbacks received from both Chevron and Mobil; in Equatorial Guinea, major U.S. companies pay revenues directly into a Riggs bank account under President Obiang's direct control; and in Congo Brazzaville, Elf Aquitaine (not Total) financed both sides of the civil war and helped to mortgage the country's future oil income in exchange for expensive loans. As Global Witness (2004) demonstrates, *none of these scandals could have happened if oil companies had been forced to disclose publicly their resource payments to petro-states.* This corruption raises the transaction costs of doing business in oil-exporting countries, negatively influences the amount of foreign direct investment, lowers the productivity of infrastructure expenditures, affects decisions about which projects to undertake, and is negatively correlated with foreign currency credit ratings, thereby damaging future performance (Sutton 2005). In the end, countries that fall at the bottom of Transparency International's corruption scale, and this includes almost all oil exporters, generate socioeconomic conditions that fuel social unrest and have more internal and external conflict.

That such outcomes generate deep and escalating grievances should not be a surprise. Both booms and busts produce intense social, identity-based, and generational tension, especially when the huge in-migrations associated with oil production add different nationalities, religious identities, and political beliefs to the mix.[27] In petro-states, this is exacerbated by sharp cleavages created by a highly visible (most often) foreign industry associated with the West and unusually noticeable extremes of wealth and poverty in what is widely perceived to be a rich country. The first point of grievance is most often the regions where oil fields are found because oil exploitation affects every environmental medium—air, water, and

land—and can endanger the health and livelihoods of communities located near installations and pipelines.[28] While these regions feel the greatest effects, they tend to get the least rewards; they suffer from lower
economic growth, higher inflation, greater dislocations,[29] and lower per capita income—all in the context of higher expectations. When communities
protest, most regimes, whether authoritarian or democratic, respond with
force, as government-sponsored public or private security forces act to protect oil operations and the future revenues of the state. Perhaps the best
known instance is Nigeria's Niger Delta, where once thriving and self-
supporting villages have been made unlivable, security forces have caused
severe human rights abuses, and communities have few ways to seek
redress—except by holding hostage the producers and the production of
oil (Human Rights Watch 1999).[30] This is a formula for almost permanent
instability, violence, and eventually, civil war and state failure.

Petro-states may appear to be remarkably stable in the face of such challenges, and indeed their regimes, whether authoritarian or democratic, often last an unusually long time. But this is a hollow stability. Their deficits
of information, monitoring, and linkages with their populations mean
that change, when it comes, is not likely to be reformist and incremental.
Instead, the unexpected ousting of Iran's powerful Shah or the sudden collapse of the party system in Venezuela portends the types of dramas waiting in the wings. In the best case scenarios, oil states already have enough
stateness in place that they can manage to reconstitute themselves after
such challenges, as Venezuela and Nigeria are trying to do. But when states
are already exceptionally weak or have been virtually destroyed, this portends the proliferation of more failed states. In turn, each regime change or
conflict in an oil-exporting country sparks new volatility in oil markets
with greater prospects for global inflation and recession as well as more fiscal chaos inside the exporters themselves. This foreshadows new failures
down the road. Thus the bundle of price volatility, global economic difficulties, environmental damage, authoritarian responses, state failures, and
increased conflict is the Achilles' heel of current arrangements, and is increasingly putting the entire industry under scrutiny.

WHY TECHNOCRATIC FIXES CANNOT BE THE FIRST STEP

Avoiding market and state failures has become the rhetorical stance of
all actors in the oil story, and the range of prescriptions offered is wide.

According to economists, petro-states should diversify away from oil and use market mechanisms (including a liberalized trade and exchange regime, privatization and deregulation) to guarantee macroeconomic stability. To prevent the Dutch Disease (see chapters 1 and 7), they ought to improve productivity in agriculture and industry and reform their financial sectors. They should "sterilize" their petroleum revenues by saving them in an oil trust fund abroad, thereby avoiding overheating by introducing them gradually into the economy. They should cut public spending and avoid popular public works programs with immediate payoffs. Finally, they should provide a stable environment of property rights and drastically limit their own role, possibly by privatizing the petroleum industry. And they should do all of this while improving their judicial systems to better fight corruption. In short, petro-states should simply remake themselves.

But such prescriptions do not take into account a fundamental reality: *what is often economically inefficient decision making is an integral part of the calculation of rulers to retain their political support by distributing petrodollars to their friends, allies, and social support bases.* Nor do they recognize that such far-reaching economic reforms can seldom be accomplished short of massive and sustained external conditionality, which is especially unlikely in oil-exporting countries. Rulers have every reason to engage in the political allocation of petrodollars and face no immediate incentives to be frugal, efficient, and cautious in their policy making. And they have no reason to decentralize power voluntarily to other stakeholders. Rather than checking the rising dominance of the state over the economy (as neo-liberals advise), avoiding the hasty industrialization, profligate overspending, and increased domestic consumption that has marked the OPEC countries (as development economists advocate), or promoting judicial reform, financial transparency and "good governance" (as both USAID and the World Bank urge), political leaders seem to believe that they can ward off immediate political and economic problems by doing precisely the opposite. This is not because leaders do not understand what might be in their own interests; rather, at least in the short run, they may understand only too well.

This is why many of the solutions proposed for overcoming the resource curse, which seem so very promising, are unlikely to work on their own and, instead, should be put forward as part of a larger process of political reform. Virtually all of these proposals are only economic and technocratic, and they are aimed solely at petro-states themselves rather than the symbiotic relationship between these states and the oil companies. To be effective, they most often rest upon extensive information, monitoring, and participation generated by an environment suffused with respect for rights as well as the consent of the population. In sum, they require at least some of the very "stateness" that is lacking in oil exporters. Even a brief look at these proposals demonstrates the importance of *prior* attention to addressing deficits in information, monitoring, and participation before they can be successful.

"SOW THE PETROLEUM": ECONOMIC DIVERSIFICATION

Perhaps the most obvious solution to the problem of the rentier state may be to diversify the tax base. Indeed economists have long argued that economic diversification, combined with better fiscal and monetary policies, can overcome the "crowding out" of other productive activities that petroleum dependence builds into the economy. By subsequently taxing these activities, this in turn could reduce the state's dependence on natural resource rents. But although this has been attempted in countries as different as Venezuela and Iran, this is unlikely to resolve the problem, at least not in the first instance. There are painfully few successful examples of diversification that can withstand the political impact of the withdrawal of huge subsidies and protective tariffs combined with increased taxation. While huge petrodollar flows perversely affect the productivity of non-oil activities, they have had the added drawback of encouraging huge industrial projects that can better hide revenue siphoning (leading to some rather astonishing "white elephants," most notably in steel and other forms of heavy investment). One central reason for the failure of such diversification is that oil-dependent governments have not combined these efforts of diversification with sound fiscal and monetary policy; thus they have been unable to mitigate the negative effects of boom/bust cycles. This budgetary instability means that in good times they are incapable of putting brakes on overspending, but in bad times they cannot stop over-borrowing.[31] The problem is that this remedy depends first and foremost on the information and monitoring generated by merit-based civil service bureaucracies that can withstand the pressures of state capture. But this type of bureaucracy is precisely what is in short supply.

"STERILIZE" OR REMOVE REVENUES
THROUGH NATURAL RESOURCE FUNDS

A second solution might be to prevent governments from relying on resource rents by putting those rents beyond their reach and into a natural resource fund. Whether modeled after Norway's State Petroleum Fund or the very different Alaska Permanent Fund, such funds are viewed as an important fiscal tool that can aid in planning. However, these funds, as they have been constituted to date, have major drawbacks. Because they are generally not transparent, and the information regarding their allocations is not available to legislatures, the press, or nongovernmental organizations (NGOs), the types of accountability mechanisms that would ensure their proper functioning do not yet exist (for more on this issue, see chapter 8). Indeed, there is little point in talking about such funds in countries like Kazakhstan, Republic of Congo, or Equatorial Guinea, where governments do not provide even the most basic information about their revenues from oil or gas. Further, while these funds may look good on paper, they are almost always set up under the direct control of the executive and thus can constitute a type of parallel budget without controls.[32] This poses the danger of simply adding to fiscal chaos while becoming a second "honey pot." Finally, claiming that it is necessary to save oil money while simultaneously attempting to raise taxes is politically difficult in countries that have become accustomed to a rentier culture or whose populations live in acute poverty. Explaining the necessity of taxation requires information and open debate, and both are in short supply.

"PRIVATIZE": REALLOCATE RIGHTS TO OIL REVENUES

A third way to prevent too singular a reliance on revenues earned directly from oil is to change the patterns of property rights either of the production process or over the ensuing revenues, for example through direct distribution. Changing the ownership structure of the production process might mean inviting significant foreign participation (Kazakhstan) or permitting domestic private interests to take over—at least temporarily (Russia). But once again, the problem with these arrangements is political. Privatization raises the acutely partisan question of who gets to be the new owner, and it runs counter to strong nationalist notions that the state is the guardian by right of oil wealth. Further, where oil rents are concerned, there is still no evidence that domestic private oil companies are any better equipped to manage petroleum than their state counterparts (see chapter 2).[33] Direct distribution to the population, modeled after Alaska, has its own problems; it threatens to abandon cherished public goods, for example, school systems and health care, while failing to create citizen engagement (see chapter 9). Alaska itself is a prime example. The distribution of petrodollars to individuals has substituted for a broad-based tax system, a personal income tax, and even a sales tax—and the results are classic: chronic budget deficits, public works projects that remain unfinished, lower than average productivity, and a pattern of favoring consumption over investment. Why should this be any different in countries with less educated populations, less rule of law, and less participation?

*　　*　　*

Perhaps any of these policies might work well if the state in question is Norway—not war-torn Angola, post-communist Kazakhstan, or ethnically divided Iraq. Norway, which is held up as the example of "best practices," has avoided the worst manifestations of the resource curse. But it did so from a point of departure of an already high level of development, with a preexisting merit-based, technically competent, and honest bureaucracy, and a strong democracy. With information, monitoring, and participation "stateness" mechanisms already available, it was able to hold a broad debate over the appropriate utilization of oil revenues, reorganize its Ministry of Industry, create the highly efficient Statoil, define explicit roles for public and private companies, sustain a diversified economy, rein in borrowing, and establish an oil fund invested abroad to sterilize excess revenues. It even protected the state's non-oil fiscal capacity by resisting the strong temptation to lower taxes and permit oil revenues to replace its normal revenue base. By bringing its oil fortune under strict control, it was able to ward off the insidious rent-seeking that followed in the wake of oil discoveries elsewhere (Karl 1997). The result speaks volumes: in recent reports of the United Nations Human Development Index, Norway ranks as the number one country.

But Norway's main lessons for other oil exporters could seem discouraging. However well it has performed under the pressures of oil wealth, even a technologically sophisticated "civil service state" has faced serious difficulties controlling its oil rents.[34] Furthermore, Norway demonstrates that the problem of managing oil wealth is essentially a problem of historical sequence: good institutions must be in place *prior* to the exploitation of oil. Good governance, transparency, and participation are *prerequisites* for the effective utilization of petrodollars to alleviate poverty and prevent conflict—not the other way around. Where serious deficits exist that block the free flow of information, monitoring, and the participation of the population, petrodollars simply cannot be spent efficaciously.[35]

The crux of the "oil trap" is this: it is much easier and faster to build a pipeline than an efficient and representative state. But since neither states nor corporations get to choose the historic sequence confronting them, what is on the table is identifying and devising the functional equivalent of crucial forms of stateness. Escaping the resource curse requires targeting the basic historic deficits of petro-states that are also characteristic of the international environment in which they operate. This means overcoming the informational, monitoring, and participation deficiencies discussed above as a precondition for the appropriate functioning of the economic and technocratic reforms discussed elsewhere in this volume.

Moreover, there is an appropriate sequence for these efforts at state and industry reform: neither monitoring nor citizen participation can be effective without prior attention to the problem of information. This is why the emerging international convergence around the notion of transparency— pushed from below by a coalition of several hundred NGOs with partners in the exporting countries and from above by the British government in particular—is so promising. Transparency in itself is no panacea and we have yet to see how effective it can be at changing deeply entrenched institutions and habits, but what differentiates the transparency initiative from other proposals is its comprehensive focus, not only on petro-states but also on the entire network of norms and practices that sustains opacity. The belief is that transparency is the essential first step in a multidimensional strategy to counteract the resource curse. In effect, it is the first manifestation of what could become a fiscal social contract for the entire energy sector.

A FAST TRACK TO STATENESS: TOWARD A FISCAL CONTRACT IN THE ENERGY SECTOR

That a convergence is growing about transparency is unmistakable. Pushed by a number of high profile scandals, the morally reprehensible prospect of the replication of devastating outcomes in the desperately poor and exceptionally violent new exporters of West Africa, and, most recently, the sharp rise in oil prices, Global Witness,[36] the Open Society Institute,[37] and (to date) more than 230 other NGOs mounted an international campaign calling for all natural resource companies to disclose their payments to the governments where they operated. The "Publish What You Pay" (PWYP) campaign, launched officially in June 2002, was joined a year later by a broad alliance of governments and most of the major players in the oil industry in the Extractive Industry Transparency Initiative (EITI). Their pledge to voluntarily develop a framework to promote the transparency of payments and revenues started a bandwagon effect. In 2004 alone, the EU parliament passed legislation to promote the publication of payments to governments by extractive companies listed on the European Stock Exchange; the "Publish What You Pay" Act, which called for the utilization of stock market disclosure rules to mandate that American companies make their payments public, was launched in the U.S. House of Representatives; and efforts were started to condition development assistance to oil exporters on transparency requirements. Even the World Bank and the International Monetary Fund, not especially noted for their own transparency, are examining plans to institutionalize transparency clauses into all of their dealings with oil and mining countries (see, for example, International Monetary Fund 2005). This transparency campaign has already shown some notable impacts, most especially in Angola, where the government and Chevron–Texaco have disclosed some of their oil receipts and where efforts have begun to improve public finance (McMillan 2005), but also in Nigeria, Chad, Gabon, Timor-Leste, Sao Tome and Principe, Trinidad and Tobago, and Azerbaijan. At least 51 governments are using an EITI template for increasing transparency within their extractive industries—each pushed from inside by domestic civil society groups linked to the international campaign.[38] BP's more transparent actions in Angola and Azerbaijan are a result of this campaign, and the Extractive Industry Review of the World Bank can also be traced in part to civil society pressure. Despite the growing indications of failure in what were poorly sequenced and very late attempts to improve transparency in the Chad–Cameroon pipeline project, certain innovative mechanisms developed in that project, especially the Oversight Management Plan and the Revenue Oversight Committee, reveal potential designs for institutions in the future. Building on notions of rights and corporate social responsibility, these halting but initial actions are predicated on the belief that all stakeholders—the companies, the people in oil-exporting countries, the taxpayers in consuming countries, the governments in consuming countries, and the international financial institutions—have an interest in turning the current "lose–lose" situation into a different set of norms: a requirement that transparency about company payments and country resource incomes and expenditures should become standard operating procedures.

But as the logic of the prisoners' dilemma suggests,[39] this is a highly contested process. None of these initiatives have proceeded smoothly,[40] and some have not proceeded at all.[41] The problem is best captured in the debate over mandatory versus voluntary revenue disclosure models, the former favored by NGOs and the latter by international corporations. The companies argue that the sanctity of contracts and traditional notions of national sovereignty make producing countries responsible for taking the first steps to remove confidentiality clauses and other widespread secret practices. They also claim that mandatory agreements would destroy a level playing field since Indian and Chinese competitors and state companies not listed on public stock exchanges would have a significant comparative advantage.[42] PWYP contends that coordination with financial institutions and petro-states themselves would ensure disclosure at the government level, obviating the advantage of a recalcitrant company. Both agree that the consent of host governments for transparency is essential and that this consent can be won only through the combined pressure of financial institutions and the governments of consumer countries. While all stakeholders nominally agree that more transparency would improve country performance, most companies' bottom lines, and the health of the whole energy sector, each is also afraid of moving first and being undercut by others.

Nonetheless, merging agendas, constant interactions and growing widespread popular concerns about global warming and high energy prices are gradually manufacturing the outlines of a new international consensus—one that is likely to result in a compromise mixing both mandatory and voluntary actions. This is being pushed at two levels: on a country-by-country basis that focuses on aiding domestic groups to create internal pressure inside oil states, and at the level of regional and international organizations that can design the necessary oversight and compliance mechanisms necessary to underwrite transparency. The weight of expectations is also moving the process forward, creating clear political constraints (rather than legal ones) against business as usual. In the end, however, it is governments, both in producing and consuming countries, that have the duty and the tools to make transparency into enforceable domestic law and (why not?) an international treaty. Certain recommendations flow from this analysis:

- *For all governments*: Both host and home governments should remove all obstacles, legal or political, to the transparent disclosure and monitoring of the oil sector. This would include removing non-disclosure clauses in contracts and providing guarantees of freedom to publish revenue amounts.
- *For producing governments*: Oil revenues should be included in the national budget. Furthermore, information regarding revenue as

well as expenditure allocations should be distributed widely within the polity through the press, the internet, and a variety of consultative fora.

- *For companies*: Companies should publicly disclose, in a regular and timely manner, all net taxes, fees, royalties and other payments made to producing states, including compensation payments and community development funding. Companies should also pledge to respect internationally recognized environmental and health standards regardless of their enforcement inside oil-exporting countries.

- *For international financial institutions*: Transparency conditionality should be attached to all loans and assistance to oil states and to all Export Credit Agency assistance to energy corporations. Countries and companies that do not abide by these conditions should receive no further assistance and those that engage in "best practices" should be rewarded.[43]

- *For NGOs*: Both nationally and transnationally, these organizations should strengthen the capacity to collect and disseminate information, develop independent monitoring, and lobby governments, companies, and international financial institutions. NGOs should also form "umbrella" coalitions that unite environmental, human rights, indigenous rights, scientific, and other constituencies affected by petroleum arrangements.

CONCLUSION

The resource curse is fundamentally a political problem about the efficient, transparent, and just distribution of the costs and benefits from the world's most valuable commodity. As such, it requires a political solution. This will not be easy. While high prices foster a growing constituency in the developed world for reform, they have the opposite effect inside the oil exporters themselves where reform proceeds furthest and fastest when governments are running out of oil rents. But negotiations in the medium term should be prompted by the desire of all concerned to avoid a worst-case scenario of violence and disorder by accepting a "second best" option. As the oil market moves from conditions of abundant and cheap supply to limited and more expensive energy, the problem of rich states and poor institutions can only heat up—with terrible consequences only too easy to foretell. And while reform may seem very unlikely to observers who may have become jaded by repeatedly witnessing the tremendous power of oil rents, its seeds are already in place. Transparency is not a stand-alone tool, and it is only a start. But if it is seen as a prerequisite to other types of state and market reforms, it promises real payoffs for managing expectations, reducing social tensions, and providing more stability. In this respect, it has the potential to provide real governance dividends in petro-states, as well in as the international energy sector. Sequence matters in this story. Greater access to information sets the framework for producing better monitoring, and both information and monitoring create incentives for the involvement of those who currently are (but need not be) adversely affected by petroleum exploitation. In a relatively short time, the interactive effects of information, monitoring, and participation can create the necessary conditions for making many of the current proposals for overcoming the resource curse begin to work. This is because overcoming information, monitoring, and participation deficits can help to create a new consciousness among rulers and citizens that dependence on petrodollars alone is not a sustainable basis for development. This in turn permits a discussion of taxation—something that is still off the radar screen—but which eventually will have to play a key role in escaping the all-too-common dynamics of rentier states. Declaring what is being paid to governments, revealing the needs of a country, and showing that plentiful petrodollars are really not so abundant after all will necessarily give rise to debate over how more revenues can be raised. At this point, another governance dividend could kick in. Direct taxes promote not only more efficient bureaucracies but also liberal governance, and they do so, as Mahon (2005) has shown, *within a very few years of their implementation*. In this respect, transparency may help to set off processes that represent a fast track to stateness.

More empirical research is imperative for developing the specific reforms that are so badly needed in the energy sector. A number of fundamental questions are evident: To what extent does transparency increase pressures for monitoring, accountability, and citizen participation? What conditions are needed for it to operate? Where oil governments are authoritarian and thus view accountability and participation as anathema, would such governments accept the necessity of building or strengthening merit-based civil service (the other basic requisite for more effective development outcomes), and how are such essential administrative apparatuses effectively created? Are there previous experiences in building more extensive taxation systems in the midst of "plenty" that might provide a learning opportunity for oil governments? What are some identifiable "best practices" within the international energy sector stemming from international oil companies or their host governments that effectively mitigate the risks of extensive environmental damage and human rights violations in regions where oil is found? What type of conflict resolution mechanisms can diffuse tensions in oil regions and begin to build a new basis of trust between companies and citizens? What types of organizational citizen-based action is most effective in mitigating the harmful consequences of dependence on oil? How will the transition from petroleum-based fuel to a bundle of different fuels be managed? Finally, what specific steps can be taken to bring about a new fiscal contract in the energy industry, and in what sequence should they be taken? These and many more questions beg for attention.

However grandiose or out of reach a "big push" to curb rent-seeking and other perverse effects of petroleum may seem, half-hearted attempts or partial efforts that single out solely one stakeholder while letting others continue their past practices simply will not work. Nor will technocratically couched reforms that seek to design and control outcomes from the outside in what is sometimes rather euphemistically referred to as "shared sovereignty" (Krasner 2005). Because partial reforms run the risk of merely moving the huge rents from petroleum from one site to another and creating new grievances in the process, a more comprehensive approach is imperative. A gradually emerging fiscal contract, especially if mandatory and backed by law, can begin to build accountability, perhaps slowing and even reversing the resource curse with its accompanying slippery slope into violence and war. Anything less is simply rearranging the deck chairs on the *Titanic*.

NOTES

1. Here, the resource curse refers to the fact that natural resource–rich economies have lower growth (Sachs and Warner 2000), worse institutions (Karl 1997), and more conflict than resource-poor economies (Collier and Hoeffler 2004). For additional important readings on the resource curse, see note 4.

2. Note that my argument does not apply to all natural resource–dependent countries but only those that live off the exports from a high rent-generating commodity. Despite their widespread utilization of the notion of rents, social scientists have been slow to understand that the "resource curse" is primarily a rentier phenomenon and thus applies differentially to natural resources depending on the very different extent of the rents they generate. This is why oil exporters must be treated as a subgroup because the nature of their rents is so qualitatively different.

3. This is why Wright and Czeslusta's (2004) example of the United States as a "successful" oil producer is misleading. The United States was never an oil exporter that lived primarily from the rents generated by this sector.

4. There is extensive documentation about these poor outcomes. See, for example, Gelb (1988), Auty (1993, 2001), Sachs and Warner (2000), and Ross (2001b) on economic outcomes; Karl (1997, 1999, 2000, 2004, 2005), Wantchekan (2000), and Ross (2001a) on political economy outcomes, including the relationship to democracy and rule of law; and Le Billon (2001), Collier and Hoeffler (2004, 2005), and Kaldor et al. (forthcoming) on the relationship between oil and war.

5. On January 31, with crude oil at over $68 per barrel, Exxon Mobil announced the most profitable year for any company in U.S. history, pocketing $36.1 billion in 2005. Later, it was revealed that its CEO's salary amounted to approximately $141,000 *per day. San Francisco Chronicle,* January 31, 2006, E.1.

6. The Arctic Sea has lost 400,000 square miles of ice in the last 30 years, equivalent to the size of the state of Texas.

7. The titles of a spate of new books make the point. See, for example, Goodstein (2004) and Roberts (2005).

8. For a more thorough explanation of the argument briefly presented here, see Karl (1997), especially chapter 2. For space reasons, none of the numerous other mechanisms affecting state-building is mentioned here. Unless otherwise cited, the arguments in this section can be found in my writings listed in the bibliography.

9. The revenues a state collects, how it collects them, and the uses to which it puts them defines its very nature. More important, variations in the sources of state revenues helps to explain differences in the form states take and the ways in which they relate to their citizens. Nonetheless, the manner in which different types of taxation and public finance shape political institutions has received surprisingly little attention, except in the field of fiscal sociology.

10. This is defined here as the attempt to design a centralized administrative system to penetrate society and the national territory in order to effect policies.

11. The manner in which this proceeded reveals important lessons. State institutional development did not progress evenly, uniformly, or in some ideal way. But numerous scholars have noted that where taxes were direct and based on property, for example, England, they were very visible, and this transparency helped to create citizens who became monitors of the public purse. Where taxes were indirect and less evident to the populace or where nobles or other powerful interests were exempt from taxation completely, for example, France and Spain, their cost was less evident and demands for either administrative efficacy, the end of absolutism, or representation were mitigated (Zolberg 1980). Nonetheless, in both cases, states had incentives to develop complex bureaucratic organizations to assess and collect taxes and to train what became a relatively honest and capable civil service.

12. Historically, even where some tax policy was attempted, there was widespread evasion, especially by the wealthy, the tax base was extremely narrow, policies were not openly debated, and collection was ineffective.

13. Note that many natural resource-rich countries in the developing world are rentier states as are those that rely on significant infusions of foreign aid over time for the bulk of state revenues. Still, oil rents are far higher and of longer duration than those enjoyed by most other rentier states. On rentier states, see, for example, Mahdavy (1970), Beblawi and Luciani (1987), Karl (1997), and Chaudry (1997).

14. The phrase is from Majon (2005). Under these circumstances, borrowing could not play the same role as a complement to taxation and, in many cases it actually retarded state-building and prevented reform (Centano 2002; Karl 1997).

15. Tugwell's (1975) description of this bargaining in Venezuela is especially enlightening.

16. Witness, for example, the well-known case of Mossadegh in 1954 in Iran.

17. Because individual governments in oil-exporting countries were initially not strong enough to extract good bargains from multinational oil companies, they soon learned to band together, even across continents, to try to build a united front against company threats to move their production elsewhere. Thus, contacts between Venezuela and the Middle East, as early as the 1940s, established accords to jointly demand "50:50" profit sharing agreements and effectively established new rules of the oil game. OPEC would continue these practices after its formation in 1960.

18. There are key differences among oil exporters, of course. While Venezuela, for example, has developed these state skills, they are far less present in, say, Kuwait. Although Kuwait has been an exporter for some time, geographic factors, especially the exceptionally easy access to getting its oil from the ground, meant that bargaining over technology never became part of its skill set—a deficit it now has to face.

19. Amuzegar (1998, 101) claims that subsidies in the Persian Gulf ran as high as 10 to 20 percent of GDP in some years.

20. One manifestation of the lack of transparency during oil booms is that there is no accurate accounting of the utilization of oil windfalls by the OPEC countries themselves. These figures are estimates by Gelb (1988) and Amuzegar (1998).

21. I am grateful to Macartan Humphreys for helping with this formulation.

22. Prices plunged to $12 per barrel in 1998, for example, more than doubled to $30 in 2000, dropped to $20 in 2002, and then exceeded $60 in 2005.

23. OPEC stopped its annual and sometimes semiannual practice of publishing these data in 1982.

24. The extent to which this is true is difficult to convey. Simmons (2005) notes that this "data vacuum" has led to the proliferation of a whole new class of energy consultants, the so-called tanker traffic counters, whose job is to estimate production based on observations of tanker traffic at the world's leading loading docks. He recounts the story of Petrologistics, which claims to have spies in all the major ports, though by some accounts has only one employee who conducts his business above a small grocery store in Geneva. Although this employee apparently feeds information to a number of prestigious places, including the all-important IEA Monthly Report, there is no way to verify what is the basis, if any, of the reported numbers.

25. Reference prices emerge from the interaction between spot markets, more liquid forward markets, and markets that trade. And the most "liquid" markets play the greatest role in oil price determination, but they are also the most removed from physical supply and demand.

26. When this description was made by an international banker to an OPEC oil minister (in the presence of this author), the oil minister retorted: "Yes, but you bankers were like drunken bartenders!" But borrow they did—more rapidly and over a longer period than other developing countries (Karl 1997). This permitted leaders

of petro-states to avoid badly needed structural changes for longer than other developing countries.

27. Some countries in the Gulf region, for example, have more foreigners than citizens!

28. Crude oil and the byproducts of extraction contain significant quantities of toxic substances and other pollutants. These include benzene (a carcinogen), toluene (a liver and kidney toxin), mercury, lead, sodium (which makes soil unfit for vegetation), hydrogen sulfide (a neuro and reproductive toxin), and sulfur dioxide (a major contributor to acid rain). Chronic small spills or the improper handling and release of waste and toxic substances can seriously damage local residents, plants, animals, and the soil.

29. This includes higher in-migration, often from other countries, ethnic groups, or religions, increased prostitution, AIDS, and crime.

30. This is also the case, for example, of the municipality of Yopal in Colombia; the Bakola/Bayeli pygmies around Kribi, Cameroon; and the communities of the Cohan indigenous people in Ecuador. For more on the case of Ecuador, see Gerlach (2003); on Colombia, see Dunning and Wirpsa (2004); on the Sudan, see Human Rights Watch (2003); and on Chad/Cameroon, see Gary and Karl (2004).

31. For a long time, Indonesia was an exception here.

32. One Venezuelan president was able to secretly buy weapons to channel to Central America; the president of Azerbaijan could tap into the fund to support the conflict with Armenia, and most observers do not know where Kazakhstan's president is spending these revenues.

33. For example, Norway's state industry is a model company, while many Russian private energy enterprises are very suspect.

34. Norwegian public policy has led political conflicts over the use of oil revenues, which some voters see as "a growing cake that voters cannot eat" (Listhaug 2005: 834). In an interesting twist, it is the bureaucracy and the permanent government that wants to save. Nonetheless, this is a far cry from the effects of the resource curse, and Norway stands in marked contrast to other oil exporters.

35. Note that the Extractive Industry Review of the World Bank Group, which issued its recommendations in January 2004, reached a similar conclusion.

36. In December 1999, Global Witness published *A Crude Awakening*, exposing the apparent complicity of the oil and banking industries in the plundering of state assets during Angola's 40-year civil war. Because the refusal to release financial information by major multinational oil companies encouraged the mismanagement and embezzlement of oil revenues by Angolan elites, the report called on the oil companies operating in Angola to "publish what you pay."

37. The other founding members included Oxfam GB, Save the Children UK, and Transparency International UK.

38. *Publish What You Pay* Newsletter, August 2004.

39. This occurs when an inability to commit makes all parties worse off relative to the best possible outcome.

40. The World Bank, for example, launched an exhaustive Extractive Industry Review, which resulted, to the leadership's astonishment, in a recommendation to

withdraw gradually from all oil and mining activities—something it is not prepared to do.

41. Efforts toward legislation in the United States do not have the support of the Bush administration and are stalled in Congress.

42. Competitiveness with non-Western companies is an especially salient concern of the companies and rightly so. In Sudan, for example, Chinese and Indian companies quickly moved in when the Canadian firm, Talisman Energy, was forced to withdraw because of human rights concerns. In Angola, China won a concession by offering a loan commitment that undercut the IMF's efforts to pressure for improved transparency.

43. See Global Witness (2005).

REFERENCES

Aizeman, J. and N. Marion. 1999. "Volatility and Investment: Interpreting Evidence from Developing Countries." *Economia* 66: 157–79.

Amuzegar, J. 1998. "OPEC as Omen: A Warning to the Caspian." *Foreign Affairs* 77 (November/December): 95–112.

Auty, R. 1993. *Sustaining Development in Mineral Economies: The Resource Curse Thesis.* London: Routledge.

Auty, R. 2001. *Resource Abundance and Economic Development.* Oxford: Oxford University Press.

Beblawi, H. and G. Luciani, eds. 1987. *The Rentier State.* London: Croom Helm.

Birdsall, N. and A. Suramanian. 2004. "Saving Iraq from Its Oil." *Foreign Affairs* 83(4): 77–89.

Centano, M. 2002. *Blood and Debt: War and the Nation-State in Latin America.* University Park: Pennsylvania State University Press.

Chaudry, K. 1997. *The Price of Wealth: Economics and Institutions in the Middle East.* Ithaca, NY: Cornell University Press.

Collier, P. and A. Hoeffler. 2004. "Greed and Grievance in Civil Wars." *Oxford Economic Papers* 56: 663–95.

Collier, P. and A. Hoeffler. 2005. "Resource Rents, Governance and Conflict." Special issue, *Natural Resources and Violent Conflict* 49(4): 625–33.

Dunning, T. and L. Wirpsa. 2004. "Oil and the Political Economy of Conflict in Colombia." *Geopolitics* 9: 1.

Gary, I. and T. L. Karl. 2004. *Bottom of the Barrel: Africa's Oil Boom and the Poor.* Baltimore: Catholic Relief Services Press. Also available at http://www.catholicrelief.org/africanoil.cfm

Gerlach, A. 2003. *Indians, Oil, and Politics: A Recent History of Ecuador.* Wilmington: Scholarly Resources, Inc.

Global Witness. 2004. *Time for Transparency: Coming Clean on Oil, Mining, and Gas Revenues.* Washington, DC: Global Witness Publishing.

Global Witness. 2005. *Extracting Transparency: The Need for an International Financial Reporting Standard for the Extractive Industries.* London: Global Witness Publishing.

Goodstein, D. 2004. *Out of Gas: The End of the Age of Oil.* New York: W. W. Norton.

Human Rights Watch. 1999. *The Price of Oil: Corporate Responsibility and Human Rights Violations in Nigeria's Oil Producing Communities.* London, New York: Human Rights Watch.

Human Rights Watch. 2003. *Sudan, Oil and Human Rights.* London, New York: Human Rights Watch.

International Monetary Fund. 2005. *Guide on Resource Revenue Transparency.* Washington, DC: International Monetary Fund.

Kaldor, M., T. L. Karl, and Y. Said. (forthcoming). *New and Old Oil Wars.* London: Pluto Press.

Karl, T. L. 1987. "Petroleum and Political Pacts." *Latin American Research Review* (January): 63–94.

Karl, T. L. 1997. *The Paradox of Plenty: Oil Booms and Petro-States.* Berkeley: University of California Press.

Karl, T. L. 1999. "The Perils of Petroleum: Reflections on *The Paradox of Plenty.*" Special issue, *Journal of International Affairs* 53(1).

Karl, T. L. 2000. "Crude Calculations: OPEC Lessons for Caspian Leaders." In *Energy and Politics in Central Asia and the Caucasus,* R. Ebel and R. Menon, eds. New York: Rowman and Littlefield, pp. 29–54.

Karl, T. L. 2004. "The Social and Political Consequences of Oil." *Encyclopedia of Energy,* Cutler Cleveland, ed. San Diego: Elsevier, pp. 661–72.

Krasner, S. D. 2005. "The Case for Shared Sovereignty." *Journal of Democracy* 16(1): 69–83.

Le Billon, P. 2001. "The Political Ecology of War: Natural Resources and Armed Conflicts." *Political Geography* 20: 561–84.

Listhaug, O. 2005. "Oil Wealth Dissatisfaction and Political Trust in Norway: A Resource Curse?" *West European Politics* 28(4): 834–51.

Mahdavy, H. 1970. "Patterns and Problems of Economic Development in Rentier States: The Case of Iran." *Studies in the Economic History of the Middle East,* M.A. Cook, ed. Oxford: Oxford University Press, pp. 428–67.

Mahon, J. E. 2005. "Liberal States and Fiscal Contracts: Aspects of the Political Economy of Public Finance." Prepared for the 2005 annual meeting of the American Political Science Association, September 1–4.

McMillan, J. 2005. "Promoting Transparency in Angola." *Journal of Democracy* 16(2): 155–69.

Moore, M. 2004. "Revenues, State-Formation and the Quality of Governance in Developing Countries." *International Political Science Review* 25: 297–19.

Roberts, P. 2005. *The End of Oil: On the Edge of a Perilous New World.* Boston: Houghton Mifflin.

Ross, M. 2001a. "Does Oil Hinder Democracy?" *World Politics* 53: 325–61.

Ross, M. 2001b. *Extractive Industries and the Poor.* Boston: Oxfam America.

Sachs, J. D. and A. Warner. 2000. "Natural Resources Abundance and Economic Growth." HIID Development Discussion Paper 517a, October 1995. Later published in *Leading Issues in Economic Development,* New York: Oxford University Press.

Simmons, M. R. 2005. *Twilight in the Desert.* Hoboken, NJ: John Wiley & Sons.

Smith, A. 1937. *An Inquiry into the Nature and Causes of the Wealth of Nations.* New York: Modern Library.

Sutton, G. D. 2005. "Potentially Endogenous Borrowing and Developing Country Sovereign Credit Ratings." Occasional Paper. Basel: Bank for International Settlements.

Tilly, C., ed. 1975. *The Formation of National States in Western Europe.* Princeton, NJ: Princeton University Press.

Tilly, C. 1992. *Coercion, Capital and European States, AD 990–1992.* Cambridge, MA: Blackwell.

Tugwell, F. 1975. *The Politics of Oil in Venezuela.* Stanford: Stanford University Press.

Wantchekon, L. 2000. "Why Do Resource Abundant Countries Have Authoritarian Governments?" Paper presented at the American Political Science Association.

Wright, G. and J. Czelusta. 2004. "The Myth of the Resource Curse." *Challenge* 47(3): 6–38.

Yergin, D. 1991. *The Prize: The Epic Quest for Oil, Money, and Power.* New York: Simon & Schuster.

Zolberg, A. 1980. "Strategic Interactions and the Formation of Modern States: France and England." *International Social Science Journal* 32: 687–716.

CHAPTER 11

Critical Issues for a Revenue Management Law

Joseph C. Bell and Teresa Maurea Faria

ABSTRACT

This chapter focuses on legal and institutional instruments that can help in the management of resource wealth. We first discuss oil accounts and ways to structure and manage them to help ensure high levels of accountability. We then address the more political question of revenue management, focusing on oversight and control mechanisms and on the roles of transparency, public governance, and integrity. Our discussion then turns to a consideration of specifically legal aspects, focusing on the integration of oil revenue management systems with the existing international obligations and concluding with a discussion of ideas on how to keep the oil revenue management law in place.

INTRODUCTION

In this chapter, we set out a number of elements that need to be addressed in any oil or mineral revenue management law, analyze the key issues, and provide some alternative solutions. Since a number of the policy questions are addressed elsewhere in this book, the focus here is on legal and institutional issues. We discuss various national laws but make particular reference to the recently enacted oil revenue management law of Sao Tome and Principe, as set out in abridged form in Appendix 1. This law was drafted by a special oil commission made up of representatives of various branches of the government with assistance from The Earth Institute at Columbia University,[1] the World Bank, the International Monetary Fund, and others. Although specific to Sao Tome and Principe and not a model in every respect, the Saotomean law illustrates the issues that any law must address and provides one set of solutions. The Saotomean law addresses oil, but similar considerations would also apply for other exhaustible natural resources.

In principle, oil or mineral revenues could be handled like any tax or other receipt, placed in Treasury accounts, and allocated in accordance with normal budgetary process. However, in a resource-dependent economy, the magnitude of the receipts and the difficulties of control suggest the need for special legislation directed to the particular problems posed by such revenues. Although the issues we discuss are common to any resource-dependent economy, the discussion is particularly addressed to developing countries with still maturing institutions.

As an initial matter, any oil revenue management law—like other laws—must be adapted to the needs, institutions, and legal framework of the country. Drafting must take place within the parameters of the local legal system and must take account of existing laws and practices. Many subjects that might be included in a revenue management law may be already addressed in other legislation and regulations. Laws or regulations governing public procurement, public information, disclosure, conflicts of interest, and judicial review, for instance, may all come into play. Any law must also be integrated with existing expenditure rules, limitations, and laws that govern budget processes. One size does not fit all, and the failure or success of any oil law is likely to depend in large measure on the way it is integrated with—or in some cases separated from—existing institutions and practices. It is also essential to understand how statutory law actually works in the country. Many times, formal codes are merely "show" laws often adopted from developed world models but in practice not enforced. This may be the result of lack of resources, lack of experience, overriding political and economic considerations, or simply the lack of a culture of compliance.[2] Details count, but drafters must be cautious to avoid excessive complexity.[3] Particularly in weak states, it is important to work through the responsibilities of each entity, its capacity to carry out its intended functions, and the possibility of using bright-line rules—which do not require or permit discretionary judgment. Moreover, one must not assume that "new" institutions will somehow master government and administrative skills that existing institutions lack.[4] Nor can one assume that the norms and mentality will necessarily change because wine has been put in new bottles.

In this context, oversight and transparency play a key role in law enforcement. The participation of a broad base of constituencies in the oversight of the oil revenue management strengthens its implementation and enforcement. Finally, a critical aspect of any law is transparency regarding the sources, amounts, and use of oil funds and with respect to the contracting processes. Without this, government officials, oversight committees, and the public will simply not have the basic information necessary to ensure responsible use of the nation's resources. On the other hand, transparency can help make up for the deficits of even weak institutions, as civil society, the press, and responsible elements of government can use such information to demand accountability and to press for reform. Transparency cannot ensure the responsible use of resource revenues, but without transparency, abuse is almost certain.

Against this backdrop, we first present an analysis of issues relating to the structuring and management of oil accounts. We then address revenue management oversight and control mechanisms and the roles of transparency, public governance, and integrity in the process. We then discuss the particular aspects of integration of oil revenue management systems with the oil-rich government's existing international obligations, and conclude with a discussion of ideas on how to keep the oil revenue management law in place. Our conclusions and recommendations are reflected throughout the chapter in the analysis of specific issues.

STRUCTURING AN ACCOUNT FOR OIL REVENUES

ESTABLISHMENT OF THE ACCOUNT

There are often important reasons for establishing a special account for managing oil revenues (see chapter 8 for a discussion of a number of the motivations). It is possible for oil funds to be held and managed in an account held by the central bank or treasury, as is the case with Norway, or in a trust fund, as is the case with Alaska. Given the central importance of oil revenues, however, the management, transparency, and protection of oil funds may be enhanced by the establishment of a separate, segregated account—an "oil fund." While most of the discussion in this chapter is oriented toward such an account, many of the considerations we discuss remain relevant, even if a special account or fund is not established.

In practice, a number of basic decisions must be made in determining how best to establish an oil account:

- Whether the account should be a trust fund, a special account, another subaccount of the reserves held by the Central Bank, or simply a segregated account or accounts held by the Treasury

- Whether the account should be held in an offshore depository or in domestic institutions
- What the qualifications of the custodian should be and how the custodian should be selected

Before actual oil production when the only receipts are signature bonuses or if the amounts otherwise are relatively limited, one could use an official institution where the Central Bank already holds an account. In that case, the oil fund will need to be segregated into a separate account or subaccount.[5] For larger amounts and a fuller range of services and capabilities, one must turn to the major international institutions. In fact, the universe of eligible institutions is quite small given the need for strong technical capacity and the highest credit rating.

If an oil fund is to be held outside of the normal government accounts, it is necessary to select a "custodian" institution. It is preferable that the funds be held in an institution outside the oil-producing country and that the holdings be denominated in international currencies. Holding the account in domestic institutions or in domestic currency would increase the vulnerability of the country to "Dutch Disease," which would result in further distortions of the economy. Also, most domestic banking systems do not have the controls and capacity necessary to ensure the integrity and safety of an oil account, particularly given its potential magnitude. Further, the selection of a domestic institution to be custodian is likely to be a highly politicized process.

The role of the custodial bank is to hold the assets of the fund as securely as possible so that the only risk is the market risk inherent in the investments of the account. In addition, the custodial institution must be able to provide a range of services to allow the efficient management of the account. This is particularly important if domestic capacity is weak, as may be the case especially during the start-up period. For instance, it can provide to the public direct Web access to information about the fund and its activities, as well as summary financial reports on the performance of the fund managers. The custodial institution may or may not be an investment advisor, as the two functions are distinct.

A number of different persons in the government could be charged with establishing the account depending on the local political structure. Ordinarily, the Central Bank would be the logical candidate to take the lead, as it would have the relevant experience. Given the importance of the custodian, however, it may be desirable to include a larger number of officials in the process, as was the case in Sao Tome and Principe. Selection between private custodians should be made on the basis of a competitive open tender.

DEPOSITS AND WITHDRAWALS

The petroleum sector may generate a large number of different cash streams that move to the government, for example, bonuses, taxes, royalties, and receipts from the sale of government oil. There is a question then about which of these should be covered by the law. In general, one would expect the definition of revenue to be as comprehensive as possible.[6] A good example is Sao Tome and Principe's Oil Revenue Law, which defines oil revenues for the purposes of the law in a very inclusive manner.[7] In the case of a national oil company, there are a number of specialized issues for the determination of payments owed to the government by the company, which should be set forth in the instructions to the custodial bank.[8]

Deposits

To enhance transparency and to avoid possible diversion or delay, payments should be made by electronic transfer directly into the oil account by the entity bearing the payment obligation. The obligation to the government should not be considered discharged until the payment is received into the account.[9] This enhances controls (such as auditability) and dovetails with transparency obligations.

Withdrawals

While ordinary accounts may be subject to electronic transfer orders simply from the Central Bank, an oil account requires a more formal structure to provide protection where institutions are not strongly and deeply established. For instance, in the case of Sao Tome and Principe, the signatures of four officials from different parts of the government are required on withdrawal orders.[10] Another possible protection mechanism is the requirement of a delay of several days between the presentation of transfer documents and the actual withdrawal of funds. This would allow for informal or formal intervention prior to the movement of funds when irregularity is suspected. Provision also needs to be made for payment of the expenses of the fund itself, such as custodial charges, payments to investment advisors, transactional charges, and possible refunds in the case of mistaken payment or overpayment.

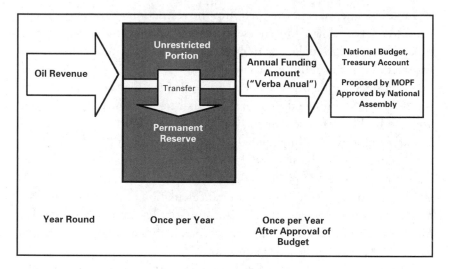

Figure 11.1   Revenue Flows in Sao Tome and Principe.

Source: The Earth Institute at Columbia University.

A further control, which might or might not be included in the instructions to the custodial institution, is to limit by law the transfer of funds to the budget to a single annual withdrawal, as was mandated by the Saotomean oil revenue law. The amount of the withdrawal each year, the "Verba Anual," is determined in the budget process and then there is only a single transfer from the oil account to the Treasury (see figure 11.1). This enhances regularity in the process and reduces the temptation to meet each short-term financial need by recourse to the oil fund.

SPENDING LIMITS, STABILIZATION, AND ENDOWMENT FUNDS

An oil account can serve a number of purposes.[11] It could be a mechanism for monitoring oil financial flows, a stabilization fund to take account of fluctuating oil prices, or a savings device to establish a permanent fund to service the state or its citizens. The policy arguments for a permanent fund are canvassed elsewhere, but if a permanent fund is to be created, a number of issues must be addressed in the law: namely, what is the desired size of the permanent fund and what should be the path to achieve the desired size, that is, how is the division of income between current expenditures and savings to be determined during the period of production.

Building a permanent fund requires the restriction of current expenditures to a level below oil revenues, at least during the initial period of oil production. A key policy and drafting issue is the determination of whether to cap expenditures by law and if so, what the cap should be and how "hard" it should be. In Norway, for example, there is no cap as such. Withdrawals from the oil fund are set equal to the deficit in the budget, and the buildup of a permanent fund depends solely on annual discretionary decisions regarding the budget. In Sao Tome and Principe, on the other hand, the law itself specifies hard limits on the amount of annual expenditures. The Timor-Leste Petroleum Fund Law takes a somewhat similar approach in requiring an annual calculation of the maximum estimated sustainable income taking account of the country's oil wealth. However, the law allows the parliament, on an annual basis, to exceed the ceiling under certain specified conditions.[12]

Setting the size of the permanent fund involves intangible choices of intergenerational equity, assumptions about the efficiency of current expenditures and public investment, and estimates about the size and value of a country's petroleum resources. One rough rule of equity, adopted by the Saotomean oil revenue management law, is to try to maintain an even revenue flow to the government or its citizens, throughout both the period of production and afterwards. The Timorese petroleum fund law uses a similar approach through its calculation of the "maximum sustainable annual expenditures." This can be done in principle by finding the present value of the oil resource and making available for current consumption the expected return on the estimated value plus the return on the balance in the oil account.[13] To do this, however, requires estimates of a number of variables and any process will provide only a rough leveling of revenues. The estimated value of the resource in particular changes over time when and if new commercial discoveries are made, and as prices change.

As part of setting a ceiling, whether mandatory or indicative, it is usually necessary to place a well defined value on the petroleum resources of the country.[14] This estimation requires a number of assumptions—the size of the petroleum reserves and extraction rates, future prices, and the discount rate to determine the present value of the reserves. Price assumptions particularly can result in widely differing values of reserves and hence widely different levels of permissible spending. The wide range of prices over the last seven or eight years—from $10 to over $70 per barrel—could allow for a great deal of discretion and thus could create the temptation to predict an increase in future prices to justify higher current expenditures.

To avoid this, we recommend that the law tie the numbers to some objective determination. In the case of Sao Tome and Principe, the projected price is based on the historical price over the prior 10 years.[15] This has three advantages. First, it is based on known numbers. Second, it will change only slowly year to year, as a new year is added to the calculation to replace the oldest figure in the prior calculation. Third, the production figures used are those in the plans that producers have to file with the government. These will usually be conservative providing a conservative bias to the estimate of oil wealth. Over time, new discoveries may increase the estimated oil wealth, and the use of a formula such as that in Sao Tome and Principe will again adjust (although if very substantial new commercial discoveries occur, the level of reserves can result in a significant increase in the amount of permitted annual spending). But since it is unlikely that such estimates must be adjusted downward, these changes, unlike projections of future prices, should not lead to the situation in which governments must decrease the level of spending year to year.[16]

The Saotomean oil revenue management law provides for a second set of spending limits unrelated to the buildup of a permanent fund. Before actual oil production, a country may receive limited oil revenues in the form of signature bonuses and possibly other payments. These amounts are relatively small but should nevertheless move through the oil fund. In the case of Sao Tome and Principe, formulas try to spread these funds over five years, the estimated period prior to commercial oil production. Of course, there may ultimately be no production as exploration may not turn up commercially producible reserves.

Even if no permanent reserve is envisioned, there is still often a need for a stabilization reserve.[17] One of the most serious problems incurred by resource-rich countries is the fluctuation in spending. When prices are high, spending increases. When prices then fall, however, the spending cannot be sustained. This may result in a stop-go pattern of development with increased pressures to borrow—the net effect being that resource-rich governments are also among the most heavily indebted. A permanent fund with annual spending limits, as in Sao Tome and Principe, helps avoid this problem since the formulas act to smooth expenditures even during periods of significant price fluctuations.[18] If there is to be no permanent fund, one can create a stabilization reserve within the oil account (or as a separate account) to address price fluctuations. In determining whether monies should be transferred in or out of the stabilization fund, one could use formulas for projecting prices and future production that would be similar to those used in determining how much to transfer to a permanent reserve. To avoid political estimates, estimates should be tied to market data, to the extent possible.[19] Because of the unpredictable nature of future oil prices, prudence would suggest building a significant reserve in connection with the stabilization fund—that is, the initial spending levels should be less than the amounts expected to be available even after stabilization, until a reasonable reserve is accumulated.[20]

USES OF REVENUES

An oil revenue management law could reasonably be restricted to the receipt, management, and control of oil revenues without addressing expenditures apart from whatever overall spending limits are imposed. Nevertheless, a number of laws establishing funds have specified some restrictions as to areas of use. For instance, the use of funds may be restricted to certain priority sectors or there may be set allocations to regional or local governments. In the case of Sao Tome and Principe, regional allocations—often a highly contentious issue—were specified,[21] but sectoral allocations were only broadly predetermined (see figure 11.2). The statute contains only a general requirement that the revenues be used in connection with a national development plan and poverty reduction strategy or, in the absence of such plan or strategy for priority, in "education, health, infrastructure, and rural development." The drafters felt that more detailed limitations on the activities of future governments were inconsistent with democratic notions, holding that parties and candidates in the future should be free to determine the details of their own expenditure choices within the ceilings.

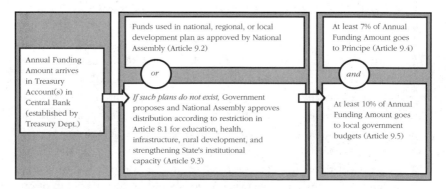

Figure 11.2   Flow of Revenues Into and Within Sao Tome and Principe.

Source: The Earth Institute at Columbia University.

Another important idea has been direct distribution of a portion of the annually available funds to citizens of the country.[22] Apart from the Alaskan fund, however, no fund has provided for direct distribution.[23] The idea was broached in Sao Tome and Principe, but was immediately rejected. For a discussion of some of the arguments in favor or against this option, see chapter 9.

OIL FUND MANAGEMENT

Central to any revenue management law is the set of rules and basic principles governing the management of the oil fund. Good governance, professional management, and broad oversight can go a long way in protecting the value of oil fund assets.

OIL FUND MANAGEMENT FUNCTIONS

The law must provide a clear governance structure covering the main oil fund asset management functions: setting investment policy, selection and oversight of investment managers, and selection and oversight of the custodial institution.[24] The oil revenue management law should establish clear mandates, compensation policy, and governance rules for the investment committee, for the portfolio managers, and for the custodial bank.

Investment policy making and oversight

The overall responsibility for the management and investment of oil fund assets should be assigned to an investment committee charged by law with creating and periodically reviewing the investment policy, and overseeing the oil fund asset management. The investment committee should have a clear mandate, advisably in the body of the law, which spells out its membership and selection process, and its main functions, powers, and responsibilities. The oil revenue management law should not charge the investment committee with making investments itself; rather, the investment committee should be charged with establishing general investment policy, and selecting and overseeing qualified professional portfolio managers who will carry out the investment policy. Many developing countries will have to look overseas for their oil fund portfolio managers as no expertise can be found locally.

The membership of the investment committee should be broad enough to ensure political support from the different branches of government and political constituencies. The committee should be structured to include people who are likely to have financial knowledge and experience. It almost certainly should include representatives of the ministry of finance and the central bank. In the case of Sao Tome and Principe, the committee also includes a member appointed by the President and two members appointed by the National Assembly, one of whom must be from the opposition. Where experience is limited, representatives of international financial institutions could participate in the investment committee as nonvoting members. In addition to providing technical assistance, international observers and other nonvoting members could act as a further check on conflicts of interest or other inappropriate activity. This idea was, however, rejected in Sao Tome and Principe.

In Timor-Leste, the executive branch has the overall responsibility for investment policy making, oversight, and management of the Timorese Petroleum Fund portfolio. The minister of finance, in particular, plays a key role in making investment decisions with the operational management delegated to the central bank, pursuant to a management agreement. Similarly, in Sao Tome and Principe, the policy making, oversight, and asset management functions are all assigned to a single committee—the Management and Investment Committee.[25] The Management and Investment Committee has the authority to delegate investment management responsibilities to qualified professionals.[26] It is yet to be seen whether the committee will delegate or exercise the investment management function directly once the country's oil fund is set up and begins operations. Kuwait's permanent oil fund, the Future Generations Fund, is also subject to executive branch policy making and management, which is carried out by the Kuwait Investment Authority (KIA). Similarly, the Norwegian Petroleum Fund is by law managed by Norway's Minister of Finance, which it does through the country's central bank, Norges Bank, pursuant to a management agreement.[27]

To promote transparency, an oil revenue management law should require the investment committee to report its activities periodically to the government and to the public, and its activities should also be subject to audits by independent international auditing firms.[28] Voting members should be subject to fiduciary duties and, in case of breach, to the appropriate sanctions. Finally, the law should address compensation of nongovernmental members.

Selection and oversight of portfolio managers

An oil revenue management law should set forth clear rules and procedures that delineate the selection process for portfolio managers. The process should be subject to open and competitive public procurement pursuant to rigorous qualification requirements, which should include proven experience in the management of large portfolios for large investors.

An oil revenue management law should also establish objective criteria for assessing the performance of portfolio managers, who should be subject to periodic performance reviews against pre-agreed benchmarks.[29] Either the law should itself establish clear benchmarking procedures with which to evaluate the investment managers' performance in managing and investing oil fund assets, or it should charge the investment committee with the task, following consultation with the portfolio managers.[30]

As the size of the oil fund grows, it may be advantageous from a performance standpoint to break the oil fund into separate investment-specific portfolios that may be more profitably managed by specialized managers. The larger the oil fund, the easier it is to justify the transactional costs and institutional burden involved with selecting, overseeing, and evaluating the performance of multiple portfolio managers. The Norwegian Petroleum Fund, for example, selects various external portfolio managers to manage different financial asset-specific portfolios,[31] and the Alaska Permanent Fund is divided into more than 40 financial asset portfolios that are managed by more than 20 managers.[32]

Be they members of the investment committee, as in the case of Sao Tome and Principe, trustees as in the case of Alaska, or outside professional asset managers, portfolio managers should be held to appropriate standards of care when carrying out management duties and exercising whatever discretion with which they are vested. In common law jurisdictions, this is often expressed as a fiduciary duty that requires trustees, for instance, to meet a "prudent investor" standard or similar rule[33] (see, e.g., the provisions in the Alaska Oil Fund).[34] Sao Tome and Principe has adopted a similar approach that provides that investment management functions shall be discharged pursuant to the "prudent investor rule," as defined in the law.[35] The Timor-Leste law, on the other hand, has opted for a more open approach[36] with no further criteria being provided but for the duty of the portfolio manager to take actions to maximize the return on the investments taking into account the appropriate risk as evidenced by the investments permitted under the applicable law.[37]

Underlying the formulation of any of these rules are the questions of who can elaborate the standard (should it be the courts or the government through contract, regulation or statute?), who can enforce whatever standard is applicable (should it be citizens or particular governmental entities?), and which institution can decide whether the standard is met (should it be domestic or foreign courts?). Although the reference for trustees or governmental investment committees may typically be domestic law and domestic institutions, it would be possible to give jurisdiction in certain instances to foreign courts that possess more developed expertise and stronger institutional history to enhance the protection of the oil fund's assets. Indeed, contracts with foreign asset managers are very likely to be governed by foreign law and subject to arbitration or some form of adjudication outside of domestic courts.

GENERAL INVESTMENT POLICY

The oil revenue management law may give broad discretion to the investment committee for devising an investment policy or it may set out a specific investment policy that gives very little room for committee discretion. The oil revenue management law of Sao Tome and Principe, for instance, charges the executive branch to submit for the approval by the National Assembly an investment policy proposed by the Management and Investment Committee. Timor-Leste, on the other hand, opts to give the executive branch greater discretion to design an investment strategy for the oil fund, subject only to statutory limits and to consultation with an investment advisory board by the minister of finance.

Where separate accounts are set up (e.g., a main oil fund account, a permanent reserve account, and a stabilization reserve account), the law may provide for a different investment policy (with the appropriate investment horizon and adequate investment requirements) for each account. Such legal flexibility will allow for the reexamination of investment strategies, horizons and restrictions, if needed, as the size of an oil fund increases and the institutional capacity and experience in oil fund portfolio management develop.[38]

SPECIFIC LIMITATIONS ON INVESTMENTS

Limitations on types of investments

An oil revenue management law should limit an oil fund's investments to certain secure and nonspeculative instruments. Both the Sao Tome and Principe oil revenue management law and the Timor-Leste petroleum fund law provide such limitations.[39] As a fund becomes larger, it may be appropriate to permit some portion of the assets to be invested in more sophisticated or more risky instruments. Again, this is an area in which rules and institutional capacity must be closely calibrated.

No domestic investment; no development fund

Investment advisers of a country's oil account should not be permitted to invest the fund in the country, or in domestic enterprises or enterprises controlled by nationals of the country. This prohibition serves two very important purposes. First, it helps limit political influence in the fund's choice of investments and enhances the likelihood of a fully professional investment regime. Second, it avoids governmental use of the oil account as an extra budgetary fund without full governmental and parliamentary oversight. Authorization of development spending should be the responsibility of the parliament, pursuant to the budget process. As recommended in chapter 7 such expenditures could draw significantly from oil revenues,[40] but development should not be done through the back door of the oil fund. The oil fund itself is supposed to be a permanent endowment for the country's future and should be invested solely from the perspective of protecting and growing that endowment. Requiring the fund to be invested in offshore assets also keeps the oil fund itself from contributing to inflationary pressures in the domestic economy, the "Dutch Disease."

The Sao Tome and Principe oil revenue management law expressly prohibits the investment of oil revenues deposited in the oil fund "in investments domiciled in Sao Tome and Principe, or in any investments controlled directly or indirectly, in whole or in part, by any national [or entity of Sao Tome and Principe], whether or not resident in Sao Tome and Principe, or who falls within [conflict of interest] circumstances." The Timor-Leste petroleum fund law also contains provisions to that effect.

No borrowing

A critical issue in any oil revenue management law is whether borrowing against oil resources or the assets held in the fund should be permitted. One can sketch scenarios, particularly before oil production commences or in the early life of oil production, when borrowing to enhance current human or capital investment would be sensible; actual experience, however, is negative.[41] The Saotomean, Norwegian, Alaskan, and Timorese oil revenue management laws all prohibit borrowing. In Sao Tome and Principe, for instance, borrowing against the assets of the fund and borrowing against the country's oil resources are both prohibited.

> Any and all acts are prohibited by the State or its Officials if such acts directly or indirectly create, permit, assume, or promise the existence of public loans, public bonds, security interests or any other

liens or encumbrances relating to the Oil Accounts or any other Oil Resources, whether existing or future, or related thereto. (Sao Tome and Principe Oil Revenue Law, Article 4.1)

In addition, an oil revenue management law should prohibit the pledge or other such use of oil resources or oil fund assets as security for loans. Such a prohibition prevents the government from borrowing against future production, which would result in the same consequences that arise from borrowing directly against natural resources.[42] Prohibiting the creation of security interests in oil fund assets does not mean that the government cannot borrow, but it does prevent the government from securing that borrowing with oil revenue or oil resources. Lenders thus must instead rely on the general creditworthiness of the country. This provides important discipline for both the country and the lenders, and gives the lenders a greater stake in stability and good government. Such discipline can be particularly important during the interval between the discovery of commercial oil and the commencement of oil production—a period in which there will be strong popular pressure to increase spending.

Narrow technical exceptions to this rule may be carved out in the law to permit the borrowing of securities in connection with prudent portfolio management,[43] subject to strict conditions, and the payment of preestablished financial charges in connection with the maintenance and the management of the account, as permitted, for example, by the Saotomean oil revenue management law. The Timorese Petroleum Fund Law, by contrast, contains a flat prohibition on any liens or encumbrances whatsoever on the Petroleum Fund.

OVERSIGHT AND CONTROLS

OVERSIGHT GROUPS

Parliamentary and governmental oversight

The collection, management, and use of all oil-derived revenues should be subject to wide and detailed oversight. In strong and well established governments, this oversight may be carried out by parliamentary commissions or other governmental bodies that already have oversight functions.[44] Traditional legislative oversight can be enhanced by requiring the publication of periodic and public reports by the various parts of government charged with carrying out the revenue law. For instance, in Sao Tome and Principe, the National Assembly is required under the Oil Revenue Law to conduct yearly public plenary sessions to discuss general oil and gas policy. Ministers, invest-ment committee members, the Auditor General, and the oversight board are required to be present to answer questions from parliamentarians, and to dis-cuss the activities of the fund including the required annual oil fund audits.

Oversight board

Given the significance of oil revenues and the limitations on existing in-stitutions, it may also be desirable to consider the establishment of addi-tional oversight groups, especially groups which may bring in civil society and elements not necessarily represented in the government. The case of Chad provides an early example. There, the management of resource rev-enue generated in connection with the Chad–Cameroon Petroleum Pipe-line Project was supervised by an oversight board, the Committee for the Control and Supervision of Oil Resources or *"Collège de Contrôle,"*[45] which included civil society representatives among its members and was moni-tored by the World Bank and the International Monetary Fund.[46] This oversight board was charged with verifying that the oil fund complied with applicable law, and with authorizing and controlling the disburse-ment of funds held in the oil fund. Chad, unfortunately, also provides an example of what can happen when oil institutions are divorced from the real power institutions of the country. In a widely criticized action, the Chadian government recently amended the revenue management law to reduce the authority of the *Collège* and to undo the basic revenue manage-ment framework. In December 2005, the Chadian parliament amended Law No. 001, providing for the deactivation of the country's oil fund, an increase in oil revenue expenditures, and a reassignment of a portion of the mandated expenditures for bureaucratic and security purposes.

In Sao Tome and Principe, the Oil Revenue Law created a new indepen-dent oversight body, the Petroleum Oversight Commission, composed of governmental and civil society members. The commission is charged with monitoring the management of oil revenues and assuring the implemen-tation of the revenue management law, and has been given significant in-vestigative powers. In Timor-Leste, the Petroleum Fund Law created a Petroleum Fund Consultative Council, made up of former officials, but its function is limited to providing opinions on major issues and acting as a medium of communication with the public.[47]

The nature, composition, and powers of any new oversight institution must be considered carefully. Such institutions have the advantage of creat-ing a sharp focus on the resource sector and of bringing into the oversight function groups that might otherwise be excluded. Moreover, the experience built up in such groups may be very important in providing continuity in oil policy and in explaining activities to the public. Further, oversight institutions may enhance public trust and understanding which may be critical to the long-term existence and management of the fund.

At the same time, such institutions could become a second "government" and thus create further civil conflict. In some instances, this conflict may be necessary given the character of the government, and the oversight commission then becomes a brake on arbitrary governmental action. There are limits to this, however, as demonstrated by the experience of the Chadian *Collège* in its attempt to deal with its own autocratic and unsupportive government. Second, unless clearly defined, such bodies may take on an amorphous legal character. The Petroleum Oversight Commission in Sao Tome and Principe, for instance, mixes investigative and administrative powers, as well as limited judicatory powers,[48] and in a number of respects overlaps existing institutional responsibilities.

Whatever the approach, the oil revenue management law should set forth a clear mandate for the oversight board. The Saotomean Petroleum Oversight Commission, for example, has broad responsibilities to monitor and ensure compliance by the government with the oil revenue management law, and it has independent administrative powers to investigate allegations of misconduct.[49] Depending on its scope, an oversight board could be accorded the power to investigate, require, and compel the production of documents and information, and to initiate and conduct investigations on its own motion or on complaints. The powers of an oversight board may also include the power to enjoin the actions of any governmental institutions or governmental officials in violation of the law, and the power to take judicial action to ensure the enforcement the law.[50] See figure 11.3 for a summary of different provisions that have been used in a sample of countries around the world.

To promote independence, membership of an oversight board should reflect the multiplicity of stakeholders in the management of a country's oil revenues. To enhance legitimacy, seats could be assigned not only to the various branches of the government at all levels (national, regional, or local) but also to the opposition and to civil society.[51] Participation of the international community in the oversight board may also be desirable, through a nonvoting observer represented by an international public institution present in the country. Note that this idea was rejected in Sao Tome and Principe.[52] Numerous organizational issues such as term length,

Country	Oversight Body	Membership	Mandate
Azerbaijan	Supervisory Board	9 members, all appointed by the President, but should represent both government and civil society.	Review and comment on draft annual budget, annual report and financials, audits.
Chad	Committee for the Control and Supervision of the Oil Resources (CCSPR) or Collège de Contrôle	9 members, multiple constituencies. Includes 4 members from civil society.	Ensure fund's compliance with finance law; authorize and control withdrawals, and oversee use of funds.
Kuwait	Board of Directors of Kuwait Investment Authority (KIA)	8 members. Includes 5 members from private sector.	Oversee and direct the activities of state oil company.
Sao Tome and Principe	Petroleum Oversight Commission	11 members, multiple constituencies. Includes 3 members from civil society.	Permanent oversight of all payment, management, and use of oil revenues and oil resources.
Timor-Leste	Petroleum Fund Consultative Council	Multiple members; exact number may vary in time. Includes former government officials, government appointees, and civil society.	Advise on matters relating to the performance and operation of the Petroleum Fund.

Figure 11.3   Oil Revenue Management Oversight Around the World—Selected Examples.

Source: Authors.

AUDITS AND REPORTING

An important mechanism of accountability is the periodic auditing of the oil fund. An oil revenue management law should specify the accounting method or methods the oil fund should follow, and require all activity of the oil account to be audited annually by an independent internationally recognized accounting firm that utilizes internationally accepted accounting methods, selected by open and public procurement. The law should also require that audits, any back-up papers, and special reports be presented to governmental agencies and be made public.[53] Moreover, any governmental agencies subject to the annual audits may be allowed to comment on them and pose any pertinent questions as such agencies see fit.

To the extent that a body of the local government has the power and responsibility to audit state accounts, such an institution should also be

composition, independence from selecting bodies, staff, and compensation also need to be addressed.

required by the law to conduct an audit of the oil account activity.[54] In Sao Tome and Principe, for example, the national oil account is subject to a dual audit requirement, with mandatory annual audits by the country's Auditor General and by the international accounting firm audit. In Chad, this internal audit is a responsibility of the General Accounting Office of the Supreme Court.[55] In Canada, the Alberta Heritage Savings Trust fund is audited by the Auditor General.[56] Similarly, Norway's oil fund is also audited by the country's office of the Auditor General.[57]

Reporting requirements should also be established. The country's oversight board and each governmental agency involved in the production, compilation, processing, or receipt of data or other information relating to oil revenue should be required to report periodically to the government and to the public. In varying levels, all revenue management laws contain reporting and reporting disclosure requirements.

PRIVATE RIGHTS OF ACTION/JUDICIAL CONTROLS

Any law must be clear as to who has standing to seek judicial enforcement of activity under the law, enforcement that could include the right to injunctive or mandamus relief. To strengthen public oversight further, some consideration should be given to private or citizens' rights of action to enforce compliance with the requirements of the oil revenue management law. The use of private litigation to enforce public rights is just beginning to emerge in developing countries, but it is a significant potential source of control over unlawful government action.[58]

PENALTIES

Legal sanctions such as those against bribery, abuse of office, and dereliction of duty may be directly applicable to actions under the petroleum law, but if not, the petroleum law will have to address these issues.

The Saotomean oil revenue management law prescribes a range of penalties applicable to violations of the law, including fines, imprisonment, the disgorgement of any monies and reversion of any improper advantages obtained, and, in some cases, the nullification of contractual agreements and documents.[59] In addition, the Saotomean oil revenue law provides enhanced penalties for both misdemeanors and criminal acts.

TRANSPARENCY

SCOPE OF PUBLIC INFORMATION

The requirement of transparency and the establishment of mechanisms that ensure such transparency are critical in any oil revenue management law. As a general rule, all oil revenue related information should be made public. Any law should provide a nonexhaustive list of items subject to transparency, and the parties responsible for making each piece of information public.[60]

Among many international efforts to foster and strengthen transparency in natural resource management are the "Publish What You Pay"[61] and the "Extractive Industries Transparency Initiative" (EITI) campaigns,[62] both of which support transparency of resource revenues through the disclosure of information on natural resource related payments made by private companies to resource exporting governments, among others.[63] Also of particular note and value is the IMF Guide on Resource Revenue Transparency published in 2005.[64]

A special issue with respect to the publication of payment data is whether such information should be available on an individual company basis or should be aggregated.[65] In countries with mature institutions, individual company data may be available, but in many developing countries there is no such disclosure.[66] While aggregate data may be the best information available in some countries, civil society or parliamentarians cannot use such data to compare directly payment data reported by the government with payments reported by the companies.

The Sao Tome and Principe Oil Revenue Law takes the preferred approach and mandates public access to individual payment data rather than to summaries or aggregations of information. Further, in the joint development zone controlled by Nigeria and Sao Tome and Principe, Presidents Obasanjo and de Menezes have signed a declaration of principles, the Abuja Joint Declaration, which requires public disclosure of individual company data and of contracts by the governing authority and the companies.[67] One of the advantages of having direct public Web access to the records of the custodial account (described in more detail later) is that payment information is available on a disaggregated basis and, without any intervention or discretionary action by the government, that all of the information can be made available to other branches of the government, civil society, and interested international groups.

A separate issue is the publication of all oil-related contracts. Although governmental oil contracts have traditionally been kept confidential in the developing world, that is not the practice in advanced democracies.[68] Moreover, the most recent practice even in developing countries is moving toward disclosure.[69] For instance, the Saotomean oil revenue management law requires disclosure and public access to "all contracts relating to the participation of the State or any enterprise or entity owned or controlled in whole or in part by the State, the scope of which directly or indirectly concerns activities related to Oil Resources or Oil Revenues."[70] Making contracts public ensures the integrity of bidding and negotiations, which in turn ensures that awards are made competitively and are consistent with whatever rules have been laid down. Without the transparency of contractual agreements, it is impossible for civil society or interested members of parliament to ensure that contracts are enforced and payments made accordingly. Making contracts public when they are entered makes possible full public oversight of those agreements that will be central to the political economy of the country in the future and is the only way to give such contracting full political legitimacy. This legitimacy is important not only for the citizenry but also for the companies because it provides protection against political second guessing when exploration prospects turn out favorably. Secrecy may protect the negotiators (government and private), but no one has identified a governmental interest in keeping agreements private. The contracts themselves are shared among industry partners; it is only the public that is excluded if they are kept confidential.

Sometimes in order not to make contracts or payments public, companies rely on confidentiality clauses and assert that it is the government that prevents them from making such information public. However, the government can and should, in the exercise of its own sovereign power, determine that such information shall be publicly disclosed. Certainly, a self-imposed confidentiality argument has no weight in the debate on a forward-looking law.

Any exceptions to the disclosure requirements should be very narrowly drawn. The Saotomean oil revenue management law specifically allows the withholding of information only if it is classified as confidential by law or treaty, and it puts the burden of claiming confidentiality on the proponent. The Saotomean law protects proprietary information from disclosure, but specifically prohibits making any payment information confidential. The Timorese petroleum fund law, on the other hand, has a general exception for confidential information without defining it. It also permits the government to use a number of other justifications for preventing the release of data.[71] Although certain of the exceptions might make sense in principle, they are drawn so generally that a determined government could use them to prevent almost any meaningful disclosure. What as a general matter should be considered confidential has been widely discussed in the literature, particularly in connection with environmental information.[72]

PUBLIC INFORMATION OFFICE

A requirement that information be made public necessitates supporting infrastructure that may not already be in place. For instance, there needs to be some form of a central, adequately financed depository, as well as a public information office where such information is readily available. In many cases, one could use existing institutions.[73] Alternatively, one could set up a new office particularly for oil-related information. In Sao Tome and Principe, an office was created under the auspices of the National Assembly to serve as depository for oil-related information. One of the shortcomings of the Timor-Leste law is the failure to provide for a public information office or Web facility where documents that are to be made public will be available; the subject may or may not be treated in other legislation.

It is important to have access to complete, readable, and comprehensible physical copies in local language. This access should include not only reports in summarized and understandable form but also access to the underlying data so that independent checks can be made.

DIRECT ACCESS TO INFORMATION THROUGH THE INTERNET

Electronic technology can greatly facilitate public access to information. All information, regardless of whether it is also available in print, should be scanned to digital format, uploaded, and maintained on the Internet. Any document received by the public information office should also be scanned and posted with its control number. This would allow for universal access to all public information both locally and internationally.

Internet access can also offer a dramatic increase in oversight of the oil account itself. In Sao Tome and Principe, the Columbia University Oil Advisory Group oil team proposed that the public be granted Web access to the financial data of the national oil account—for example, deposits, withdrawals, and holdings. Such access would be similar to the access an individual account holder has to his or her private account. If extended to the oil account, such access would provide greater transparency. In the case of Chad, there was a monthly posting of the account's activity as well as of quarterly reports. Timor-Leste has implemented a quarterly reporting system regarding holdings and aggregate receipts for its fund.[74] The proposal in Sao Tome and Principe, by providing real-time access to the oil account's financial data, would go well beyond that.

RESPONSIBILITY FOR DISCLOSING INFORMATION

An oil revenue management law could reinforce a transparency regime by requiring private parties to publicly disclose governmental contracts and oil-related payments. This would provide an independent check on government reports and would help ensure that such information is available even if the government fails to carry out its obligations to make such information public. The Saotomean oil revenue management law requires disclosure by both the government and the payer. The oil law further enforces such mandatory disclosure by requiring that the obligation to disclose agreements be included in all oil resource contracts either explicitly or by operation of law.[75]

PUBLIC GOVERNANCE AND INTEGRITY

Matters such as public governance and integrity may be already addressed by existing legislation; if not, they should be addressed in the oil revenue management law or in ancillary regulation. At a minimum, the basic principles of public governance and integrity, as applicable to the management of oil revenues, should be included in the revenue management law unless clearly addressed elsewhere.

CONFLICTS OF INTEREST

If not already defined by law, an oil revenue management law should set forth the elements of impermissible conflicts of interest and the basis rules for handling situations of unacceptable conflicts of interest. Laws and regulations governing ethics in public service often include mechanisms such as mandatory disclosure, temporary and permanent limitations, anti-nepotism rules, blind trusts, and mandated divestiture or liquidation of a public official's interest.[76] Again, one should be cautious about establishing rules that require or permit discretionary judgments; for example, the term "abuse of office." It may be better to provide bright line rules, for example, "no employment of a relative" (with "relative" carefully defined).

In Sao Tome and Principe, the oil revenue management law sets out strict conflict-of-interest standards that prohibit government officials from holding interests in oil revenues or representing any entity in which the oil revenues deposited into the oil fund are held or invested,[77] and also provides for the Petroleum Oversight Commission to establish its own conflict-of-interest regulations. Ethics rules aimed at avoiding unacceptable conflicts of interest also exist in Alaska, Azerbaijan, and elsewhere. Having the rules and enforcing them, however, are two different things.

BRIBERY AND CORRUPTION

The Saotomean oil revenue management law also requires all oil-related agreements and contracts to include no-bribery and procurement compliance representations, public disclosure obligations, and prevailing language (Portuguese) provisions, as well as a provision conditioning the effectiveness of the agreement or contract on full compliance with applicable government contract law. Under the law, agreements and contracts are to be construed to include these provisions, even if such provisions are not expressly written therein. Where the standards are included in the contract, any violation will constitute a breach of contract, allowing for an additional cause of action in case of bribery or corruption. The law can go even further (which the Saotomean law does) and can make any contract voidable in case of violation. As this is a severe sanction and could itself be abused by the government, further elaboration may be necessary in order to limit voidability to situations of gross abuse or bribery related to the contracting process itself.

In any event, it is recommended that the oil revenue management law itself contain an express prohibition of bribery and any illegal or undue advantages in the oil sector.[78] Note that most Western companies will already be subject to penal sanctions for bribery in their home country so that one effect of antibribery provisions is to equalize, at least in principle, the standard for all companies.[79]

PUBLIC PROCUREMENT

Public procurement is one of the areas in public governance most prone to corruption. With a view to reducing the opportunities for corruption and undue favoritism and patronage in public procurement, an oil revenue management law should stipulate that all significant contracts and agreements relating to oil revenues or to oil resources must be subject to open competitive public procurement. Under the Saotomean oil revenue management law, oil contracts—which are defined very broadly—are void unless entered into pursuant to the competitive provisions required by the Act.[80] The law requires that oil contracts be awarded pursuant to competitive public tenders in accordance with general legislation. In the absence of such legislation—and to the authors' knowledge currently no such general legislation exists—contracts are supposed to be approved by the Petroleum Oversight Commission. This may present an issue until the Petroleum Oversight Commission is fully implemented and operating.

INTEGRATION WITH OTHER INTERNATIONAL OBLIGATIONS

Frequently, oil resources may be shared with adjacent countries, and in such cases any oil management law must take account of the regime that governs such resources. If care is not taken, the joint zone can become a separate pocket of off-budget activity with limited control. In the case of Sao Tome and Principe, which shares oil resources with Nigeria, a preexisting treaty prevented Sao Tome and Principe from prescribing rules for the zone shared by the two countries, but the Saotomean oil revenue management law was able to regulate and reinforce the commitment of the two countries with respect to the joint development zone.

Domestic law, while it cannot always directly control a joint development zone, can control the activities of domestic officials acting on behalf of the government with respect to the joint zone.[81] In particular, no official is authorized to approve any contribution to the budget for the administration of the joint zone without such contribution being approved by the National Assembly. Officials are also subject to the conflict of interest and other legal provisions that apply to all government officials and representatives. As per the Sao Tome and Principe Oil Revenue Law, for instance, no Saotomean official could agree to or authorize any document encumbering the oil resources of the joint zone that are allocable to Sao Tome and Principe. Moreover, Saotomean officials are directed by the law to work with the Nigerian representatives to implement the provisions of the Abuja Declaration agreed to by the two Presidents.[82] Since such provisions are generally consistent with the Saotomean law, this provides some coherence between the two regimes.

While a problem area in the case of Sao Tome and Principe, joint resources could, with some imagination, be an opportunity for enhanced and more secure oil management. For instance, it would be much easier to set up a truly independent international trust account with fixed rules that neither country could arbitrarily void even if its government changed or was subject to instability. The rules could be changed by agreement of all participating parties, but the account would not be subject to change simply because of instability of one of the parties.

KEEPING THE LAW IN PLACE

A central issue for an oil management law is how to create practical and legal barriers that will inhibit subsequent governments from abandoning or evading the law while at the same time maintaining flexibility to meet changing conditions. Sovereignty means that any law passed by the current government is in principle subject to amendment or repeal by any future government. The action in Chad is a case in point. Still, measures can be taken even legislatively that may make it harder to change the law. For instance, in certain countries, it is possible to create special supermajority legislative approval and referenda requirements for changes in the law.[83]

Another way to reinforce the oil law is to adopt a constitutional amendment addressing certain key elements. A constitutional amendment would significantly strengthen the controls over the collection and use of oil revenues, and would inhibit—but not prevent—the ability of any party or subdivision of the state to arbitrarily or unilaterally change the rules governing the oil account. In the unlikely event that an unconstitutional government attempts to seize power, such an amendment might also help protect the country from the seizure of funds, especially if the funds are held in an international institution outside of the country.

An amendment could reaffirm key principles of the oil revenue management law. For instance, the amendment might state that all petroleum resources and the revenues derived from them are the property of the state and cannot be pledged or encumbered,[84] that all revenues from such resources must be deposited in the oil account, that all transfers from the oil account to the general funds of the Treasury must be approved by the appropriately designated institution or institutions, that the activities of the oil account, including all deposits and withdrawals, shall be public, that monies from the oil account can be made available only for particular specified uses and, possibly, that pledges or other encumbrances on the petroleum resources of the state are prohibited. The constitutional amendment could be passed separately or in conjunction with the oil law.[85]

The state constitution of Alaska for example provides in Article IX, Section 15, that "[a]t least 25 percent of all mineral lease rentals, royalties, royalty sale proceeds, federal mineral revenue sharing payments and bonuses received by the State shall be placed in a permanent fund, the principal of which shall be used only for those income-producing investments specifically designated by law as eligible for permanent fund investments. All income from the permanent fund shall be deposited in the general fund unless otherwise provided by law."[86]

The Alaskan fund is interesting in another respect and that is its use of a trust. Trusts, at least at common law, are frequently used to put assets beyond the control of either the party establishing the trust or the beneficiary of the trust. The trustee or manager of the trust is then required to act in accordance with the instructions setting up the trust, and the beneficiaries of the trust can sue the trustee if it fails to act as required.[87] In the oil fund context the difficulty is the sovereign binding future sovereigns.[88] More generally, it is hard to imagine any government being willing to commit large sums to a foreign trust and then to throw away the key.

Even though the government maintains full control of a fund, the stability of a fund could also be enhanced by the involvement of regional or international institutions such as NEPAD[89] or the World Bank. Chad provides a good example of the power of such involvement and the limitations on that power.[90] Even where such institutions have simply observer status or nonvoting membership, they can provide an additional degree of professionalism, transparency, and accountability. Apart from enhancing management, their presence could be especially helpful in resisting domestic pressures driven by short-run political advantage.

Whatever form the fund takes, however, legislators and those assisting them must recognize that the law without strong supporting institutions may become just paper. In the end, popular support rather than good drafting is the most important sustaining mechanism, but a well constructed law may help increase and build that support. There is a possibility of a virtuous circle in which a workable and effective law creates stronger popular constituencies who in turn will act to support and maintain the law.

NOTES

1. The "oil" team of the Earth Institute was made up of the authors and Macartan Humphreys, Martin Sandbu, and Peter Rosenblum, all of Columbia University. This chapter relies heavily upon the work of the team.

2. See Greenspan Bell (2000).

3. The Saotomean oil law is telling in this respect. Not only does the new law impose a number of requirements that current institutions may not be equipped to carry out, but, contrary to recommendations, the law itself calls for additional laws to establish a public information office and an oversight board. The need for these additional laws has significantly delayed the startup of both these institutions.

4. Indeed, there is some research suggesting that in the face of limited resources, focusing on new rules for existing institutions may be more fruitful than focusing on the establishment of new institutions. See, for example, Posner (1998), and sources cited therein.

5. Sao Tome and Principe is provisionally using the New York Federal Reserve to hold its account.

6. Chad's petroleum revenue management law, for example, was severely criticized because in its original form it covered only a portion of the oil stream although partial coverage may have been the most that was politically feasible. See Catholic Relief Services (2005).

7. Art. 1(ii).

8. Pursuant to the Timor-Leste Petroleum Fund Law, any state-owned oil company receipts shall be included as Petroleum Fund gross receipts (Art. 6.2). Selected provisions of the Timorese Petroleum Fund Law are transcribed in Appendix 2.

9. Such electronic transfers should be free of any transfer or exchange taxes.

10. In the draft discussed among the Saotomean lawmakers the officials were also required to certify as part of the withdrawal order that it was in accordance with the provisions of the oil law.

11. See chapter 8 for a discussion of natural resource funds.

12. Pursuant to Article 9 of the Timor-Leste Petroleum Fund Law: "No transfer shall be made from the Petroleum Fund in a fiscal year in excess of the Estimated Sustainable Income for the Fiscal Year unless the Government has first provided the Parliament with" certain reports and explanations. However, "[i]f required under the law of Timor-Leste, transfers from the Petroleum Fund are exceptionally permitted for the purposes of refund of tax, in the event of overpayment of tax. . . . This amount represents a reduction of the Petroleum Fund receipts, and shall not be considered as part of the appropriation [the amount approved by the Parliament for the relevant fiscal year]." Article 10.

13. For example, the Saotomean oil revenue management law limits expenditures based on a formula that is essentially equal to 5 percent (i.e., the expected earnings on the fund) multiplied by the amount in the permanent fund plus 5 percent of the remaining estimated oil wealth. There is a further limit to make sure that the amount calculated as 5 percent of the remaining oil wealth does not exceed the unrestricted portion of the account in the prior year. The latter restriction is intended to avoid any invasion of the principal amount of the permanent fund.

14. If all revenues are put into a fund and then only earnings from the fund are used to support current expenditures, such estimates would not be necessary, but this would result in a very low level of initial spending. While in some cases this may be consistent with absorptive capacity, it is very unlikely to be consistent with political pressures for rapid development and spending that arise, once commercial petroleum is found.

15. For new oil streams, it is necessary to look at comparables to obtain the historical figures, but this can be done by using some sort of basis adjustment which, while not entirely free of subjective elements, will cause only modest variations in the calculated average price.

16. For examples of the calculations under various assumptions, see the Earth Institute Web site at http://www.earthinstitute.columbia.edu/cgsd/STP/index_oillaw.htm.

17. See, for example, Davis et al. (2001b). For estimates of the required size of a stabilization fund for Nigeria, see IMF (2005b).

18. If in the first year or two of commercial oil production prices are very low compared to historical prices, initial revenues may not be able to support expenditures at the level calculated at historical prices. The Saotomean oil revenue management law addresses this problem in part by incorporating an initial one-year lag after the commencement of commercial oil production into the determination of the limit on revenue expenditures, and by limiting the amount to be spent to actual prior year revenues plus expected earnings on the permanent fund balance. Article 8.3(b). The effect of various buildup patterns is illustrated at the Earth Institute Web site, available at http://www.earthinstitute.columbia.edu/cgsd/STP/index_oillaw.htm.

19. It would also be possible to incorporate forward markets into a hedging strategy to provide more stability of income flows (see Dodd 2004).

20. If only a stabilization fund is used, the estimate of future prices becomes more critical. A permanent fund, except in its earliest years, provides a much larger fund balance or "reservoir" from which current expenditures can be financed. Hence, the inevitable difference between forecasted or current prices and the prices used to calculate the limits is much less likely to result in a liquidity or funding problem.

21. Regional allocations are highly political and have been the central focus of much conflict regarding the use of oil revenues. This is true for example in Nigeria, where greater disclosure is needed for the special oil revenue allocations made to oil-producing state and local governments. On this topic, see Brosio (2000, 24–25). In Sao Tome and Principe there is a mandated allocation of 7 percent of the Verba Anual (Verba Funding Amount) to Principe, an autonomous region, and 10 percent to local autarchic governments. Although Principe and local regions are allocated funds, their budgeting and appropriation procedures are subject to national supervision.

22. See chapter 9 for a discussion of distributive aspects of resource revenues.

23. Although frequently pointed to as a model, the constitutionally required allocation of revenues to the fund and direct distribution have been criticized for diverting revenues from the general fund and depressing expenditures for education, infrastructure and other social needs. For a more general discussion of the topic, see Davis et al. 2001a. Conditional cash transfers, a variant of direct distribution has apparently been successful in Mexico where payments are made to families whose children are enrolled in school. See Gertler and Boyce (2001), Davis (2003) and Rawlings (2004).

24. The custodial function encompasses solely the custody of the oil fund assets, and is carried out by the account custodian.

25. Articles 11 and 13 of the Sao Tome and Principe Oil Revenue Law.

26 Article 13.4 of the Sao Tome and Principe Oil Revenue Law.

27. See Act No. 36 of June 22, 1990, relating the Norway's Government Petroleum Fund available at the Norges Bank Web site at http://www.norges-bank.no/english/petroleum_fund/management/actno36.html, and Management Agreement between the Minister of Finance and Norges Bank dated as of February 12, 2001, as most recently amended on December 1, 2004, at http://www.norges-bank.no/english/petroleum_fund/management/agreement-2004.html.

28. The Timor-Leste Petroleum Fund provides for quarterly reports on the fund performance. The initial reports through the third quarter of 2005 are available at http://www.transparency.gov.tl/PR/PFQR.htm.

29. Specific benchmarks can facilitate the oversight of government spending and thus help protect against political manipulation and diversion of funds. A clear benchmark also provides a specific guide to the ministry of finance for developing the budget.

30. Pursuant to Timor-Leste's Petroleum Fund Law, the Investment Advisory Board is responsible for developing performance benchmarks of desired returns on, and appropriate risks of, the investments of the Petroleum Fund. Article 10.1(a). In addition, the annual report for the Petroleum Fund shall contain a comparison of the income derived from the investment of Petroleum Fund assets with benchmark performance indices provided to the Minister of Finance by the Investment Advisory Board for the relevant fiscal year. Article 14.2(f).

31. According to the Norwegian Central Bank, this strategy was devised with "the objective of achieving the highest possible return within the guidelines and framework set by the Ministry of Finance." See Norges Bank Web site at http://www.norges-bank.no/english/petroleum_fund/mandates/.

32. A list of managers and specific mandates, portfolios managed and respective benchmarks is available at the Alaska Permanent Fund Corporation Web site, at http://www.apfc.org/investments/MANAGERS.cfm.

33. In the United States, virtually all states have adopted their respective versions of the Uniform Prudent Investor Act, which sets out the required standard of care for the fiduciary investment in trust of another's assets. See Trillos (2005).

34. In Alaska, the "prudent investor rule" means that in making investments, the portfolio manager should exercise the judgment and care, under the circumstances then prevailing, that an institutional investor of ordinary prudence, discretion, and intelligence exercises in the management of large investments entrusted to it not in regard to speculation but in regard to the permanent disposition of funds, considering probable safety of capital as well as probable income.

35. Pursuant to Article 1(ll) of the Sao Tome and Principe Oil Revenue Law, the "prudent investor rule" shall mean that an agent shall ensure high quality and efficiency standards in the performance of any investment transactions or services, and shall discharge his duty to protect the legitimate interests of the state with the diligence of a discerning and orderly manager, pursuant to the risk sharing principle and

the safety of the investments, in accordance with the investment rules approved by the Management and Investment Committee.

36. Article 11.4 of the Timor-Leste Petroleum Fund Law.

37. Article 12.5 of the Timor-Leste Petroleum Fund Law.

38. See Article 14.3 of the Petroleum Fund Law of Timor-Leste, which provides for the range of specified permitted investments to be reviewed by the government and approved by the Parliament at the end of five years taking into account the size of the oil fund and the level of institutional capacity.

39. See Article 13 of the Sao Tome and Principe Oil Revenue Law and Article 15.1 of the Petroleum Fund Law of Timor-Leste (Appendix 2).

40. Chad's oil revenue escrow account was used as a development fund. In Timor-Leste, certain constituencies claim that the oil fund should be used as a development fund.

41. Angola's recent history, for example, illustrates how oil-backed financing can exacerbate oil price fluctuations and further weaken already poor accountability and public governance in oil exporting countries. Angola has mortgaged much of its future oil production by using it to secure international short-term, high-interest financing, the proceeds of which were not used in development or poverty alleviation programs, but rather often wasted or lost to corruption (Global Witness 1999, 2002).

42. Some commentators have expressed concern about whether such an account might be subject to attachment by private creditors, but under existing international and U.S. law and longstanding doctrines of sovereign immunity, a governmental account is generally immune from attachment.

43. Investments held by the oil account can in certain instances be used to collateralize other securities held in the account where such securities are of short duration.

44. Pursuant to the Saotomean Oil Revenue Law, the country's Auditor General also performs certain oversight functions, being responsible for auditing the oil account on an annual basis and for reviewing oil contracts ex ante and ex post. It is not clear, however, that the Auditor General has been able to fully carry out these functions.

45. The Chad Revenue Management Plan is available under "Revenue Management Plan" on the Chad-Cameroon Development Project Web site, at http://www .esso.com/Chad-English/PA/Files/20_ch16.pdf.

46. Despite the active monitoring of international financial institutions, the effectiveness of the Collège de Contrôle has proven weak at best in view of lack of enforcement of the law, insufficient human capacity and political pressures and influences. See, for example, Catholic Relief Services (2005).

47. In a number of sections of the Timorese law, parties are required to "advise" or to provide an opinion to others.

48. The language of Article 24.2(d) of the Saotomean Oil Revenue Law provides the Petroleum Oversight Commission with the power to "carry out searches, inspections, and seizure of any documents or personal property that are the object, tool, product of any infraction, or that are necessary to the opening of the respective process." In drafting the Petroleum Oversight Commission's implementing legislation, however, Saotomean legislators have expressed their concern that the Petroleum

Oversight Commission not usurp judicial functions from the judiciary branch, and that the implementing laws should clearly provide that any such search and seizures be subject to the appropriate judicial proceedings.

49. Art. 24.

50. In Sao Tome and Principe, the drafting committee considered, but then rejected, giving the oversight board the power to suspend any transfers out of the oil account in exceptional circumstances of "grave" violation, subject to the review of the country's highest court or to action by a supermajority of the National Assembly.

51. The oil revenue management law should leave the procedure of nongovernmental member selection to the discretion of the selecting constituency.

52. The Petroleum Oversight Commission includes 11 members appointed or elected, as the case may be, by the President of the Republic, the National Assembly (including one member selected by the opposition), the Superior Judiciary Council, the Autonomous Region of Principe (the island of Principe), local governments, business associations, trade unions, and nongovernmental organizations.

53. The Sao Tome and Principe Oil Revenue Law provides that all audit backup documents and reports shall be made public. Similarly, the Timorese law provides in Article 24.2 that the sources of information required by the law to be disclosed and made public shall be annexed to the Petroleum Fund's Annual Report, whatever its form, and including all reports and statements, in unedited form.

54. A list of existing supreme audit institutions is available at the International Organization of Supreme Audit Institutions (INTOSAI) Web site, at http://www .intosai.org/Level2/2_DIRECT.html.

55. Catholic Relief Services (2005).

56. See Alberta Heritage Savings Trust Fund Act, Queen's Printer Web site, at http://www.qp.gov.ab.ca/Documents/acts/A23.CFM.

57. See Norges Bank Petroleum Fund Web site, at http://www.norges-bank.no/ english/petroleum_fund/reports/1998/1.html.

58. An example is the evolving use of citizen suits to enforce environmental laws in developing countries. See Baydo et al. (2004) for an overview of the recent experience in the Philippines. See also Roberts et al. (1992).

59. Penalties could also include reprimands and warnings, removal from office in the case of public officials, temporary or permanent loss of contractual rights, termination of contract, non-imprisonment sentences, etc. Penalties can include nullification of agreements and documents entered into, in violation of the law, the disgorgement of any monies and reversion of any advantages improperly obtained. Penalties may also include fines, expatriation or expulsion of foreign residents, deemed aggravation of relevant crime or misdemeanor, and imprisonment in appropriate cases.

60. The Timor-Leste Petroleum Fund Law, however, follows the inverse approach, establishing a general principle of transparency and listing all exceptions to the principle.

61. Publish What You Pay, http://www.publishwhatyoupay.org.

62. Extractive Industries Transparency Initiative, http://www.eitransparency.org.

63. Other international transparency initiatives include the OECD Guidelines for Multinational Enterprises; the OECD Project on Revenue Transparency in the

Democratic Republic of Congo; the World Bank Extractive Industries Review; the International Monetary Fund Code of Good Practices and Fiscal Transparency.

64. International Monetary Fund (2005a).

65. While EITI reporting guidelines provide for the disclosure of oil revenues on an aggregate basis by oil-rich governments, the level of aggregation is contentious in that many argue that only with the disclosure of payment information on an individual company basis would accountability be possible and transparency effective.

66. For a discussion of host government-mandated disclosure of oil company payments to governments see Save the Children (2005a), which notes that Canada is the only country with any mandatory requirements on disclosure on a country-by-country basis. See also Save the Children (2005b).

67. A copy of the Abuja Joint Declaration is available at the Nigeria-Sao Tome and Principe Joint Development Zone Web site, at http://www.nigeriasaotomejda .com.

68. For a discussion of the recent progress in the oil industry transparency see Olsen (2005).

69. The government of Congo-Brazzaville, for example, has recently published on its Web site all of its Production Sharing Agreements, recent production figures and audits of the state owned oil company. See Catholic Relief Services (2005). Information on and excerpts of such production sharing agreements are available (in French) at the Congo-Brazzaville government's Web site at http://www.congo-site.net/v4x/MEFB/home.php.

70. Art. 17.2(k).

71. Timor-Leste Petroleum Fund Law, Article 32.

72. See, for example, the Aarhus Convention, http://www.unece.org/env/pp/welcome.html.

73. In Sao Tome and Principe, the Columbia University Oil Advisory Group proposed the establishment of a public information office as a subdivision of an already existing governmental body, in the physical form of an office where documents would be filed, indexed, kept, and made readily available to the public. The head of the public information office would be appointed and dismissed as provided for in the oil revenue management law, and have the legal obligation to appear before the government (the National Assembly, in the case of Sao Tome and Principe) on an annual basis to testify about the compliance of the country's authorities with the information disclosure provisions of the oil revenue management law.

74. See http://www.transparency.gov.tl/PR/PFQR.htm.

75. Art. 21.

76. OECD/IDB Forum on "Implementing Conflict of interest Policies in the Public Service," Rio de Janeiro, 5–6 May 2004. Background papers and presentations are available at the OECD Web site, http://www.oecd.org/document/11/0,2340,en_2649_33735_31419595_1_1_1_1,00.html.

77. Art. 30.

78. Sample language outlawing bribery can be found in the United Nations Convention Against Corruption (UNCAC), the Organization of American States Inter-American Convention Against Corruption, the OECD Convention on Combating Bribery of Foreign Public Officials, the Council of Europe's Criminal Law Convention

on Corruption and Civil Law Convention on Corruption, the Convention of the European Union on the Fight Against Corruption involving officials of the European Communities or officials of member states, the African Union Convention on Preventing and Combating Corruption the United Nations Convention Against Transnational Organized Crime, and the United Nations Convention Against Corruption.

79. See in the United States the Anti-Bribery and Books and Records Provision of the Foreign Corrupt Practices Act (15 USC 78) and in the United Kingdom the Anti-Terrorism, Crime and Security Act of 2001 (ACTSA). See also the OECD Convention on Combating Bribery of Foreign Public Officials in International Business Transactions (1997), the Council of Europe Criminal and Civil Conventions on Corruption (1999), the Inter-American Convention Against Corruption (OAS Convention) (1996), and the United Nations International Convention Against Corruption (2003).

80. Art. 22.

81. The Treaty governing the joint zone requires the parties in the first instance to try to make decisions by consensus, but this requirement, which is not absolute, does not relieve the Saotomean officials of their obligations under Saotomean law.

82. The full text of the Abuja Declaration is available at the Joint Development Authority Web site, at http://www.nigeriasaotomejda.com/Pages/Publicity.html. The Declaration was not self-implementing and in spite of the commitment of the two Presidents, the administrators of the joint zone have failed to enforce all of its provisions. Among other items, the recently negotiated joint production agreement with Chevron and Exxon has not been made public although the authors understand that payments and certain provisions of the contract will be made public. Even this limited compliance had not occurred as of February 2007.

83. Recent experience in Bolivia shows that referenda may be abused. Referenda are two-edged swords and may be used to compromise legislative prudence and weaken effectiveness of the existing revenue management framework.

84. Such amendments need to be carefully drafted so as not to be construed as creating a monopoly on drilling and production by the state. Such restrictions in Mexico and elsewhere have resulted in significant distortions.

85. It is worth noting that certain countries allow for the creation of unchangeable constitutional provisions, which may not be amended. The German Constitution, for example, contains immutable clauses. Similarly, Article 89 of the French Constitution, which sets forth the process of constitutional amendment, provides that the republican form of government may not be subject to amendment ("La forme républicaine du gouvernement ne peut faire l'objet d'une révision"), and earlier French Constitutions purported to be entirely immutable. Along the same lines, Article 60 of the Brazilian Constitution provides that no proposal of amendment shall be considered which is aimed at abolishing the federative form of state; direct, secret, universal, and periodic suffrage; the separation of the three branches of government; and individual rights and guarantees. Article 60 also provides that the Constitution shall not be amended during a federal intervention, the state of defense, or the state of siege.

86. Alaska Constitution, Article IX, Section 15.

87. Although trusts are typically a common law institution, a somewhat similar arrangement can be established in civilian systems through the use of a "foundation" controlled by a self-perpetuating board of directors. The arrangements are more subject to the oversight of the state and the board of directors would usually have much more power to control the disposition of funds than the typical trustee.

88. The case is different where there are third-party rights. In those instances the trust is likely to be set up under foreign law and the third parties have the right to enforce the terms of the trust. Such a trust has been used in the case of the Chad–Cameroon pipeline, where the payments are initially made to a trust in which the lenders including the international institutions have an interest. The trust is not subject to the control or the laws of Chad and cannot be unilaterally changed by Chad. Chad's amendment of Law No. 001 and the ensuing default under its financing agreements led to the suspension of World Bank loans and distributions from the accounts to Chad. The oil fund balances themselves remained beyond the reach of unilateral action by the Chadian government. See "CHAD: Government and World Bank Struggle to Save Face in Oil Row," Reuters (Source: IRIN), February 6, 2006. A solution to the impasse was achieved in July 2006 when the World Bank and the government of Chad executed a Memorandum of Understanding whereby the Chadian government committed to invest 70% of its budget in priority poverty alleviation programs, committed 5% of its oil revenues to regional distribution, created a stabilization fund, and committed to strengthen the Collège de Contrôle. See the World Bank press release archived at http://www.reliefweb.int/rw/RWB.NSF/db900SID/EKOI-6RT5GY (accessed March 2007).

89. NEPAD, The New Partnership for Africa's Development, http://www.nepad.org/.

90. See World Bank press releases on Chad on the World Bank Web site, at http://web.worldbank.org/WBSITE/EXTERNAL/COUNTRIES/AFRICAEXT/CHADEXTN/0,,menuPK:349881~pagePK:141159~piPK:141110~theSitePK:349862,00.html. See also public statements by the International Monetary Fund and the European Investment Bank on their Web sites, respectively.

REFERENCES

Baydo, K. E., G. Bathan-Baterina, M. M. Legera, and M. A. Mendoza. 2004. "A Test Case on the Citizen Suit Provision of the Clean Air Act: The IBP Experience." Paper presented at the Second Alternative Law Groups Conference on Public Interest Lawyering, at the Malcolm Hall of the University of the Philippines College of Law, October 20.

Bell, R. G. 2000. "Building Trust: Laying the Foundation for Environmental Regulation in the Former Soviet Bloc." *Environment* 42. Reprinted in *Environment in the New Global Economy (The International Library of Writings on the New Global Economy)*, Peter M. Haas, ed. Northampton, MA: Edward Elgar Publishing.

Brosio, G. 2000. "Decentralization in Africa." Working Paper, International Monetary Fund.

Catholic Relief Services. 2005. *Chad's Oil: Miracle or Mirage? Following the Money in Africa's Newest Petro-State*. Baltimore: Catholic Relief Services and Bank Information Center.

Davis, B. 2003. "Innovative Policy Instruments and Evaluation in Rural and Agricultural Development in Latin America and the Caribbean." In *Current and Emerging Issues for Economic Analysis and Policy Research (CUREMIS II). Vol. I: Latin America and the Caribbean*, ed. Benjamin Davis. Chapter 3. Rome: Economic and Social Department, Food and Agriculture Organization of the United Nations.

Davis, J., R. Ossowski, J. Daniel, and S. Barnett. 2001a. "Oil Funds: Problems Posing as Solutions?" *IMF Finance & Development Magazine* 38(4). Also available online at http://www.imf.org/external/pubs/ft/fandd/2001/12/davis.htm#author.

Davis, J., R. Ossowski, J. Daniel, and S. Barnett. 2001b. *Stabilization and Savings Funds for Non Renewable Resources*. Washington, DC: International Monetary Fund.

Dodd, R. 2004. "Protecting Developing Economies from Price Shocks." Special Policy Brief 18, Financial Policy Forum, Derivatives Study Center. http://www.financialpolicy.org/fpfspb18.htm.

Gertler, P. and S. Boyce. 2001. "An Experiment in Incentive-based Welfare: The Impact of PROGESA on Health in Mexico." http://faculty.haas.berkeley.edu/gertler/.

Global Witness. 1999. *A Crude Awakening, The Role of the Oil and Banking Industries in Angola's Civil War and the Plunder of State Assets*. London: Global Witness. http://www.globalwitness.org/reports/show.php/en.00002.htmlhttp://www.globalwitness.org/reports/show.php/en.00016.html.

Global Witness. 2002. *All the Presidents Men: The Devastating Story of Oil and Banking in Angola's Privatized War*. London: Global Witness. http://www.globalwitness.org/reports/show.php/en.00002.html.

International Monetary Fund. 2005a. *Guide on Resource Revenue Transparency*. http://www.internationalmonetaryfund.com/external/pubs/ft/grrt/eng/060705.htm.

International Monetary Fund. 2005b. *Nigeria Selected Issues*. IMF Country Report No. 51303 (August). Washington, DC: International Monetary Fund.

Olsen, W. H. 2005. "The Oil Industry and Transparency." Unpublished manuscript, Revenue Watch, Open Society Institute.

Posner, R. A. 1998. "Creating a Legal Framework for Economic Development" *The World Bank Research Observer* 13(1): 1–12.

Rawlings, L. 2004. "A New Approach to Social Assistance: Latin America's Experience with Conditional Cash Transfer Programs." World Bank Social Protection Discussion Papers Series (No. 0416). http://www1.worldbank.org/sp/safetynets/Conditional%20Cash%20Transfer.asp.

Roberts, E., J. Dobbins, and M. Bowman. 1992. "The Role of the Citizen in Environmental Enforcement." Presented at the Second International Conference on Environment Compliance and Enforcement, September 22–25, in Budapest. Also available online at http://www.inece.org/forumspublicaccess_documents.html.

Save the Children. 2005a. *Beyond the Rhetoric: Measuring Revenue Transparency—Home Government Requirements for Disclosure in the Oil and Gas Industries*. London: Save the Children.

Save the Children. 2005b. *Beyond the Rhetoric: Measuring Revenue Transparency—Company Performance in the Oil and Gas Industries*. London: Save the Children.

Trillos, J. C. 2005. *Investment Products Deskbook: Banking Rules and Regulations*. Washington, DC: A. S. Pratt & Sons.

CHAPTER 12

Future Directions for the Management
of Natural Resources

Macartan Humphreys, Jeffrey D. Sachs, and Joseph E. Stiglitz

The chapters in this volume identify steps that governments of resource-rich countries can take to increase the benefits that their countries derive from their holdings of oil, gas, and other resources. The focus on governments is natural: these actions will work only if governments lead the way. We believe these reforms should attract the support of their populations. Moreover, in some cases, these reforms will be brought about only with concerted pressure from civil society.

But the "resource curse" afflicts not just host country governments and their populations; it also affects the operations of major international corporations, their home governments, and those in consuming nations. We believe that reforms that bring an end to the resource curse are also in the interests of the oil companies and consumer states. The chapters in this book have identified associations between resource extraction and civil wars, human rights abuses, corruption, poor governance, and environmental damage, sometimes at catastrophic levels. Governments of resource-rich states cannot resolve these problems alone if the relevant environment is prohibitive.

Responses are therefore needed not only from host countries but also at the level of the international system. And this is in the interests of both oil companies—which suffer considerable direct and reputational costs owing to their perceived complicity with autocratic regimes, human rights abuses, and environmental havoc[1]—and their home governments—which sometimes find themselves following compromised foreign policies, backing despots in order to secure advantageous access to oil and gas fields, pipelines, and sea routes, often with long-run damage to the reputation and true national interests of the consuming countries. These responses must ensure not just more equitable relations between producer nations and private corporations but also better domestic economic management of resources and better handling of the difficult political economy issues that invariably arise in the presence of large amounts of resource wealth.

If we are to make progress in dealing with the resource curse, governments in both consuming and producing countries will have to change what they do; the international community will have to act in concert. Corporations will have to take an active role. And so too will civil society. We can ask corporations to act more ethically, in a more "socially responsible way," but they are more likely to do so when pressure is brought to bear. We cannot rely on goodwill alone.

We summarize here a core set of responses, many of which are drawn from and supported by the chapters in this volume. Key recommendations for action by national governments include the following:

- *Condition the "deal" on future prices and other economic circumstances.* In the past, oil and gas contracts have not taken sufficient account of how the share of profits accruing to governments change as prices and output change. Oil companies often made sure that they were protected if oil prices fell, but they garnered the extra profits that resulted from soaring prices. No democratic government can accept a deal in which the corporation receives an unconscionably high return, and the country receives a pittance for its natural resource. Companies must be fairly compensated for their investments—but rates of return that are not commensurate with the risk will never be accepted. The mathematics is relatively simple. Ignoring costs of extraction, consider a deal with a fixed gross royalty of 50 percent. If the oil company was willing to undertake extraction when it expected prices of oil at $20 a barrel, then, if prices soar to $80 a barrel, the company receives four times the required return ($40 compared with $10). If such price increases are deemed unlikely, "progressive" deals that increase the country's share as prices rise may have only a minor impact on the ex ante value of a deal but can eliminate grossly inequitable situations ex post. But the deals made in the 1980s and 1990s were not sufficiently progressive—in many cases, the rising value of oil and gas holdings has not resulted in a rising share of benefits for the owners of these resources. Instead, oil and gas contracts should specify returns to governments under a wide range of price, cost, and production scenarios. Otherwise, once prices start rising without a corresponding rise in the returns to resource nations, there will be a predictable rise in tensions between countries and corporations and a corresponding rise in resource nationalism.

- *Tailor the auction design to the context.* Countries need to take whatever actions possible to increase the level of competition between corporations. Doing so will not only increase the value received by countries but also reduce the risks of cronyism. This can in part be done by better auction design. Auction design, along with contract design, can affect the magnitude of information asymmetries and their consequences. And they can affect the number of bidders in the market and the fierceness with which they bid. The choice of design can be very important for revealing information about the value of assets and generating competition. Contract and auction design also affect cash flows of governments—in badly designed arrangements, governments borrow implicitly at high interest rates from corporations when they can borrow at lower interest rates on the market. There is no one best auction format for auctioning rights to oil and gas, however. Popular formats such as first-price sealed bid are good in some contexts, but in others, particularly where there are complementarities and asymmetric information, the recently developed auction designs described in chapter 5 may perform much better.

- *Require transparency of negotiated outcomes.* Although having domestic constituencies evaluate contracts during or after negotiations may seem like a constraint on government negotiators, it is a constraint that can in fact increase the bargaining power of domestic negotiators and help produce a better and more durable deal; it is essential if one is to avoid corruption. In general, there is no good reason for contracts to be kept secret.

- *Use bonding to prevent environmental damage.* To mitigate the problem of corporations saddling countries with large environmental costs, governments should require that corporations post bonds in anticipation of future cleanup costs. This becomes more feasible as it becomes easier to ascertain in advance the size of possible cleanup costs. For example, we now know more about the risks of some of the tailings than we knew a quarter century ago, and advances in technology have enabled better monitoring of pollution and possibly even lower costs in pollution abatement.

- *Calculate national wealth correctly.* Rather than following standard approaches that treat oil and gas revenue as income, national accounting standards should be employed that accurately reflect the true economics of oil and gas production, taking account simultaneously of earnings and of the depletion of stocks, and the degradation of the environment. A clear understanding of the true wealth of a resource-rich nation can help counter temptations to spend too much too quickly and to rely too narrowly on a depletable asset. Focusing on net national production (NNP) rather than gross domestic product (GDP) will direct attention to the benefits to the developing country—a project that increased GDP, but in which most of the profits went to a foreign owner, would look far less attractive from the aspect of NNP.

- *Stabilize expenditures.* Many resource-rich countries suffer greatly from boom-bust patterns. Resource prices are volatile; but when incomes are high, international lenders are willing to lend them more, so they even spend beyond their ample current flows, getting increasingly in debt. Money spent in this way is often poorly spent; and there are huge economic costs to such macroeconomic volatility. Some countries have found it desirable to create stabilization funds, credibly committing themselves to steadier patterns of expenditure. But if such funds are to be effective, incentives need to be built in so that political leaders are not tempted to raid them. In addition, at the international level, accounting frameworks have to be appropriately adapted, so that countries that spend out of their stabilization funds in a period of economic downturn are not penalized. Rainy day funds are designed to be spent when there is a rainy day.

- *Use earnings for investment rather than consumption to avoid Dutch Disease problems.* Dutch disease effects arise largely from the rapid conversion of resource wealth (in the form of stocks of assets) into domestically produced consumption or investment goods. The effects of this are adverse impacts on non-oil exporting sectors, lower growth, and great readjustment costs once production stops. One solution is to rely on taxation for mobilizing domestic resources. More generally, to ensure sustained growth as natural resources get depleted, earnings have to be invested in financial, physical, and human capital. Investing in alternative export sectors, in agriculture, and in education can help sustain growth and diversify risk. It may be desirable, almost necessary, to pace investment inside the country, holding some financial assets abroad in the meanwhile.

- *Take steps to avoid inequities.* While there is in principle more scope for pursuing aggressive equalitarian policies in resource-dependent countries (without normal adverse effects on incentives), we have seen that resource-rich countries are often characterized by great inequality. The political crises associated with oil wealth can likely be mitigated by ensuring a fair distribution of benefits within a country. The decentralization of revenue collection to subnational entities, however, can often result in an exacerbation of resource curse effects. The capacity of subnational entities to manage extreme volatility of income streams and to ensure oversight is often weaker than that of central governments. Thus it is better in most cases to centralize revenue collection and the intertemporal smoothing of expenditures, while allowing for the possibility of decentralizing expenditure to subnational bodies. There remain, of course, the highly contentious issues of how to divide proceeds. Producing regions in particular should not be faced with the environmental or other damages that may accompany production without seeing evidence of the benefits that derive from the production. In all cases, a first step to confronting the distributive repercussions of oil wealth is to collect and disseminate better information on the impact of oil and gas production on patterns of income distribution within producing countries.

- *Strengthen state–society linkages.* As oil revenues flow in, multiple forces act to unlink governing elites from their populations. They no longer, for instance, require revenues from taxes on their citizens. These dynamics can be countered politically by expanding the scope for broad-based participation in decision making. Broad based participation in oversight mechanisms can increase policy predictability and reduce the incentives and scope for misuse of revenues. This oversight can be strengthened by integrating the management of oil revenues with regular budgetary processes, and—contrary to the trends we observe in many countries—by continuing to rely on classic forms of taxation, such as income taxation, rather than relying exclusively on oil and gas revenues.

In addition to these recommendations there is a series of ways in which *international action* can help countries seeking to increase their capacity for the management of oil and gas revenues. Recommendations that arise from the chapters in this volume include the following:

- *Develop a mechanism for providing access to the services of skilled negotiators.* Better outcomes could arise for countries if they could draw on the skills of professional negotiators with extensive experience in the industry. Lack of access to such negotiators is in part due to a financing problem. This could be resolved through arrangements that bring together a pool of experts in negotiation that are remunerated according to fair standards from a fund that receives reimbursement only once earnings accrue.

- *Develop a third-party natural resource fund management service.* International bodies could create and support a "global clearinghouse" for natural resource revenue funds. This clearinghouse could deal with both the logistical and, more importantly, the difficult commitment issues associated with fund management in a way that respects and strengthens the sovereignty of producing nations. It could, for example, accept only accounts that come with strict rules on the magnitude of funds that could be withdrawn every year, disburse funds only when the required signatures of several branches of government are provided, and prevent the nonconstitutional raiding of revenues.

- *Enforce stricter standards on multinationals.* Foreign resource companies working in developing countries should be subject to the same environmental and ethical standards they face at home. To ensure high standards there should be both individual and corporate accountability. The international community needs to make it easier for producer states to collect damages from multinationals—which often have few assets in the countries where they inflict the damage. This may mean piercing the corporate veil: allowing a parent company that owns more than 20 percent share in a mining company that has damaged the environment to be sued for the damage inflicted will provide strong incentives for it to exercise oversight. Limited liability was introduced to increase economic efficiency, not to be a shield against bad behavior. Firms (and their agents) that violate environmental standards or engage in corrupt practices should be liable to criminal prosecution, with a full agreement on extradition for violations of such acts. In all cases, action in the home country of the multinational should be facilitated, which in many cases will entail legal reforms that enable pursuing firms across borders (such as through a more expansive version of the U.S. Alien Tort Claims Act).[2]

- *Create and maintain a global public information office on oil and gas revenue management.* A global information office can be established that collates and posts basic data on contracts and payments for oil and gas around the world. Such a center could create a standardized system for filing contracts on-line and maintaining information on payments and public expenditures on a country-by-country basis. The generation and publication of comparable data on oil deals can facilitate negotiations, and improve oversight once deals are concluded.

TRANSPARENCY

We close this volume with a special note on the role of transparency in reversing the resource curse. A remarkable number of the chapters in this volume have identified the importance of transparency for resolving the multiple problems emanating from oil and gas holdings. This is all the more striking as these authors come from a range of different professions, disciplines, and perspectives.

In the first section of this book, the chapters by Joseph Stiglitz, Daniel Johnston, Jenik Radon, and Peter Cramton all point to the role of transparency in relationships between country governments and oil corporations. Joseph Stiglitz in chapter 2 emphasizes the loss of competitiveness that can arise in weak informational environments. In such cases, all bidders—both the informed and the uninformed—may offer less to governments. Yet he also emphasizes the costs to corporations arising from a lack of transparency; chief among these is the possibility that the ensuing rights over oil and gas reserves will not be secure.

In chapters that examined some of the details of oil contract negotiation, David Johnston and Jenik Radon both emphasized that even in settings where competitive bidding may not be optimal, transparency in negotiations will likely render multiple benefits. As illustrated by David Johnston, the complexity of evaluating contracts can result in great confusion over what one would expect to be a simple question: did a government get a bad deal? A lack of transparency may give rise to exaggerated fears that a government did not in fact get a good deal and that foul play or exploitation was present. The case of Chad prior to renegotiations in

2006 is illustrative. By common measures, the country got a bad deal. The Government Take figure was low in Chad compared to other countries, and it is likely that, under the original deals, the benefits to the country would not adequately capture the increased rents that are now accruing from rising oil prices. However, it is difficult to assess with any certainty just how bad the deal was. The measures commonly used to assess the deal fail to take account of key aspects of Chad's situation, such as the cost of transportation and the quality of the oil and, even though the deal is often described as a model of transparency, basic details of the deal are not in fact publicly available.

More transparency can also allow for more effective public oversight. As Jenik Radon emphasizes, more oversight can actually strengthen a government's hand during negotiations: If the domestic negotiator requires the ratification of a watchful public this can serve as a credible demonstration of resolve to get a good bargain.[3] While this may make striking a deal more difficult, it may also raise the value of a deal for corporations, since any deal struck will have stronger public approval and less chance of being overturned.

In chapter 5, Peter Cramton similarly emphasizes the importance of a transparent auction design for competitive bidding. He emphasizes that transparency, even in the design of the auction process, is likely to be beneficial both to companies and governments as it allows for the selection of more appropriate rules for different settings.

Geoffrey Heal in chapter 6 notes one key difficulty for countries aiming to get the best value out of oil resources: poor access to capital markets. This arises in part from the fear of default associated with the political instability and policy uncertainties that are linked to oil and gas producers. If transparency can help allay these concerns and reduce the chances for default, increased access to capital markets can be of general benefit. Jeffrey Sachs in chapter 7 emphasizes the importance of transparency for avoiding the Dutch Disease. Avoiding the adverse effects of oil income on non-oil tradable sectors requires coherent, longer-term, transparent planning to render growth in these sectors more predictable. The logic of these arguments is taken up again in chapter 8 by Macartan Humphreys and Martin Sandbu, who argue that political uncertainty about actions of future governments can lead to faster than optimal expenditure by incumbents. As argued by Paul Collier (2004), saving in such an environment—through a fund or otherwise—may simply produce a transfer from a wise present government to a foolish government in the future. Greater policy transparency, by subjecting governments to more oversight and by encouraging the alignment of policies between alternating governments, might reduce unpredictability in the future and thereby reduce incentives for present governments to overspend.

Further arguments for greater transparency are found in chapters 9, 10, and 11, which explicitly deal with the political and legal implications of resource wealth. While other chapters emphasized the importance of transparency for negotiations, auctions, and fiscal management, Michael Ross stresses the role transparency can play in improving relations between corporations and populations from producing areas. These relationships are habitually fraught with difficulties that are unlikely to be resolved simply by increased investments in local projects. Transparency can help to improve these relations not only directly but also indirectly, by changing the focus of activity of local groups. Rather than lobbying extraction companies, these groups might instead direct their activities toward the central government, thereby taking pressure off companies while strengthening government through the institution of increased accountability. Greater transparency can also insulate states against the possible assumption among populations in producing regions that revenues are greater than, in fact, they are. Terry Karl in chapter 10 places these questions of transparency at the very center of her analysis. A fundamental source of political decay in oil-rich countries, she argues, is the absence of productive relations between governments and their citizens; technocratic fixes are likely to have little effect absent a basic level of trust between citizens and rulers. A first step toward establishing this trust, she argues, is the provision of basic information about what monies governments receive and how it is used. Joseph Bell and Teresa Faria provide yet another argument in chapter 11. Transparency, they contend, is a precondition for the enforcement and implementation of a law; if information is not available on basic details such as government revenues, the agencies of oversight that are central to the rule of law will be unable to function effectively.

These arguments derive specifically from studies by practitioners and researchers of the oil and gas industries. Interestingly, however, research on transparency within the field of economic theory points to more mixed results. According to economic theorists, transparency could in principle reduce competition if it allows for easier collusion among firms. Further, while more information about the actions of "agents" is typically better for "principals,"[4] the lack of transparency can, under some conditions, lead to greater effort by political leaders to perform well in order to over-come the informational problem and demonstrate their capacity.[5] For these reasons, much recent empirical work has focused on the effects of transparency. Does transparency *in fact* lead to better outcomes? The re-sults are quite striking. While the theory is mixed, the empirics support the case for greater transparency quite clearly. In one experimental study of the impact of information on competitor behavior, economists found that posting information about competitor actions leads to greater, not weaker, competition (Huck et al. 2000). Another study found that fiscal transparency induces greater effort on the part of politicians, and that this in turn is rewarded with higher approval ratings and a willingness of vot-ers to trust politicians with significantly larger budgets. Strikingly, this re-search suggests that on average more oversight makes governments more, not less, popular (Alt et al. 2001). Other work supports the claims made here that transparency can help avoid the linkages between state and soci-ety that occur in the presence of natural resource wealth. One study, us-ing a natural experiment, concludes that voter turnout rises when voters have more information about policy debates—a strong indicator of more vibrant political competition (Lassan 2005).[6] Another recent analysis of radio access confirms that voters with more information are more active and successful in ensuring the political processes do in fact benefit their areas (Stromberg 2005). Yet another study found that increased access to information on education expenditure in Uganda led directly to less mis-use of funding at the local level (Reinikka and Svensson 2005). The vol-ume of research supporting the purported benefits of greater transparency appears to be growing rapidly.

In short, the arguments in favor of transparency range from the im-pacts that it might have on competition between firms when seeking rights to explore and drill; to the enhanced efficiency of negotiation pro-cesses; to the credibility of a government's negotiating position and its ability to guarantee the longevity of a deal; to the stability of a political environment and the effects of that on access to capital markets and on the incentives of leaders to spend optimally over time; to the attitudes of popu-lations toward governments; to the ability of basic mechanisms of ac-countability, be they governmental or nongovernmental. These arguments are compelling and are supported by existing empirical work on transpar-ency. They suggest that *the first step toward reversing the oil curse is to re-move the layers of secrecy that continue to surround so many aspects of the industry.* This secrecy, while hugely beneficial to the few, comes at great cost to publics inside and outside of producing countries and ultimately to the governments and companies that promote them.

In trying to increase transparency, numerous operational problems arise. The most basic is determining what exactly should be transparent. Clearly, not all documents could or should be made publicly available. Without a clearer identification of what should be transparent, the call for increased transparency may have little content. The chapters in this volume propose the institution of a *transparency principle* subject to specified exceptions. That is, there should be a strong presumption in favor of rights to access to information. Petitioning for limitation of access to particular information should be allowed, but with well-defined constraints on what can and cannot remain confidential.[7]

A second difficult question is how to achieve compliance. Some advocate a voluntary approach. The problem with a voluntary approach (on the part of companies and governments), however, is that it is precisely in the difficult cases where voluntary compliance will be less forthcoming that transparency is likely to be most important. Corrupt governments will put pressure on corporations not to disclose. Further, with voluntary compliance, individual corporations may be slow to comply simply because they believe that other firms will be slow to comply.[8] There have, however, been a number of relatively simple mechanisms proposed to enforce compliance. Host governments are in a particularly strong position to declare a transparency principle imposing a legal requirement on firms to make all payments and contracts public subject to the threat of invalidating contracts should the transparency principle not be applied. This approach has been taken by Sao Tome and Principe. It places responsibility on firms to provide information to a public information office; should they fail to do so, they risk losing the contracts they hope to protect. There are also a number of mechanisms that can be adopted by home countries. Publication of payments could, for example, be a requirement on companies in order to be listed on a stock exchange, or alternatively home country governments could demand that multinationals make all payments transparent: any payments made to a host country government that is not "published" would simply not be tax deductible. Further pressure could be imposed by banks and banking regulators. Clearly, it can be risky for banks to lend to firms that do not disclose; this is especially the case if, as in Sao Tome and Principe, such oil contracts could be subject to abrogation. Accordingly, international financial institutions could also require transparency of payments and contracts for any companies that benefit directly from loans made by these institutions; and financial regulators could require this of the banks over which they have oversight.

A third issue centers on how to prevent violations of a transparency principle through the introduction of ad hoc confidentiality clauses within the contracts themselves. One solution found in the Sao Tome and Principe law is to use legal means to render these legalistic attempts to violate transparency null and void. The Sao Tome and Principe law in fact specifically renders such attempts invalid.

A final issue involves preventing information overload and allowing interested parties to manage information efficiently. With high levels of transparency comes the risk that locating key documents can become a complex task. Indeed, in some situations, a glut of unimportant information may conceal a lack of transparency. For instance, with the wealth of information on the Cameroon–Chad agreement on the World Bank Web site it can take a considerable search to realize that key documents, notably the agreements between the governments and the oil consortium, are not in fact available.[9] The Joint Development Authority (JDA) of Nigeria and Sao Tome and Principe posts a number of documents about transparency, including the Abuja declaration, which declares that all contracts will be published on-line, but the contracts themselves do not appear on the JDA's Web site.[10] Thus, one relatively easy solution, as proposed above, involves creating a Global Public Information Center on oil and gas contracting. The advantage of a standardized system of this form is that it not only makes information easier to deposit and to access, but also makes it obvious when information that ought to exist, in fact, does not.

Much more can be done then to increase the transparency of the oil and gas industry, and this is likely to have beneficial effects. However, as emphasized in many of the chapters of this volume, transparency may well be a necessary condition for better management of oil and gas wealth, but it is unlikely to be a sufficient condition.

* * *

The experience of the last quarter century has provided surprising and sobering lessons regarding the impact of wealth from natural resources on the politics and economies of producing countries. These countries hold assets of great value, ones for which there is increasing competition. This competition should lead to tremendous benefits to producing countries. The news of new finds in developing countries, from Mauritania, to Guinea Bissau, to Chad should be sources of hope for the populations of these countries. Yet we know that if business continues as usual these hopes will not be fulfilled. In some cases, we may expect to see countries failing to capture the true value of their assets, seeing the profits instead move overseas. In other cases, we may expect to see rising corruption, political fragmentation, increased poverty, and environmental damage. Yet, as shown in the chapters of this volume, averting these trends is possible. The economics and politics of the "resource curse" are not especially complicated. Many of the principles that should be applied to counter these adverse patterns are also relatively simple. The difficulty is applying these principles in an environment in which greed and secrecy dominate. At a moment in which it is becoming increasingly clear that past policies have not provided the benefits they promised either to the governments or the populations of producing countries, and at a time in which bargaining power is likely shifting toward producing nations, there is a great potential, finally, to change the way collectively we manage our endowments of energy and other natural resources.

NOTES

1. Those operating in Nigeria, for example, suffer materially on a continual basis from political unrest, thefts of oil, and the kidnapping of personnel. The reputational costs are perhaps more important: British Petroleum and Occidental have been criticized for their links with security forces in Colombia (Human Rights Watch, 1998); Elf, for reportedly giving direct military support to belligerents in the Republic of Congo (Amnesty International 2002); Shell, for apparent complicity in the execution of Ken Saro-Wiwa, as well as slow responses to massive oil leakages in the Niger Delta (Human Rights Watch 1999); and Texaco for soil and groundwater contamination in the Ecuador Amazon. As a result of continued criticism of its activities in Sudan, Talisman eventually was forced to pull out (on Sudan see Human Rights Watch 2002).

2. In the United States there are legal grounds to take action against corporations in cases of corruption (through the Foreign Corrupt Practices Act [FCPA]) and of egregious human rights abuses (through the Alien Tort Claims Act [ATCA]) but not for environmental damage overseas (see Open Society Justice Initiative 2005). While such efforts need to be expanded and strengthened in the United States, the introduction and use of such legislation should be universalized through the introduction of compatible legislation in other countries also.

3. This logic has been elaborated by Thomas Schelling (1960).

4. See Holmström (1979).

5. See Holmström (1999) and Dewatripont et al. (1999). See also Prat (2005) for a different theoretical argument against transparency over actions when outcomes are observable. In this model agents that are rewarded on the basis of actions taken may

become more conformist and fail to act on private information that could result in better outcomes.

6. Interestingly work by Gentzkow (2006) shows that access to television reduces turnout, in part because voters substitute away from richer sources of information.

7. Such allowances are made for example in Article 20 (sections 2 and 3) of the Sao Tome and Principe law (Appendix 1).

8. Experimental work (see Bloomfield and O'Hara 2000) suggests, for example, that, when given the choice, dealers choose to withhold information even when there are benefits to releasing it; in doing so they drive out higher information dealers from the market. This simple logic can lead to universal noncompliance even in situations where all firms would in fact be willing to comply if others did also.

9. http://www.worldbank.org/afr/ccproj (last accessed August 2006).

10. http://www.nigeriasaotomejda.com/ (last accessed August 2006).

REFERENCES

Alt, J., D. Lassan, and D. Skilling. 2001. Fiscal Transparency, Gubernatorial Popularity and the Scale of Government: Evidence from the States. EPRU Working Paper. University of Copenhagen.

Amnesty International. 2002. "Following the Oil: French Arms Deals in Africa." *The Terror Trade Times* 3, June 3. Available at http://web.amnesty.org/web/web. nsf/pages/ttt3_oil (accessed August 2006).

Bloomfield, R. and M. O'Hara. 2000. "Can Transparent Markets Survive?" *Journal of Financial Economics* 55(3): 425–59.

Collier, P. 2004. "Petroleum and Violent Conflict," keynote address at the World Bank ESMAP Petroleum Revenue Management Workshop (March 2004).

Dewatripont, M., I. Jewitt, and J. Tirole. 1999. "The Economics of Career Concerns. Part I: Comparing Information Structures" *Review of Economic Studies.* January 66(1): 183–98.

Gentzkow, M. 2006. "Television and Voter Turnout." *Quarterly Journal of Economics* 121(3): 931–72.

Holmström, B. 1979. "Moral Hazard and Observability." *Bell Journal of Economics.* 10(1): 74–91.

Holmström, B. 1999. "Managerial Incentive Problems: A Dynamic Perspective." *Review of Economic Studies.* January 66(1): 169–82.

Huck, S., H.-T. Normann, and J. Oechssler. 2000. "Does Information about Competitors' Actions Increase or Decrease Competition in Experimental Oligopoly Markets?" *International Journal of Industrial Organization* 18(1): 39–57.

Human Rights Watch. 1998. "Colombia: Human Rights Concerns Raised by the Security Arrangements of Transnational Oil Companies." New York: Human Rights Watch (April).

Human Rights Watch. 1999. *The Price of Oil: Corporate Responsibility and Human Rights Violations in Nigeria's Oil Producing Communities.* New York: Human Rights Watch.

Human Rights Watch. 2002. "Talisman 'Human Rights' and Development Efforts, 2000–2002." New York: Human Rights Watch.

Lassen, D. 2005. "The Effect of Information on Voter Turnout: Evidence from a Natural Experiment." *American Journal of Political Science* 49(1): 103–18.

Open Society Justice Initiative (Ingrid Tamm, Christian Lucky, and Stephen Humphreys). 2005. *Legal Remedies for the Resource Curse.* New York: Open Society Institute.

Prat, A. 2005. "The Wrong Kind of Transparency." *American Economic Review* 80: 21–36.

Reinikka, R. and J. Svensson. 2005. "The Power of Information: Evidence from a Newspaper Campaign to Reduce Capture of Public Funds." World Bank and IIES Working Paper.

Schelling, T. C. 1960. *The Strategy of Conflict.* Cambridge, MA: Harvard University Press.

Strömberg, D. 2004. "Radio's Impact on Public Spending." *Quarterly Journal of Economics* 119(1): 189–212.

APPENDICES

Abridged Sao Tome and Principe Oil Law*

NATIONAL ASSEMBLY
Law No. 8/2004
Oil Revenue Law

PREAMBLE

The Democratic Republic of Sao Tome and Principe shall soon be starting to receive oil revenues resulting from the exploitation of its oil resources. Related to this reality are complex strategic matters that must be anticipated, resolved and regulated so that such revenues can foster progress and sustainable social and economic development in Sao Tome and Principe.

Based on these principles, this law is adopted, guided by two fundamental ideas. The first idea is centered on the payment and management of oil revenues. An attempt was made to address the concerns shown by the international experience taking into account the national reality and the need for the Sao-Tomean people to make strategic decisions regarding their future.

For that purpose an account is established—the National Oil Account—in which all oil revenues shall be deposited directly, and mechanisms are introduced which are intended to ensure that such revenues will not be used indiscriminately. Thus, limits are set forth for the use of the oil revenues, such limits not excluding, however, the need to make decisions about spending on priority sectors on which expenditures will focus and the respective revenue allocation.

Similarly, this law introduces mechanisms to prevent the revenues being channeled to other accounts. Revenues may only be deposited in the

---

*Unofficial translation. The translated law is available at http://www.earthinstitute.columbia.edu/cgsd/STP/documents/oilrevenuemanagementlawgazetted_000.pdf. A copy of the gazetted law is available at http://www.earthinstitute.columbia.edu/cgsd/STP/documents/OilRevenueLawGazetted_000.pdf (accessed 3 March 2007).

State Treasury Accounts or in accounts established for that specific purpose in the name of the State, as authorized by the National Assembly.

This law establishes quantitative and qualitative limits on the amount of oil revenues that shall be used for annual budgetary expenditures. The quantitative limits define, in certain breadth, the maximum amount of annual expenditures to be financed by oil revenues. The qualitative limits determine the basic principles for the calculation of the annual expenditures within the maximum fixed limits, as follows: (I) planned and forecasts of future revenues; and (II) absence of distortions in the economy.

The finite nature of oil resources was also taken into account, as well as the need to introduce mechanisms that will allow Sao Tome and Principe to face the post-petroleum era with minimum economic distress. For that purpose, a reserve sub-account was established—the Permanent Fund of Sao Tome and Principe—in which part of the oil revenues shall be deposited, and whose use shall be strictly conditioned, except for the earnings generated from investments of its funds. Thus, it is intended for the Sao-Tomean people to continue to benefit from the yields generated by the investments of the reserve sub-account even after the oil resources come to an end.

The management and investment of the oil revenues are assigned to an Investment and Management Committee, which is the institution with the authority ascribed by law for that purpose. The Investment and Management Committee shall act pursuant to the prudent investor rule, the principles established by this law and by the management and investment policy.

This law introduces mechanisms to ensure the effective management and investment of oil revenues, and establishes different priorities according to their allocation. All revenues allocated to finance public expenditure shall be managed aiming immediate liquidity, while the revenues deposited in the permanent fund shall be managed for medium- and long-term profitability. The management and investment policy, which will guide revenue management and investment, shall reflect these principles.

The second fundamental idea of the law is centered on oil revenue management auditing, transparency and oversight mechanisms, which are considered to be of great importance to ensure that this law be enforced according to its objectives.

Two annual audits of the oil accounts, in which the oil revenues shall be deposited, shall be carried out: one by the Auditor General and the other by an internationally recognized international auditing firm.

The law establishes clear transparency and publicity rules with respect to all acts and documents related to the oil activity. On one hand, mechanisms are introduced that limit the confidentiality of contracts concerning oil resources or oil revenues, mandatory registration and disclosure is introduced for all documents and information related to the oil sector. On the other hand, all people have ample rights to access the information.

The law also creates a Petroleum Oversight Commission, with independence and administrative and financial autonomy to ensure its effectiveness, with oversight, investigative and sanctioning powers.

Finally, this law clarifies that its dispositions apply to the Joint Development Zone; it establishes a range of irreconcilable conflicts with regard to the exercise and placement in positions in the bodies created by the law; and it aggravates by one third, in their minimums, the penalties established by the general law to punish behaviors that violate the provisions of this law.

In these terms, the National Assembly sets forth, pursuant to Article 97(b) of the Constitution, the following:

CHAPTER I

DEFINITIONS AND SCOPE OF APPLICATION

Article 1
(Definitions)[1]

1. For the purpose of this law:
   a) "Administration" or "State Administration"—shall mean the direct, indirect, autonomous or independent administration of Sao Tome and Principe, including all ministries, entities, agencies, departments, offices, institutes, services, support services to the sovereignty bodies, as well as local and regional branches of the state and all their services, departments and all entities, companies and production unities controlled, in whole or in part, directly or indirectly, by the central, regional or local administration.
   b) "National Petroleum Agency"—shall mean the governmental legal entity with authority to regulate the national petroleum industry;
   c) "Official" or "State Administration Official"–shall mean any individual occupying any position in, employed by, contracted by or otherwise acting on behalf of or representing the State Administration,

---

[1]Translator's Note: For the purpose of this translation, the terms and expressions defined in this Article are listed in the same order as they appear in the original Portuguese language alphabetical order.

including ministers, directors, administrators, managers, attorneys-in-fact, commissioners or concessionaires of any entities controlled by the Public Administration;

d) "Year"—shall mean the period between January 1st and December 31st.

e) "Business Association"—shall mean any permanent association of entrepreneurs or professionals created in order to defend and promote their business or professional interests;

f) "Joint Development Authority"—shall mean the collective body established for the purposes described in the Treaty.

g) "Central Bank"—shall mean the Central Bank of Sao Tome and Principe, as established by Law No.8/92, dated as of August 3, 1992.

h) "Custody Bank"—shall mean any financial institution, or its branches or agencies, in an international foreign center, which is rated the highest by two internationally recognized risk analysis agencies, able to receive and hold cash balances in an internationally convertible currency, act as the custodian itself or by an Official, keep operation records of the National Oil Account, and provide to the public, directly or through competent entities, the information subject to the transparency principle under the terms of this law;

i) "Approved Bank"—shall mean any foreign commercial bank, or its branches or agencies, in an international financial center, which is rated the highest by two internationally recognized risk analysis agencies.

j) "Management and Investment Committee"—shall mean the committee organized to ensure the management of the Oil Accounts and the investment of the oil revenues deposited in such accounts;

k) "Petroleum Oversight Commission"—shall mean the independent organization that ensures the oversight of all the activities related to the national oil resources and revenues;

l) "Oil Accounts"—shall mean the National Oil Account and the Permanent Fund of Sao Tome and Principe, when collectively referenced;

m) "Treasury Account"—shall mean any account or sub-account referred to as Public Treasury Account, established by the Treasury with the Central Bank, pursuant to Decree No. 51/96, dated as of October 29, 1996;

n) "National Oil Account"—shall mean the account established and held by the Central Bank with the Custody Bank, pursuant to this law;

o) "Oil Contracts"—shall mean transaction instruments having Oil Resources or Oil Revenues as an object.

p) "Abuja Joint Declaration"—shall mean the declaration regarding transparency and good governance signed on June 26, 2004 by the Presidents of the Federative Republic of Nigeria and the Democratic Republic of Sao Tome and Principe.

q) "State" or "Sao-Tomean State"—shall mean the Democratic Republic of Sao Tome and Principe, as defined in article 1 of the Constitution;

r) "Permanent Fund" or "Permanent Fund of Sao Tome and Principe"—shall mean the sub-account established with the Custody Bank, with the purpose of establishing a permanent savings reserve, pursuant to paragraph 1 of Article 3, and to Article 10 of this Law;

s) "Public Registration and Information Office"—shall mean the public registration and information service, as defined in Article 18 of this law;

t) "Natural gas"—shall mean all hydrocarbons that are gaseous at atmospheric pressure and temperature;

u) "Approved Foreign Government"—shall mean the government of any foreign country or any agency or instrumentality of such foreign government, which is rated the highest by two internationally recognized risk analysis agencies;

v) "Production Commencement"—shall mean the date on which the commercial production of hydrocarbons shall commence in any block of the national territory, including the Exclusive Economic Zone and the Joint Development Zone.

w) "Hydrocarbons"—shall mean the hydrocarbons as defined in the Treaty, the Treaty Regulations, and sub-paragraph (m) of Article 1 of the Oil Activities Law;

x) "Oil Activities Law"—shall mean Law No. 4/2000, dated as of August 23, 2000, and all amendments thereto;

y) "State General Budget"—shall mean the State General Budget as defined in Law No.1/86, dated as of December 31, 1986;

z) "Non-Governmental Organizations"—shall mean any association, organization, legal entity, foundation, institution or company and other bodies deemed as legal entities represented in Sao Tome and

Principe, not-for-profit, that predominantly pursue scientific, cultural, charitable, aid, social solidarity, social and economic development, human rights protection, environmental protection goals, and other related goals;

aa) "Unrestricted Part of the National Oil Account"—shall mean the balance of the National Oil Account, excluding the Permanent Fund of Sao Tome and Principe;

bb) "Person"—shall mean any individual or legal entity, whether national or foreign, resident or non-resident of Sao Tome and Principe;

cc) "Petroleum" or "oil"—shall mean all hydrocarbons that are liquid at atmospheric pressure and temperature;

dd) "Management and Investment Policy"—shall mean the document containing the management and investment rules for the Oil Revenues deposited in the Oil Accounts, pursuant to the principles set forth in this Law;

ee) "Expected Average Prices"—shall mean the price calculated according to paragraph 1(a) of Article 7 of this law;

ff) "International Reference Prices"—shall mean, for the period of ten[2] years as from the Production Commencement Year, the official price of hydrocarbons publicly rated by the Brent FOB Sullom Voe, and, and for the seventh[3] year after Production Commencement and subsequent years, the actual sale price of crude oil in Sao Tome and Principe, including the sales of hydrocarbons of the Joint Development Zone;

gg) "Oil Production"—shall mean the commercial production of oil or any other hydrocarbon in the Exclusive Economic Zone or in the Joint Development Zone;

hh) "Field Development Program"—shall mean the detailed document, which, pursuant to the Treaty, the Treaty Regulations or Oil Revenue Law, as the case may be, is submitted by an oil operator for the establishment, construction and operation of facilities and services for the recuperation, processing, storage and transportation of hydrocarbons in the contracted operator's block;

---

[2] Translator's Note: Discrepancy between periods in first and second clauses in original.

[3] Id.

ii) "Oil Revenue"—shall mean any payment or payment obligation owed by any Person to the State, directly or indirectly, with respect to the oil resources of Sao Tome and Principe, including, but not limited to:

    I) Any and all payments from the Joint Development Authority arising out of hydrocarbon-related activities developed in, or in connection with, the Joint Development Zone,

    II) All payments arising out of activities related to Exclusive Economic Zone Oil Resources, namely, but not limited to Sao Tome and Principe's share of crude oil and gas sales; signature bonuses and production bonuses; royalties; rents; proceeds from sale of assets; taxes; fees; duties and customs taxes; public service fees; net profits of state-owned oil companies; revenues from State share rights in oil contracts; crude oil sales; commercial activity resulting from transaction of oil, gas, or refined products; return on investments of the oil revenues; any and all payments generated in connection with the commercial production of hydrocarbons;

    III) Other revenues of analogous nature or revenues deemed as having an analogous nature by law.

jj) "Extraordinary Oil Revenue"—shall mean, for the period after the Oil Production Commencement, any signature bonus or any other payment, including the payments received from the Joint Development Zone related to an area that is not yet in production;

kk) "Oil Resource"—shall mean any deposit, block or area where hydrocarbons can be found, regardless of its commercial potential, within the national territory, including the Exclusive Economic Zone, and pursuant to the terms of the Treaty, in the Joint Development Zone;

ll) "Prudent Investor Rule"—shall mean that in performing any investment transactions or services, the agent shall ensure high quality and efficiency standards, and shall discharge his or her duties protecting the legitimate interests of the State with the diligence of a discerning and orderly manager, pursuant to the risk sharing principle and the safety of the investments, in accordance with the investment rules approved by the Management and Investment Committee pursuant to this Law;

mm) "Operation Rules"—shall mean the document containing the operation rules for the Oil Accounts;

nn) "Treaty Regulations"—shall mean the regulations approved by the competent authorities in accordance with the Treaty;

oo) "Royalties"—shall mean the liquidated revenues from the sale or disposition of crude oil or natural gas, as defined in the Treaty, in the Treaty Regulations and in the Oil Activities Law;

pp) "Long Term Real Rate of Return"—shall mean the rate calculated pursuant to paragraph 4 of Article 8 of this law;

qq) "Service Fee"—shall mean any charges for Oil Accounts administration, management and maintenance services, as well as by the investments of the Oil Revenues deposited in such accounts;

rr) "Treaty"—shall mean the treaty dated as of February 21, 2001, between The Federative Republic of Nigeria and The Democratic Republic of Sao Tome and Principe concerning the Joint Development Zone for petroleum and other resources;

ss) "Union"—shall mean any permanent workers association formed to defend and promote their social-professional interests;

tt) "Expected Present Value of Future Oil Revenues"—shall mean, for any period, the amount calculated pursuant to paragraph 1(c) of Article 7 of this law;

uu) "Annual Funding Amount"—shall mean the amount to be transferred to the Treasury Account pursuant to this Law;

vv) "Joint Development Zone"—shall mean the area defined for the purposes of the Treaty;

ww) "Exclusive Economic Zone"—shall mean the maritime area as defined by Law No. 1/98, dated as of March 31, 1998;

2. The terms listed above may be used in the singular or in the plural, provided the adequate alteration, unless the context clearly indicates otherwise.

Article 2
(Scope of Application)

This law shall regulate the payments, management, use and oversight of oil revenues resulting from oil operations in the entire national territory, including its terrestrial and maritime areas, including the Exclusive Economic Zone and the Joint Development Zone created by the Treaty.

CHAPTER II

OIL ACCOUNTS

SECTION I

GENERAL PROVISIONS

Article 3
(Establishment of Oil Accounts)

1. The Central Bank, acting in the name of the State, shall establish and hold the Oil Accounts with a Custody Bank selected by the Government pursuant to this law.
2. The Central Bank shall deliver to the Custody Bank upon execution of the Oil Accounts opening and management agreement the Operation Rules, which shall be an integral part of such agreement, and the Treasury Account number into which the Annual Funding Amount shall be transferred.

Article 4
(Prohibition on Liens or Encumbrances)

1. Any and all acts are prohibited by the State or its Officials if such acts directly or indirectly create, permit, assume, or promise the existence of public loans, public bonds, security interests or any other liens or encumbrances relating to the Oil Accounts or any other Oil Resources, whether existing or future, or related thereto.
2. The prohibition contained in paragraph 1 above shall not apply to financial charges in connection with the maintenance and management of the Oil Accounts maturing no more than one year after the date on which such lien is initially incurred.
3. Any attempt to violate paragraphs 1 and 2 above shall be null and void.

Article 5
(Operation Rules)

1. All transfers out of and in to the Oil Accounts shall be effected electronically.
2. The Central Bank shall prepare and present to the Government, who will submit to the National Assembly for approval by statute the Operation Rules of the Oil Accounts, which shall include:

a) Authorization for transactions and transfers between the National Oil Account and the Permanent Fund;
b) Deadlines for transfers to the Oil Accounts;
c) Certification, registration and proof of transactions;
d) Authorizations for Oil Accounts investment transactions;
e) Payment of fees, commissions, emoluments, and other Service Fees for bank services and operations;
f) Other rules regarding deposits and remittance of oil revenues to the State.

3. Oil Accounts debt transactions will require signature of the following persons:
a) President of the Republic;
b) Prime-Minister;
c) Director of the Treasury and Patrimony;
d) Director of International Transactions of the Central Bank;

4. The contract referred to in paragraph 2 of Article 3 above shall provide that no transfer of the Oil Revenues deposited in the Oil Accounts may be effected to any bank account that is not held in the name of the Sao-Tomean State, or any other account not authorized by a law approved for that purpose by the National Assembly.

SECTION II

NATIONAL OIL ACCOUNT

Article 6
(Deposits)

1. All monies owed to the State as Oil Revenue shall be deposited directly into the National Oil Account by the Persons liable to pay such monies. The Central Bank and other institutions that are currently or in the future in charge of the matter shall approve all necessary regulations and instructions.

2. Any Oil Revenue shall be considered paid by the Persons when fully and effectively deposited in the National Oil Account.

Article 7
(Forecast of the Oil Revenues)

1. No later than June 30 of each Year, the National Petroleum Agency shall calculate and make public:

a) The expected average price of the oil barrel which shall be the average international reference price of Brent FOB Sullom Voe publicly quoted in the 10 prior years, which reference price shall be adjusted by a price differential resulting from the difference in quality between Brent and the different types of Sao Tome and Principe oil. The expected future average price for natural gas shall be the reference future average price adopted in natural gas contracts and adjusted pursuant to the terms set forth for oil.

b) The expected future sales of hydrocarbons by or on behalf of the State, based solely in the production in the blocks under production or commercial development and consistent with the production estimates updated by the block operators.

c) The Expected Present Value of Future Oil Revenues, as estimated by the sum of the revenues deposited in the National Oil Account during the previous twelve months ending on June 30 of such Year, plus the expected revenues for all future Years, with the proper discounts. Expected future revenues shall be estimated using the expected average future price of oil and natural gas, as defined in paragraph (a) and the expected future hydrocarbons sales, as defined in paragraph (b) of this article. A rate of not less than 7% shall be used to discount expected future revenues.

2. The National Petroleum Agency shall submit the calculations in writing to the President of the Republic, the National Assembly, the Government, the Governor of the Central Bank, the Petroleum Oversight Commission, and shall effect the respective registry.

3. Within 30 days from the date of submission of the calculations by the National Petroleum Agency pursuant to this Article, the Petroleum Oversight Commission shall check if the calculations were done according to the provisions of this law.

Article 8
(Determination of and Limits on the Annual Funding Amount)

1. The Government shall include in the proposed State General Budget an Annual Funding Amount that shall be transferred out of the National Oil Account for the expenditures set forth in Article 9 of this law, and which shall only be transferred out of the National Oil Account to the Treasury Account after the definitive approval of the State General Budget.

2. The Annual Funding Amount for 2005 will be as set forth in the National State Budget as approved by the National Assembly.
3. In the following years, the Annual Funding Amount shall be subject to the following limits:
   a) Starting in 2006, for each Calendar Year until the end of the first Year after the Production Commencement, the Annual Funding Amount shall not exceed the greater of the following amounts:
      I) 20% of the balance of the National Oil Account on December 31, 2005, as estimated by the Central Bank;
      II) 20% of the total estimated balance of the National Oil Account at the end of previous Year, as estimated by the Central Bank;
      III) Each Year, after the date of announcement of commercial hydrocarbon discovery and after the assurance of production, the amount equal to the total forecast balance for the National Oil Account at the end of the immediately preceding Year, as estimated by the Central Bank, *divided* by the number of remaining years until the end of the first Year after the expected Production Commencement Year.
   b) For each Year starting with the second Year after the Production Commencement, the Annual Funding Amount shall not exceed the lesser of the following amounts:
      I) An amount equivalent to the sum of:
         A) The Long Term Real Rate of Return multiplied by the balance of the Permanent Fund on June 30 of the previous Year, and
         B) The Long Term Real Rate of Return multiplied by the Expected Present Value of Future Oil Revenues on June 30 of the previous Year.
      II) An amount equivalent to the sum of:
         A) The Long Term Real Rate of Return multiplied by the balance of the Permanent Fund on June 30 of the previous Year, and
         B) The balance of the unrestricted part of the National Oil Account on June 30 of the previous Year.
4. For the purpose of this Article, the Long Term Real Rate of Return shall be the Real Rate of Return expected on a portfolio composed of assets proportionate to the assets held in the Permanent Fund during the same period. The Long Term Real Rate of Return shall never exceed 5%. The inflation adjustment shall use the variation rates of the

official price indexes of the currencies in which the Permanent Fund asset portfolio is invested.

Article 9
(Allocation of the Annual Funding Amount)

1. The allocation of the Annual Funding Amount shall be decentralized with respect to sectors and territory, and aimed at the elimination of poverty and the improvement of the quality of life of the Sao-Tomean people, the promotion of good governance, and social and economic development. In addition, such allocation shall be used, namely, to strengthen the efficiency and effectiveness of the State Administration, to ensure a harmonious and integrated development of the Country, a fair sharing of the national wealth, the coordination between economic policy and social, educational and cultural policies, rural development, preservation of the ecological balance, environmental protection, the protection of human rights, and equality among citizens before the law.

2. The Annual Funding Amount may only be used pursuant to the policies and actions defined in a national, regional or local development plan and a national poverty reduction strategy.

3. Should the policies, plans and strategies referred to in paragraph 2 above not be in place, the Annual Funding Amount shall be allocated essentially and in first priority for the education, health, infrastructure and rural development sectors, as well as in the strengthening of the State's institutional capacity, as proposed by the Government and approved by the National Assembly.

4. An amount not less than 7% of the Annual Funding Amount shall be annually reserved to the public expenditures of the Autonomous Region of Principe.

5. An amount not less than 10% of the Annual Funding Amount shall be annually reserved for the State share of local budgets, and shall be distributed pursuant to the Local Finance Law.

6. The allocation of the reserves provided in this article shall be part of the State General Budget. The National Assembly shall approve budgetary and accounting procedures and mechanisms that are sufficient to ensure efficient monitoring of such use.

7. The proposals for the allocation of the Annual Funding Amount shall be accompanied by explanatory reports.

SECTION III

PERMANENT FUND OF SAO TOME AND PRINCIPE

Article 10
(Permanent Fund)

1. No later than the first Production Commencement Year, the Central Bank shall establish a sub-account of the National Oil Account that shall constitute the Permanent Fund, and whose transactions may only be effected pursuant to the following paragraphs.

2. No later than January 31 of each year starting in the second Year after the Production Commencement, and after the transfer from the National Oil Account of the Annual Funding Amount and the Service Fees owed, the balance of the National Oil Account on June 30 of the previous Year shall be transferred to the Permanent Fund.

3. After the Production Commencement, any Extraordinary Oil Revenue deposited in the National Oil Account shall be transferred to the Permanent Fund within 30 days from the date of such deposit.

4. No later than January 31, as from the second Year after the Production Commencement, an amount not greater than the amount set forth in subparagraphs (b)(I)(A) and (b)(II)(A) of paragraph 3 of Article 8 of this law may, if necessary, be transferred from the Permanent Fund to the National Oil Account for the payment of the Annual Funding Amount.

5. Any and all transfers of Oil Revenues deposited in the Permanent Fund in violation of paragraph 4 above shall be prohibited and shall be null and void, without prejudice to the transfers explicitly and exclusively authorized for investments pursuant to the Operation Rules and the Management and Investment Policy.

SECTION VI

MANAGEMENT AND INVESTMENT OF THE OIL ACCOUNTS

Article 11
(Management principles and rules)

The management and investments of the Oil Revenues deposited in the Oil Accounts shall be the responsibility of a Management and Investment Committee, which shall act according to the Prudent Investor Rule, following the principles and rules set forth in this law and in the Management and Investment Policy.

Article 12
(Management and Investment Committee)

1. A Management and Investment Committee shall be established, chaired by the Minister of Planning and Finance and also including the Governor of the Central Bank as the deputy chair, and three other members, one appointed by the President of the Republic and the other two appointed by the National Assembly, one of the latter appointed by the opposition parties.

2. The Persons appointed by the President of the Republic and the National Assembly shall be nationals, individuals or legal entities, resident or legally represented in Sao Tome and Principe, and shall have proven previous experience in managing international investment portfolios.

3. Each one of the members appointed by the President of the Republic and the National Assembly shall serve a two-year term commencing on the date of the respective appointment, renewable only once for an identical period.

4. In case of vacancy, the new member shall commence a new term.

5. The Management and Investment Committee may only meet if the majority of its members is present, and decisions shall depend upon the affirmative vote of at least three of its members.

6. The members of the Management and Investment Committee, with the exception of the Minister of Planning and Finance and the Governor of the Central Bank, shall be paid a fee to be fixed by the Government, and shall receive no other remuneration other than reimbursement of previously authorized expenses.

7. The Management and Investment Committee shall establish its internal operating rules, subject to the approval of the National Assembly.

8. The State General Budget shall include an allocation for the annual budget of the Management and Investment Committee.

Article 13
(Management and Investment Policy)

1. The Management and Investment Committee shall design and propose to the Government, which shall submit it for approval by the National Assembly, the Management and Investment Policy which shall meet on the following objectives:

a) Sufficient investment liquidity to ensure the availability of cash for the Annual Funding Amount;

b) Maximum profitability of the Permanent Fund of Sao Tome and Principe, subject to specified levels of acceptable risk for the investment horizon;

c) Transparent, modern and diversified management of the financial assets that are part of the investment portfolio of the Oil Accounts.

2. The Management and Investment Policy shall apply to each one of the Oil Accounts and shall include, at a minimum:

a) The types of permitted investments, including categories of assets and instruments;

b) Minimum required ratings and classifications for permitted high-risk investments, based on classifications proposed by expert firms of international reputation;

c) The rules relating to asset diversification by sector and issuer;

d) The rules to determine and monitor market risks, notably currency risks and interest rates risks;

e) The acceptable level of market value fluctuation during the term of the investment;

f) The rules established to ensure sufficient liquidity according to the Annual Funding Amount requirements.

3. The National Oil Account investments shall be held only in internationally convertible currency, in the form of the following instruments:

a) Cash bank deposits with an Approved Bank;

b) Negotiable direct obligations issued by any Approved Foreign Government;

c) Securities issued or directly guaranteed or insured by any Approved Foreign Government, maturing no later than two years after the date of acquisition, provided that the full faith and credit of such Approved Foreign Government is pledged in support thereof;

d) Bankers' acceptances, and floating rate certificates of deposit issued by the Approved Bank, maturing no later than two years after the date of acquisition;

e) Investment funds, the assets of which shall comprise securities of the type described in sub-paragraphs (a) and (c) above, regardless of the maturity date of such assets;

f) Other financial instruments of similar risk, profitability and liquidity to the ones referred to in the preceding sub-paragraphs, as approved by the Management and Investment Committee.

4. The Management and Investment Committee may delegate to managers specialized in investments the operational aspects of their powers and duties.

5. It is prohibited to invest the Oil Revenues deposited in the Oil Accounts in investments domiciled[4] in Sao Tome and Principe, or in any investments controlled directly or indirectly, totally or partially, by any national Person, whether or not resident of Sao Tome and Principe, or who falls within the circumstances described in paragraph 1 of Article 30 of this law.

CHAPTER III

AUDITING

Article 14
(Annual Audits)

1. The management and activity of the National Oil Account, including all investments, deposits, withdrawals and transfers, shall be subject to two annual audits, one by the Auditor General and the other, external and independent, by an international auditing firm, and such audits shall be concluded within six months of the end of each audited Year.

2. The audits referred to in paragraph 1 above shall assess compliance with this law and with other laws relating to the financial administration of the State, the Investment Policy, the Operation Rules, as well as all other rules relating to the Oil Accounts management and operation in the previous Year, namely, any investments, deposits, withdrawals and transfers.

3. Audit reports shall be simultaneously sent to the President of the Republic, the National Assembly, to the Government, to the Petroleum Oversight Committee, to the Sao Tome and Principe's Solicitor's Of-

---

[4]Translator's Note: Original Portuguese version refers to "investments domiciled" (*sic*) in the country, likely meaning investments "located" in the country or "companies" domiciled in the country.

fice and to the Public Registration and Information Office, within 30 days upon completion, under the terms of this article.

4. The reports mentioned in paragraph 3 of this Article shall include, necessarily, all documents, notes and observations that contribute to the full understanding of such reports.

Article 15
(Selection of the Auditing Firm)

1. The auditing firm shall be selected by the Petroleum Oversight Commission pursuant to competitive public procurement open to internationally recognized accounting firms with international experience.

2. Without prejudice to the requirements of paragraph 1 above, the competing audit firms shall present proof of their technical competence to audit corporations listed in official stock markets, according to international auditing and accounting standards.

3. The provisions of Article 22 shall be applicable accordingly.

Article 16
(Public Debate)

1. After the beginning of each legislative session, the National Assembly shall schedule and debate, in separate plenary sessions, according to its internal organization:

   a) General policy concerning hydrocarbons, to which members of the Government shall be present to answer the Deputies' questions and clarification requests;

   b) The Oil Accounts audit reports, to which the ministries in charge of finance and hydrocarbons matters, the members of the Management and Investment Committee, the Governor of the Central Bank, the President of the Auditor General, the President and the members of the Petroleum Oversight Commission, one administrator from the external auditing firm that should have participated in the audit, the Executive-Director of the National Petroleum Agency, shall all be present and shall have the right to address the floor.

2. The topics mentioned in paragraph 1 above shall be discussed with civil society in public sessions organized by the Petroleum Oversight Commission prior to the debates at the National Assembly.

CHAPTER IV

PUBLIC INTEGRITY

SECTION I

TRANSPARENCY AND PUBLICITY

Article 17
(Transparency)

1. All payments, management, use and investment of Oil Revenues or Oil Resources shall be subject to the transparency principle.
2. The transparency principle implies disclosure of, and public access to, namely:
   a) Payments and respective receipts, management, and debit and credit transactions, as well as balances of the Oil Accounts;
   b) The agreement for the opening and management the Oil Accounts entered into between the Central Bank and the Custody Bank;
   c) The distribution of revenues arising out of the oil activity carried out in the Joint Development Zone;
   d) The Operation Rules of the Oil Accounts and any amendments thereto;
   e) The forecast of Oil Revenues prepared by the National Oil Agency;
   f) All liens and encumbrances levying on the Oil Accounts, as permitted under paragraph 2 of Article 4;
   g) Reports and other audit-related documents prepared by the Auditor General and the auditing firm with respect to the management and execution of the Oil Accounts;
   h) The Investment Policy concerning the Oil Accounts;
   i) The annual report of the Petroleum Oversight Commission;
   j) All budgets that benefit from transfers from the Annual Funding Amount, including the State General Budget and the Joint Development Authority Budget;
   k) All contracts relating to the participation of the State or any enterprise or entity owned or controlled in whole or in part by the State, the scope of which directly or indirectly concerns activities related to Oil Resources or Oil Revenues;

l) Conflict matters as described in Article 30, as well as related lawsuits and sanctions.

3. All activities subject to the transparency principle shall be made public through a website in the Internet for inquiry purposes.

Article 18
(Public Registration and Information Office)

1. A Public Registration and Information Office shall be established, where all documents and information about activities related to Oil Resources and to the management of the Oil Revenues mentioned in the previous Article shall be filed, compiled, kept and made available to the public.

2. The documents and information referred to above shall be submitted for filing purposes to the entity in charge of the organization and maintenance of the Public Registration and Information Office, by the entities of the State Administration or Persons responsible for the elaboration, submission, receipt or approval of such documents and information, within ten business days of the occurrence of the event subject to registration.

3. The organization and maintenance of the Public Registration and Information Office shall be under the responsibility of the National Assembly.

4. A special law shall regulate the establishment and operation of the Public Registration and Information Office.

Article 19
(Publicity and Access to Information)

1. Information subject to transparency shall be conveyed in such a way that an addressee with basic comprehension and knowledge can apprehend its meaning and scope, and such information shall:
   a) Be presented in the Portuguese language;
   b) Be complete, whole, clear, objective, truthful and current;
   c) Be of universal and free access.

2. Without prejudice to the universal and free access to information, the Government shall regulate the forms of public disclosure and access, and shall establish the fees for the provision of certificates, shipping or copies, as well as the time for the information to be obtained and the guarantees of the public access to information.

OIL CONTRACTS

Article 20
(Confidentiality Clauses)

1. Confidentiality clauses or other mechanisms included in Oil Contracts or in any other transaction instrument concerning any Oil Revenue or Oil Resource that prevent or attempt to prevent access to documents and information pursuant to Article 17 of this law shall be null and void, and contrary to public policy.

2. Information concerning proprietary industrial property rights shall be exempted from the scope of mandatory disclosure to the extent that confidentiality in such cases is protected by a national law, by the Treaty, by the Treaty Regulations or by any an international law.

3. In no case shall the provision of the above paragraph apply to any financial information.

4. Any Person intending to avail itself of the protection granted in the above paragraph shall have the burden to prove its right to confidentiality protection pursuant to the rules of evidence applicable to documents contained in the Civil Code.

Article 21
(Implicit contract clauses)

1. All Oil Contracts or other transaction instruments concerning Oil Resources or Oil Revenues shall contain, and in the absence thereof shall be construed to imply, the following provisions:

   a) "No loan, reward, advantage or benefit of any kind has been given to any Official or to any person for the benefit of such Official or person or third parties, as consideration for an act or omission by such Official in connection with the performance of such person's duties or functions or to induce such Official to use his or her position to influence any acts or decisions of the Administration with respect to this Agreement. Any breach of this representation shall cause this Agreement to be invalid and voidable by the State Administration";

   b) "The validity and effectiveness of this agreement shall be subject to the full compliance with all applicable administrative procurement rules relating to State contracting."

c) "This Agreement is elaborated and filed in the Portuguese and English languages, in case of non-conformity, the Portuguese language version shall prevail.";

d) "This Agreement shall be made public and a copy hereof shall be provided to the Public Registration and Information Office within 10 days from its execution."

Article 22
(Public Competition)

1. All Oil Contracts or other transaction instruments to be entered into with the State Administration concerning Oil Resources or Oil Revenues, services relating to Oil Resources or in any way related to the oil sector or related activities, shall be preceded by public competitive tender pursuant to general law.

2. In the absence of legislation applicable to public tender, Oil Contracts or any other instruments mentioned in paragraph 1 above shall be approved by the Petroleum Oversight Commission prior to execution.

3. All Oil Contracts or other transaction instruments mentioned in paragraphs 1 and 2 above shall be made public by the State or by any Person, no less than ten days prior to execution, without prejudice to the terms of paragraphs 2, 3 and 4 of Article 20.

4. Oil contracts and other transaction instruments entered into in violation of this Article shall be considered void and without any effect, without prejudice to the liability of Officials and Persons perpetrating such violation.

5. The provisions of this Article shall not exempt any Person or State Administration Official of any legal obligation, except those obligations that are not consistent with this Article.

CHAPTER V

ENSURING PUBLIC OVERSIGHT AND ENFORCEMENT

SECTION I

PETROLEUM OVERSIGHT COMMISSION

Article 23
(Establishment of the Petroleum Oversight Commission)

1. A Petroleum Oversight Commission having legal entity status and administrative and financial autonomy shall be established to ensure the

permanent oversight of all payment, management and use of the Oil Revenues and Oil Resources.

2. The Petroleum Oversight Commission shall be composed of eleven members, appointed or elected as follows:

 a) One member appointed by the President of the Republic;

 b) Three representatives of the National Assembly, one necessarily appointed by the parliamentary groups from the opposition;

 c) One counselor judge with at no less than five years of professional experience, appointed by the Superior Judiciary Council;

 d) One representative from the Autonomous Region of Principe;

 e) Two representatives from local governments;

 f) One representative from Business Associations;

 g) One representative from the Unions;

 h) One representative from Non-Governmental Organizations.

3. The decisions of the Petroleum Oversight Commission shall require the affirmative vote of at least six of its members.

4. The organic law regulating the Petroleum Oversight Commission shall regulate the form of appointment and dismissal of the members of the Petroleum Oversight Commission, the duration of their terms, their compensation, and internal rules and conflicts of interests, as well as the organization and operation of the Petroleum Oversight Commission.

Article 24
(Authority and Powers of the Petroleum Oversight Commission)

1. Without prejudice to the oversight powers provided by the law to other government bodies, the Petroleum Oversight Commission shall have the authority to oversee the compliance of all activities with this law, namely:

 a) The verification and regularity of the expenditures of the Annual Funding Amount;

 b) Management and investment of Oil Revenues, including the exchange operations to the credit and debit of the Oil Accounts and their respective flow of funds in accordance with the Operation Rules and the criteria defined in the Investment Policy;

 c) The enforcement of the transparency rules;

 d) The external auditing firm's audit;

 e) The certification of the Production Commencement date.

2. To carry out its duties, the Petroleum Oversight Commission shall have the power to:
   a) Request relevant information and documents from any Person;
   b) Inquire about violations of any nature related to oil resources or oil revenues;
   c) Initiate investigations and inquiries based on its own knowledge or on third parties' complaints of irregularities or violations of the requirements of this law;
   d) Carry out searches, inspections, and seizure of any documents or personal property that are the object, tool, product of any infraction, or that are necessary to the opening of the respective process;
   e) Present reports that may include detailed description of any act subject to oversight, the investigation process, and inquiries initiated and closed, as well as recommendations as to the appropriateness of the adoption of new procedures;
   f) Hear, judge and enforce administrative proceedings and minor infractions consisting of violations of this law;
   g) Report to the competent authorities any irregularities or apparent violations of the provisions of this law that are subject to disciplinary, civil or criminal sanctions;
   h) Act as a party to judicial actions.

SECTION II

ENSURING THE ENFORCEMENT OF THE LAW

Article 25

(Mechanisms for law enforcement)

The mechanisms to ensure the enforcement of this law shall be defined by a special law, which shall regulate, in particular, the civil, criminal, and administrative responsibilities for acts performed in violation of the requirements of this law.

Article 26

(Public Prosecutor's Office and Police Authority)

1. Upon knowledge of violation of this law, the Public Prosecutor's Office shall on its own motion initiate judicial action to enforce the

responsibilities of Officials or Persons pursuant to the Public Prosecutor's Office's organic law, as well as criminal, civil, and other applicable law.

2. Police authorities shall cooperate as may be requested by the Petroleum Oversight Commission in the exercise of its oversight functions.

Article 27
(Injunctions)

1. At any time prior to the issuance of a final decision, a governmental body with decision-making authority shall on its own motion, or upon request, issue any necessary injunction in case of a justifiable fear of grave injury to the public interest which would be difficult to repair.

2. Any decision to issue or amend any injunction shall set out the grounds therefor and the term of any injunction shall be fixed.

3. The grounds for the revocation of any injunction shall also set out the grounds therefor.

4. The appeal of injunctions shall stay the effectiveness of the appealed decisions, except when the appellate body shall determine otherwise.

5. Except as expressly provided otherwise, any injunction shall expire:
   a) When a definitive decision is made;
   b) If the fixed term of the injunction or its extension has expired;
   c) If the deadline for a definitive decision has elapsed;
   d) If the injunction is revoked by a judicial decision that becomes *res judicata*.

Article 28
(Court actions)

1. Any Person whose rights are protected under this law may appeal final decisions made by any Administration body to judicial courts with jurisdiction.

2. Any appeal filed pursuant to paragraph 1 above shall stay the appealed decision unless such stay results in grave injury to public interest and the court so declares in a reasoned decision.

3. In the case of appeal of decision made by the Petroleum Oversight Commission in the exercise of its oversight power, it is presumed that any stay of any Petroleum Oversight Commission's decision constitutes grave injury to public interest.

CHAPTER VI

FINAL DISPOSITIONS

Article 29
(Joint Development Authority)

1. Without prejudice to the provisions of the Treaty, the provisions of this law shall apply to all Oil Revenues of the State arising out of the Joint Development Zone and all State Administration Officials or any other Person employed, hired, or otherwise acting on behalf of or representing the Sao-Tomean State Administration in the Joint Ministerial Council or in the Joint Development Authority.

2. In particular, such Persons and Officials mentioned in paragraph 1 above shall act so as to implement, jointly with the Federative Republic of Nigeria, the Abuja Joint Declaration as applicable to the Joint Development Authority.

3. All information that shall be made public pursuant to the Abuja Joint Declaration shall also be made public in accordance with paragraph 3 of Article 17 and paragraph 2 of Article 18 of this law.

4. In no case shall the State make any financial contribution to the budget of the Joint Development Authority or carry out any other obligation under the terms of the Treaty, without the approval of the National Assembly.

Article 30
(Conflicts)

1. No Person may be appointed or stay in office if such Person holds, directly or indirectly, on its own or through a third party, any economic, financial, participatory or other interest in activity related to Oil Revenues, or if such Person serves on boards, or is a representative, attorney-in-fact, agent or commissioner of, or otherwise represents any Person in which the Oil Revenues deposited into the Oil Accounts are held or invested.

2. Any Person in a situation described in paragraph 1 of this Article shall refuse his or her nomination, or shall resign from the position he or she has been appointed to, as the case may be.

3. Any person or entity who nominates, appoints, accepts or serves terms with the State Administration having knowledge of a conflict as described in paragraph 1 of this Article shall be punished with a fine equivalent

to three times the amount such Person earned as compensation from the time he or she engaged in such activity until the time the conflict was uncovered.

4. Any Official who, due to the interest or resulting from his or her appointment, receives directly or through a third party, by any way or nature, an economic advantage from the violation of the provisions of this Article, will be punished with a fine equivalent to three times the economic advantage received.

5. In addition to the fines prescribed in this Article, the Official shall disgorge to the State the amount equivalent to the economic benefit including all proceeds earned by him or her or by a third party in connection with the violation.

6. Attempted violations shall always be punishable with a fine equivalent to half of the fine established for the consummated illegal act.

Article 31
(Violation of the law)

1. Until the law defined in Article 25 is approved, and without any prejudice to the penalties explicitly prescribed by this law, any violations of this law that constitute either a crime or a misdemeanor shall have their minimum terms increased by one third if related to Oil Resources or Oil Revenues.

2. For the purposes of this law, the daily fine is equivalent to the amount of three national minimum wages in effect at the time when the action or omission occurs.

3. Any violations of the mandatory provisions of this law shall be void and shall not bind or produce any legal effect against the State, except for the rights of bona fide third parties, as provided for and protected under applicable law, and the liability of Officials.

Article 32
(Secondary Application)

Matters not specifically addressed in this law or in regulations pursuant to this law shall be subject to the rules applicable to analogous matters specifically subject to this law and regulations pursuant to this law. In the absence or insufficiency of rules in this law and in regulations pursuant to this law, such matters shall be subject, by secondary application, to the provisions of the Oil Activities Law.

Article 33
(Effectiveness)

This law shall become effective five days after its publication in the Official Gazette.

Approved by the National Assembly of Sao Tome and Principe on November 26, 2004.—The *acting* President of the National Assembly, *Jaime Jose da Costa.*

Promulgated on December 29, 2004.

For publication.

The President of the Republic, *Fradique Bandeira Melo de Menezes.*

Abridged Timor-Leste Oil Law*

1. OVERVIEW

PREAMBLE

This Act establishes a Petroleum Fund which seeks to meet with the constitutional requirement laid down in Article 139 in the Constitution of the Republic. Pursuant to this provision, petroleum resources shall be owned by the State, be used in a fair and equitable manner in accordance with national interests, and the income derived therefrom should lead to the establishment of mandatory financial reserves.

The Petroleum Fund shall contribute to a wise management of the petroleum resources for the benefit of both current and future generations. The Petroleum Fund shall be a tool that contributes to sound fiscal policy, where appropriate consideration and weight is given to the long-term interests of Timor-Leste's citizens.

Efficient planning and proper execution of public sector budgets are key components of a sound management of the petroleum wealth. The Petroleum Fund is to be coherently integrated into the State Budget, and shall give a good representation of the development of public finances. The Petroleum Fund shall be prudently managed and shall operate in an open and transparent fashion, within the constitutional framework.

This Act lays down the key parameters for the operation and management of the Petroleum Fund. The Act governs the collection of and management of receipts associated with the petroleum wealth, regulates transfers

*Unofficial translation. Available at http://www.transparency.gov.tl/PA/pf_act .htm (accessed 3 March 2007).

to the State Budget, and provides for Government accountability and oversight of these activities.

2. OIL REVENUE RECEIPTS

Article 6
Petroleum Fund Receipts

"6.1 The following amounts are Petroleum Fund gross receipts:

(a) the gross revenue, including Tax Revenue, of Timor-Leste from any Petroleum Operations, including prospecting or exploration for, and development, exploitation, transportation, sale or export of petroleum, and other activities relating thereto;

(b) any amount received by Timor-Leste from the Designated Authority pursuant to the Treaty;

(c) any amount received by Timor-Leste from the investment of Petroleum Fund Receipts;

(d) any amount received from direct or indirect participation of Timor-Leste in Petroleum Operations; and

(e) any amount received by Timor-Leste relating directly to petroleum resources not covered in paragraphs (a) to (d) above.

6.2 In the event that Timor-Leste participates in Petroleum Operations indirectly, as provided for in paragraph 6.1(d), through a national oil company, the receipts of the Petroleum Fund shall include the following:

(a) any amount payable by the national oil company as tax, royalty or any other due in accordance with Timor-Leste law; and

(b) any amount paid by the national oil company as dividend.

6.3. From the amount received in accordance with Section 6.1, the Central Bank shall be entitled to deduct, by direct debit of the Petroleum Fund account, any reasonable management expenses, as provided for in the operational management agreement referred to in Section 11.3."

3. PETROLEUM FUND INVESTMENT AND PROTECTION

Article 11
Management of the Petroleum Fund

"11.1 The Government is responsible for the overall management of the Petroleum Fund.

11.2   The Minister shall not make any decisions in relation to the investment strategy or management of the Petroleum Fund without first seeking the advice of the Investment Advisory Board in accordance with Article 16.

11.3   The Minister shall enter into an agreement with the Central Bank for the operational management of the Petroleum Fund and the Central Bank shall be responsible for the operational management of the Petroleum Fund.

11.4   The Petroleum Fund shall be managed prudently in accordance with the principle of good governance for the benefit of current and future generations."

Article 12
External Investment Managers

"12.1   The Central Bank may propose to the Minister, either of its own motion or at the request of the Minister, the appointment of one or more external Investment Managers to be responsible for managing the investment of amounts in the Petroleum Fund.

12.2   The Central Bank may select and appoint an external Investment Manager proposed under Article 12.1 only if the Minister is satisfied that:

(a) the external Investment Manager is a legal person with sufficient equity capital and adequate guarantees and insurances against operational risks;

(b) the external Investment Manager has a sound record of operational and financial performance; and

(c) the references and reputation of the external Investment Manager in the field of fund management are of the highest standard.

12.3   The Central Bank shall be responsible for the tendering procedures required for any appointment made pursuant to Article 12.1, as well as for the contracting of any other professional services under the operational management agreement referred to in Article 11.3, and shall in doing so comply with the substantive provisions of Timor-Leste law.

12.4   The procedures for terminating a contract with an external Investment Manager shall be laid down in the operational management agreement referred to in Article 11.3.

12.5   The duty of the Investment Manager is to maximise the return on the Petroleum Fund investments having regard to appropriate risk as indicated by the investments permitted under Articles 14 and 15, any subsidiary legislation under this Act, any instructions by the Minister and the operational management agreement referred to in Article 11.3."

Article 14
Investment Rules

"14.1 Not less than ninety per cent (90%) of the amounts in the Petroleum Fund shall be invested only in qualifying instruments described in Article 15.

14.2 Not more than ten per cent (10%) of the amounts in the Petroleum Fund may be, in accordance with all procedures laid down in this present Act, invested in financial instruments other than those mentioned in Article 15.1, provided that such instruments are:

(a) issued abroad;

(b) liquid and transparent;

(c) traded in a financial market of the highest regulatory standard.

14.3 The range of instruments included as qualifying instruments in Article 15.1 shall be reviewed by the Government, and approved by Parliament, at the end of the first five (5) years of the Petroleum Fund existence, having regard to the size of the Petroleum Fund and the level of institutional capacity."

Article 15
Qualifying Instruments

"15.1 Subject other provisions of this present article, a qualifying instrument is:

(a) a debt instrument denominated in United States Dollars that bears interest or a fixed amount equivalent to interest, that is:

(i) rated Aa3 or higher by the Moody's rating agency or rated AA– or higher by Standard & Poor's rating agency; and

(ii) issued by or guaranteed by the World Bank or by a sovereign State, other than Timor-Leste, provided the issuer or guarantor is rated Aa3 or higher by the Moody's rating agency or rated AA– or higher by Standard & Poor's rating agency; or

(b) a United States Dollars deposit with, or a debt instrument denominated in United States Dollars that bears interest or a fixed amount equivalent to interest issued by:

(i) the Bank for International Settlements;

(ii) the European Central Bank; or

(iii) the Central Bank of a sovereign State, other than Timor-Leste, with a long-term foreign currency rating of Aa3 or higher by the Moody's rating agency or AA– or higher by the Standard & Poor's rating agency;

(iv) a bank designated by Moody's rating agency with a long-term foreign currency rating of Aa3 or higher or designated by Standard & Poor's rating agency with a long-term foreign currency rating of AA– or higher.

15.2 The Investment Manager shall dispose of an instrument if it ceases to be a qualifying instrument because of a change in the rating of the instrument or the issuer of the instrument within one month of the instrument ceasing to be a qualifying instrument.

15.3 The average interest rate duration of Petroleum Fund qualifying instruments under Article 15.1 shall be less than six (6) years.

15.4 A derivative instrument is a qualifying instrument only if:

(a) it is solely based on instruments that satisfy the requirements of Article 15.1; and

(b) its acquisition reduces the financial exposure to the risks associated with the underlying instrument or instruments."

4. NO LIENS OR ENCUMBRANCES ON THE PETROLEUM FUND

Article 20
No Encumbrances on the Assets of the Petroleum Fund

"20.1 Any amount that is invested pursuant to Articles 14 and 15 shall, at all times, remain the property of Timor-Leste.

20.2 Any contract, agreement or arrangement, to the extent that it purports to encumber the assets of the Petroleum Fund, whether by way of guarantee, security, mortgage or any other form of encumbrance, is null and void."

5. PETROLEUM FUND OVERSIGHT

Article 21
Maintenance of Petroleum Fund Accounts and Records

"21.1 The Director of Treasury is responsible for maintaining the Petroleum Fund accounts and records in accordance with the International

Accounting Standards in force, to reflect the operations and financial condition of the Petroleum Fund.

21.2   The Director of Treasury shall submit to the Minister quarterly management information reports and analyses on the performance and activities of the Petroleum Fund no later than twenty (20) days after the end of each quarter.

21.3   The Director of Treasury is responsible for reporting on the performance and activities of the Petroleum Fund for the purpose of the annual financial statements of Timor-Leste."

Article 24
Information Contained in the Annual Report

"24.1   The Annual Report for the Petroleum Fund shall be prepared in a manner that makes it readily adaptable for public information, and shall contain in particular the following information for the fiscal year for which the Report is prepared:

(a)   audited financial statements certified by the Independent Auditor, comprising:

   (i)   an income and expenditure statement;

   (ii)   a balance sheet, including a note listing the qualifying instruments of the Petroleum Fund, valued at market value;

   (iii)   details of all appropriations and transfers from the Petroleum Fund; and

   (iv)   notes to the financial statements, as appropriate;

(b)   a report signed by the Minister describing the activities of the Petroleum Fund in the year, including all advice provided by the Investment Advisory Board, any reports prepared by the independent auditor under Article 35 and drawing attention to particular issues or matters that may be of concern or interest to Parliament;

(c)   a statement by the Director of Treasury drawing attention to any accounting issues or practices arising from the Report that may materially affect the interpretation of amounts or activities shown within it;

(d)   the income derived from the investment of Petroleum Fund assets during the Fiscal Year compared with the income of the previous three Fiscal Years;

(e) a comparison of the nominal income on the investment of Petroleum Fund assets with the real return after adjusting for inflation;

(f) a comparison of the income derived from the investment of Petroleum Fund assets with the benchmark performance indices provided to the Minister pursuant to Article 16.1;

(g) a comparison of the Estimated Sustainable Income for the Fiscal Year with the sum of transfers from the Petroleum Fund for the year;

(h) in the event of Government borrowings, the liabilities shall be reflected in the presentation of Petroleum Fund accounts so as to give a true representation of the past and expected future development of the Government's net financial assets and rate of savings; and

(i) a list of persons holding positions relevant for the operation and performance of the Petroleum Fund, including:

(i) the Minister;

(ii) the Director of Treasury;

(iii) the members of the Investment Advisory Board;

(iv) the external investment managers;

(v) the Head of the Central Bank; and

(vi) the members of the Petroleum Fund Consultative Council.

24.2 The sources of the information described in Article 24.1, whatever their form, and including all reports and statements, shall be annexed to the Annual Report in unedited form."

6. SUSTAINABLE INCOME CALCULATION

SCHEDULE 1

CALCULATING ESTIMATED SUSTAINABLE INCOME FOR A FISCAL YEAR

"I.   Estimated Sustainable Income for a fiscal year is the maximum amount that can be appropriated from the Petroleum Fund in that Fiscal Year and leave sufficient resources in the Petroleum Fund for an amount of the equal real value to be appropriated in all later Fiscal Years as determined in accordance with the formula in paragraphs II and III below.

II. Estimated Sustainable Income for a Fiscal Year is calculated according to the following formula:

$r \times$ *Petroleum wealth*

where:

r　　　　　is the estimated average real rate of return, or real interest rate, on Petroleum Fund investments in the future and, for the purposes of these calculations, shall be 3.0%.

III. In this Schedule, "petroleum wealth" is calculated according to the following formula:

$$V + \textit{Present value }(R_0, R_1, \ldots, R_n) = V + \sum_{t=0}^{n} \frac{R_t}{(1+i)^t}$$

where:

V　　　　　is the estimated value of the Petroleum Fund at the end of the prior Fiscal Year

$R_0, R_1, \text{etc.}$　are the published budget projections for expected annual Petroleum Fund receipts minus investment returns for that Fiscal Year (R_0) and future Fiscal Years (R_1, etc.)

i　　　　　is the estimated nominal yield on a U.S. government security, averaged over the years in which Petroleum Fund Receipts are expected

n　　　　　is the number of years until no further Petroleum Fund Receipts are projected to be received.

IV. All assumptions upon which the calculations made pursuant to paragraphs II and III above are based shall be clearly identified and explained, and any changes made in these assumptions in subsequent calculations shall be clearly pointed out.

V. All assumptions made shall be prudent, reflect international best practice and be based upon internationally recognized standards.

VI. The amount determined in accordance with the formula in paragraphs II and III above shall be certified by the Independent Auditor."

APPENDIX 3

Glossary of Oil Terms*

Accelerated depreciation   Writing off an asset through *depreciation* or *amortization* at a rate that is faster than normal accounting straight-line depreciation. While there are a number of methods of calculating accelerated depreciation, they are usually characterized by allowing for higher rates of depreciation in the early years of an asset's lifespan. Accelerated depreciation allows for lower tax rates in the early years.

Acreage   Amount of land area (or offshore area) under lease or associated with and/or governed by a *production sharing contract.*

Amortization   An accounting convention designed to emulate the cost or expense associated with reduction in value of an intangible asset over a period of time (see *Depreciation*). Amortization is a non-cash expense.

Block   A license area or contract area; each individual parcel of acreage held by an international oil company or a government.

Bonuses   Typically, a payment to the government for the right to conduct petroleum operations. A bonus can take many forms, including:

- **Signature bonus** Typically due and payable within 30 days of contract signature

*This glossary was largely written and assembled by David Johnston and Daniel Johnston, and previously published by Daniel Johnston. See, for instance, Johnston, D. 1994. *International Petroleum Fiscal Systems and Production Sharing Contracts.* Tulsa: PennWell Publishing. Words that appear in a given definition in *italics* are defined separately in the glossary.

- **Discovery bonus** Triggered in the event of a discovery
- **Commerciality bonus** Triggered when a discovery is deemed to be a *commercial discovery*
- **Production bonus** Triggered when certain production levels have been achieved, such as 10,000 barrels of oil per day (BOPD)
- **Cumulative production bonus** Triggered when certain cumulative production levels have been achieved, such as 100 million barrels (MMBBLS)

Booking barrels   The practice of adding barrels of oil to a company's list of assets.

Capitalize   (1) In an accounting sense, the periodic expensing of capital costs such as through *amortization, depreciation,* or *depletion.* (2) To convert an (anticipated) income stream to a present value by dividing by an interest rate. (3) To record capital outlays as additions to asset value rather than as expenses.

Carried interest   When a working interest partner in the exploration or development phase of a contract pays a share of costs and expenses that is disproportionately lower than its working interest share (see *Working interest*). Typically, government agencies, such as the oil ministry or national oil company (NOC), are "carried" through the exploration phase of a contract, at which point the government takes up a working interest. The NOC is thus said to be "carried," through exploration, or is said to have an option to "back in" to a discovery.

Cash call   The situation in which *working interest* holders in a petroleum venture are required to pay their share of operating costs and capital costs according to their percentage holdings and the terms of the joint operating agreement governing members of the consortium.

Cash flow   Gross revenues less all associated capital and operating costs. Contractor cash flow is equal to gross revenues less all costs, government royalties, taxes, imposts, levies, duties, *profit oil share,* and so forth. Contractor cash flow represents the contractor's share of profits. Government cash flow typically consists of royalties, taxes, imposts, duties, *profit oil share,* and so forth. In a financial sense, cash flow represents net income plus *deprecia-*

tion, depletion and *amortization*, and other non-cash expenses; an analysis of all the changes that affect the cash account during an accounting period. Usually synonymous with cash earnings and operating cash flow.

Commercial discovery   In popular usage, the term applies to any discovery that would be economically feasible to develop under a given fiscal system. As a contractual term, it often applies to the requirement on the part of the contractor to demonstrate to the government that a discovery would be sufficiently profitable, from both the contractor's and government's points of view, to merit development. A field that satisfied these conditions would then be granted commercial status and the contractor would then have the right to develop the field. Also referred to as "commercial success."

Commercial success   (see *Commercial discovery*)

Commerciality point   The point at which a commercial discovery has been appraised and a government, typically the national oil company, must decide whether to "back in" (see *Carried interest*).

Concession   An agreement between a government and a company that grants the company the right to explore for, develop, produce, transport and market hydrocarbons or minerals within a fixed area for a specific amount of time. The concession, production, and sale of hydrocarbons are then subject to rentals, royalties, *bonuses*, and taxes. Under a concessionary agreement, the company takes title to gross production, less government *royalty oil*, at the *wellhead*.

Consortium   A group of companies operating jointly, usually in a partnership with one company as *operator*, in a given permit, license, contract area, block, and so forth.

Contractor   An international oil company operating in a country, on behalf of the host government, under a *production sharing contract* or a *risk service agreement*, for which it receives either a share of production or a fee.

Contractor take   The total contractor after-tax share of *cash flow*.

Cost of capital   The minimum rate of return on capital required to compensate debt holders and equity investors for bearing risk. Cost of capital is computed by weighting the after-tax cost of both debt and equity according to their relative proportions in the corporate capital structure.

Cost oil   Used especially in *production sharing contracts*, the oil (or revenues) used to reimburse the contractor for exploration, development, and operating costs incurred.

Cost recovery   The means by which companies recover costs.

Cost recovery limit   Typically with *production sharing contracts*, in any given accounting period, there is a limit to the amount of deductions that can be taken for cost recovery purposes. The limit is usually quoted in terms of a percentage of gross revenues or gross production. Unrecovered costs are carried forward and recovered in subsequent accounting periods, if there is sufficient production.

Country risk   The risks and uncertainties of doing business in a foreign country, including political and commercial risks. Also referred to as "sovereign risk."

Crypto tax   A less conventional (direct) means by which a government imposes duties, levies, or financial requirements on an international oil company. Examples include social welfare development funds; hostile audits; mandatory currency conversions; customs duty exemptions that are not honored; unreasonable hiring quotas; inordinately long depreciation rates; inefficient procurement requirements; excessive immigration/visa requirements, etc. These elements are rarely captured in typical published *Government Take* statistics.

Depletion   (1) The reduction in value of a wasting asset caused by the removal of minerals. (2) Depletion for tax purposes deals with the reduction of mineral resources due to removal by production from an oil or gas reservoir or a mineral deposit (see also *Depletion allowance*).

Depletion allowance   Provision that allows a company a deduction for tax calculation purposes based on some percentage of gross revenues; a type of "incentive" that a government can use to encourage investment. For instance, the Filipino Participation Incentive Allowance (FPIA) allows the contractor group 7.5 percent of gross revenues as part of the service fee.

Depreciation   An accounting convention designed to emulate the cost or expense associated with reduction in value of a tangible asset due to wear and tear, *deterioration,* or obsolescence over a period of time.

Development costs   Costs associated with placing an oil or gas discovery into production; these typically consist of drilling, constructing production facilities, and transporting goods and materials.

Direct tax   A tax that is paid directly by an individual or corporation, such as income and property taxes. The opposite of an *indirect tax,* such as a value-added tax (VAT) or sales taxes, which is levied on goods or services.

Discounted cash flow analysis   Economic modeling of anticipated income versus expenditures over time. It is based on estimated production rates, oil prices and costs, as well as on royalties, taxes, and other means of *Government Take.* The net result is a stream of cash flow over time. Cash received in the distant future is not as valuable as cash received now; therefore, the time value of the cash flow is calculated factoring in time value of money to arrive at a "present value" equivalent (see *Discounted present value*).

Discounted present value   The total value of a product (such as oil) over its lifetime, in which future cash streams are discounted at some appropriate interest, or discount, rate. For example, with 5 percent interest rates, a $1 payment to be received next year has a discounted present value of $1/1.05 = $.95.

Domestic market obligation (DMO)   The situation in which governments or national oil companies have an option to purchase a certain portion of the contractor's share of production (also referred to as "domestic requirement"). Typically the purchase price for DMO crude is less than market price. Also, local currency may be part of the price formula.

Economic profit   Gross project revenues minus total costs, which include exploration, development, and operating costs.

Economic rent   While there are a number of definitions, economic rent is commonly defined as the difference between the value of production and the cost to extract it. The extraction cost consists of normal exploration, development, and operating costs as well as a share of profits for the industry.

Effective royalty rate   The minimum share of revenues (or production) the government will receive in any given accounting period from royalties and its share of *profit oil.*

Entitlements   The shares of production which the operating company, the working interest partners, and the government or government agencies are authorized to lift. Entitlements are based on royalties, *cost recovery, production sharing, working interest percentages,* and so forth (see also *Lifting*).

Expected monetary value   (see *Expected value*)

Expected value   A weighted average financial value of various possible outcomes, such as either a discovery or a dry hole, weighted according to the estimated likelihood (estimated probability of success or failure) that either outcome might occur.

Expense   (1) In a financial sense, a noncapital cost associated most often with operations or production. (2) In accounting, costs incurred in a given accounting period that are charged against revenues. In other words, to "expense" a particular cost is to charge it against income during the accounting period in which it was spent. The opposite would be to "capitalize" the cost and charge it off through a depreciation schedule.

Fiscal system   The legislated taxation structure for a country, including royalty payments. In popular usage, the term includes all aspects of contractual and fiscal elements that comprise a relationship between a government and international oil company.

Gold plating   When a company or contractor makes unreasonably large expenditures due to a lack of cost-cutting incentives. This kind of behavior could be encouraged where a contractor's compensation is based in part on the level of capital and operating expenditure.

Government participation   Many governments provide the national oil company (NOC) an option to participate as a working interest partner in the development of a discovery. The NOC participation usually begins at the *commerciality point*, and from that point on it meets *cash calls* like any other working interest partner. The NOC may or may not reimburse the contractor for its share of *past costs* associated with the discovery.

Government Take   There are a number of definitions but the most succinct is: Government Take = Government cash flow/Gross project cash flow. Hence, the government share of economic profits (*cash flow*), typically expressed as a percentage (%); or the total government share of production or gross cash flow from royalties, taxes, *bonuses, profit oil*.

Gross benefits   The benefits to a country, including *Government Take*, that come with having foreign companies operate in-country. Gross benefits include outcomes, such as employment gains, that are valued by the government but that are not counted as part of *Government Take*.

Incentives   Fiscal or contractual elements provided by host governments that make petroleum exploration or development more economically attractive. Incentives can include royalty holidays, tax holidays, tax credits, reduced *government participation*, lower *Government Take*, investment credits/uplifts, accelerated depreciation, depletion allowances, and interest expense deductions (*cost recovery*).

Inconvertibility   Inability of a foreign contractor to convert payments received in local currency into home country or hard currency, such as American dollars or British pounds.

Indirect tax   A tax that is levied on consumption rather than income. Examples include value-added taxes, sales taxes, or excise taxes on luxury items; see also *Direct tax*.

Intangibles   All intangible assets such as goodwill, patents, trademarks, unamortized debt discounts and deferred charges. Also, for example, for fixed assets, the cost of transportation, labor and fuel associated with construction, installation, and commissioning.

Interest cost recovery   This is considered to be a type of incentive by allowing the contractor to recover financing costs associated with capital investment. The interest rate allowed can be a statutory rate, it can be negotiated, or it can be an item that is bid upon. The "base" is usually the average unrecovered cost recovery balance during an accounting period.

Internal rate of return (ROR)   A capital budgeting method, it is the discount rate that results in a net present value of zero for future cash flows.

Levy   To impose or collect a tax or fine.

License   An arrangement between an international oil company and a host government regarding a specific geographical area and petroleum operations. In more precise usage, the term applies to the development phase of a contract after a commercial discovery has been made (see also *Block*).

License area   A block or concession area governed by a *production contract* or other type of contract between an international oil company and a host government.

Lifting   When a company takes physical and legal possession of its *entitlement* of crude oil, which ordinarily consists of two components under a *production sharing contract*: *cost oil* and *profit oil*. Lifting agreements govern the rules by which partners will lift their respective shares and how adjustments are made if a party lifts more than it is entitled to ("over lifted") or less than it is entitled to ("under lifted"). Liftings may actually be more or less than actual entitlements, which are based on royalties, working interest percentages, and a number of other factors (see also *Entitlement*).

Lifting agreement   (see *Lifting*)

Net back   Many royalty calculations are based upon gross revenues from some point of valuation, usually the *wellhead*. The point of sale, however, may be different than the point of valuation, and the statutory royalty calculation may allow the transportation costs from the point of valuation to the point of sale to be deducted from the actual sale price (i.e., "netted back"). Downstream costs between the wellhead and the point of sale are sometimes referred to as "net back deductions."

Operating profit (or loss) The difference between business revenues and the associated costs and expenses, excluding interest, other financing expenses, and other extraordinary items or ancillary activities. Synonymous with net operating profit (or loss); operating income (or loss); net operating income (or loss); *economic profit* (or loss); and *cash flow*.

Operator The company directly responsible for day-to-day operations, for maintaining a lease or license, and for ensuring the rights and obligations of the other members of the contractor group are met.

Pareto optimal An allocation is Pareto optimal if there is no way to make one person better off without simultaneously making another worse off.

Past costs Costs associated with a discovery prior to the *commerciality point*. About half of the governments with participation options (see *Government participation*) will reimburse their working interest share of past costs. The governments that do reimburse typically will do so up to a certain percentage of their entitlement, for instance approximately 65 to 70 percent.

Prisoners' dilemma In game theory, a social problem in which all individuals have incentives to take actions that, while in each individual's own interest, collectively make everyone worse off than they otherwise would have been.

Production sharing agreement (see *Production sharing contract*)

Production sharing contract (PSC) Same as a production sharing agreement but increasingly commonly used terminology. A contractual agreement between a contractor and a host government whereby the contractor bears all exploration costs and risks, as well as development and production costs, in return for a stipulated share of the production resulting from this effort. See chapters 3 and 4.

Profit oil In a *production sharing contract*, the share of production remaining after *royalty oil* and *cost oil* have been allocated to the appropriate parties to the contract.

Profit oil split   The way in which *profit oil* under a *production sharing contract* is divided ("split") between the various parties—typically the government and the contractor.

Progressive taxation   Taxation in which tax rates increase as the base to which the tax is applied increases (or, where tax rates decrease as the base decreases); the opposite of *regressive taxation.*

Prospectivity   Informally, both the chances for making commercial discoveries and the risks associated with exploration. An area with the potential for large discoveries, low costs, and low risks would be considered highly "prospective."

"R" factors   Some tax rates (as well as royalties, *domestic market obligations,* and *government participation*) are governed by predetermined "payout" thresholds. "R" stands for "ratio." Typically the contract defines "R" as the ratio of an oil company's cumulative receipts to its cumulative expenditures. Cumulative expenditures include both capital and operating costs. For example, when "R" equals 1 (one) this is the point at which the company has achieved "payout." Usually multiple thresholds are established. For example:

"R"	Tax Rate (%)
0–1	40
1–1.5	50
1.5–2	60
>2	70

The "R" factor is calculated at the end of each accounting period; when a threshold is crossed, the new tax rate would apply beginning with the next accounting period.

Rate of return contracts   Also referred to as "resource rent royalties (or taxes)"; "trigger taxes"; or the "World Bank Model." Those contracts in which the government collects a share of company cash flows in excess of specified *internal rate of return (ROR)* thresholds. These thresholds are determined either by statute, bidding, or negotiation. The government share is calculated by accumulating negative net cash flows at the specific threshold rate of return (using a method called "compound uplifting"). Once the accumulated value becomes positive, the government takes a specified share. An example is shown below:

ROR (%)	Tax Rate (%)
<20	0
20–25	30
25– 30	50
>30	70

This is a typical design found in the 1980s and 1990s. This construction, however, could result in *gold plating*, in which a company spends more than it otherwise would because with terms like these, under some scenarios, the more it spends the more the company makes.

Recoverable reserves   The hydrocarbon volumes expected to be produced economically and not be left behind in the reservoir.

Regressive tax   Taxation in which tax rates become lower as the basis to which the applied tax increases (or, where tax rates increase as the basis decreases); the opposite of *progressive taxation*.

Relinquishment   The requirement that a certain percentage (often around 25 percent) of the original contract area be returned to the government at the end of the first phase of the exploration period. Usually, additional relinquishment is required at the end of the second phase of the exploration period. Contracts typically have specific provisions for the timing and amount of relinquishment prior to entering the subsequent phases of the contract. Also referred to as "exclusion of areas."

Resource rent tax (RRT)   Term that some economists use to refer to additional profits taxes (peculiar to the oil industry). Australia, for instance, has a specific tax based on profits and that is so referred. Normally, the RRT is levied after the contractor or international oil company has recouped all capital costs plus a specified return on capital that supposedly will yield a fair return on investment (see *Rate of return contract*).

Ringfencing   A fiscal (or contractual) device that forces contractors or concessionaires to restrict all *cost recovery* and or deductions associated with a given license (or sometimes a given field) to that particular cost center. The cost centers may be individual licenses or on a field-by-field basis. For example, with typical ringfencing, exploration expenses in one non-producing block cannot be deducted for tax calculation purposes in another block. Most countries use ringfencing—particularly countries that use *production sharing contracts* (PSCs). Under a PSC, ringfencing acts in the same way—cost incurred in one ringfenced block cannot be recovered from another block outside the ringfence. Ringfencing ordinarily refers to "space" (i.e., area and/or depth) but can also be based on "time" and categories of costs.

Risk Service Agreement   Also referred to as a "service agreement" or "service contract." The arrangement in which a contractor is paid a cash fee in return for performing the service of producing mineral resources. All production belongs to the state. The contractor is usually responsible for providing all capital associated with exploration and development. In return, if exploration efforts are successful, the contractor recovers costs through the sale of oil or gas plus a fee. Figure 3.1 [Classification of Petroleum Fiscal Regimes] highlights the difference between a Risk Service arrangement and a "Pure" Service arrangement.

Royalty oil   A percentage of the production (or revenue) paid to the mineral rights' owner (typically a country government) independently of the costs of production. This represents the government oil *entitlement.*

Saturation   This term applies to accounting periods where there are un-recovered costs carried forward; the cost recovery mechanism is at its maximum (saturated).

Service agreement or service contract   (see *Risk service agreement*)

Sliding scales   A mechanism in a fiscal system that varies effective taxes and/or royalties based upon profitability or some proxy for profitability. There are three main families of sliding scales: production-based, *"R" factor*, and *rate-of-return*. The most common type of sliding scale is the production-based sliding scale. Ordinarily, each tranche of production is subject to a specific rate and the term "incremental" sliding scale is sometimes used to further describe this. For example:

Typical Production-Based Sliding Scale Royalty

		Royalty (%)
First tranche	Up to 10,000 BOPD	5
Second tranche	10,001–20,000 BOPD	10
Third tranche	20,001–30,000 BOPD	15
Fourth tranche	> 30,000 BOPD	20

Royalty rate determination in a given accounting period is based upon a weighted average. For example, with this sliding scale, if production averages 40,000 BOPD, then the overall royalty will be 12.5 percent during that period. Some of the production will be subject to the 5 percent royalty but some will also be subject to the 20 percent royalty, producing a weighted average of 12.5 percent. (Sometimes also referred to as "gliding scales," e.g., in Kazakhstan.)

Sovereign risk   (see *Country risk*)

Tax loss carry-forward   (TLCF) In systems in which expensing of preproduction costs is allowed a negative tax base can arise, and is referred to as a tax loss carry-forward. A TLCF can also originate in systems where bonuses are deductible for tax calculation purposes and may be expensed.

Taxes in lieu   Under some *production sharing contracts,* the arrangement in which the contractor's taxes are paid "for and on behalf of the contractor" out of the national oil company's (NOC's) share of *profit oil.* Typically the NOC will pay taxes directly to the taxing authority and provide the contractor a receipt that can be used as evidence in its home country for double taxation purposes so that the contractor can receive a tax credit against home-country taxes.

Uplift   A fiscal incentive whereby the government allows the contractor to recover some additional percentage of tangible capital expenditure. For example, if a contractor spent $10 million on eligible expenditures and the government allowed a 20 percent uplift, then the contractor would be able to recover $12 million dollars. The uplift is similar to an investment credit. The term often implies, however, that all costs are eligible where the investment credit applies to certain eligible costs. Also used at times to refer to the built-in rate of return element in a *rate of return contract.*

Wellhead   The last valve off of a production platform from which oil is extracted; the point of valuation.

Withholding tax   A direct tax on a foreign corporation by a foreign government, levied on dividends or profits remitted to the parent company or to the home country, as well as interest paid on foreign loans.

Work commitment   The drilling and/or seismic data acquisition and processing obligation associated with any given phase of a *production sharing contract*.

Work program bidding   Bidding in which bidders submit a competitive plan for production in a particular *block* or *license area*.

Working interest   The percentage interest ownership a company (or government) has in a joint venture, partnership, or consortium. The expense-bearing interests of various working interest owners during exploration, development, and production operations may change at certain stages of a contract or license. For example, a partner with a 20 percent working interest in a concession may be required to pay 30% of exploration costs but only a 20 percent share of development costs (see *Carried interest*). With *government participation*, the host government usually pays no exploration expenses but will pay its pro-rata working interest share of development and operating costs and expenses.

Web Site References

RESOURCES AT INTERNATIONAL FINANCIAL INSTITUTIONS

International Monetary Fund Code of Good Practices and Fiscal Transparency: http://www.imf.org/external/np/fad/trans/code.htm

International Monetary Fund Fiscal Transparency Code: http://www.imf.org/external/np/fad/trans/index.htm

International Monetary Fund Guide on Resource Revenue Transparency: http://www.imf.org/external/pubs/ft/grrt/eng/060705.pdf

World Bank: Extractive Industries Review: http://www.ifc.org/eir

World Bank: Oil, Gas, Mining and Chemicals Section: http://www.worldbank.org/mining/

UNIVERSITY RESOURCES

Columbia University Earth Institute Documents on the Sao Tome and Principe Oil Law: http://www.earthinstitute.columbia.edu/cgsd/STP/index_oillaw.htm

Aberdeen University Oil and Gas Center: http://www.abdn.ac.uk/oilgas/

NONGOVERNMENTAL GROUPS WORKING ON GAS MANAGEMENT OF OIL AND TRANSPARENCY INITIATIVES

Extractive Industry Transparency Initiative: http://www.eitransparency.org/

Global Witness: http://www.globalwitness.org
Publish What You Pay: http://www.publishwhatyoupay.org
Revenue Watch: http://www.revenuewatch.org/
   For Azerbaijan: http://www.revenuewatch.org/azerbaijan/activities/
   For Iraq: http://www.iraqrevenuewatch.org/
   For Kazakhstan: http://www.kazakhstanrevenuewatch.org/

Joseph C. Bell is a senior partner at Hogan & Hartson LLP with more than 35 years of experience in the energy sector. Drawing on his economics and legal background, he is currently advising in a number of developing countries in Asia, Africa, and the Middle East regarding oil and natural resource policy or the negotiation of individual concession agreements. He is a member of the Council on Foreign Relations, a director of the International Senior Lawyers Project providing pro bono international service, and Chair of the Advisory Board of the Revenue Watch Institute.

Peter Cramton is Professor of Economics at the University of Maryland. Over the last 20 years, he has conducted research on auction theory and practice, which has appeared in the leading economics journals. The main focus of this research is the design of auctions for many related items, the applications of which include spectrum auctions, electricity auctions, and treasury auctions. On the practical side, he is Chairman of Market Design Inc., an economics consultancy focused on the design of auction markets. Over the past five years, he has played a lead role in the design and implementation of electricity auctions in France and Belgium, gas auctions in Germany, and the world's first auction for greenhouse gas emission reductions in the United Kingdom. He has advised numerous governments on market design and has advised dozens of bidders in high-stake auction markets. Since 1997, he has advised ISO New England on electricity market design and was a lead designer of New England's forward capacity auction. He has advised market makers in California and PJM on electricity market design as well.

Teresa Maurea Faria is Associate General Counsel at Conservation International. She practices law in the area of international transactions, with particular emphasis on project and international finance, energy, and matters relating to Latin America. In addition, she has advised the government of Sao Tome and Principe with respect to the management of the country's expected oil revenues, including the drafting of an oil revenue management law ensuring transparency, accountability, and public oversight of oil funds. Before joining Conservation International, she worked at Hogan & Hartson law firm, where she focused on international finance, international project finance, domestic corporate finance, and secured transactions. She has also participated in cross-border mergers and acquisitions in the energy and telecommunications industries in Latin America.

Geoffrey Heal teaches Managerial Economics and is the Director of Columbia's Center for Economy Environment and Society and of the Union of Concerned Scientists, a group founded by eminent scientists to promote sound scientific thinking about the environmental problems facing society. His current research interests include modeling the impact of markets for derivative securities on the allocation of risks in the economy, modeling the pricing of derivatives in a general equilibrium framework, and studying ways of controlling the impact of economic activity on the environment and ways of valuing the economic services provided by environmental assets. He served as a Commissioner of the Pew Oceans Commission, established by the Pew Charitable Trusts to review the management of U.S. fisheries and coastal zones, and is a Director of the Beijer Institute of the Royal Swedish Academy of Sciences and an International Research Fellow of the Kiel Institute of World Economics. In addition, he is Chair of the National Research Council's Committee on the Valuation of Ecosystem Services, whose report was published in October 2004. He was a founder of the Coalition for Rainforest Nations and chairs its advisory board.

Macartan Humphreys is Assistant Professor of Political Science at Columbia University. His research focuses on political economy, formal political theory, and the linkages between natural resources and violence. Recent research includes experimental work on public goods in Uganda, game theoretic work on ethnic politics, survey work of ex-combatants, and field research in Senegal, Liberia, Mali, and Sierra Leone on civil conflict. He has published in leading political science journals including the *American Political Science Review, World Politics*, the *British Journal of Political Science*, and the *Journal of Conflict Resolution*. He is a research scholar at the Center for Globalization and Sustainable Development at the Earth Institute and has served as an advisor to the governments of Liberia and Sao Tome and Principe and to the United Nations.

David Johnston is a Director with Daniel Johnston & Co., Inc., working with governments and oil companies on upstream exploration, development, and Enhanced Oil Recovery contracts worldwide. His work includes contract design, economic/financial analysis, negotiations, and expert witness work. He teaches courses in "Economic Modeling and Risk Analysis" and "International Petroleum Fiscal System Analysis and Design" at the University of Dundee and has published two books through the University, *Economic Modeling and Risk Analysis Handbook* and *Maximum Efficient Production Rate*. He also published *Introduction to Oil Company Financial Analysis* (PennWell Books, 2006) and has written a number of articles on the subjects of energy and technology.

Terry Lynn Karl is Gildred Professor of Latin American Studies and Professor of Political Science at Stanford University. Her research interests include the impact of oil on oil-exporting countries, comparative democratization, and the global politics of human rights. Most recently, she is a co-editor of *New and Old Oil Wars*, with Mary Kaldor and Yahia Said (Pluto Press, forthcoming). She is the author of many other works, including *The Paradox of Plenty: Oil Booms and Petro-States* (University of California Press, 1997).

Jenik Radon has been Adjunct Assistant Professor at Columbia University's School of International and Public Affairs since 2002. He co-founded the Afghanistan Relief Committee in 1980, served as the Vice Chair of the U. S.-Polish Economic Council from 1987 to 1992 and was an advisor to the Estonian government, including the ministries of reform, economy, and justice from 1988 to 1995. In 1990, prior to Estonian independence, he founded the Estonian-American Chamber of Commerce in Tallinn and served as its Founding Chair. From 1996 to 2005, Radon was an advisor to the government of the republic of Georgia and the key negotiator for Georgia for the multi-billion-dollar oil and gas pipelines from Azerbaijan through Georgia to Turkey. For his achievements, he was awarded the Medal of Distinction by the Estonian Chamber of Commerce in 1990 and the Order of Honor of Georgia, the highest civilian award and one of the first awarded to a foreigner, in 2000. He is a visiting professor at the Indira Gandhi Institute for Development Research (an economics institute supported by the Reserve Bank of India) in Bombay, heads the international law firm of Radon & Ishizumi and is trustee/executor of Vetter Pharma, a leading German pharmaceutical company. Radon is the author of numerous articles, including "'Hear No Evil, Speak No Evil, See No Evil' Spells Complicity" (UN Global Compact's Compact Quarterly, Vol. 2005, Issue 2); "The ABCs of Oil Agreements" (*Covering Oil: A Reporter's Guide to Energy and Development,* ed. Anya Schiffrin and Svetlana Tsalik, 2005); "Sovereignty: a Political Emotion, Not a Concept" (*Stanford Journal of International Law,* Vol. 40, 2004); and "Negotiating and Financing Joint Venture Abroad" (ed. N. Lacasse and L. Perret, Wilson & Lafleur Itee, 1989).

Michael L. Ross is Associate Professor of Political Science and Chair of International Development Studies at the University of California, Los Angeles (UCLA). He is the author of *Timber Booms and Institutional Breakdown in Southeast Asia* (Cambridge University Press, 2001) and articles on the political and economic problems caused by resource abundance, the causes and consequences of democratization, and Southeast Asian politics.

Jeffrey D. Sachs is the Director of The Earth Institute, Quetelet Professor of Sustainable Development, and Professor of Health Policy and Management at Columbia University. He is also Special Advisor to United Nations Secretary-General Ban Ki-Moon. From 2002 to 2006, he was Director of the United Nations Millennium Project and Special Advisor to UN Secretary-General Kofi Annan on the Millennium Development Goals, the internationally agreed goals to reduce extreme poverty, disease, and hunger by the year 2015. Sachs is internationally renowned for his work as economic advisor to governments in Latin America, Eastern Europe, the former Soviet Union, Asia and Africa, and his work with international agencies on problems of poverty reduction, debt cancellation for the poorest countries, and disease control. He is a Research Associate of the National Bureau of Economic Research. Sachs has been an advisor to the IMF, the World Bank, the OECD, the World Health Organization, and the United Nations Development Program, among other international agencies. During 2000 and 2001, he was Chairman of the Commission on Macroeconomics and Health of the World Health Organization, and from September 1999 through March 2000 he served as a member of the International Financial Institutions Advisory Commission established by the U.S. Congress.

Martin E. Sandbu is a lecturer in business ethics at the Wharton School of Business at the University of Pennsylvania. His research ranges from the political economy of development through the economics of fairness and the political philosophy of distributive justice. Among his publications is an institutional proposal for increasing the accountability of governments in resource-rich countries, entitled "Natural Wealth Accounts: A Proposal for Alleviating the Resource Curse" (*World Development* 2006). He has advised governmental agencies and nongovernmental organizations in Bolivia, East Timor, and Sao Tome and Principe on natural resource management.

Joseph E. Stiglitz is University Professor at Columbia University in New York and Chair of Columbia University's Committee on Global Thought. He also holds a part-time appointment at the University of Manchester as Chair of the Management Board and Director of Graduate Summer Programs at the Brooks World Poverty Institute. In 2001, he was awarded the Nobel Prize in economics for his analyses of markets with asymmetric information. Stiglitz was a member of the Council of Economic Advisers from 1993 to 1995, during the Clinton administration, and served as CEA chairman from 1995 to 1997. He then became Chief Economist and Senior Vice-President of the World Bank from 1997 to 2000. His book *Globalization and Its Discontents* was translated into 35 languages and has sold more than one million copies worldwide. His latest book is *Making Globalization Work* (W. W. Norton 2006).

INDEX